Renaissance Architecture

Oxford History of Art

Christy Anderson is an architectural historian with a special interest in the buildings of Renaissance and Baroque Europe. The author of *Inigo Jones and the Classical Tradition* (2006), she has taught at Yale University, the Courtauld Institute, and MIT, and is currently an Associate Professor at the University of Toronto.

Oxford History of Art

Titles in the Oxford History of Art series are up-to-date, fully illustrated introductions to a wide variety of subjects written by leading experts in their field. They will appear regularly, building into an interlocking and comprehensive series. In the list below, published titles appear in bold.

WESTERN ART

Archaic and Classical Greek Art
Robin Osborne

Classical Art From Greece to Rome
Mary Beard & John Henderson

Imperial Rome and Christian Triumph
Jas Elsner

Early Medieval Art
Lawrence Nees

Medieval Art
Veronica Sekules

Art in Renaissance Italy
Evelyn Welch

Northern Renaissance Art
Susie Nash

Art in Europe 1700–1830
Matthew Craske

Modern Art 1851–1929
Richard Brettell

After Modern Art 1945–2000
David Hopkins

WESTERN ARCHITECTURE

Roman Architecture
Janet Delaine

Early Medieval Architecture
Roger Stalley

Medieval Architecture
Nicola Coldstream

Renaissance Architecture
Christy Anderson

Baroque and Rococo Architecture
Hilary Ballon

European Architecture 1750–1890
Barry Bergdoll

Modern Architecture
Alan Colquhoun

Contemporary Architecture
Anthony Vidler

Architecture in the United States
Dell Upton

WORLD ART

Aegean Art and Architecture
Donald Preziosi & Louise Hitchcock

Early Art and Architecture of Africa
Peter Garlake

African-American Art
Sharon F. Patton

Nineteenth-Century American Art
Barbara Groseclose

Twentieth-Century American Art
Erika Doss

Australian Art
Andrew Sayers

Byzantine Art
Robin Cormack

Art in China
Craig Clunas

East European Art
Jeremy Howard

Indian Art
Partha Mitter

Islamic Art
Irene Bierman

Japanese Art
Karen Brock

Native North American Art
Janet Berlo & Ruth Phillips

The Pacific Arts of Polynesia and Micronesia
Adrienne L. Kaeppler

WESTERN DESIGN

Twentieth-Century Design
Jonathan Woodham

Design in the USA
Jeffrey L.Meikle

Fashion
Christopher Breward

PHOTOGRAPHY

The Photograph
Graham Clarke

American Photography
Miles Orvell

WESTERN SCULPTURE

Sculpture 1900–1945
Penelope Curtis

Sculpture Since 1945
Andrew Causey

THEMES AND GENRES

Landscape and Western Art
Malcolm Andrews

Portraiture
Shearer West

Eroticism and Art
Alyce Mahon

Beauty and Art
Elizabeth Prettejohn

REFERENCE BOOKS

The Art of Art History: A Critical Anthology
Donald Preziosi (ed.)

Oxford History of Art

Renaissance Architecture

Christy Anderson

OXFORD
UNIVERSITY PRESS

OXFORD
UNIVERSITY PRESS

Great Clarendon Street, Oxford, OX2 6DP,
United Kingdom

Oxford University Press is a department of the University of Oxford. It furthers the University's objective of excellence in research, scholarship, and education by publishing worldwide. Oxford is a registered trade mark of Oxford University Press in the UK and in certain other countries

First Edition published in 2013

British Library Cataloguing in Publication Data
Data available

ISBN 978–0–19–284227–5

Printed and bound by CPI Group (UK), Ltd, Croydon, CR0 4YY

Contents

Acknowledgements

The first idea for this book seemed straightforward enough: a study that embraced Renaissance architecture in all its diversity and wonder. Those good intentions, however, faced the reality of difficult choices and an ocean of literature on each national tradition. Many friends and colleagues came to my aid.

A number of students have helped with the project: Ellen Chang, Alexis Cohen, H. G. Masters, Katherine Sims, Kimberley Skelton, and Christopher Worme. They sorted slides (back in the day), scanned images (more recently), found bibliography, tracked down images, read sections, and were the audience I always had in mind. For one important summer Jacob Roscoe ably assisted with the research on French and Flemish architecture. Over the years I developed several courses out of this material at Yale University and the University of Toronto. I am grateful to all of my students for their interest and excellent ideas.

David Karmon offered advice on all fronts, and was a kind and insightful reader of early drafts. Ellen Chirelstein and Lucy Gent each took on the task of reading a later draft, and helped me in many ways to adjust the tone and language. I am especially thankful to Deborah Howard for her extraordinary help at many stages of the book, at its very beginning and closer to the end, when her careful reading saved me from many errors. Needless to say, any errors that remain are mine alone. Other friends helped in ways personal and professional: Elaine Contant, Bob Hemmer, Maurice Howard, Nancy Lustgarten, Sarah McPhee, Lyndy Pye, and Lorin Starr. Thank you to all these good friends and colleagues.

When possible, I have selected buildings that survive, and almost all of these I have seen first hand. Some trips (several through England, France, the Netherlands, Portugal, and Germany) I made by myself. Yet the book is infinitely richer for the trips taken to see buildings in the excellent company of Hilary Ballon, Howard Burns, Tracy Cooper, Paul Davies, Louise Durning, David Friedman, David Hemsoll, Deborah Howard, Krista de Jonge, Matt Kavaler, Alex Nagel, Scott Opler, Koen Ottenheym, Charles Robertson, and Clare Tilbury. Katie Jakobiec organized an extraordinary trip for me in Poland that left me wanting to see more. Georgia Clarke has been a travelling companion to many of these buildings; and I have always returned from our adventures filled with ideas and information, hundreds of photographs, and many good stories which did not make their way into the text.

Several of these field trips were funded through the generosity of the Griswold Family Fund of Yale University and the Connaught Fellowship at the University of Toronto. A Fellowship from the Massachusetts Center for Renaissance Studies gave me the restful surroundings to write and edit. A Fellowship from the John Simon Guggenheim Foundation coincided with the completion of this manuscript.

Many other friends and colleagues helped with their own areas of expertise, and offered suggestions on interesting buildings and approaches. Hannah Chapelle Wojciehowski kindly allowed me to see her book on groups in the Renaissance before it appeared in print. Nicola Camerlenghi shared his article on architecture and time.

Simon Mason commissioned this book, and Matthew Cotton kindly and patiently saw it to completion. Jackie Pritchard took special care in the final details of editing. With a wonderful eye, Deborah Protheroe found just the right images that conveyed my meaning. And Emma Barber steered the book through production and helped to keep me on track.

As always, Kevin Gallagher was my most important collaborator, listening patiently as I tried to work out problems and always reminding me to back up my laptop. Our son, Innis Odin Gallagher, luckily discovered Harry Potter just as I pushed through to the end.

My deepest thanks, however, are due to my own teachers who offered models of the rigorous, passionate, and open-minded study of architecture. To one of them, Henry A. Millon, I dedicate this book.

Glossary

Terms explained in the glossary are highlighted in bold wherever they occur in the text.

Aedicule: A building in miniature, framed by an architectural element on a smaller scale. An aedicule may be a recess in a wall, intended to focus attention on an important object, or it may more commonly be the frame around a window or door. The use of columns or Gothic arches refers back to the larger building in which the aedicule is located.

***Bimah*:** In a synagogue, the Torah is read from a platform called a *bimah*, meaning in Hebrew 'elevated place'. The *bimah* can be located in the centre of the synagogue, or at the side of the hall and parallel with the ark, the cupboard where the Torah is kept.

***Cantiere*:** In Italian, the building site is called the *cantiere*. As construction on major buildings might take generations, as at St Peter's in Rome, work sites were often persistent parts of a city. Construction demanded workers with various skills, and at any one time there would be craftsmen with the knowledge of materials as various as wood, stone, metal, and tile. Temporary buildings, including the mason's lodge, provided work space for the trades. Master craftsmen and architects had responsibility for the project overall, including the schedule and finances.

***Cryptoporticus*:** In ancient Roman architecture, the *cryptoporticus* is a covered passageway, usually vaulted, that supports a structure above. It might be lit from openings in the vault, or with piers along one side opening onto a hill. In hot climates, it was a cool and protected place, and well suited for villas and country buildings. For Renaissance architects, the architectural form evoked all the qualities of ancient Roman architecture in its massive forms, vaulted open space, and structural sophistication.

***Fondouks*:** Inns that provided housing for merchants and storage for their goods in cities along the major trade routes. Also known as *fondaco* in Venice and *caravanserai* in Persian, there was usually stabling for animals on the ground floor and rooms for the merchants upstairs.

***Lierne*:** Comes from the French 'lier' meaning to bind, and in architecture it is a tertiary rib that connects two other ribs in a vaulted ceiling. The *lierne* rib does not spring either from the central boss in the centre of the ceiling or from one of the major ribs that rise from the floor or wall. Thus it has an additive quality and the effect is a highly ornamented pattern of vaults spanning the ceiling, often in the shape of stars or flowers, looking like a mesh fabric stretched overhead.

Lunette: A semicircular space framed by an arch or vault, which may contain ornament and decoration.

Metopes: Alternating with triglyphs (see below) in the Doric order, metopes are sunken, squarish panels that often contain sculpted or painted decoration.

***Muqarnas*:** Three-dimensional ornament used in Islamic architecture, often applied to pendentives (see below), vaults, and other places of transition from one part of the building to another. A *muqarna* can be made of wood, stucco, or stone, and the cascading appearance refers both to its origins in geometry and natural forms. For European architects, *muqarnas* were one of the most distinctive and exotic features of Islamic architecture, though comparable to the elaboration of Gothic vaulting and tracery.

Orthogonal: In mathematics, lines are orthogonal if they are perpendicular at their point of intersection. In architectural drawing, orthogonal refers to a mode of representation that aimed to show three-dimensional objects in two dimensions, and was used by the ancient writer Vitruvius in connection with sundials that show longitude and latitude. This mode of drawing shows all aspects of a building projected onto a flat, frontal plane so that measurements are accurate and can be taken from the drawing.

Pendentive: The triangular space that marks the transition between a dome and the square, structural space below.

***Piano nobile*:** Refers to the main level of a house or palace where the grandest rooms were located, on the first main floor above the ground storey.

***Qibla*:** In Arabic, *qibla* means 'direction', and refers to the direction one should face when praying to Mecca. In mosques, the *qibla* wall points toward Mecca and often contains a niche, a *mihrab*, that marks the direction one faces while praying.

Quatrefoil: A medieval ornament of four leaf-shaped forms [a *trefoil* had three leaf forms joined together], and often included as part of Gothic tracery framing windows or in open stonework. As with much of Gothic ornament, this motif derives from plant forms yet became standardized as a regular pattern of architectural ornamentation.

Roundel: A disk or circular form that often contains decoration or figural imagery in paint or sculpture. Roundels may also be openings in a wall used to let in light, especially within curved or vaulted spaces.

Spandrel: The space between two arches or between an arch and its rectangular enclosure. That triangular space may be a wall and thus solid, or left open. As with pendentives, the spandrel is the space in between two architectural forms and is often highlighted with ornament.

Stereotomy: The theory and practice of cutting solids, especially wood and stone, into precise geometric shapes for their use in buildings. Although an ancient practice, new developments in stereotomy emerged in the fifteenth century as craftsmen and architects revisited classical mathematical and geometrical texts by Euclid and others. Albrecht Dürer, Piero della Francesca, Philibert de l'Orme, and Alonso de Vandelvira all wrote treatises on the use of geometry in the design of objects and architecture.

Triglyphs: In classical architecture, in the Doric order, a part of the frieze above the columns and capitals. The triglyph has three vertical grooves, regularly spaced, that may refer back to the origins of classical architecture as a wooden structure: the triglyphs are a reference to the ends of the wooden beams that would have supported the roof. Triglyphs alternate with metopes (see above) in the frieze and create a recognizable and rhythmic pattern associated with the Doric order.

***Trompe*:** An example of the complex geometry developed by masons and architects in late medieval and Renaissance architecture, a *trompe* is an elaboration of an arch that connects two walls and provides extra space to the rooms above. The arch, which could then be enclosed with masonry, could be used, as Philibert de l'Orme did at the Château d'Anet (1547–52), to allow an additional room, added after the completion of the chateau, for the King to write and meet in private. The technical complexities of designing the *trompe*, which projects assertively out into space, demanded a high level of theoretical and practical experience in stereotomy (see above) and masonry.

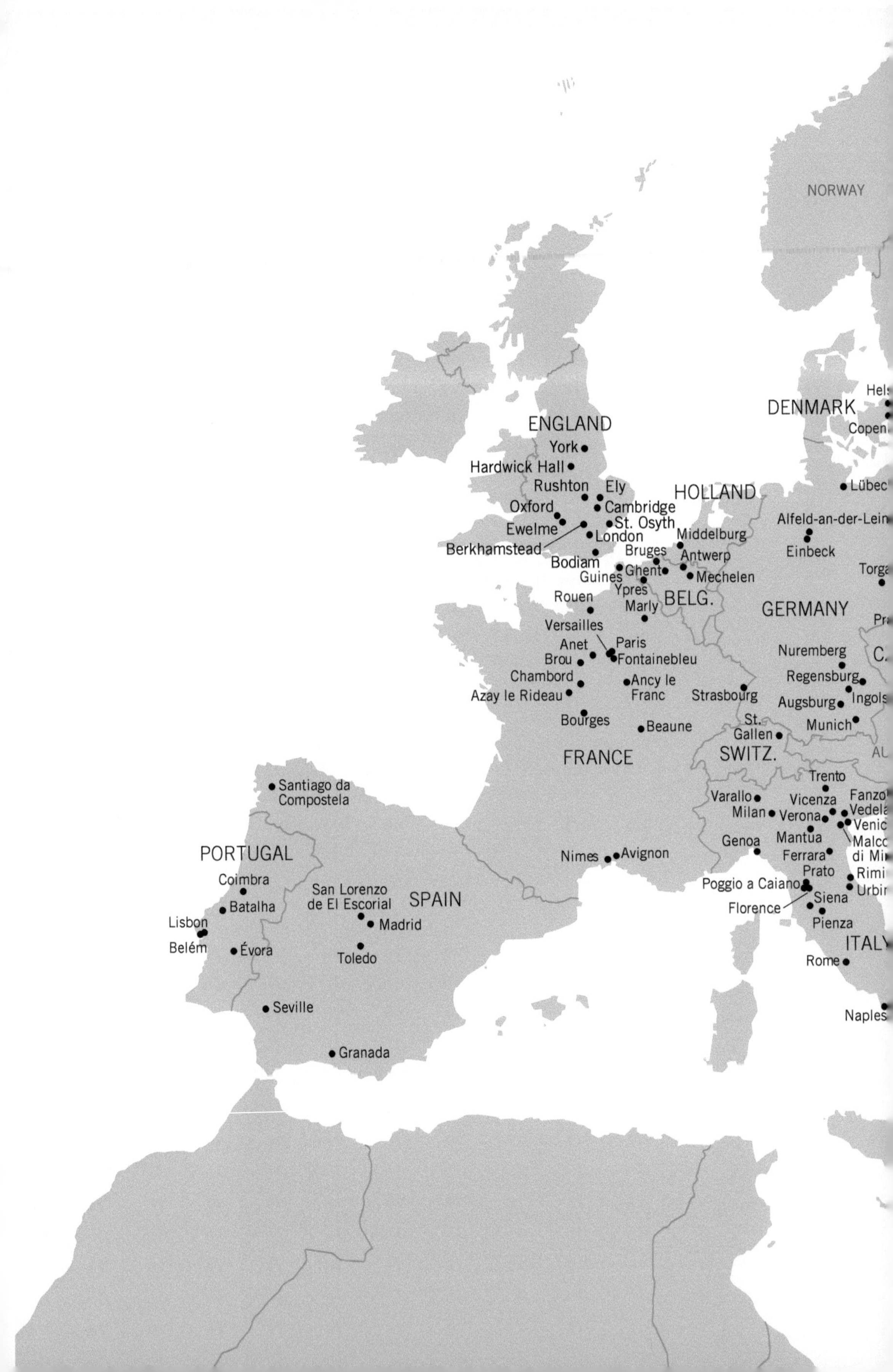
NORWAY
DENMARK
Hels
Copen
ENGLAND
York
Hardwick Hall
Rushton
Ely
Oxford
Cambridge
Ewelme
St. Osyth
London
Berkhamstead
Bodiam
HOLLAND
Middelburg
Bruges
Antwerp
Ghent
Guines
Mechelen
Ypres
BELG.
Rouen
Marly
Lübec
Alfeld-an-der-Lein
Einbeck
Torga
GERMANY
Versailles
Anet
Paris
Brou
Fontainebleu
Chambord
Ancy le Franc
Azay le Rideau
Strasbourg
Bourges
Beaune
Nuremberg
Regensburg
Augsburg
Ingols
Munich
St. Gallen
SWITZ.
FRANCE
Santiago da Compostela
Trento
Varallo
Vicenza
Fanzo
Milan
Verona
Vedela
Venic
Mantua
Malco di Mi
Genoa
Ferrara
PORTUGAL
Nimes
Avignon
Prato
Rimi
Coimbra
Poggio a Caiano
Urbir
San Lorenzo de El Escorial
SPAIN
Siena
Batalha
Florence
Lisbon
Madrid
Pienza
Belém
Évora
Toledo
ITALY
Rome
Seville
Naples
Granada

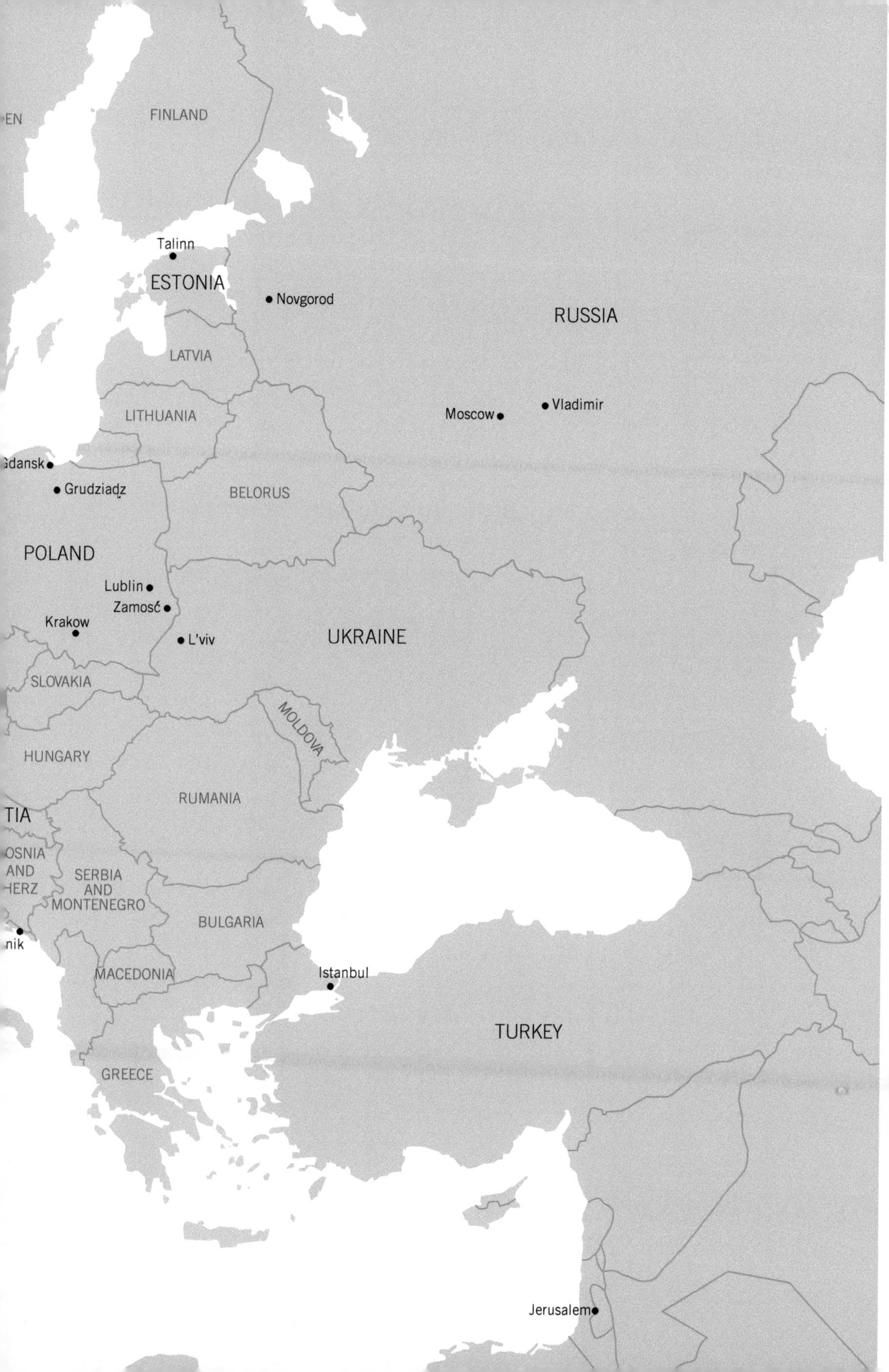

EN
FINLAND
Talinn
ESTONIA
Novgorod
RUSSIA
LATVIA
LITHUANIA
Moscow
Vladimir
Gdansk
Grudziadz
BELORUS
POLAND
Lublin
Zamosć
Krakow
L'viv
UKRAINE
SLOVAKIA
MOLDOVA
HUNGARY
RUMANIA
TIA
OSNIA
AND
HERZ
SERBIA
AND
MONTENEGRO
BULGARIA
nik
MACEDONIA
Istanbul
TURKEY
GREECE
Jerusalem

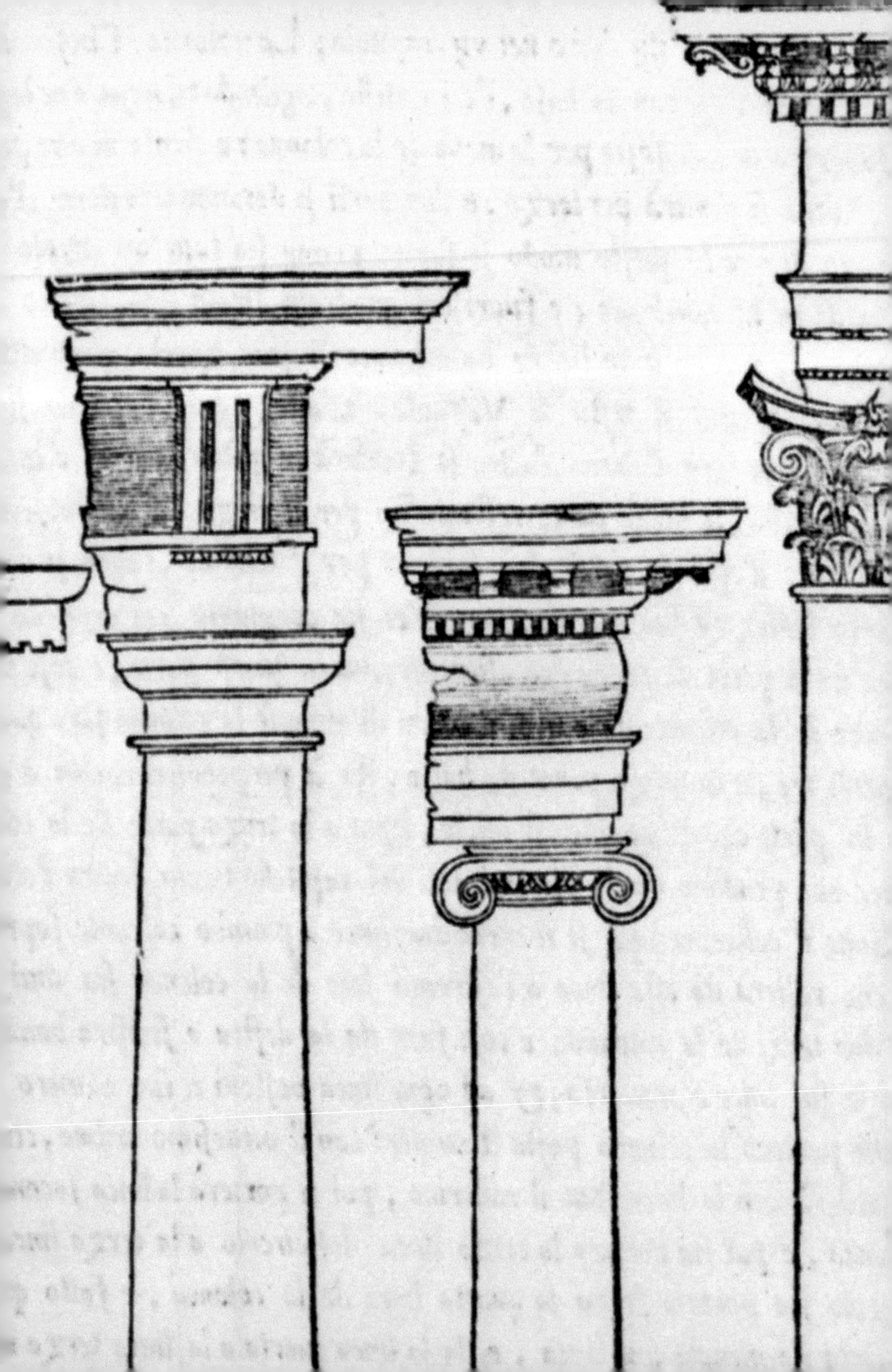

Introduction

Renaissance architecture can be hard to love. It may be respected or admired, or even understood on an intellectual level, but these days it rarely evokes the impassioned response of the great medieval cathedrals or the awe of the vast Baroque palaces. In his book on *Renaissance Architecture in Italy* (1963), Peter Murray said that we have to take Renaissance buildings on their own terms, that we need to have the knowledge of ancient culture and Renaissance learning in order to see the architecture as it was meant to be seen. This is a tall order. Many of the patrons responsible for the most famous buildings of the period were great scholars, often with vast libraries and a deep knowledge of ancient cultures. They understood architecture, along with the arts of poetry, music, painting, and sculpture, to be a part of that learned culture. Architects too understood that architecture could participate in these elevated discussions.

Certainly a knowledge of ancient philosophy, Renaissance literature, theological debates, and recent scientific discoveries can all contribute to an understanding and deep appreciation of architecture in the fifteenth and sixteenth centuries. This book brings in that background to the discussion of the buildings. Yet the same intellectual context of Renaissance architecture that helps us to understand the fascination with particular forms, such as the column as a sign of ancient Roman culture, can also inhibit the very physical and material pleasures of the buildings. For all their scholarly seriousness and detail, architectural treatises that emerged during this period provided an enveloping theory that only tells part of the story. These buildings were meant to be enjoyed, and at many levels. The rich and sensuous details of a classical capital, the extravagance of polished marbles on the façade of a Venetian palace, the brazen display of the woodcrafter's art in panelling, were all intended to astound the viewer. It is a curious thing, therefore, that this period of intense intellectualism in the arts was also one of profound sensual delight. Aesthetic experiences, through the mind as well as through the body, were thought to increase the efficacy of a building, whether its purpose was to display the power of a great ruler or to enhance religious practice. Further, architecture was intended to fulfil the agenda of beauty, and beauty

Detail of 35

had a purpose; the choice of ornament, material, and style could make a building more effective, better able to fulfil its function in the world. This book addresses both the sensual appeal and the intellectual and historical context of Renaissance architecture. While modern scholars have shied away from acknowledging the emotional impact of architecture, Renaissance craftsmen, like their medieval predecessors, found ways to move the viewer to delight or wonder. What was the point of the time and expense of building if like eloquent language it did not affect the viewer?

The Lure of Classicism

The history of Renaissance architecture has primarily been the story of architectural classicism as it developed in central Italy in the fifteenth and sixteenth centuries. Often beginning with the work of Filippo Brunelleschi in Florence and culminating in the buildings of Andrea Palladio in Venice, the overarching narrative describes a growing interest in the ancient architecture of Rome, the emergence of the architect as the controlling force of design, and the increasing sophistication of architectural theory. The focus is on the dominant individuals, architects and patrons, who jointly created the major works of architecture in a select group of cities and court centres. The dominance given to central Italian traditions can be traced back to the sixteenth-century author Giorgio Vasari, who famously condemned Gothic architecture (what he called 'German') as debased.

> We come at last to another sort of work called German, which in both ornament and proportion is very different from both the ancient and the modern. Nor is it adopted now by the best architects but is avoided by them as monstrous and barbarous, and lacking everything that can be called order. Nay, it should rather be called confusion and disorder. In their buildings, which are so numerous that they sickened the world, doorways are ornamented with columns which are slender and twisted like a screw, and cannot have the strength to sustain a weight, however light it might be. Also on all the facades, wherever else there is enrichment, they build a malediction of little niches one above the other, with no end of pinnacles and points and leaves, so that, not to speak of the whole erection seeming insecure, it appears impossible that the parts should not topple over at any moment. Indeed they have the appearance of being made of paper rather than stone or marble. In these works they made endless projections and breaks and corbellings and flourishes that throw their works out of all proportion; and often, with one thing being put on top of another, they reach such a height that the top of a door touches the roof. This manner was the invention of the Goths, for, after they had ruined the ancient buildings, and killed the architects in the wars, those who were left constructed buildings in this style. They turned the arches with pointed segments, and filled all Italy with these abominations of buildings, so in order not to have any more of them their style has been totally abandoned.[1]

Vasari's condemnation of the Gothic bolstered his own belief, at the centre of his book, that important and noble architecture was the product of great individuals. His book is organized around biographical studies of artists, sculptors, and architects, culminating in the singular figure of Michelangelo.

If the term 'Renaissance' has subsequently become a shorthand for the history of architectural classicism in the post-antique period, it has also become synonymous with architecture in central Italy. In Florence, Rome, and the court cities of Mantua, Urbino, Ferrara, and other centres historians have been able to compose a narrative that was forward moving and developmental. The story goes something like this: architects and patrons increasingly used classical architectural forms for a wide variety of building types, transforming their ancient architectural models to suit contemporary needs and in a desire to create an ever more sophisticated and refined language of classical design. The protagonists in the story were the enlightened patrons as well as the educated architects. For an English-speaking audience, this history of Renaissance architecture has been best presented in the translations of books by the German scholars Ludwig Heydenreich and Wolfgang Lotz, and more recently, Christoph Frommel.

The difficulty with this canonical history of Renaissance architecture lies in what is excluded. The central Italian experiments with architectural classicism were only one area of interest during this period. For others Gothic architecture continued to be a vital and relevant style of building, infinitely adaptable to new buildings and fully expressive of the material wealth of urban centres. Other communities assimilated the architectural traditions of older groups, as in southern Spain with the Islamic traditions from the south and east. For some, the political and religious turmoil of the period provoked a return to local styles and traditions as a way to reiterate the strength of the past. From our vantage point, certain moments in the fifteenth and sixteenth centuries may seem prescient of today's architectural situation: ever more complex theoretical discussions, an increasingly sophisticated professional class of architects, and a public ever more willing to see architecture as a vehicle of political and social messages.

If the narrative of classical buildings produced by great architects in central Italy has the dominant place in most histories of Renaissance architecture, a second theme has been the dissemination of these ideas throughout the Italian peninsula and Europe as artists emigrated due to war and greater opportunities abroad. Architectural tourism, often a sideline activity for pilgrims or political emissaries, developed as popular interest in architecture grew, and those travellers helped to disseminate information throughout Europe and beyond. The printing of books and images, as well as drawings and even models, helped architectural ideas to travel.

Seeing Renaissance Architecture on Its Own Terms

The great variety of architecture in Europe during the fifteenth and sixteenth centuries makes it impossible to designate any one area as the stylistic centre out of which all good architecture emerged. There are too many interesting and complex buildings across Europe to cling to any idea that architectural style flowed from central Italy alone. Such a model of architectural history marginalizes the importance of local traditions that continue alongside classical practice. Rather it might be possible to locate a number of places where rich and well-developed local traditions produced architecture of exceptional interest and inventiveness. From the notion of one centre there might instead be many. Wherever Italian ideas found a new home, they were always understood in the light of local practice. Classical architecture, the modern style in Vasari's terms, might be included on a palace façade as a sign of a new and exotic style. Columns in particular were a reference to humanist learning and education, appropriate for architectural patrons seeking to display their status and family antiquity.

Recent work on the continuity of the Gothic in the fifteenth and sixteenth centuries has explored the continuing vitality of that mode of building throughout Europe, perhaps with the exception of central Italy where classicism was dominant. The Gothic that was used in castles, churches, domestic buildings, and civic structures was not the same as what had been developed in the Middle Ages. This new style adapted its forms and references to account for cultural and social changes, as well as the presence of classicism itself. Gothic architecture absorbed a range of other elements including vegetal imagery, or the incorporation of columns and classical forms, as well as exotic forms derived from the east.[2]

A Road Map

This book takes a broad view of architecture, and includes buildings from across Europe in the fifteenth and sixteenth centuries. While historians may not agree on the precise time period of the Renaissance, what connects the buildings included here is their response to a series of economic, political, religious, and cultural changes of the period. The design of religious architecture, for example, responded to the great upheavals in liturgical practice and belief brought about by the Reformation. New church plans were developed to allow for an increasing involvement of the laity in worship in those places where the reforms were adopted, such as the German princely states. Elsewhere there was an entrenchment of old patterns of building as a way to ensure spiritual fealty to the canonical faith. Similar varieties of architectural response can be seen in the changing political and social circumstances. It would be misleading to present only those buildings that had the greatest long-term effect on the centuries following. Within the limits of one volume, I have thrown the net wide, including buildings that are significant as milestones in the long history of architecture in Europe as well as relatively unknown examples that demonstrate the tremendous variety and vitality of architectural traditions of the time. This approach is a conscious corrective to the dominance of Italy in existing scholarship. Following the lead of historians such as Peter Burke who have written about the cultural variety of Europe in and outside of Italy, I too have given a great deal of space to places and buildings that are rarely discussed, and almost never in a book of this kind.

Readers will find unexpected architecture from places far beyond the central Italian cities that are the usual monuments in books on Renaissance architecture. At the same time, my choice of buildings was shaped by a series of new questions that have arisen in recent years, such as issues of gender and class. While architects were almost without exception men in this period, women had an important role as patrons of buildings on a grand and smaller scale. Their ideas about architecture directly affected the design of buildings from the layout of houses, cityscapes, gardens, and estates to the smaller-scale arrangement of interiors and domestic settings. Women's own labour can also be seen in all aspects of architecture, as they worked in parallel with their male counterparts on the construction and maintenance of buildings.

Issues of gender are only one of the new approaches to architecture. Other scholars have similarly looked at architecture developed for working classes that may have little of the visual splendour of the great palaces but is no less important for the people it served, its effect on the urban scene, and its attention to the actual social demands of the period. If Renaissance architecture has traditionally been a history of building by and for elites, this book offers a broader story that is more representative of the types of buildings constructed in cities and towns.

The diversity of conditions and precedents throughout Europe, from Denmark to Sicily, Portugal to Moscow, may seem to allow for no points of convergence. And yet one theme that does tie the buildings in this book together is the ways in which architecture in this period is used as a way to structure relationships between people and their world. Each chapter in the book addresses a building type, or typology, a kind of structure that serves a particular function. Religious architecture offered a means to connect man and God in a very real and operational way. A new villa or country residence substantiated land ownership with all of its economic and seigneurial privilege. Renaissance architecture, in a thousand different ways, was the medium of connection and dialogue, a mediation between people and things that increasingly seemed to have their own identity and to be less part of a cosmic whole held together under a divine rule. Usually the Renaissance is seen as a period of strong individuals, consciously seeking to establish their identity on a local and sometimes international scale; architecture can be seen as an active participant in this playing out of power.

The development of new modes of architectural drawing and the development of the architectural treatise as a practical and literary genre changed the practice of architecture in this period. In fact, the complex dialogue between theory and practice is one of the central themes in any history of Renaissance architecture, as it is here. I use the design and construction of St Peter's in Rome as a case study to explore some of these issues—although it would have been possible to look at, for example, the building of the great mosque of the Süleymaniye by Sinan in Istanbul as an equally rich example of a complex design process and the resulting monument.

Renaissance princes used architecture, unabashedly, for their political ends. Building was a means to display power by displaying their ideals and aspirations for their family, their empire, and themselves. One generation of courtly families flowed into another, and their buildings often reflect their ancestors and their building projects. In the chapter on architecture and politics I look at a series of European courts, with special attention to the buildings around the Spanish monarchies and the Hapsburg kings. Powerful female patrons come to the fore in this chapter, and allow us to see what women were building with their money, time, and power.

A common trope in the history of the Renaissance, as we have noted, is that it saw the rise of the individual as a powerful force in the world. Individuals rarely operated alone, however, and groups of people commissioned architecture to serve their collective needs. In the chapter on corporate architecture, I present a group of buildings that would rarely be discussed: housing for the elderly and lay religious organizations, schools and universities, hospitals and halls for trade companies and guilds. Although sometimes grand, more often modest, these buildings show the various ways groups achieve communal goals by building.

Cities were the engines of economic growth, much as they were in the Middle Ages, and they were the sites of much of the building in the Renaissance. Chapter 6, however, looks at urban architecture as the product of (and stimulus for) the economic activities of trade and exchange. Goods flowed into and out of cities, and the rich palaces of the merchants as well as the small houses of the artisans all depended upon this tide of material wealth. Cities could not function without an adequate infrastructure of water and streets that allowed for the expansion of populations and the movement of people and products through what was, in most cases, a dense urban fabric that had been established in an earlier period.

Although most of the population of Europe lived in cities, it was the countryside that provided the raw materials for the production of goods, wool for textiles for example; the food for the city's inhabitants; and the raw stuff for the making of architecture. Chapter 7, 'Architecture in the Natural World', examines buildings in the country, some built for protection, others for pleasure, all for the exploitation and use of nature.

The final chapter takes us forward, in and out of Europe and towards a new age. For the Renaissance is also the beginning of the age of exploration, and the discovery of a world beyond Europe.

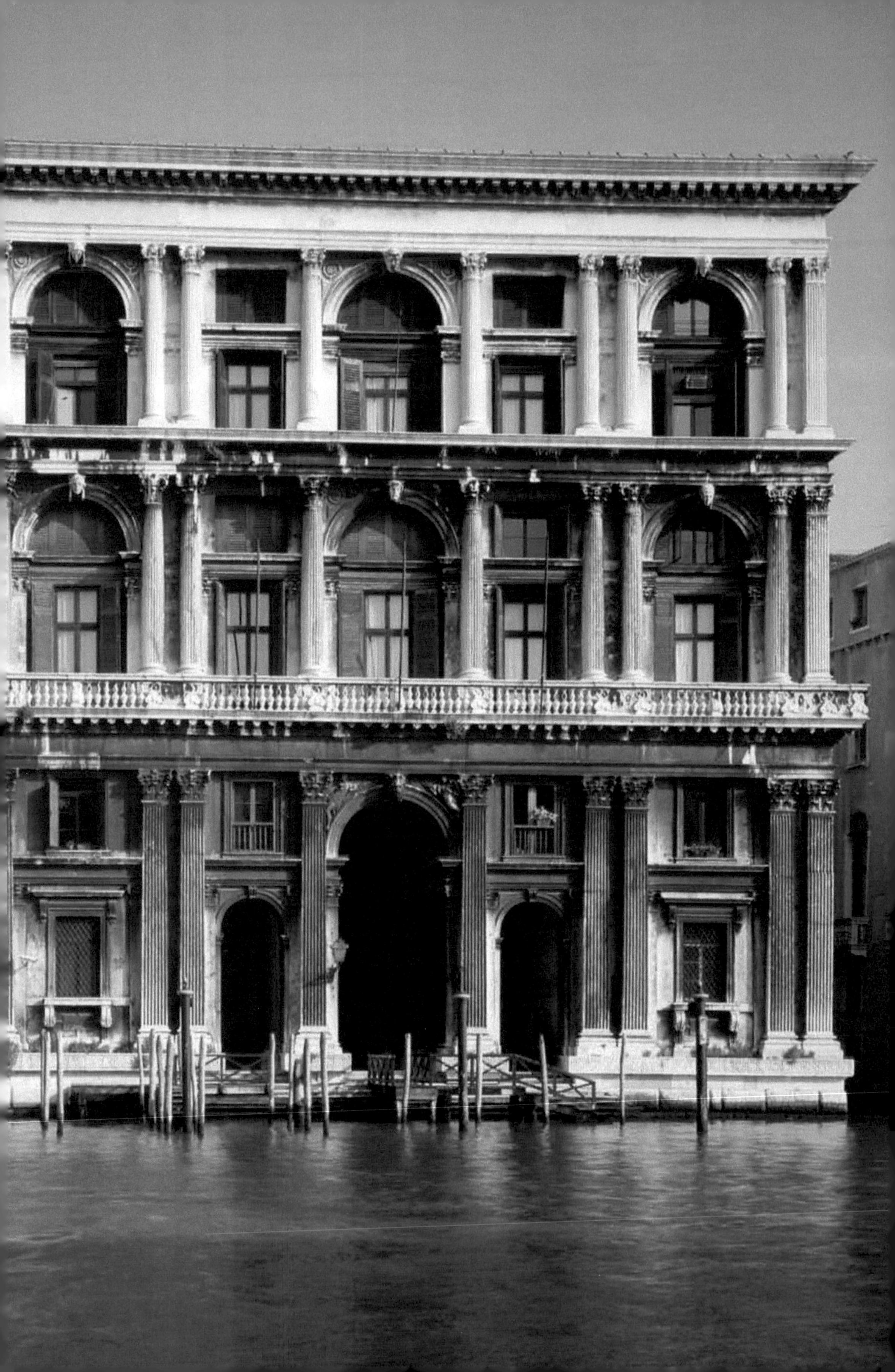

The Voluptuous Pleasure of Building

1

Despite the destruction of war and the natural course of ageing, Europe is filled with Renaissance architecture. Almost every small town has buildings from this period, witnesses to the pleasure of building. Some are masterpieces; more are minor examples, in a local style, somewhat altered over time and adapted to new use. A new history of Renaissance architecture cannot begin to cover all of these buildings, or even all of the variations on the themes of each building type that I cover here. Yet a first step must be to recognize the variety of forms and materials, as well as the innovation of local craftsmen and patrons. One needs to account for both inventions on a small and grand scale, as well as the continuity of styles and practices that continued from the Middle Ages. While innovation can tell us a lot about what made the world change, the tenacity of local practices says much about attitudes toward the past and social cohesion. Both are important.

'A Glorious and Beautifull Shew'

In May of 1608 Mr Thomas Coryat set sail from Dover to Calais. He hoped that the account of his journey through France, Germany, and Switzerland and into Italy would encourage other young men to travel, 'for the description of many beautiful Cities, magnificent Palaces, and other memorable matters that I have observed in my travels, may infuse (I hope) a desire to them to travel into transmarine nations, and to garnish their understanding with the experience of other countries'.[1] Like anyone on a tour through Europe, Coryat was amazed at the variety of foreign buildings he saw there. He thought that the architecture in Venice was the best in all Europe. The palaces, he writes, 'stand very neare to the water, and make a very glorious and beautifull shew. For many of them are of a great height three or foure stories high, most being built with bricke, and some few with faire free stone. Besides, they are adorned with a great multitude of stately pillers made partly with white stone, and partly of Istrian marble.'[2] [1] Every aspect of these glistening palaces was different from the buildings that Coryat knew in England. Some roofs in

Detail of 1

1

Michele Sanmicheli, Palazzo Grimani, commissioned 1556–7, completed 1575, Venice

Boats arrived at the palace entrance that was modelled after a Roman triumphal arch with Corinthian fluted pilasters. That regular pattern of columns continues in the upper floors, and gives no hint of the irregular building site that lies behind the façade. Sanmicheli's classical solution for the palace was innovative and a radical break from Venetian traditions.

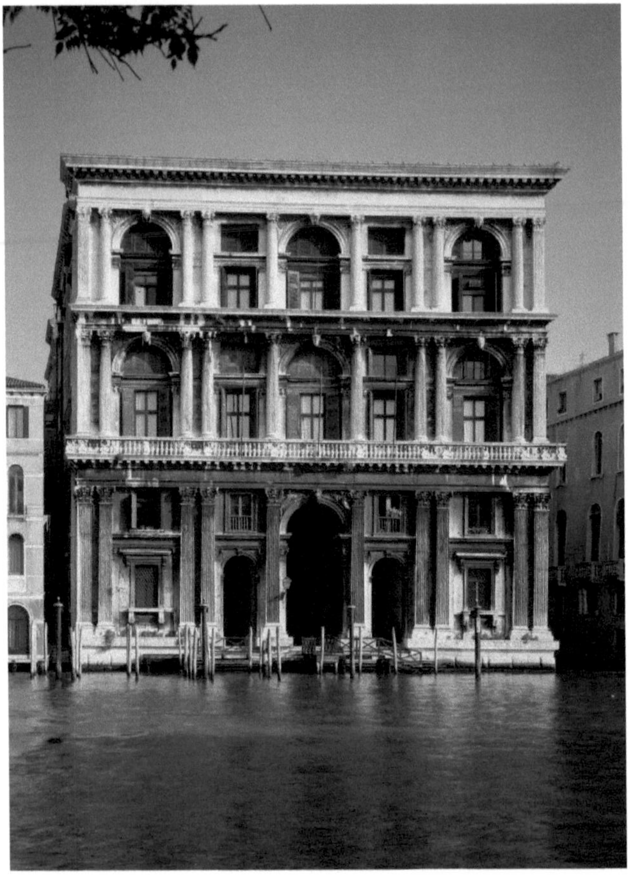

Venice had flat terraces, called *altane*, 'built in that manner as men may walke upon them'.[3] And even more remarkable, the houses directly on the canal were built on pylons. Coryat found Venetian palaces remarkable for their costly materials and construction just as much as for the view they provided along the Grand Canal.

In each city and country that Coryat visited he noticed that it was built in a local style, using the materials available nearby and adapting the traditional forms to their local needs. Architecture identified a region both to outsiders and to its residents. Modern visitors will have much the same experience. Palaces in Venice differ in materials, plan, and detail from those found in other parts of Italy, or those found in northern Europe.

Coryat's enthusiasm for Venetian architecture, in all of its material splendour, was typical of travellers' responses to buildings that were different from what they knew at home. They saw that each country in Europe had a variety of architectural forms that reflected local custom, patterns of living, materials, craftsmanship, and history. For travellers then and now, the differences in architectural styles and types were part of a place's identity.

The Language of Architecture

Language is a powerful metaphor for architecture, and in the fifteenth and sixteenth centuries has a close parallel to developments in the creation of national languages and literatures. The interest in the literature of antiquity spurred the translation of those works into national languages. On the Italian peninsula, for example, scholars debated which version of Italian (that of the courts, Tuscany, or of Dante) should be the new literary language.[4] What was certain was that there was a new interest in the development of national identity through language. Children should be taught their 'birth-tongue', argued one English author in the late fourteenth century, and not French in order to appear more aristocratic.

The use of architectural forms derived from ancient Roman models, what we now call classicism, began first where the ancient buildings were most plentiful, where they were the local (if distant) past. Not the domain of the architect alone, the study of ancient architecture emerged as one aspect of the study of ancient cultures, including literature, history, coins, and sculpture. The study of architectural antiquities, therefore, was enmeshed with an entire cultural project: the recuperation and revitalization of the classical past for present-day purposes. Antiquarian study was not an idle pursuit of scholars working away in their studies but a political process with an agenda to bolster political power, ensure the power of the Church, and reform culture. Architecture was a fully committed part of this project. Any discussion of style, therefore, must also take into account that the decisions about what seem to be aesthetic matters alone had political, religious, and social implications and motivations.

There are reasons to agree with historians that classicism should play the lead role in any history of architecture during this period. First, with the vantage of historical distance, classicism did indeed become the dominant architectural form throughout Europe, and in the New World, in the centuries following. Through the publication of treatises on the orders, and in the association of that architecture with specific political agendas, classicism became an international style. Further, as the 'Latin' of architectural form, classicism was most clearly associated with the educational ideals of humanism. In contrast to the multiplicity of the regional vernaculars (the use of classicism in combination with other forms in France, England, and Germany for example), there was an argument to be made that classicism was the only truly *literate* style. And accusations of illiteracy, in a European culture that increasingly valued education as the route to public success, could be a damning criticism. But was classicism truly a sign of literacy?

Attention only to classicism places too much of an emphasis on style, as opposed to the use of buildings, their materials, their role within the city or in the agricultural landscape. It skews the categories by which we understand architecture too much toward abstract notions of appearance and away from a broader sense of how the buildings functioned, in both a visual and social way, for people at the time.

In fact, while classicism later became the dominant architectural language, it was only one of many styles during the Renaissance. In Venice, for example, rich and colourful materials used in patterns across the façade tied any new architecture in with local traditions [2].[5] The patron of this large house on the Grand Canal hoped to establish his political power in the city by confirming his ties to political traditions. So too his new house reused the Byzantine and Gothic forms of earlier Venetian architecture, as well as some of the very materials from earlier buildings.[6]

The use of classical architectural forms, which coalesced into a group of architectural practices, became one dominant system of creating architecture. Yet we must remember that it was only one language of building, with no inherent dominance over other equally valid languages. We should not, as some authors before have done, see the choice to build in the Gothic or some combination of the two as the inability of the French, or English, or German architects to 'get it right' and understand the language of classicism.[7]

There was a similar interest in the creation of national architectural forms that would reinforce national identity.[8] Architectural treatises,

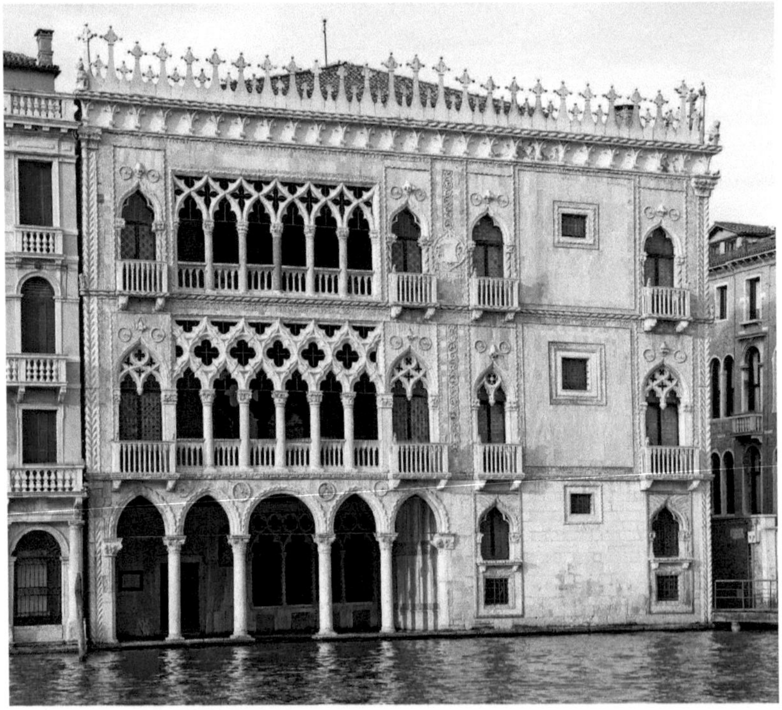

2

Giovanni and Bartolomeo Bon, Ca d'Oro, 1420s, Venice

The patron, Marino Contarini, commissioned a new house on the site of an older palace. He reused some of the earlier decorations and built in the well-established Venetian traditions using rich marbles over the façade and an open loggia on the *piano nobile*, a reference to the ducal palace. Located on the Grand Canal, and directly across from the Rialto market, Contarini employed the best craftsmen to create a grand house suitable for a prominent merchant.

written in national languages, not surprisingly advocated national architectural forms for their readers. Philibert de l'Orme (b. Lyons 1510, d. 1570) proposed a sixth architectural order that would be French and derived from nature, as the columns are the transformation of trees supporting the building. In addition to the national French order, the rest of the treatise marries French building traditions derived from masons' practice with the new sciences of geometry and **stereotomy**.

Thinking of architecture as a language allows us to tie the building practices in with local traditions and histories, which were certainly as powerful as any international classical style. If we think of architecture as a kind of language that 'spoke' to both local citizens of their needs in building as well as visitors from abroad, we can see how it was an active participant in the creation of regional identity through acts of building. However, the experience of architecture is often far more than words or language can express. The soaring spaces of a church that inspires the faithful to prayer, or the fortified exterior of a chateau rising above the Loire Valley, is more than words translated into stone. During the Renaissance architecture became a discipline in its own right. Architects and patrons alike expressed a new belief in the very act of building to speak in subtle ways about their political power or national identity.

The Matter of Materials

The first concern of any architect, or anyone wishing to build, was the acquisition of the proper materials, in sufficient quantity, and appropriate for the job at hand. Building could not begin until materials were collected, whether from local sources or more exotic materials brought in from abroad.

For the ancient writer Vitruvius, building materials defined the nature of architecture as its indivisible unit, 'for there is no kind of material, no body, and no thing that can be produced or conceived of, which is not made up of elementary particles' (*De architectura*, Bk. II, ch. 1). So, too, for the Renaissance architectural theorists for whom Vitruvius was a primary inspiration, a knowledge of brick, stone, lime, and wood was essential not only to the practical aspects of construction but also to a thorough understanding of the origins and significance of architecture. The appropriate materials, well chosen and correctly used, were necessary for architecture to be 'convenient, durable and beautiful' (Andrea Palladio, *I quattro libri*, 1570, Bk. I, ch. 1). According to Vitruvius and later writers, the forms of architecture derived from their materials and methods of construction.

Materials matter in architecture because they determine its physical characteristics, they identify the building with the site and the locality, they create the physical experience of the architecture that ties it to those who use the building and its physical setting. They are the means by which the building comes to give enjoyment. Architects and masons had to have knowledge of the physical capabilities and limitations of materials: what could stone be made to do? How much weight could it support? What kind of carving was best for wood? How long should mortar cure before it was used? Not all things were possible with each material, and the judicious and skilled architect could exploit the richness of the materials he had at hand.

Materials were the most obvious expense in building. Labour was cheap but large blocks of stone were a statement of great extravagance and luxury. The interest in rustication in Florentine architecture of the fifteenth-century, as at the Palazzo Medici in Florence [**108**], reveals this close association between massive masonry and splendour. Large stones were expensive, costly to transport, and a sign of status when left in their rough form.

Stones also connected architecture back to the organic and fertile world of nature. Renaissance architectural and scientific texts dealing with building materials suggest that rough stone would also have evoked widely held beliefs that organic forces are present in all raw materials from the earth. Later in the century Andrea Palladio would write about two kinds of stone: *pietra cotta*, or cooked stone, that is, bricks; and *pietre vive*, living stones from the ground. Building stones, like gems, were believed to contain innate qualities derived from the fecundity of the earth.

The interest in the possibilities of various materials extended from the most important buildings to the much more ordinary ones in small towns. Throughout Europe there was an interest in using local materials in ever more expressive ways. In the south-east of England, for example, flint is one of the most common stones. It is a form of the mineral silica, and is extremely hard with a glossy black interior. Traditionally, it had been used for the basic construction of every kind of building, from walls to houses to churches, the uneven stones held in place with large amounts of mortar. However, in the fifteenth century there was a new interest in the decorative potential of flint by knapping, or flaking, the flint to produce a flat surface and a regular shaped stone. These knapped flints were then set into patterns on the surface of the building, often filling in the spaces between dressed stone tracery [**3**]. The exterior of the building glistens from the metallic black edges of the flints, the most common of building materials used in the most extraordinary way. Not all buildings would have this treatment; it was reserved for the most important public buildings or private houses. Through the judicious use of materials, architecture distinguished one group from another and showed levels of social hierarchy and wealth.

3

Gatehouse, St Osyth Priory, late 15th century, Essex, England

The priory was founded in the 12th century, and the gatehouse added later as a sign of the institution's wealth and importance. The wall towards the town is covered with stone tracery, filled with the glassy black of the knapped flints. The battlements are filled with stone and flints, set in a chequerboard pattern. Flints are a local material, the result of a chemical process occurring in the chalk deposits that run along south-eastern England. Erosion releases flint nodules, looking like smooth or sometimes sharp rocks, covered in a white skin.

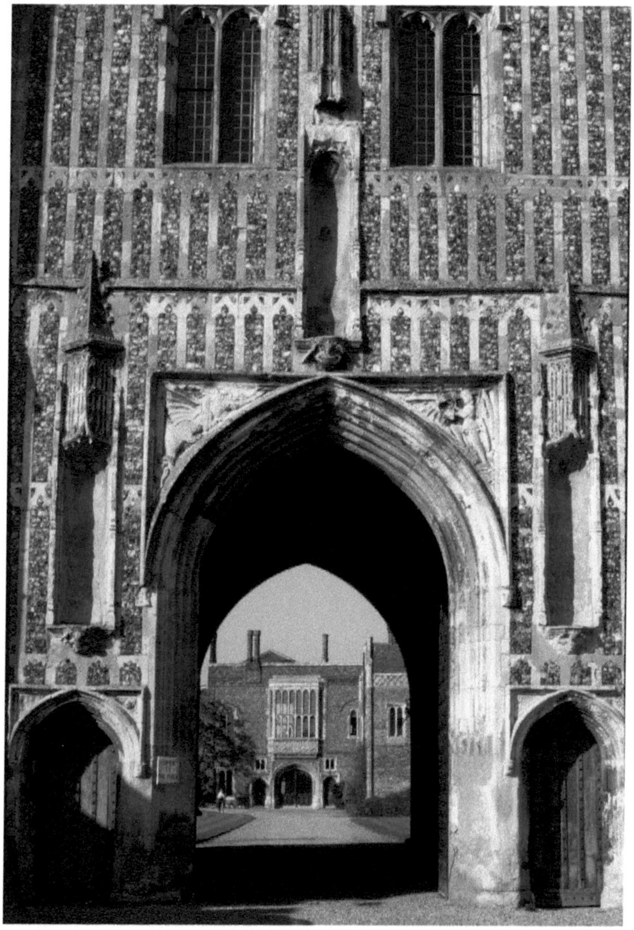

The Building of Time

Buildings tell stories about time. Through building, patrons engage an illusion of eternal present, holding time at bay as they live on in the structure they have commissioned.[9] Architecture offers the space for the reliving of past glories, military and otherwise, a memorial to events that cannot be forgotten. But buildings also exist in a much more fluid relationship to time. The construction of a large building often takes multiple generations to complete. When Julius II ordered the early Christian basilica of St Peter's in Rome torn down, and a new church begun, he began a project that would extend far beyond his lifetime. The early architects of St Peter's, Bramante, Michelangelo, and Raphael, sought, through recording their ideas in drawings, to ensure that their designs would be continued long after they had died. For any visitor to the city, the construction of the huge piers and vaults of St Peter's prompted a strange comparison between the new building rising and the ruins of the ancient city that lay all around. The popes were creating a suitably grand church to match their territorial ambitions and a new monument to rival the remains of the great Roman emperors. St Peter's made comparisons between the antique and the modern world inevitable.

Architects and patrons in Rome might well look to the ruins that lay all around the city and those that were being excavated as interest developed in antiquarian studies of the history and meaning of ancient objects. Through the study of historical documents, coins that showed ancient buildings, and the ruins themselves, scholars sought to restore Rome to her former beauty and grandeur. One merchant, Cyriac of Ancona, wrote that through the study of ancient inscriptions 'It is obvious... that we are able by our art not only to raise from the depths monuments which have been destroyed, but also to bring the names of cities back into the light. Oh what a great, what a divine power has this art of ours.'[10]

Any use of the classical orders evoked the splendours of ancient Rome in the mind of an educated viewer. Roman ruins, along with coins and statues, were the physical remains of that ancient civilization and the tangible reminder of history. Architecture could be directly connected to texts as a mnemonic device. Advice books urged young men to read before they travelled and then to study ancient monuments abroad in order to be 'an eye witness of the verie same things which he hath red in bookes, or heard of by others'. Especially in travelling to Italy, one manual goes on to urge, 'where shall you set your feet, or cast your eie: but you shall have occasion to call into remembrance, that which is set downe in Livie, Salust, Polibius, Plyny, Tacitus, Dion, and Dionisius'.[11] At least in theory, classical ruins could evoke texts read earlier and thus stimulate a mental recitation. The study of architecture became in the Renaissance part of a broader arts curriculum based in ancient texts and modern commentaries.

When available, ancient buildings were mined for usable materials, especially finely wrought columns, and capitals and bases. Craftsmen and architects could also model their new work on earlier examples, though the remnants of ancient architecture had a value in their material and workmanship that was difficult to reproduce.

Classical architecture could make the ancient gods live again, but other builders and patrons also sought to renew an ancient past that could take the form of castles as well as of temples, drawing on local building history as well as classical tradition for inspiration. When Gilles Berthelet built a new chateau on the site of the old fortress at Azay-le-Rideau (1518–28), he looked back to the medieval architectural traditions [**4**]. Berthelet rose from the middle classes to become the General of Finances for Normandy, one of the four Treasurers of France under Francis I. His chateau in the Loire Valley

4

Azay-le-Rideau, 1518–28, near Tours, France

The construction of the chateau ended abruptly when Gilles Berthelot was accused of financial wrongdoing and the property seized by the King. Only two of the four wings planned by Philippe Lesbahy, Berthelot's wife and supervisor of the project, were completed. With its steep roofs and setting along the River Indre, Azay-le-Rideau evokes the form of earlier chateaux. Classical decoration is confined to the entrance porch and the staircase.

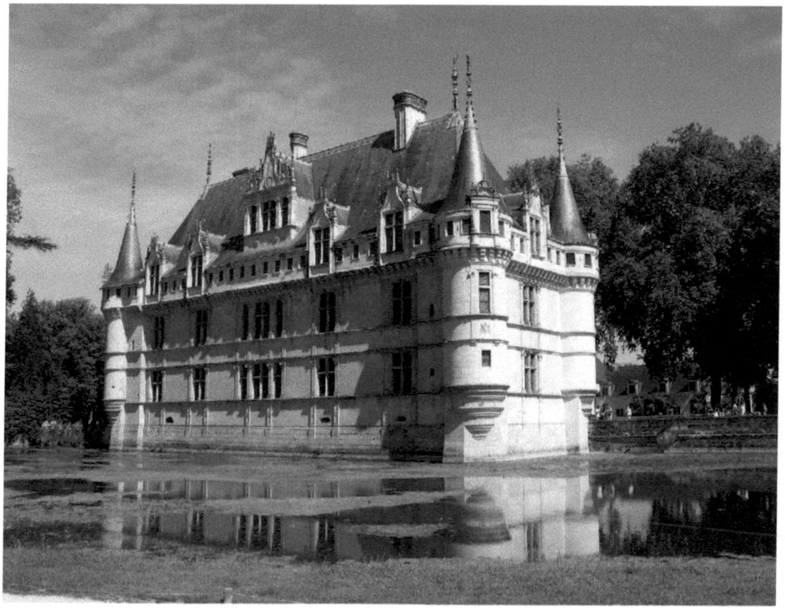

gave him an unimpeachable architectural pedigree: a newly built and grand house, yet closely resembling the earlier traditions of castle architecture. While Azay-le-Rideau uses the architectural language of fortresses, the corner towers and moat, and even the medieval plan with one room leading directly into the next, it is a very up-to-date building. The main entrance is marked by a tower of the classical orders, set off against a symmetrical façade, and leads to a grand staircase. The elements of fortification are decorative and not defensive, linking this new building to a French chivalric tradition that Berthelet wanted to claim as his own.

The architectural historian James Ackerman has suggested that every great architect finds his own antiquity.[12] Yet, as we have seen in these few examples, antiquity can take many forms. It can be the antiquity of ancient and Imperial Rome, a potent architectural language for the papal court. Or it can be a chivalric past connected with the medieval castles of landed nobility. The continued use of the Gothic tied any new building in that style to the buildings of the more recent past. And the period that we define as the Renaissance, that is the fifteenth and sixteenth centuries, is marked by just such an awareness of the rebirth, or *renovatio*, of an earlier history. The historian Arnold Toynbee (1889–1975) described 'renaissance' more broadly as 'one particular instance of a recurrent phenomenon'.[13] Architecture could contribute to this process of historical awareness because buildings can define the present through their connections to the past.

Love and Longing

In 1611 the painter Robert Peake wrote a preface to a new English edition of Sebastiano Serlio's multi-volume treatise on architecture (1537–47). He addressed it to 'The Lovers of Architecture'. When that book appeared, classical architecture, the mode of building presented by Serlio, was a relatively new phenomenon in England and other parts of Europe where Roman buildings were uncommon and mostly irrelevant to the current building practices. Columns and other elements from ancient and modern architecture had been used in limited parts of buildings such as loggias or decorative screens where craftsmen could freely adapt the models of ancient buildings. Yet Peake knew his audience. As a painter to the Tudor and Jacobean court he knew that there was a growing passion for building in England. Everyone who could afford to, and many who could not, wanted to have a building project under way: a new house, if that were possible, but even a garden gateway offered the opportunity to be builders. The desire to build, and to talk about buildings and visit the architecture of one's neighbours, had risen almost to the level of a cultural disease.

In the fifteenth century, the Italian artist and author Filarete identified this malady in its earlier phase.

> Building is nothing more than a voluptuous pleasure like that of a man in love. Anyone who has experienced it knows that there is so much pleasure and desire in building that however much a man does, he wants to do more.[14]

Why was building so addictive? For a start, in England, Italy, and other places with powerful court cultures, building offered one of the most public forms of political display.[15] Like clothing, architecture presented the self to society. It stood in for the body of the patron (in contrast to clothing which required the presence of the individual to have an effect), and engaged many people in both an intimate and less direct way.

If architecture had a political use, then it could also as Filarete suggests become a psychological compulsion. Once you begin, it's almost impossible to stop. Some of that delight must come from the physical beauty of building, the seduction of the smooth marble, wood lusciously carved, tile reflecting light back into the room. It is this kind of sensual enchantment that weaves through the romance of the *Hypnerotomachia Poliphili* (Venice, 1499), the story of the love of young Poliphilo for Polia. Their love is played out for several hundred pages and illustrated with elegant woodcuts that contribute to the exotic quality of the tale itself [**5**]. In the descriptions of architecture, gardens, and sculpture, Francesco Colonna (the likely author of the book) lingers over the materials of these objects, and the delight they arouse for the protagonists.

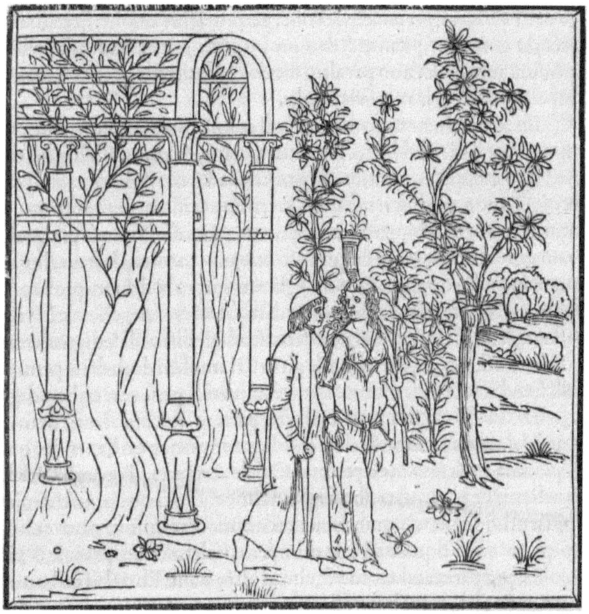

5
Francesco Colonna, *Hypnerotomachia Poliphili* (Venice, 1499)

With its elegant woodcuts, hybrid language, and dream-induced narrative, Colonna's story of love and desire plays out in an architectural setting of ruins and lush palaces. Although the long book is filled with paraphrases of Alberti and earlier architectural authors, it offers an alternative view of Renaissance architecture as a mysterious, emotional, and powerfully physical experience.

I gazed insatiably at one huge and beautiful work after another, saying to myself: 'If the fragments of holy antiquity, the ruins and debris and even the shavings, fill us with stupefied admiration and give us such delight in viewing them, what would they do if they were whole?' And then I thought again, reasoning with myself: 'Perhaps inside there is the venerable altar of mysterious sacrifices and sacred flames, or even the statue of divine Venus and the holy of holies of Aphrodite and her Son, wielder of the bow and arrow.'... The walls to right and left were cased in glossy marble, and a large disc was attached to the centre of the wall, surrounded by a leafy coronet excellently carved. This, like the one opposite, was of the black stone that resists hard iron, and polished like a mirror. As I heedlessly passed between the discs I was filled with sudden fright at the sight of my own reflection, but was reassured by an unexpected pleasure, for they offered a clear view of the scenes that were depicted there in splendid mosaic work.[16]

The *Hypnerotomachia Poliphili* offers a way into Renaissance architecture as more than simply an intellectual exercise in classical references and design solutions. Buildings were intended to engage us on every level, move us to spiritual devotion, mourning the passage of time and delighting in the stimulation of the senses.[17]

That delight is not, however, without its dangers. Poliphilo tells us as much in the passage I quote above. At one point in his study of the beautiful portal he becomes frightened, taken aback by his own reflection in the polished stone. We can imagine that for a second he does not recognize himself, reflected in the black stone, familiar yet changed. But the pleasure of the building consoles him, and he pushes on. Quickly his attention is once more held by the material of the architecture, beautiful scenes in mosaic.

The psychological engagement that Poliphilo feels, we too may experience with Renaissance architecture. In the soaring bowers of Gothic vaulting or palaces painted with familiar myths or local legends, Renaissance buildings transformed everyday experience. Classical ornament seems, for example, so recognizable in its forms derived from antiquity. That familiarity is a false sense of security and denies the subtle strangeness of these buildings. The use of classicism, similar to yet different from the ancient monuments on which it is based, should make the viewer look closely and study its subtleties. Its insistence on order, regularity, and modulation is not an imitation of life but a translation of everyday experience into a new disposition. These cunning transformations happen in other architectural languages as well, and always, in the best buildings, with a nudge urging us to stay alert.

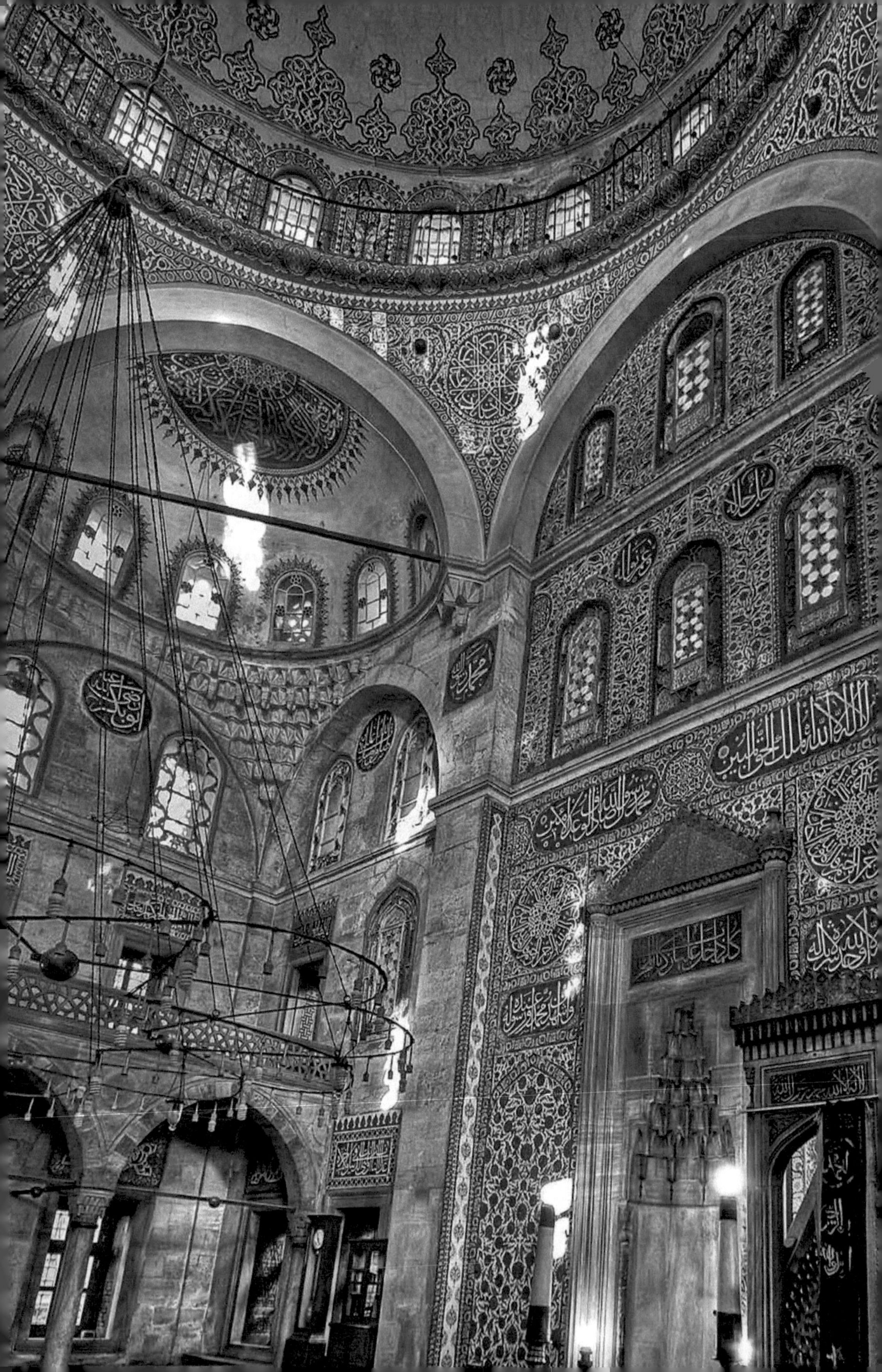

The House of God

2

No type of architecture demanded more from the architect than buildings made for worship. By equating the modern devotional building with the ancient temple, Alberti wrote that 'In all architecture there does not exist any work which requires greater talent, care, skill, and diligence than that needed for building and decorating the temple. Needless to say, a well-tended and ornate temple is without doubt the foremost and primary ornament in the city.'[1] Alberti refers to temples, rather than churches, connecting modern-day religious buildings back to their ancient precedents.

Churches and other religious buildings may not have been the most numerous within a city but they were the most important. In addition to being the institutional centre for worship, the economic and political power of the Church was a powerful force within the city and region. The physical body of the church was often at the centre of the city, close to markets and government buildings, and closely tied through its patronage to the important families of the area. The spires of the church projected up above the body of the church, proclaiming its importance to all within and without the city walls.

After the peak of the Black Death, around 1350, during which little was built, a new period of great building energy began. New churches were started in many areas of Europe, and earlier buildings were renovated and updated to meet new devotional requirements. Many of these buildings, however, took many generations, sometimes centuries, to complete and their construction continued well into the fifteenth and sixteenth centuries and beyond.

The basic plans of most religious buildings had been long established by 1400. Following on the ancient model of the Roman basilica, a longitudinal space designed to hold large crowds—though intended in the Roman period as law courts, not religious buildings—the longitudinal building remained the most frequent plan for Christian buildings.

In an early modern context, it is not possible to make a clear separation between the religious function of the buildings and the more secular activities of the local residents. Churches, as well as synagogues

Detail of 24

and mosques, were often community centres as well, serving as the site for schools, hospitals, and markets. The church was often the largest indoor space in a community and could serve as a meeting place when needed. Constructing the building was a community effort requiring not only local labour but also the finances and organizational ability of many groups within the town, including guilds and families who provided the economic strength to see the religious project through to completion.

Churches were the most common religious building in early modern cities, the structures that stood out on the urban and religious landscape. But the designation 'church' cannot sufficiently account for the variety of religious buildings constructed for quite different purposes during this period. Private chapels and pilgrimage shrines, for example, must be seen in conjunction with large public churches such as St Peter's in Rome, a building which was not only relevant to its own city but also held a position as the mother church that served the entire body of the faithful across Europe and beyond. While Christianity was the dominant religion throughout Europe, the sixteenth century was a time of great religious turmoil that resulted in the establishment of reform churches both within the Catholic faith and in the Protestant north. Although Jews were often severely controlled through official decrees and urban policy, within these prescribed limits their communities could construct synagogues in many cities. The conquest of Constantinople by Mehmet the Conqueror in 1453 meant that the city that had competed with Rome for dominance within the Christian world was now in the control of Muslims. Christian churches in Istanbul did not disappear, and many were transformed into mosques. New mosques were built as well, following the course of that religion's own reform movements in the sixteenth century.

Batalha

In 1385, King João I of Portugal won a great victory over the Spanish forces from Castile. João had been appointed king on the death of his half-brother Ferdinand, and King John of Castile felt the Portuguese monarchy was insecure, and ripe for an attack. Although greatly outnumbered, the Portuguese defeated the Spanish at the Battle of Aljubarrota, and secured the monarchy against the Spanish forces. In thanks to God for their victory, João ordered the construction of a great monastic cathedral at Batalha, three miles from the site of the battle.

The Dominican monastery, dedicated to S. Maria da Vitória, is a sprawling and unfinished complex, with all of the elements necessary for religious devotional practice: the main church building, cloister, chapter house, and chapels dedicated to its patron [**6**]. Built of the local cream limestone, the smooth surface of the exterior walls

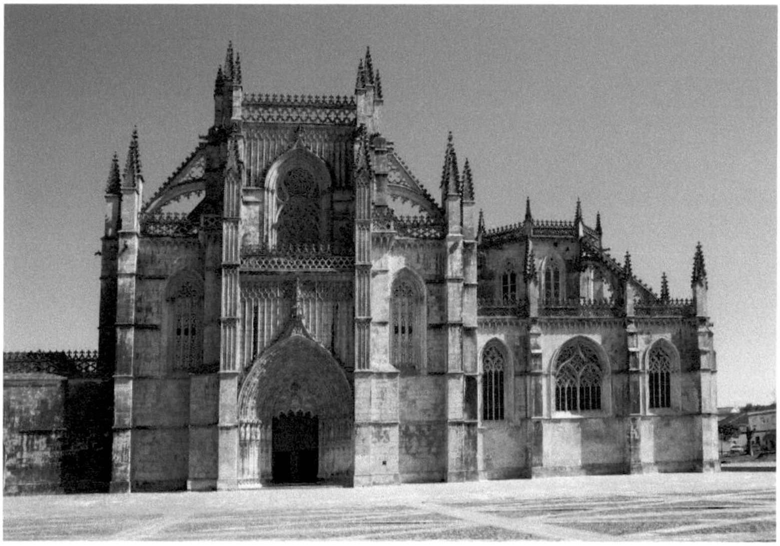

6

Alfonso Domingues and Huguet, S. Maria da Vitória, 1388–1438, Batalha, Portugal

At Batalha the ornamental language of Gothic architecture reached a new level of refinement, in ways that were distinctive to Portuguese building traditions. The strong horizontal emphasis across the façade and concentration of sculpture along the roofline and at the main portal are found in earlier buildings as at Alcobaça Abbey. Given the role of Batalha as a symbol of national identity and autonomy, the choice of Gothic ornament used in traditional ways was a powerful political statement.

contrasts with the pinnacles and tracery around the entrance door and along the roofline. The first architect, Alfonso Domingues (active at Batalha 1388–1402), and later Huguet (active at Batalha 1402–38), created a great Gothic cathedral that combined the decorative elements common to northern European buildings with distinctive Portuguese traditions in the tall proportions of the building and treatment of ornament. Consistent with much of the earlier medieval architecture in Portugal, the ornament along the façade has a strong horizontal organization that reveals the distinct blocks of the building construction beneath.

The cathedral at Batalha was considered both a gift to God and a glorification of its donor. The Capella do Fundador (Founder's Chapel) just inside the main door of the church served as the burial chapel to the house of Avis, which after the Battle of Aljubarrota held power in Portugal for the next 200 years [**7**]. The 20-metre-square room rises up to an octagon dome supported by eight piers. The rib vaults form a star vault punctuated with tracery in the form of rosettes. Underneath the dome is the tomb of King João I and his wife Philippa of Lancaster, for English support assured Portugal's victory, and was bound in to the dynasty through João's marriage to the daughter of John of Gaunt, Duke of Lancaster. Those political links are apparent in the architecture itself, and especially in the Founder's Chapel, which recalls the broad vaulted spaces of English cathedrals such as the Lady Chapel at Ely Cathedral (begun in 1321, resumed in 1342). Work continued at Batalha for several centuries, though many elements remained incomplete. A second royal mausoleum was begun by Edward, King of Portugal (reg. 1433–8), and continued by his grandson Manuel I (reg. 1495–1521).

7

Huguet, Capella do Fundador, S. Maria da Vitória, 1402–38, Batalha, Portugal

The royal pantheon contains the tombs of João I and his wife Philippa of Lancaster under the central octagon, and four of their children in altar-tombs along the south wall. The octagonal burial chapel became a standard building type in both Portugal and Spain into the 15th and 16th centuries, asserting the unity of a political dynasty.

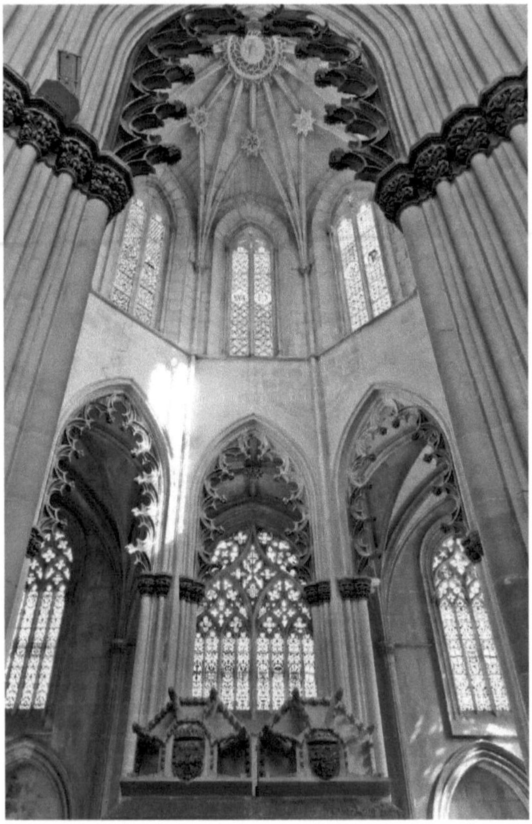

The combination of international trends and local traditions, religious dedication and political purpose, marks the cathedral at Batalha as a very powerful starting point for a study of religious buildings in the Renaissance. Batalha may have few if any references to the classical architecture in Italy of the same period. Yet Gothic ornament and traditions were still a powerful architectural language connecting this building both to Portuguese and European traditions.

Mathematics of God: Brunelleschi

When a new sacristy was built at the church of San Lorenzo, its innovation and beauty caused a sensation in fifteenth-century Florence [**8**]. It was a 'marvel' according to a biographer of its architect, Filippo Brunelleschi, attracting such crowds that 'the many people assembling there caused great annoyance to the workmen'.[2] Its innovative and awe-inspiring appearance was due to many factors, including its rich materials and ornament such as bronze on the doors and sculpture marking this private space off as rich and distinctive. The sacristy, a sacred space which held the consecrated host and precious relics, was built as an integral part of the church function. Yet this particular

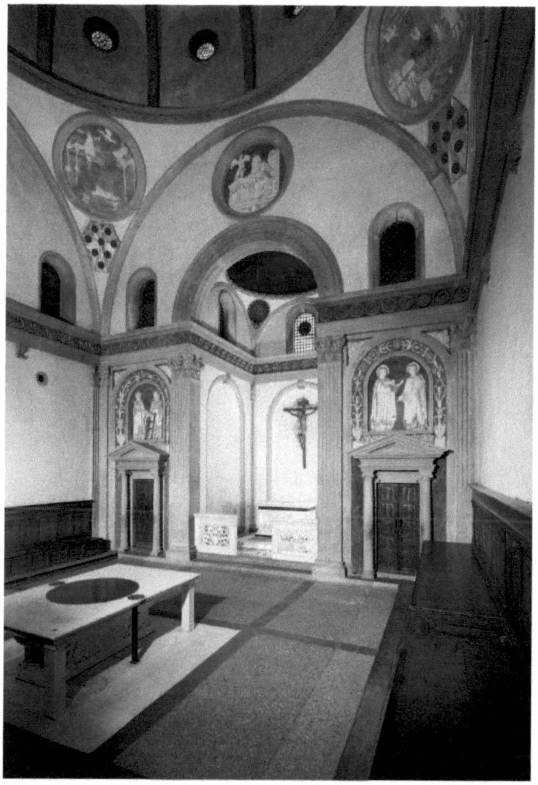

8

Filippo Brunelleschi, Old Sacristy, 1419–28, San Lorenzo, Florence, Italy

For a 15th-century viewer, the Sacristy would have evoked a number of recent and distant architectural models, including the Holy Sepulchre (begun 326, Jerusalem), Santo Stefano Rotondo (468–83, Rome) and the baptistery in Padua (13th century). The repetition of the dome over the main space and the altar recalled architecture from the eastern Mediterranean, especially buildings in Constantinople. Brunelleschi's ability to fuse these varied sources into a highly charged personal monument for the Medici marks a turning point in Renaissance architecture.

example was especially planned as a memorial chapel for the powerful Medici family who controlled this quarter of the city and in effect ruled the city of Florence.

One of its most remarkable innovations was the way in which the architect appropriated the architectural forms associated with the city itself for use in a private chapel. The dome over the central space would have specific resonances for Florentines. It evoked the baptistery of San Giovanni, the highly charged space adjoining the cathedral where individuals were baptized both as Christians and as citizens of Florence, St John the Baptist being the patron saint of the city. The dome would also have called to mind the not-yet-complete dome of the cathedral itself, a competition for the design of which was under way in 1418–20, exactly the date of the sacristy project.

It was also innovative in the choice of ornament used to commemorate the patrons. Private chapels, more often included within the space of the church overall, were often decorated with interrelated scenes attesting to the virtues of the patron. Here this form of ornament was executed in terracotta reliefs and restricted to only a small part of the chapel: the **lunettes** and **pendentives** containing scenes of saints and the Medici coat of arms. More astonishing, however, was the absence of decoration on much of the dome and wall surfaces.

Brunelleschi's architecture synthesized local, Tuscan architectural traditions in the use of a limited colour palette of grey-green stones against white stucco walls, with a new sensibility toward ornamental details. Only a few architectural elements are used throughout the architectural space. This restrictive vocabulary focuses attention on the considered alignment and placement of each form. The Renaissance, as well as the modern, viewer of Brunelleschi's buildings is invited to believe that there is an underlying order and system to the building, an almost innate order that regulates each aspect of the building. Perhaps this is a divine presence, mediated through the hand of the architect, but Brunelleschi's architecture evokes a rational calm that shapes the interior space. Against such a reduced programme of decoration as originally planned by Brunelleschi was an architectural vocabulary of ornament based on antiquity and local precedent as well as Roman and northern Italian references. A series of Corinthian pilasters along the lower storey support arches which in turn support the dome over the entire square of the ground plan.

If the decoration of the sacristy eschewed the more traditional frescoes one would expect in a late medieval chapel, its forms could well be understood in symbolic and representational terms. As a funerary chapel for Giovanni de' Medici and his wife, the cubical base was the more earthly of forms, transformed in the light of the dome into the heavenly realm. The dome itself had twelve ribs, and thus twelve oculi (lights), referring perhaps to the twelve apostles. Certainly none of these readings of the space was prescribed, but rather they were available to a viewer accustomed to reading symbolic meaning in these religious spaces.

The technical difficulty of dome construction was part of its appeal. It was known at the time that the dome of Hagia Sophia had collapsed. When the cathedral of Santa Maria del Fiore in Florence

The Dome of Heaven

As the best preserved of all ancient Roman monuments, the Pantheon was a powerful model for Renaissance architects, especially those wishing to evoke the glory of the imperial past [9]. The most recognizable element of the Pantheon was its vast and intact dome with an oculus at the centre, open to light and the elements. As a temple, the Pantheon was an obvious model, and challenge, to all later builders of religious architecture, especially for Christian churches. Medieval architects had already taken on the dome as a symbol of the dome of the heavens and the infinite power of the one Christian God over the universe. The Justinian church of Hagia Sophia (dedicated 537) in Constantinople (now Istanbul) was described at the time as having a dome that was not supported from below but held up by a great golden chain from heaven. A great dome was at the centre of all the designs for the new St Peter's, given Julius II's desire for the Roman Church to triumph over all adversaries, past, present, and future.

9

Pantheon [Palladio, *I quattro libri dell'architettura*, Venice 1570; Bk. IV, p. 81]

The Pantheon was the best preserved of all temples in Rome, and described as perfect both in form and in its effect. In his earlier treatise, Sebastiano Serlio placed it first in his book on antiquities, writing that 'it is that much more remarkable than the others because, although it has many members, those members are so well proportioned to the body that whoever sees such correspondence feels great satisfacion' (Bk. III, 50').

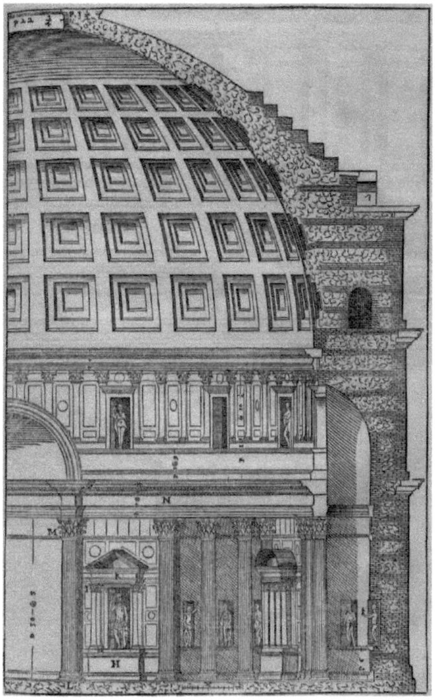

remained incomplete in 1410 after more than a century of construction, the completion of the dome was a matter of civic pride and concern [**10**].[3] Filippo Brunelleschi won the competition to solve the construction and design problems, and devised ways to hoist the heavy materials up to the level of the dome and construction solutions for the scaffolding and vaulting. The solution for the dome included the use of a double shell, bricks laid in a herringbone pattern, and pointed arches derived from medieval building practices. The importance of the dome to the status of the city, especially given its rivalry with neighbouring Siena, ensured the fame of the building and its architect in the history of Renaissance architecture.

Every aspect of the dome could take on religious significance, from its very shape to the manipulation of lights through windows, all read through Christian theology and liturgical practice. Domes also had an important function in the acoustic properties of churches. They shaped the experience of music and helped to project the spoken word of sermons and prayers. Secular buildings increasingly included the dome as a more general reference to ancient architecture. Andrea Palladio made the radical move to include domes, as well as temple fronts, in designs for villas, giving the house of the landowner the

10

Brunelleschi, Santa Maria del Fiore, dome constructed 1420–36, Florence, Italy

Although a rival to the great dome of the Pantheon in size and grandeur, the shape and solutions to the dome at Santa Maria del Fiore derive from earlier Gothic architectural solutions. The dome is essentially a rib vault structure, with lighter infill material, and a double shell construction. Brunelleschi's role as inventor, overseer, designer, and public figure marked a new moment in the history of the design profession.

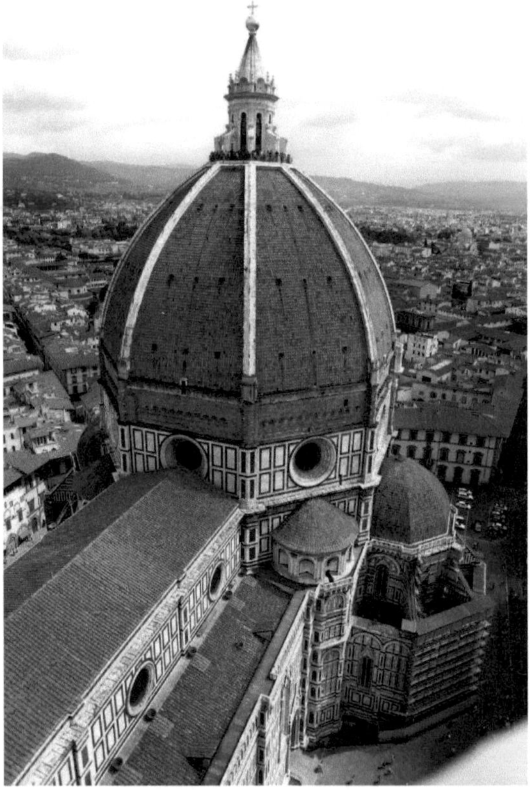

status that could come from a connection to antiquity and the references to religious architecture.

Centralized Plan Churches

On 6 July 1484, Jacopino d'Antonio de Seringo Lapovera, a young boy from the central Italian town of Prato, saw the Virgin Mary while he was chasing a cricket near the castle. The Virgin came to life for him from an image of her that was painted on the wall of an old prison. The fame of the miracle inspired the civic authorities to build a church in her honour, Santa Maria delle Carceri, and to establish Prato as the patron city of the cult.[4] Pilgrimage churches had a long medieval tradition, housing miracle-working images or religious relics. Church design took into account the increased number of pilgrims through separate ambulatories and chapels.

A competition was held for the design of the church and by April 1485 a committee selected the design of Giuliano da Maiano, although his project never proceeded much beyond the foundation. Lorenzo de' Medici, the patron at Prato, intervened that summer and appointed his own architect, Giuliano da Sangallo, to build the project to a new

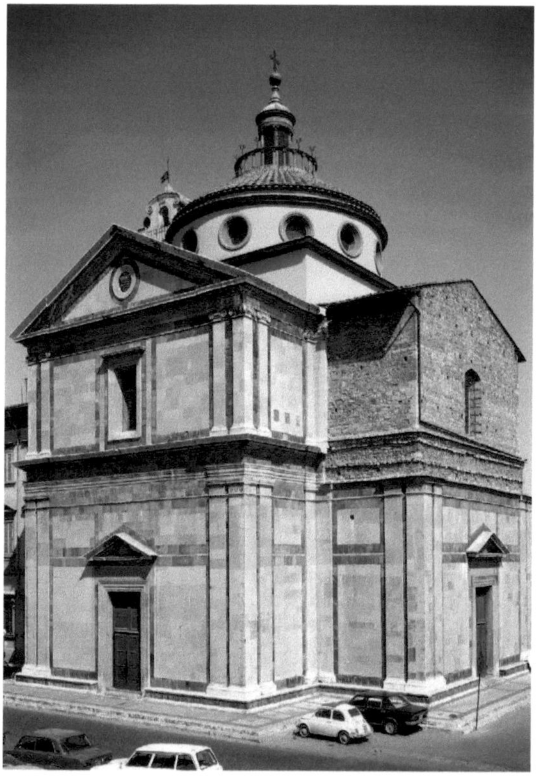

11

Giuliano da Sangallo, Sta Maria delle Carceri, 1485–99, Prato, Italy

Sangallo began his career as a woodworker, and that understanding of ornament, material, and composition can be seen in many of his architectural projects. Many drawings of ancient Roman architecture survive, and those designs appear in details of this church in the column capitals and balustrades. As a woodworker, Giuliano da Sangallo also created architectural models, including one for Santa Maria delle Carceri. Models allowed the architect and patron to evaluate the building as a three-dimensional object, and understand its overall design.

design. The revised scheme, followed in the church as built, was for a centralized church of a Greek cross plan, covered by a dome, and with each of the four arms the same width as the crossing [**11**]. The effect of the church from the outside is of a subtly controlled unity, conceived as a whole and intended as a monument as well as a place of worship.

Other pilgrimage churches in nearby towns had similar features to the church in Prato, and a certain amount of emulation, as well as civic competition, shaped the design decisions. Lorenzo de' Medici had requested a plan of Leon Battista Alberti's recent church in Mantua, S. Sebastiano (1460), also built according to a centralized plan. Another pilgrimage church in the Tuscan town of Bibbona housed a miracle-working image of the Virgin, and may have been a more likely source as it would have been seen as competition for the shrine at Prato.

Several features at Prato, however, were a response to the specific function of this church as a pilgrimage site. The bench around the outside provided seating for tired travellers. Identical portals on the three arms (the fourth holding the altar) allowed pilgrims to process into and through the church in an orderly fashion. Inside, the balustrade around the base of the dome holds candles, allowing the entire interior to be illuminated on important festivals and feast days.

Prato's Santa Maria delle Carceri is relatively unusual among fifteenth-century churches having been planned as a Greek cross plan, although many churches built during this period were designed as centralized buildings, more usually as round, square, or octagonal. An interest in centralized plans has been extensively studied in the history of Renaissance architecture, especially by Rudolf Wittkower in his book *Architectural Principles in the Age of Humanism*. For Wittkower, Leon Battista Alberti's programme of the ideal church in his *De re aedificatoria* (written about 1450) sets out principles for religious buildings emphasizing how the building would be seen. It should be monumental, according to Alberti, visible from all sides, and with the interior and exterior given equal importance. Each of these qualities of the building suggests a particular design decision, and a necessity for the architect (or a single individual) to be in charge of the conception of the building. If the interior and the exterior were to have equal importance, for example, then the plan and the elevation of the building must be thought about in tandem as interrelated elements. A wish for monumentality suggests a relationship to what was considered the most impressive architecture known at the time, that of ancient Rome. The Christian church of the Renaissance, therefore, was to be a new version of the ancient Roman temple. Wittkower notes that Alberti promotes centralized churches, and is no advocate for the basilican or longitudinal church—which was the most common church plan of the medieval period. Alberti must certainly have known that the basilican church had obvious advantages in its ability to hold large crowds and the ease of conducting Christian processions in the long nave. The emphasis on the circle as an ideal form leads Wittkower to relate this preference for a particular architectural plan in the writings of Alberti, Filarete, and later architectural theorists of the sixteenth century to broader issues of religious symbolism, philosophical discussions, and habits of the Renaissance mind. In discussing Sangallo's church of Santa Maria delle Carceri in Prato, Wittkower writes passionately of the synthesis he sees between the design of the building, Alberti's ideas, and Renaissance cosmology.

> The church, standing here like a precious jewel, is conceived, as it were, in Alberti's spirit. Its majestic simplicity, the undisturbed impact of its geometry, the purity of its whiteness are designed to evoke in the congregation a consciousness of the presence of God—of a God who has ordered the universe according to immutable mathematical laws, who has created a uniform and beautifully proportioned world, the consonance and harmony of which is mirrored in His temple below.[5]

It is difficult to say whether visitors to any centralized plan would have been aware of the symbolic references that Wittkower believes are at the root of the geometrical design, and fully available to the eye. Yet his method of understanding the choices of Renaissance architecture between competing designs certainly alerts us to the complex way that some Renaissance viewers could look at architecture. The attention to details by Renaissance architects, the subtle evolutions of the classical architectural vocabulary, the search for sources and antecedents, all suggest how even the most minor design decisions might be emotional and cultural triggers for a contemporary and later viewer. That these signals are sometimes difficult for us to recover at such a historical distance does not diminish our ability to intuit how much was at stake for architects and patrons.

Reform: Torgau Chapel

The great project by Pope Julius II to rebuild St Peter's in Rome outraged many who felt that the expense of the new church, raised mostly through the sale of indulgences, only served to glorify the power of the Pope over any true religious expression. St Peter's was to be a more magnificent and regal church than the early Christian basilica it replaced, which was, by the time of the Renaissance, in very poor condition and in need of repair. The new church was also, needless to say, to be a monument to the popes who commissioned it and raised funds for its completion. (See Chapter 3.)

Anger at the amount of money being raised, and the lavishness of the project, extended beyond St Peter's itself into a condemnation of all Roman (and courtly) architecture. As the crossing of the new St Peter's rose above the shell of the early Christian basilica, it began to resemble in its unfinished state an ancient Roman ruin [**42**]. Although on the one hand this could be understood as a sign of the resurrection, and thus fully a Christian theme, it could also be read another way: as an architecture comparable to the remnants of pagan culture, and therefore a sign that the Church was sinking to a level of decadence brought on by the ambition and grandeur of its leaders. The focus on the artistic qualities of the church in Rome, and the secular buildings of antiquity, fuelled charges that the papacy was interested in creating not so much a city of faith but primarily a showplace for private ambition.

One visitor caught up in the fury over the buildings in Rome was an Augustinian canon, Martin Luther, who visited Rome on a pilgrimage in 1510. The Pope was at the centre of his condemnations, Luther claiming that no German prince would dare to wear the rich vestments that he did and live in such worldly splendour.

Luther's anger at the grandeur of papal Rome suggests that he saw what were to him corrupt values embodied in the buildings. The idea that architecture could embody a morality, and communicate that morality to a viewer, was something new in the Renaissance; and marks a change in how a contemporary viewer might understand or read the architecture as a sign of the society which constructed it.

Luther's calls for reforms in the Christian Church and Christian liturgy had a profound effect on the creation, renovation, and use of religious space in the sixteenth century and after. Not only was there a surge of iconoclasm, the destruction and removal of sacred images, by avid reformers who believed them to be idolatrous. There was also the reorganization of existing churches in order to take account of the changes in liturgy. Pulpits were given prominence for preaching, and pews installed to allow congregants to listen to lengthy sermons. The structure of the Catholic Church, in both its theology and its spatial organization, enforced rigid hierarchies, differentiating between lay member and priest in the divisions within the church plan.

From the 1530s new Protestant churches were built in the first place within the castles erected by German princes who adopted the new reformed religion. Such princes took advantage of the religious dissention to assert control over ecclesiastical matters. The first newly built Protestant chapel was the project of the Saxon princes at Hartenfels Castle in Torgau [**12**]. Prince John Frederick began this

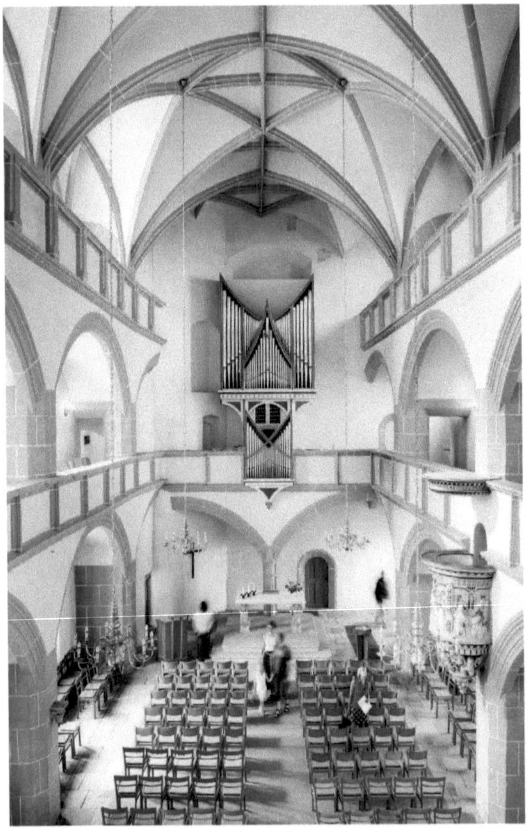

12

Nicholas Gromann, Chapel, Schloss Hartenfels, 1543–4, Torgau, Germany

The castle was begun in 1470, and additional wings added to it over time. Although the chapel was the first newly built Protestant worship hall, the design derives from local types with traditional Gothic ornament.

in 1533 as part of large-scale renovations to the castle by the Saxon court architect, Nicholas Gromann, in order to further establish the importance of the castle as a centre of the newly reformed religion. The chapel incorporated aspects of the reformed religion into its design, creating an architectural space ideally suited to the practices of worship.[6]

The space has no aisles; it is one large open space with all attention directed toward the simple altar at the far end. The pulpit is given prominence along the side of the nave, and the galleries provided space for groups of varying ranks to listen to sermons. All attention during the Eucharist, now presented directly to the lay congregation, was on the altar at the far end of the space. The centrality of the priest, and the focus of the event, was reinforced through the architecture, for just behind him was a single, unadorned column supporting the two arches west of the gallery, immediately below the organ.

The Castle Chapel was dedicated by Luther on 5 October 1544, and his sermon praised the 'new house built for the office of preaching God's word'.[7] In contrast to existing churches and cathedrals, the chapel was notably plainer and less ornamented, more in fact like a house than the rich and otherworldly spaces of Catholic worship. The smaller space was better too for acoustics, important for the new emphasis on preaching, and it allowed more direct views to the altar and preacher. Luther's reference to a 'house', however, also indicates his belief in the presence of God wherever his words are heard. No special conditions are necessary for his worship, other than a community of believers and attention to the religious teachings.

Protestant Temples

In 1598, King Henry IV of France signed the Edict of Nantes, ending the Wars of Religion (1562–98) and giving Protestants in that country limited rights. Huguenots, members of the Protestant Reformed Church of France, were allowed to build places to worship on the outskirts of cities; these halls could not be called either churches or temples, though the latter name would be used later. Almost all of these early places of worship were destroyed later, though images survive that show the arrangement of the altar, pulpits, and seating [**13**].

In his 1601 book on fortifications and architecture, Jacques Perret compared the Protestant churches to theatres and assembly halls.

> Inside there are three tiers of pews against the walls in the manner of a theatre, and in front of them a spacious aisle all the way around. There are chairs for the gentlemen and places for the ladies and, in the middle, benches for the countrywomen. Above the three tiers of pews galleries line the walls, one *toise* in breadth. Here, too, the seats are arranged in the manner of a theatre.[8]

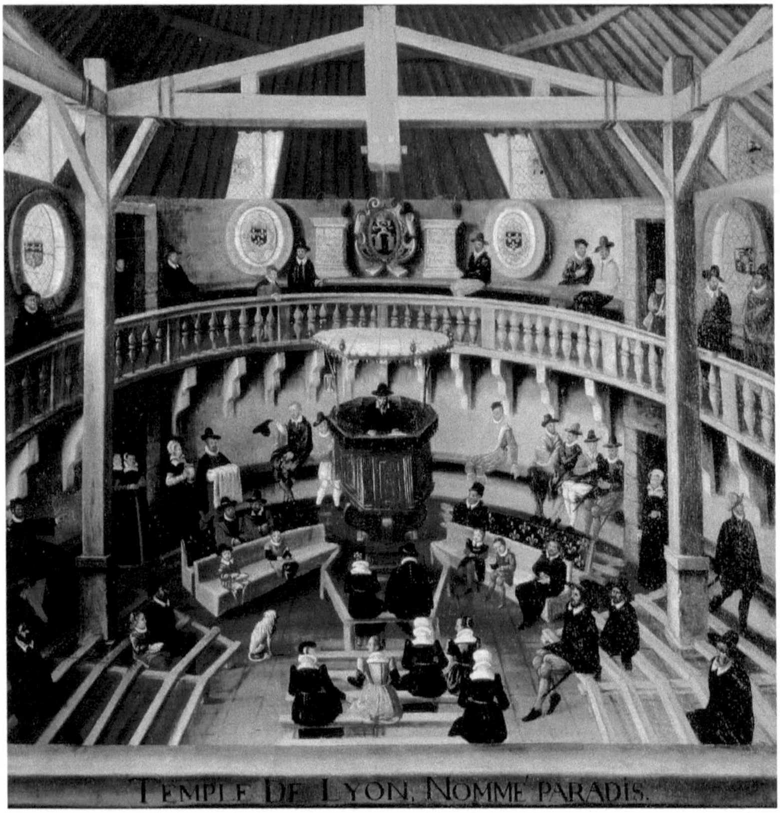

13

Le Paradis, a Calvinist Temple, 1564

Some of the pews are little more than wooden slats that serve as benches; other members of the congregation listen to the preacher from more comfortable pews with backs or set against the wall. The newly built Protestant church, as depicted in this painting, resembled a meeting room that emphasized the communal nature of worship. There are no religious decorations. The only ornament is the coats of arms of France and the town of Lyons. The straightforward building displays the supporting beams and joinery, a mirror of the tenets of the reform faith.

Distinctions between classes of people and the genders were embodied in the types of seating described by Perret and seen in the Temple of Paradise.

Synagogue

Jewish populations were often segregated to specific areas of cities, the ghettos, and built their homes, businesses, and communal buildings in that area with each forced relocation. (The urban aspects of the ghettos will be dealt with more thoroughly in the chapter on cities.) The construction of permanent places for worship was begun as soon as possible. From the outside the early synagogues were not readily noticeable or particularly grand. This may have been to protect them and deflect attention. It may also have been because the importance of the buildings was not on the façades but on the interior, the arrangement of sacred spaces and the objects held within. When permanent structures were not possible because they were not permitted by local regulations, illegal synagogues were fashioned in basements or upstairs rooms or places that could be kept well hidden.[9] The two specific elements that shaped the space of the synagogue were the

14

Old Synagogue, 16th century, Kazimierz [Krakow], Poland

Now the Jewish Museum in Krakow, the Old Synagogue is one of the best preserved synagogues in Poland. King Jan Olbrecht I moved all Jews from Krakow to Kazimierz beginning in 1495. This separate section of the city became a vital centre for Jews from Poland and beyond, with a population of about 4,500 by 1630. The *bimah* in the centre of the main space is original, probably done by the metalwork artisans from Krakow.

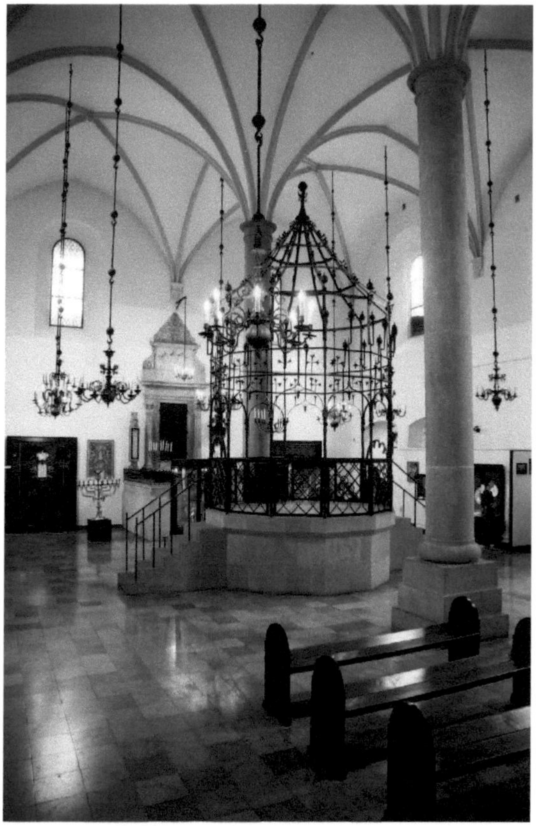

Torah ark, the cabinet for the holy scrolls, and the ***bimah***, the platform from which the Torah was read.[10]

Given the painful history of the Jews in Europe, with limited civic rights, expulsions, and the tragic pogroms and brutality of the Nazis in the Second World War, few synagogues survive from this early period, and fewer still are now used for their original purpose. Where they do remain, those areas have become places of pilgrimage for modern-day visitors. One such place is Kazimierz, which was a suburban town in the Grand Duchy of Krakow (Poland).[11] This section of the city has an important history within Jewish religion and culture as a centre for Kabbalistic scholarship and Jewish law as the home of Moses Isserles, known as ReMO (1520–72). His synagogue, built in 1556–7, its interior vaulted and simple in plan, was one of the first Polish synagogues built in masonry and incorporating elements of Renaissance planning.

The Old Synagogue in Kazimierz is a much larger structure than the ReMO synagogue, probably dates from some time after 1494, and was much rebuilt around 1570 [**14**]. The architect may have been an Italian, Matteo Gucci, who is associated with many buildings in Poland during this time. There is little evidence of Jewish designers or builders of synagogues; most were the product of Christian workers and masons because of restricted access to building guilds. The changes from the late fifteenth-century building to the sixteenth-century structure probably reflected changes in Polish architecture generally during this period: the shift away from late Gothic elements such as exposed buttresses and rib vaults to a more rectangular profile and simpler details. The interior plan is for a two-aisled building, with three bays, a relatively traditional form and common throughout synagogues of eastern and central Europe. The general proportions of the building are also broader, typical of architecture overall during this period. The ***bimah*** is towards the centre of the building, marked off by an elaborate iron cage. Other interior fittings would have included chandeliers, and inscriptions and reliefs on the walls. As with many synagogues, a women's gallery was added later, after 1600. This movement to make the specific ritual spaces within the synagogue more distinctive, and readily recognizable for their function, was a corollary effect of general trends in the planning of religious and secular spaces of all types during this period, a desire to codify and make clearly legible the various parts of building through planning, ornament, and materials.

Devotional Buildings: Tempietto, Tresham, Coimbra

In addition to churches, there was also a need for other types of devotional buildings more closely focused on a particular cult or devotional practice during the Renaissance. These buildings, often substantially smaller than the more public church, were often more visually and spatially inventive.

Adjacent to San Miniato al Monte, the Spanish church in Rome, was the site where St Peter was believed to have been crucified. Ferdinand II, King of Sicily and Aragon, and Queen Isabella of Castile and León commissioned a building called the Tempietto (or little temple) to commemorate the location and increase pilgrimage to the site. The location of the base of the cross in the crypt, visible through an opening in the main floor above, was the organizing principle for the Tempietto and its planned courtyard [**15**]. Everything radiates from this central point. The building is circular, appropriate for housing a relic yet also unmistakably related to a number of ancient circular temples such as the Temple of Vesta by the Tiber in Rome (late second century BC).

From a plate in Sebastiano Serlio's treatise, we know that there was a scheme for the building to be placed within a circular courtyard, surrounded by a colonnade. The unrelenting centrality would have emphasized the exact location of St Peter's crucifixion and added a devotional intensity to the building beginning as soon as a visitor entered into the space. This setting was never executed.

15

Donato Bramante, Tempietto, San Miniato al Monte, *c.*1505, Rome

Bramante's small temple, both ancient and modern in conception and execution, quickly achieved fame. Andrea Palladio included it in his treatise among his reconstructions of ancient temples, the only Renaissance building so honoured.

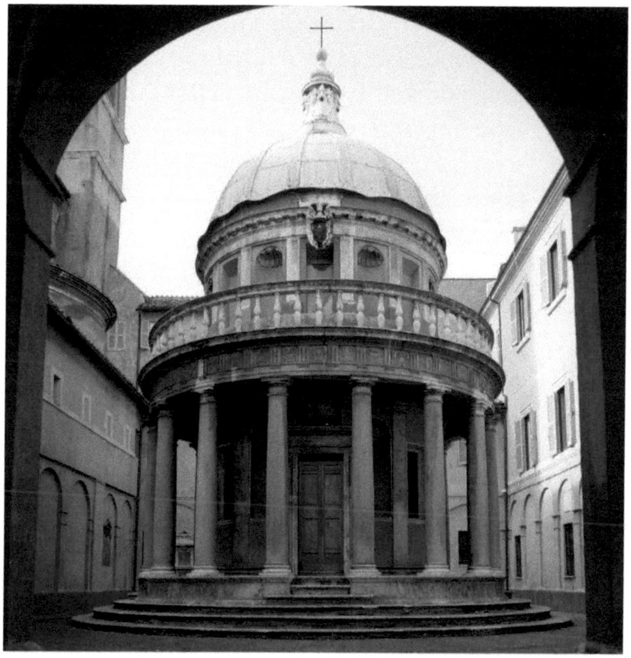

Bramante chose the Doric order for the Tempietto, and based all dimensions on the diameter of the sixteen columns ringing the central space on the exterior. This was the first building after antiquity to be built in the Doric order using the full accompaniment of ornament with **triglyphs** and here appropriately with symbols of Christian passion in the **metopes**, and it called for meticulous control from the architect. The columns, which were *spolia*, that is, taken from ancient buildings, support a continuous entablature with a balustrade above. A ring of space surrounds the enclosed room, only 4 metres in diameter. The dome is raised on a tall attic storey, thus increasing its prominence. Different parts of the building are connected through their reflection in other parts of the building: columns are mirrored in the pilasters against the inner wall, balustrades continue the line of the columns, and interior ornamentation is a mirror of what one sees on the exterior.

The design's intensity was Bramante's calling card in Rome; the Tempietto remained his most famous building and has received acclaim as a masterpiece of Renaissance architecture ever since. The tremendous focus of the building, all centred around the supposed spot of St Peter's crucifixion, and mediated through the Doric order, demanded a kind of looking which was devotional in its intensity and made the highest claims on the viewer to match the performance of the architect.

Churches and shrines were only one kind of devotional building, and individual patrons could include public signs of their faith in more everyday structures. Sir Thomas Tresham was a recusant in Elizabethan England, that is he refused to adopt the state faith of the Church of England and remained a practising Catholic. Throughout his life he was imprisoned for his faith, paying large fines, yet continued to express his loyalty to the Church of Rome in often public ways. Tresham was an avid builder with a large collection of architectural treatises in his library. He paid for a new market hall in his town, Rothwell in Northamptonshire, and planned several new buildings on his extensive properties. In Rushton, he built an elaborate lodge to be used in connection with his extensive rabbit warren [**16**]. In plan and ornament, however, the lodge is a statement of religious belief and a means for devotional meditation. The Triangular Lodge is an exploration of the symbolism of the Trinity, central to Catholic faith, and a simultaneous play on Tresham's own name and coat of arms: *tres* meaning three. On each of the three sides of the building, and on its three levels, and three gables on each side, are signs of the Trinity. A series of inscriptions run around the building, each a key to a longer passage that was frequently used as part of Jesuit meditation, and that Tresham knew well.[12]

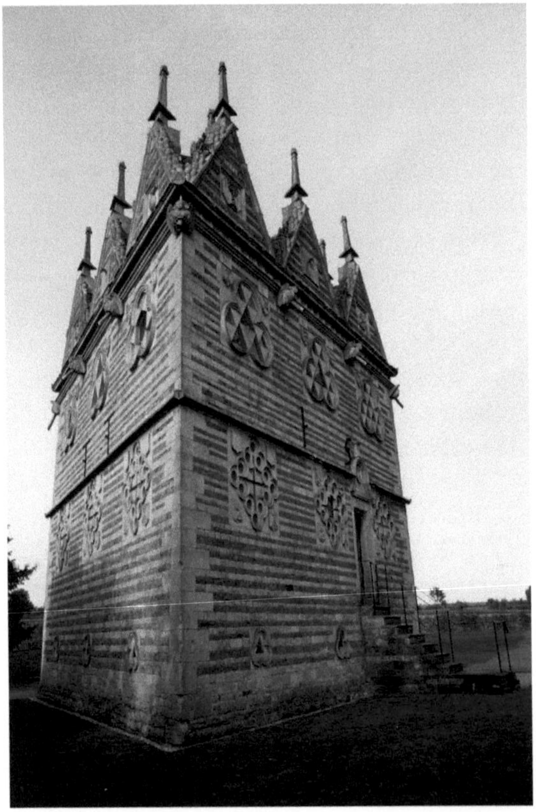

16

Triangular Lodge, Rushton, 1595, Northamptonshire, England

Sir Thomas Tresham's motto, *Tres testimonium dant*, 'There are three that bear witness', is carved over the entrance. Made from local materials, though with highly charged religious symbols, the Triangular Lodge is a kind of architectural rebus, and meant to engage the viewer in self-reflection and religious meditation.

While it may seem strange that this building was used as part of Tresham's rabbit warrens there may be a connection with its religious meaning. While the building was not a Catholic chapel or church, rabbits were an important symbol in Christian iconography of the faithful and of Christ himself. Even more, the prominent place of this building alongside a road, and close by Tresham's house at Rushton, indicate its importance for him personally and publicly. Devotional buildings did not need to be only churches or shrines; they could exist right in the midst of the everyday activities of their users. Rabbits and signs of the Catholic Trinity are not obvious neighbours, but their coexistence tells us much about the creation of sacred space in the everyday.

Such integration of devotional spaces into everyday life was most clearly accomplished in the context of religious houses. Following a long medieval tradition, the cloister was a space for religious contemplation as well as a place for relaxation and the enjoyment of nature. In a monastery or convent, all activity was understood to be in the service and devotion of God, and the practices of this world were to be a mirror of a heavenly world beyond. Fountains, in particular, were a rich site of religious meaning in addition to their very worldly functions of providing water for the brethren.[13] For example, the fountain in the Manga Cloister at the Augustinian monastery of Santa Cruz in Coimbra, Portugal, is a multipart structure, a central domed pavilion over the water linked by four small footbridges to four outer cells [**17**]. The domed pavilion on columns evokes classical buildings, especially garden buildings, in Italy; and King João III, ruler at

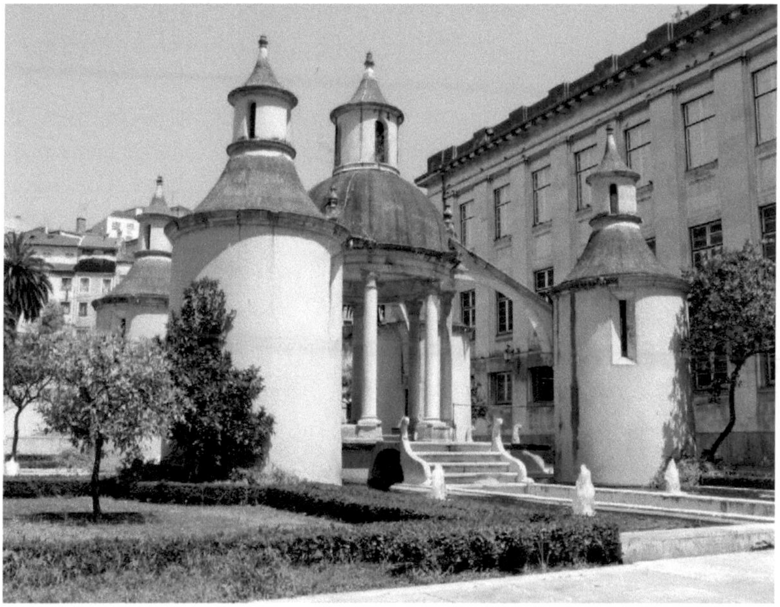

17

João de Ruão, Fountain, Manga Cloister, *c.*1535, Santa Cruz Monastery, Coimbra, Portugal

The fountain was probably the work of a French sculptor, Jean de Rouen (called João de Ruão in Portuguese; born in Rouen 1500, died in Coimbra 1580). He worked extensively in Coimbra and for the Monastery of Santa Cruz, designing funerary sculpture, retables, and chapels as well as larger architectural works. He brought a more classicizing style to this important university town and the important patrons connected with the intellectual culture fostered there. His large workshop helped to promote these ideas to a wider audience.

the time, was promoting closer ties to the papal court. That classicism, however, is combined with cupolas and an overall plan that is both Islamic and Moorish in inspiration. Typically, Portuguese architecture draws on a variety of cultures and traditions.

Fr. Jerónimos Roman visited the monastery in 1589, fifty years after it was built, and described how the fountain was used for contemplation and solitude. In each of the smaller buildings was an altar with relief carvings of an eremitic saint, St John the Baptist, St Jerome, St Paul, and St Anthony. The experience of walking up the stairs and onto the central island, and moving into the semi-darkness of the devotional cells, was part of a meditational practice facilitated through the architecture. All of the senses were engaged in this process, the sound of the splashing water and the smells of the garden cloister beyond.

Recreating the Holy Land

A pilgrimage to the Holy Land was an important concept of medieval religious practice, and continued into the Renaissance. Journeys to holy sites as part of individual devotional practice linked the three major religions of Europe, Judaism, Christianity, and Islam, creating a common experience. Jerusalem and Mecca were the most important destinations in order to see the places described in the sacred texts. These frequently perilous and always difficult journeys were often highly social events, as described by Geoffrey Chaucer in *The Canterbury Tales*, involving shared religious (and sometimes quite secular) experiences along the way. Seeking redemption for sins or sometimes healing, the pilgrim hoped for an intense spiritual experience at the end of his or her journey.[14]

If Muslim control of the eastern Mediterranean made voyages to Jerusalem even more difficult, then sites in Europe such as Santiago de Compostela remained popular alternatives, though still an arduous journey across the Alps into northern Spain. Pilgrimage could also be folded into new devotional practices. The Franciscan monk Bernardino Caimi (1425–1500) planned a series of chapels in the foothills north of Milan that would recreate the experience of a journey to the Holy Land and that he called the New Jerusalem (Caimi had previously served as patriarch of the Holy Land). Construction of the Sacro Monte, or sacred mountain, at Varallo began in 1480, and eventually included forty-three chapels set into a dramatic landscape [**18**]. As elaborations of the Stations of the Cross, in each of the chapels is a scene from the life of Jesus Christ, including polychrome life-size figures, fresco paintings, and props such as tables and chairs that make the scenes seem as if they are appearing directly in the same space as that occupied by the viewer. As originally planned, visitors to the chapels could move into the space, and walk among the sculptures. The spatial

18

Sacra Monte, Varallo, Italy

The sequence of chapels allowed visitors to move from scene to scene, and therefore participate in the unfolding drama of Christ's life. The experience was intended to be deeply emotional and engage all of the senses through the recitation of prayers that focused on the physical experience of the Passion.

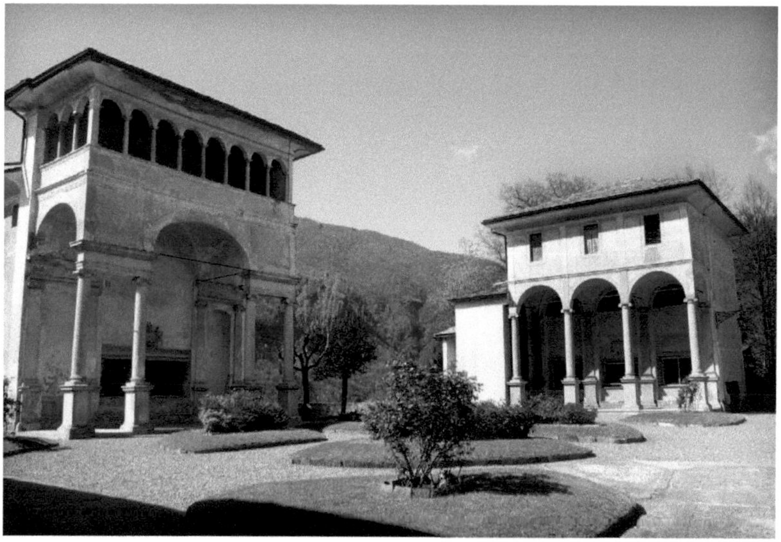

ambiguities and lifelike qualities of the sculpture heightened the emotional experience and religious intensity for the visitor, dissolving at least temporarily the distance between their everyday experience and the presence of the sacred.[15] In order to dissolve the distance between the sites in Jerusalem and the chapels in Varallo, special attention was given to creating the material qualities of the Holy Land. Devotional literature by Franciscan friars (the same order responsible for the Sacro Monte at Varallo) described in great detail aspects of Christ's life in order to encourage the faithful. After his visit to Varallo in 1507, the humanist Girolamo Morone wrote to a friend that 'I never saw anything more pious or devout; anything that can move the heart in the same way. On this Holy Mountain one is compelled to follow only Christ and to forget about everything else. Everything you see here is superior to all antiquity.'[16] Even the spacing between the buildings recreated the original, according to a guide who led Morone through the site.

Sacro monte in various forms developed throughout northern Italy, prompted by the expansion of the Muslim empire throughout the eastern Mediterranean and into Europe. A secondary threat was perceived from the Protestant reformers to the north, and in this way the chapels were also like religious bastions in the foothills of the Alps. San Carlo Borromeo, the Catholic religious reformer from Milan, was the later patron for many of these sites. Several chapels at Varallo are dedicated to scenes from his life.[17]

Venice and the East

In 1576 over 70,000 people in Venice died from the plague. In thanksgiving to God for the end of the plague, the Doge and council

19

Andrea Palladio, Il Redentore, begun 1576, Venice, Italy

The classical façade of Il Redentore was a theme that Palladio had earlier developed at Santa Maria Maggiore, prominently located across the lagoon between the Giudecca and the Palazzo Ducale. Yet both façades were not completed until long after Palladio's death in 1580. White Istrian stone marked out the façade in contrast to the brick side elevations.

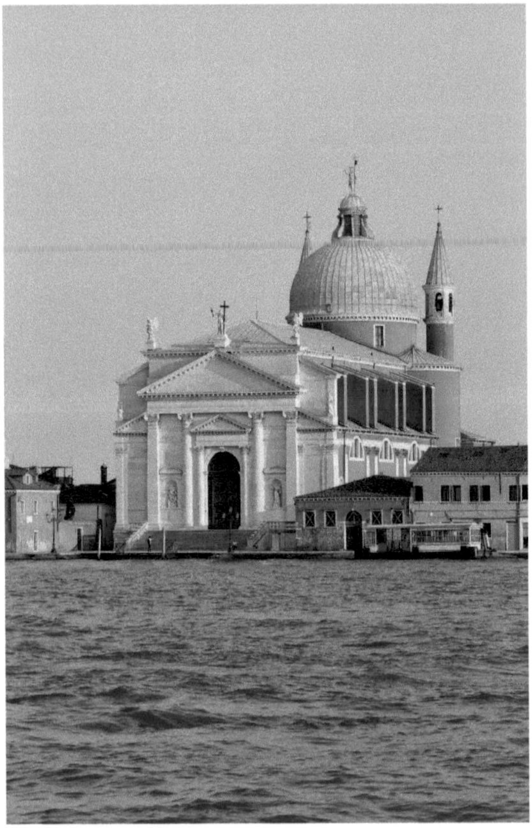

commissioned a new church dedicated to Christ the Redeemer (Il Redentore) to be built on the island of Giudecca, across from the Doge's Palace and San Marco. Andrea Palladio seems to have been the only architect considered for the commission of the church Il Redentore, probably due to the success of his earlier Venetian church of San Giorgio Maggiore (1565) [**19**].

Each year the Doge would visit the church on the feast day of the Redeemer, 15 July, walking across a pontoon bridge from the Doge's Palace to the Giudecca. As a reminder of divine intervention on behalf of the city, this festival reinforced the specific connection between civic authority and religious life in Venice. As the Doge approached the church straight on, he and his council would mount a wide, theatrical flight of stairs, set off against the gleaming white façade. The front of the church was made of Istrian stone, and stands out in sharp contrast to the brick of the building's side elevation or the mixed materials of the other buildings in the area. The design of the façade itself was a meditation on Palladio's study of the ancient Roman temples, in particular the portico of the Pantheon in Rome [**9**]. From his studies of temples when he travelled to Rome and later in his drawings of it for his treatise *I quattro libri dell'architettura*, Palladio had looked attentively at the portico as a model and motif for the use of basilican churches. In his book Palladio showed the Pantheon in **orthogonal** projection, where it seems to have multiple pediments that intersect. By shifting the proportional relationships of the pediment and the columns, making each taller or wider, he could compose a façade of interlocking temple fronts. Thus one motif could be used for the parts of the façade related to the side aisles as well as for the higher nave of the church.

In thinking about the plan of the church Palladio had to take into account not only the ceremonial and civic requirements, but also the needs of the Capuchin brothers for whom the church was also built [**20**]. The wide nave without aisles could accommodate the procession of the Doge and the large number of people in his retinue. For the Capuchin brothers, the very plain architecture of the choir, marked off from the nave and altar by a screen of columns, was more in keeping with the order's devotion to poverty and serving the poor. Passages through the side chapels along the nave allowed the order to worship and to move throughout the church without participating in the more public patterns of worship.

20

Plan, Andrea Palladio, Il Redentore, begun 1576, Venice, Italy

The plan shows three distinct types of spaces: the longitudinal nave, semicircular transepts, and rectilinear choir.

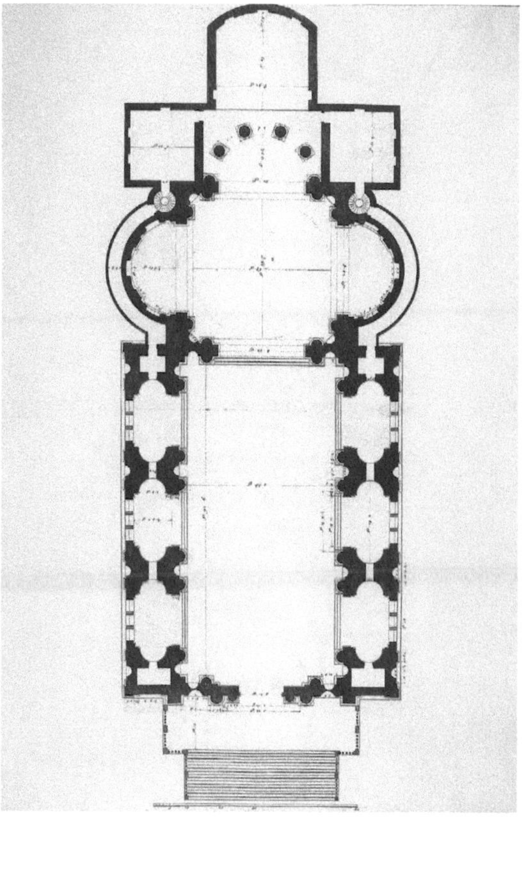

All members of the congregation would have been struck by the unified and organic ornament on the interior, the reduction of colours to a simple grey and white, and the interior flooded with light [**21**]. In his treatise Palladio had stated that white was the colour most pleasing to God, and that is apparent here in both the white façade and the monochromatic scheme on the interior. Even more, however, the experience of entering the church is of an interior space filled with light, as if that light were an almost tangible object. The light picks out the refinement of Palladio's details in the mouldings and ornament of the orders, and all of the interior spaces appear part of a unified interior space. What could also be thought as another version of the whiteness that Palladio praised, the presence of so much light was made possible because large semicircular windows are filled with clear glass. These were a version of those Palladio had studied in the ancient Roman baths in Rome. In Venice, he used them as a suitable form along the nave chapels and around the dome. They were also an ideal shape to highlight a Venetian manufacturing product. The workshops on Murano were renowned for their clear glass, called *cristallo*, whose formula no glassmaker was allowed to divulge. In creating a particularly Venetian church, Palladio transforms

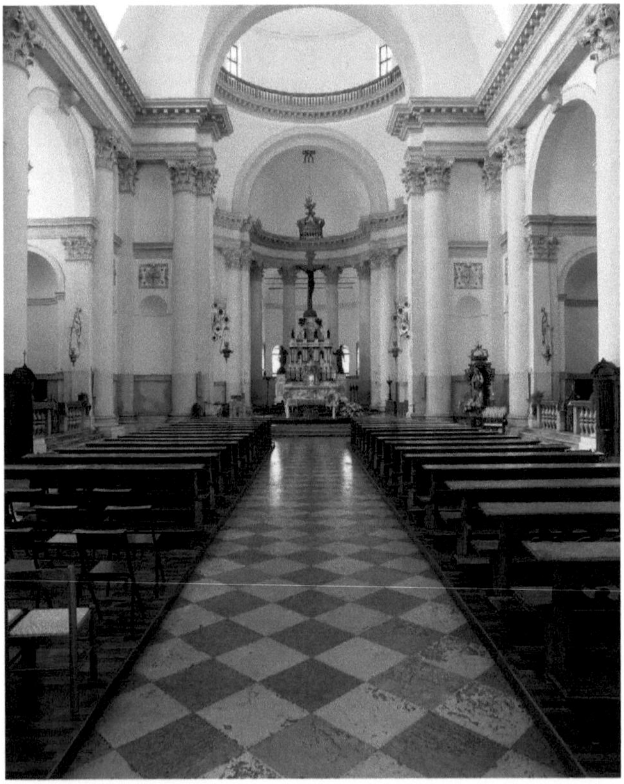

21

Interior, Andrea Palladio, Il Redentore, begun 1576, Venice, Italy

Palladio used columns and classical architectural details to unify the space and mark out areas of special importance. The Corinthian columns down the nave, supporting the complex entablature, evoke the procession of the Doge that happened once a year. Closer to the crossing, under the dome, and near to the altar, the columns increase in number.

ancient Roman models in order to accommodate very local needs and promote Venetian materials.

The simplified and light-filled interior, unified ornament, and visibility of the altar may also have been a response to the effect of the Counter-Reformation. Venice had always maintained a more distant posture in regards to the authority of Rome, claiming for herself both the authority of the 'new Rome' and a greater openness to reform theology. The Redentore incorporates many of these liturgical changes in the plan that allows a clear view of the altar and the unified ornament based explicitly on ancient models.

As much as Palladio looked to ancient Rome for models of ornament or specific details, such as the windows taken from ancient baths, the local models were particularly strong exempla for the architect and framework for a visitor. The palatine church of San Marco, visible across the water from the small piazza outside the Redentore, was the ever present architectural authority. Palladio looked to compress the richness of individual elements at San Marco into a more simplified form, allowing the two buildings to speak to one another as variations on similar themes. So, while San Marco has five domes, one over the nave and each arm of the Greek cross, the Redentore has one dome centred over the crossing of apse and transepts. If San Marco has multiple entrances and discrete façades associated with each door, the

The Light of God

Alberti wrote that churches should be dark in order that chapels can be lit on specific holy days. Lighting contributed to the drama of religious practices, and all religious buildings took this into account. Entering into the darkened space of the religious sanctuary created a space that was different from the world outside, while the lighting of candles or lamps had specific religious meanings.

Artificial as well as natural light was an important form of illumination. Lamps and reflective mirror balls were hung from the central dome of Ottoman mosques, and therefore articulated the upper space within the lower zone. When the lamps were lit at night, the mosque would have radiated light from its numerous windows out over the city. The building itself would have become symbolically like a lamp, as in the passage from the Koran 'The lamp in a glass, the glass as it were a glittering star' (24: 35).

Stained glass continued to be made well into the Renaissance, and as with medieval buildings, these windows changed the quality of light in the interior while also conveying a story for those within the building.

A change in lighting was one of the effects of the religious reform movements to church architecture. Windows were added to existing churches, especially in Venice, to make the interiors brighter and more evenly lit. A more luminous interior allowed the mass to be more clearly seen by the laity, especially at the moment of the elevation of the host.

Candles were an essential part of the liturgy, a major expense for the church but often donated by lay groups as part of their good works. Their light shimmered on the gold and silver plate that was an essential part of the service, and transformed the space of the church into a living and breathing space for the mass.

Redentore has one door and a series of interwoven temple façades that focus attention on the only entrance.

One of the most unusual aspects of the Redentore is the two thin bell towers that flank the central dome. Seen from the apse end, from the gardens of the monastery, the towers are closer to eastern Mediterranean examples, and may even be a response to the close contact Venice had with Istanbul to the east. The *campanili* of the Redentore recall the minarets of mosques in Istanbul that Marc'Antonio Barbaro knew well from his time as Venetian ambassador to the Ottoman court in 1568 to 1573. Barbaro was closely involved in the commission of the Redentore, with a clear preference for a centralized plan that would have recalled, even more clearly, the great mosques of the architect Sinan in the Ottoman Empire.

'Superbissime Fabbriche': Sinan and Istanbul

Architectural ideas circulated freely around the great cities of the Mediterranean. Ambassadors such as Marc'Antonio Barbaro brought back reports of the great buildings built by the rulers and courtiers that they had seen abroad. Merchants, pilgrims, and even soldiers were all conduits for information about architecture in foreign places. So it is not surprising that architects knew of the work of their counterparts abroad.

Venice and Istanbul shared a long history that made their architectural similarities more likely.[18] Both cities were the capitals of great military empires. The setting on the sea, with its possibilities for great views, inspired architects in both places to make much of the skyline's impact in the design of their buildings. And in the fifteenth and sixteenth centuries, both cultures were deeply involved in the crafting of Renaissance identities that looked back at earlier buildings for models and inspiration.

Sinan (*c.*1500–1588) was the chief architect for the Ottoman court for fifty years, designing hundreds of buildings throughout the empire.[19] Trained as a carpenter, and originally serving in the military, he developed a style of architecture that was flexible and visually arresting, classical in its simplicity and attentive to the demands of the site and the needs of the patron. Marc'Antonio Barbaro described Sinan's architecture as 'superbissime fabbriche' ('extraordinary and awe-inspiring buildings'), and in particular praised the mosque complex that he designed in Istanbul for the Grand Vizier, Sokollu Mehmet Pasha.

Sokollu rose to power through his service to three Ottoman sultans, and was rewarded with marriage to the daughter of Prince Selim, İsmihan, forty years his junior. When Selim rose to the sultanate in 1566, Sokollu's fame also reached its height, and it was in those years that he commissioned his most important architecture from Sinan.

22

Sinan, İsmihan-Sokollu mosque, 1571–2, Kadırgalimanı, Istanbul

A wide porch of seven domes leads into the mosque, beyond the onion dome of the fountain covering. Domes also cover each room of the *madrasa*, the slightly lower wings on three sides as well as on the mosque itself. Sinan repeats forms, in various guises, focusing attention as you climb the hill to the plateau on the marble courtyard. In a similar way, arches appear in the façade of the mosque, the arcade of the *madrasa*, and the porch. Yet each architectural element is marked by a different type of arch that helps to distinguish the various functions of the building complex.

23

Sinan, Plan, İsmihan-Sokollu mosque, 1571–2, Kadırgalimanı, Istanbul

The plan shows the strong axial orientation through the classroom (2), fountain, mosque (1), and the ritual hall of the convent (3) at the top.

The Friday mosque complex at Kadırgalimanı (1571–2) overlooks the Sea of Marmara in Istanbul [**22, 23, 24**]. It was a project of both Sokollu and his wife İsmihan, each of whom claims patronage for the project in their *waqfiyya*, or deed, describing the conditions for the upkeep of religious buildings and charitable

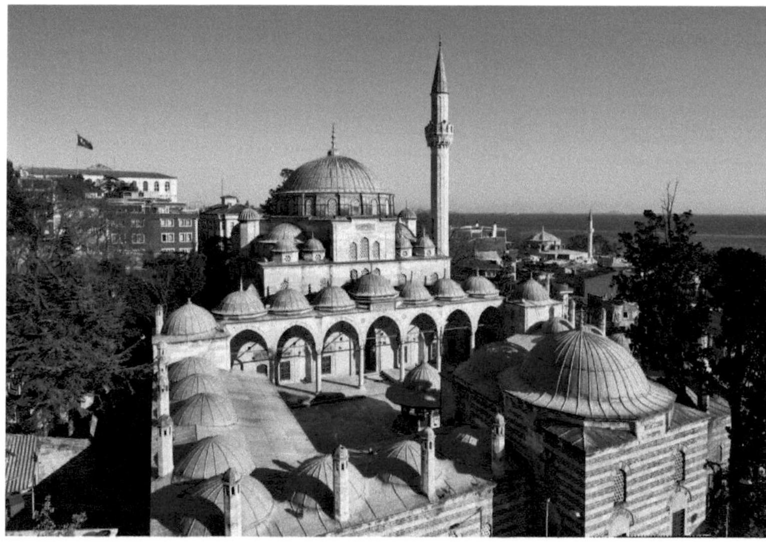

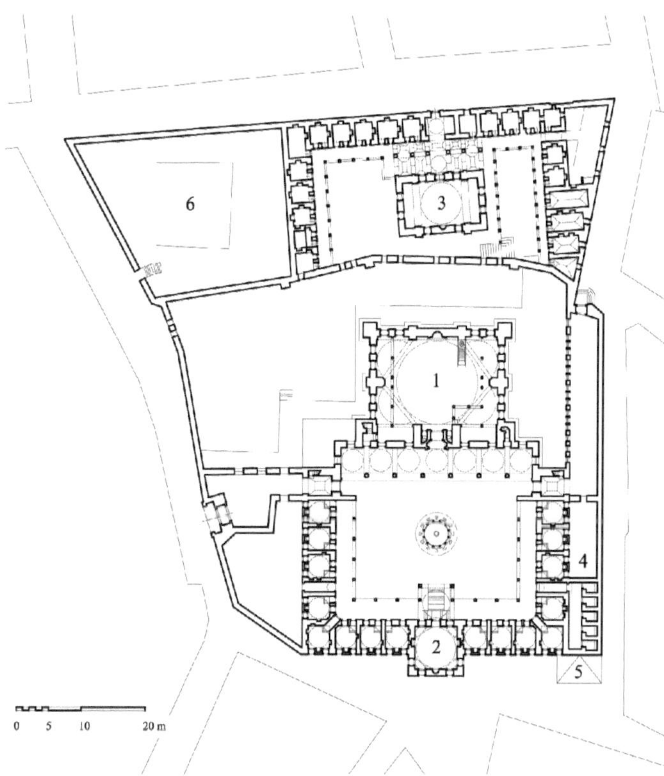

24

Sinan, View of the *qibla* wall, İsmihan-Sokollu mosque, 1571–2, Kadırgalimanı, Istanbul

Ornament is an integral part of the mosque's interior, articulating junctures between parts of the building and highlighting the most important areas used for religious practice, especially on the *qibla* wall. The exquisite Iznik tiles were planned in conjunction with the painting, stained glass, carpets, lamps, and wood inlay, incorporating both natural and abstract forms as well as inscriptions.

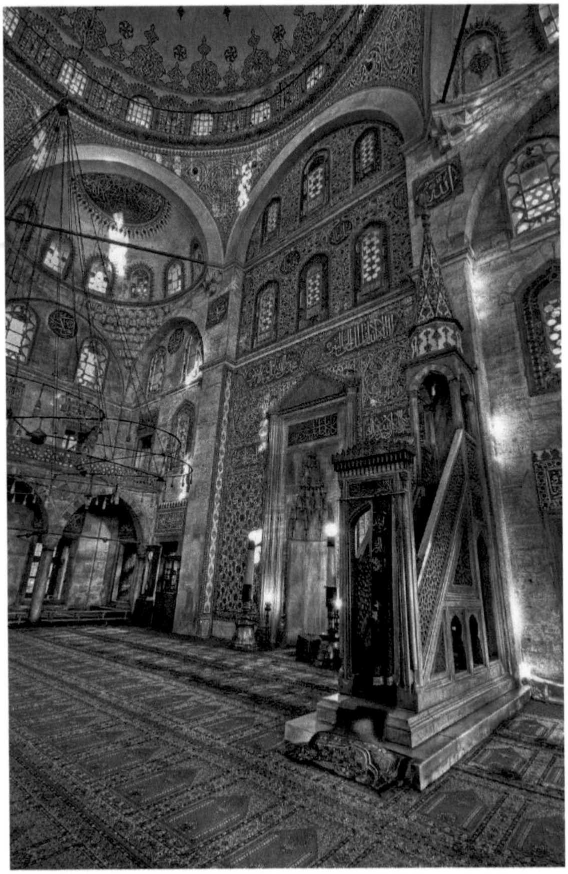

foundations. Set in a residential area of the city, Sinan used the hilly location to his advantage, raising the main courtyard on a substructure of shops. One enters the mosque complex from below, rising up steep stairs to the courtyard with its ablution fountain set on axis with the entrance to the mosque. The *madrasa*, or school, surrounds the courtyard on three sides, framing the seven-bay portico leading into the mosque itself. On higher ground, and behind the mosque, is the convent with thirty rooms for dervishes and various communal spaces. Each element of the complex is distinguished by different architectural forms and materials. To the street, the exterior is made of alternating strips of masonry and brick. The convent uses wood and less expensive materials. The mosque and courtyard is built from smooth ashlar stone, marble pavements, lead on the roofs (reserved for buildings associated with the royal court), and the richest decoration on the interior. Sinan uses both form and materials to mark the transition from public space to the sacred interior.

At the İsmihan-Sokollu mosque, Sinan created an interior that unifies structure with ornament, creating a prayer hall with a single open space, uninterrupted with columns. The dome rises above the rectangular ground plan, supported by piers pulled into the lateral walls and supported on the exterior by smaller domes and towers. Six arches support the dome, with ***muqarnas*** marking the transition area to the wall below. One hundred windows control the flow of light into the interior, highlighting the unity of the central space. The clarity of the building's structure is set off with painting and, most importantly, the highest quality of glazed Iznik tile on the ***qibla*** wall and in the dome **pendentives**. Inscriptions throughout the mosque complex urge the practice of the faithful as a turning toward God through education and prayer. On the classroom door is inscribed 'Striving for knowledge is a sacred duty of all Muslim men and women.' İsmihan Sultan's *waqfiyya* describes the creation of the universe as a perfectly decorated mosque. At the Sokollu Mehmet Pasha mosque, all the inscriptions, decorations, and structural choices of her architect, Sinan, make that vision a reality.

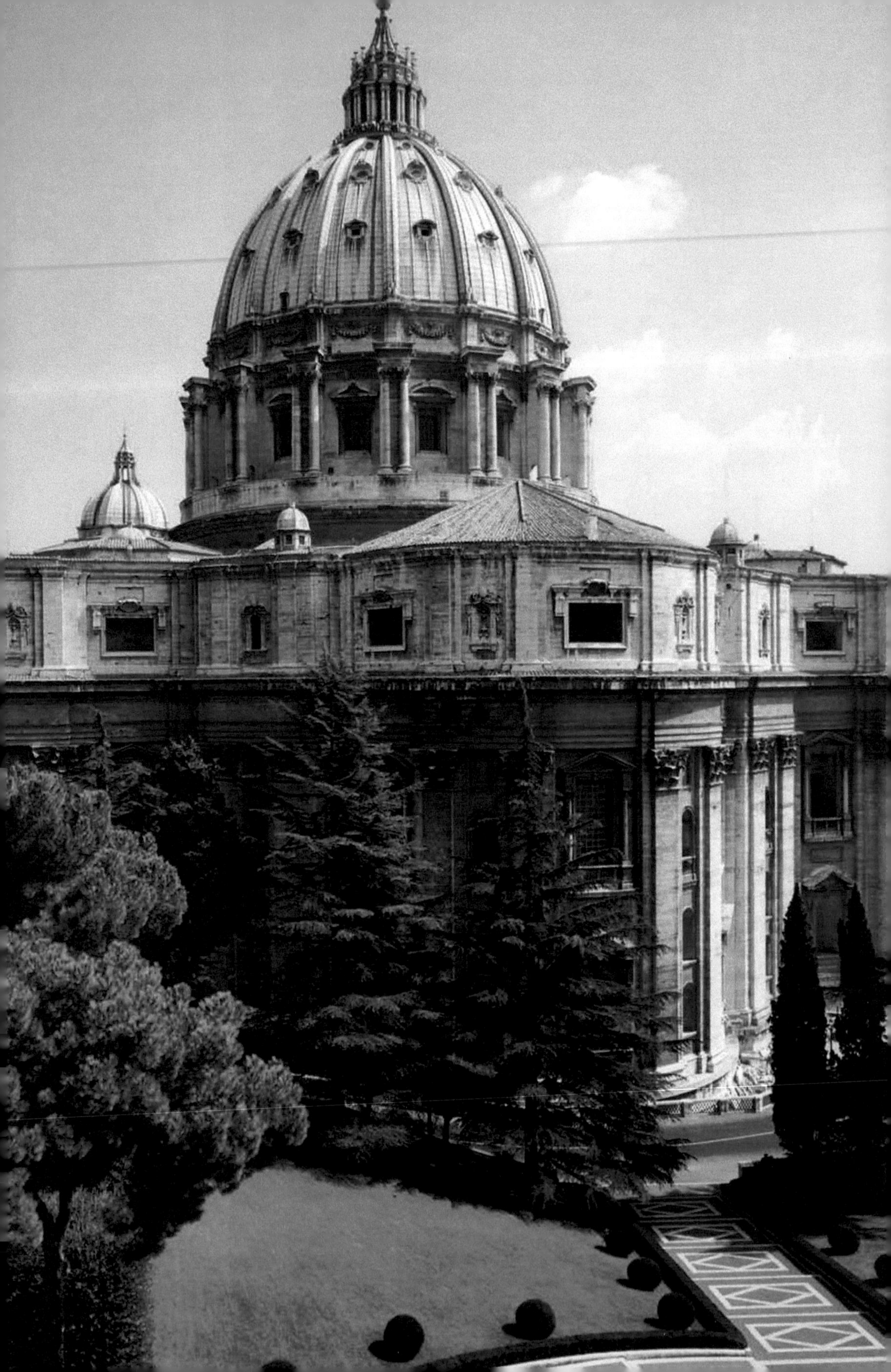

Theories and Practices

The Case of St Peter's, Rome

3

> But how congenial and instinctive the desire and thought for building may be to our minds is evident—if only because you will never find anyone who is not eager to build something, as soon as he has the means to do so; nor is there anyone who, on making some discovery in the art of building, would not gladly and willingly offer and broadcast his advice for general use, as if compelled to do so by nature.
>
> (Leon Battista Alberti, *On the Art of Building* (1450), prologue)

In his treatise on all things related to architecture, Alberti identifies an uncontrollable urge to build, or if building is not immediately possible, then the desire to think and talk about building. We cannot help ourselves from thinking about architecture, he writes, and, inevitably, from giving our opinion. By the mid-fifteenth century, when Alberti is writing, the interest in architecture was widespread among the educated classes. Yet Alberti is actually identifying a relatively new social phenomenon, the rise of architecture as a topic of conversation. His treatise addresses a new audience for architecture: the enthusiastic patron, the learned reader wishing to know more about the art of building as part of a culture of learning.

Architecture had evolved into its own discipline with publications, professional training, and competing theories. Opinions on the best form of building were passionately held. Dialogues and debates could be followed in the multiple treatises that offered diverse ideas on the best models from the antique, variations of ornament, or innovations in building technologies. Architects and authors may never have met in person but they could communicate via their publications. Readers could even communicate with authors long dead: translations of the ancient author Vitruvius included the translator's commentary.

Detail of 25

With architectural drawings and the architectural treatise new methods of architectural communication appeared in the Renaissance. While such ways of communicating existed to some degree before, they rose to a new level of importance and complexity in the fifteenth and sixteenth centuries. These highly evolved and to some extent new forms of architectural communication changed the way that buildings were thought about and ultimately designed. Printing, invented around the middle of the fifteenth century, was changing access to architectural information that had previously been closely held by guilds and craftsmen wary of revealing trade secrets to those outside the guild system.

Architectural theory is more properly thought of as part of an ongoing conversation about issues at the heart of building on both the philosophical and practical level. Architectural discourse developed through the study in other disciplines including history, theology, antiquarian studies, and especially the scientific practices of mathematics, surveying, and fortification design.[1]

Interest in architecture developed as patrons, architects, and the general public increasingly took an interest in major building projects, and the possibility of building for their own purposes. The construction of St Peter's in Rome, at the epicentre of Christianity, attracted the attention of not only the population of the city but also the numbers who came to the city on pilgrimages as well as state visits. Like the construction of the Süleymaniye mosque in Istanbul in 1550–8 (built in only eight years compared to the hundreds needed for the completion of St Peter's), imperial building projects engaged the attention of a wide public.

At the same time, despite all this intellectual ferment surrounding architecture and the remarkable novelty of these designs, actual building practice changed little. New ideas were generated by the study of classical antiquity that had a transformative impact on building design through the recovery of classical forms and the study of archaeological details, creating projects that consciously echoed ancient buildings. At St Peter's the shell of the new building was greatly expanded, resulting in a more stable design (roofed by stone vaults rather than wooden trusses). Yet to raise this structure masons continued to employ standard masonry technology used for centuries in Italy and other parts of Europe.

St Peter's will serve as a case study in this chapter for a discussion of the new ways of communicating ideas about architecture in the Renaissance (books, drawings, models) and the ongoing practice of building that proved amazingly resistant to change [**25**].

Vitruvius

Given the deep interest that Renaissance architects had in the buildings from the past, it was a mixed blessing that the only treatise to survive from antiquity was *De architectura libri decem* by Vitruvius. Written some time around 20 BC, and dedicated to the Emperor Augustus, Vitruvius' text established the topics and organization of Renaissance treatises. The ten books covered architectural issues as diverse as the training of the architect, the shape and ornament of temples and theatres, building materials, ornament, the mythical origins of architecture, hydraulics, astronomy, and machines. Vitruvius offered later readers not only details about ancient buildings, that is, how they were constructed or the varieties of ancient temple types, but also a more comprehensive theory about the principles for understanding architecture. His proposal that all buildings must satisfy the three requirements of *firmitas* (strength), *utilitas* (utility), and *venustas* (beauty) was general enough to be broadly useful and by the same token difficult to pin down. Through such a broad range of topics, Vitruvius set an agenda for architecture as an all-encompassing cultural programme that Renaissance writers took as their starting point.

His treatise survived down to the Renaissance through a number of manuscript copies, each with variations of the text making an authoritative version difficult to determine. Yet more complicated for a Renaissance reader was that it only existed in Latin, and many of the technical terms did not have a modern equivalent. Even Renaissance readers with a thorough knowledge of Latin, such as Alberti, found Vitruvius' text vague and incomplete. Giovanni Sulpicio da Veroli published a modern Latin edition in 1486 in Rome, yet given the growing interest in all areas of antiquity, including architecture, there was still a need for a translation into the vernacular.

In the first decades of the sixteenth century, Pope Julius II's desire to recreate Rome as the centre of a great Christian empire fuelled many projects of classical scholarship. A lavish and large edition of Vitruvius by Fra Giovanni Giocondo appeared in 1511, dedicated to Pope Julius II, with all the scholarly apparatus of commentary and illustrations that was also included in medical treatises and biblical studies [**26**].[2] Although Julius admitted that he himself was not a scholar, he encouraged the translation of Latin and Greek texts into Italian editions, both scholarly and lavish, for a courtly audience. A group of artists, scholars, and entrepreneurs around the artist Raphael began a translation of Vitruvius into vernacular Italian, spurred by the earlier edition by Fra Giocondo and their own scholarly interests in reconstructing Rome as it existed under the ancient Romans. The scholar Marco Fabio Calvo was responsible for the translation, supported by Raphael and the papal

25

St Peter's, Rome

This view from the east shows the apse designed by Michelangelo with the use of the giant order of Corinthian pilasters layered over piers. He wanted a 'clear, simple, luminous' design, following Bramante's designs from the first stages of the building of the new St Peter's.

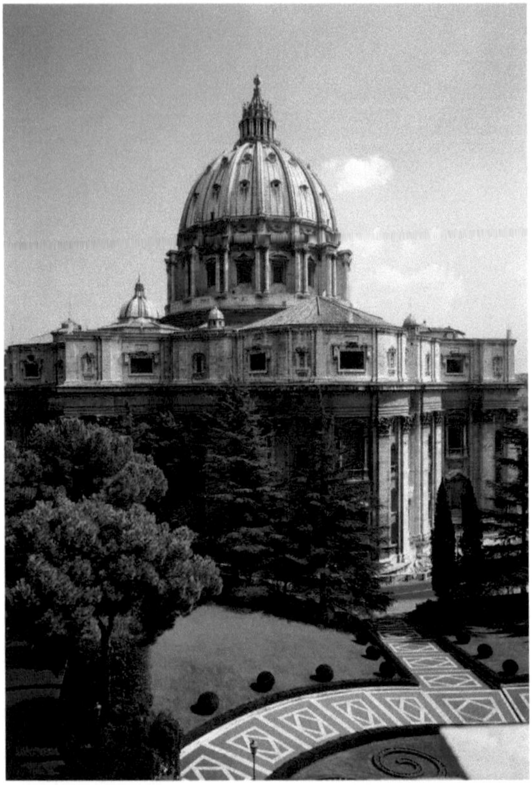

official Angelo Colocci. The project was never completed, however, stopped short by the sudden death of Raphael in 1520.[3]

The first Vitruvius translation to make it into print was started in northern Italy at the court of Ludovico Sforza. Cesare Cesariano, described by Vasari as a 'good geometer and architect', was also inspired by the lavishness and large-scale publication by Fra Giocondo. The commentary and accompanying illustrations placed Vitruvius' text in a local context, relating the ancient architectural principles to northern Italian architecture. Thus for Cesariano, Milan Cathedral, a late Gothic building, illustrated Vitruvius' triad of *firmitas*, *utilitas*, and *venustas*, although the building was far from a classical building in origin or appearance [**27**].

Architecture and the Body

St Peter's was conceived as a shrine to the apostle Peter, and planned as a holy covering for his body. Each renovation and new building to the church in the Renaissance had at its heart the belief that great architecture would further glorify the apostle through the expansion of the Church. Christianity, and especially the Church in Rome under Pope Julius II, embraced the resurrection of Christ as a tenet that

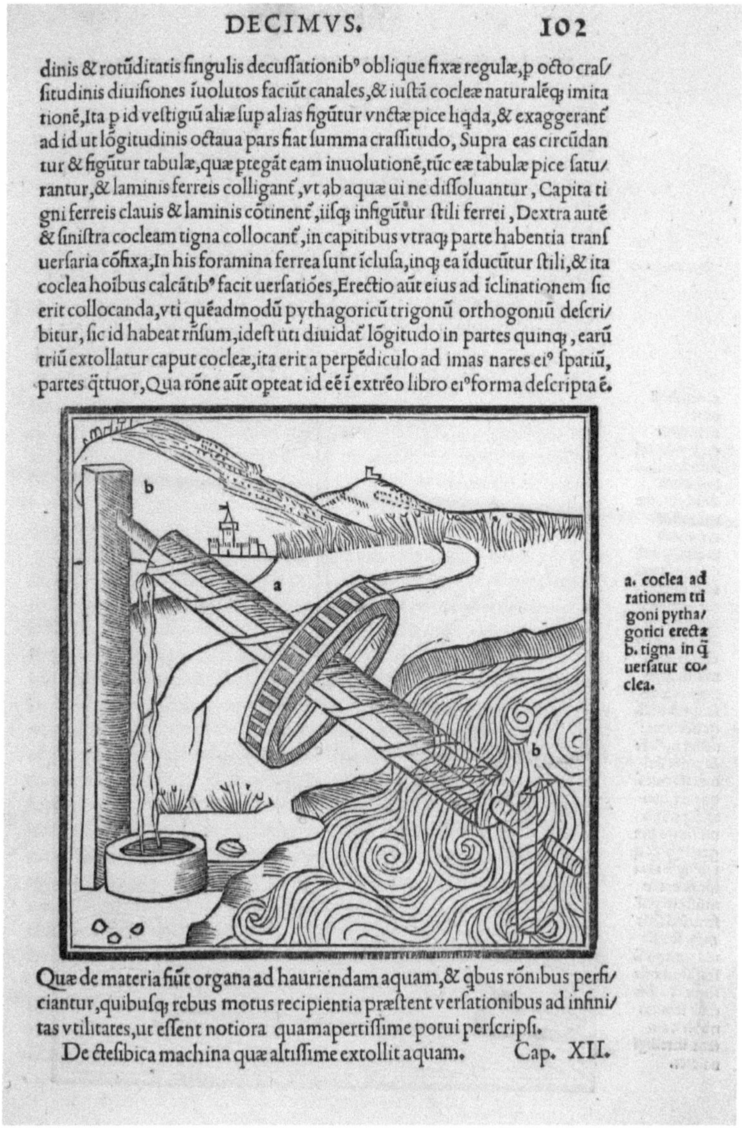
DECIMVS. 102

dinis & rotūditatis singulis decussationib⁹ oblique fixæ regulæ, p octo crass/
situdinis diuisiones īuolutos faciūt canales, & iustā cocleæ naturalēq; imita
tionē, Ita p id vestigiū aliæ sup alias figūtur vnctæ pice liqda, & exaggerant
ad id ut lōgitudinis octaua pars fiat summa crassitudo, Supra eas circūdan
tur & figūtur tabulæ, quæ ptegāt eam inuolutionē, tūc eæ tabulæ pice satu/
rantur, & laminis ferreis colligant, vt ąb aquæ ui ne dissoluantur, Capita ti
gni ferreis clauis & laminis cōtinent, iisq; infigūtur stili ferrei, Dextra autē
& sinistra cocleam tigna collocant, in capitibus vtraq; parte habentia trans
uersaria cōfixa, In his foramina ferrea sunt īclusa, inq; ea īducūtur stili, & ita
coclea hoībus calcātib⁹ facit uersatiōes, Erectio aūt eius ad īclinationem sic
erit collocanda, vti quēadmodū pythagoricū trigonū orthogoniū descri/
bitur, sic id habeat rn̄sum, idest uti diuidat lōgitudo in partes quinq;, earū
triū extollatur caput cocleæ, ita erit a perpēdiculo ad imas nares ei⁹ spatiū,
partes q̄ttuor, Qua rōne aūt opteat id eē ī extrēo libro ei⁹ forma descripta ē.

a. coclea ad rationem tri goni pytha/ gorici erecta b. tigna in q̄ uersatur co/ clea.

Quæ de materia fiūt organa ad hauriendam aquam, & q̄bus rōnibus perfi/
ciantur, quibusq; rebus motus recipientia præstent versationibus ad infini/
tas vtilitates, ut essent notiora quam apertissime potui perscripsi.

De ctesibica machina quæ altissime extollit aquam. Cap. XII.

26

Vitruvius, *De architectura*, Fra Giovanni Giocondo edition, published in Venice in 1511

Fra Giocondo used both his practical experience as engineer and architect as well as his knowledge of antiquities and ancient texts in creating his edition of Vitruvius, as can be seen here in this image showing various systems for harnessing the power of flowing water. This, the fourth printed edition of Vitruvius, included 136 illustrations as well as a glossary of technical terms to help the modern reader. In France (he was in Paris from 1495) he designed fortifications and fountains for King Charles VIII. In Italy, his projects were equally varied. Pope Julius II appointed him in 1514 to serve with Raphael as architect for St Peter's.

guided not only theology and liturgy but also the Vatican's cultural policy. The rebirth of Christ, therefore, became the paradigm for the renovation of Rome from a pagan city, and then a diminished medieval city, into the *caput mundi*, the centre of the Christian world. This almost seamless shift, from religious belief to architectural practice and back again, revolved around ideas of the body: the body of Christ, the fabric of the city, the corpus of the church building. If Christ were raised from the dead, then so too could the city be born again to the glory of its classical apogee but now in a purely Christian context.

Architectural theory in the fifteenth century had already begun to equate the building with the body, seeing in the architectural forms

27

Cesare Cesariano, *Di Lucio Vitruvio Pollione de architectura*, Como, Italy, 1521

Cesare Cesariano published the first Italian translation of the ancient Latin text, Vitruvius' *De architectura* (*c.*20 BC). In addition to a commentary on the text he also added detailed illustrations, drawing on the architecture that he knew in his native northern Italy. In this illustration he shows Milan Cathedral overlaid with a geometric diagram, as if Vitruvius could offer a modern reader a method for understanding architectural complexity according to a series of clearly defined principles.

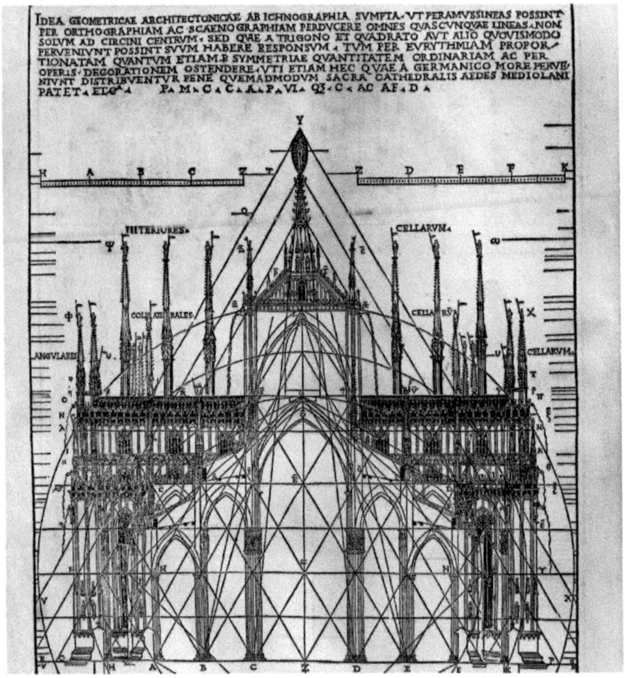

derived from classical models an equivalent to the human body. The Latin cross plan for churches, with its shorter cross arms (or transepts) and a longer nave, reiterated the figure of Christ on the cross. The overlay of body and architectural plan or section, as seen in the treatise of Francesco di Giorgio, made the analogy on proportional grounds [**28**]. A beautiful building, also described in the treatise of Alberti, followed the proportions of an elegant body. This similarity could be extended down to the level of the architectural detail, even in its most abstract form.

Individual members of the building could be compared to the human form because on a more fundamental level, buildings were understood to be objects in their own right, animated and infused with life. To begin with, buildings were constructed of objects from nature—clay in the form of brick, stone, wood, metal. All these materials, in the primal form as matter and in their transformed use as architectural materials, retained the organic vitality that they had in nature. A Renaissance audience then brought this vitalism to the buildings themselves. Alberti described this life force as the *animans*, the animated organism. Several aspects of Renaissance architecture can be understood in these terms. As we have previously seen, the forms of classicism were parallel forms to the human physique, the cornice like the forehead of the buildings, and so on. Even when following ancient exempla, architects made choices about the invention and imitation of classical details. In the garden loggia of the Villa

28

Francesco di Giorgio, Face inscribed within entablature, *c.*1490

The human body was similar to architecture not because the numerical proportions were exactly the same but rather because buildings and the body shared characteristics and qualities in common. Bodies and buildings both had clearly definable parts that existed in relationship to other parts. Although buildings were not 'alive', they were a kind of organism with interrelated elements, and the power to interact with its surroundings.

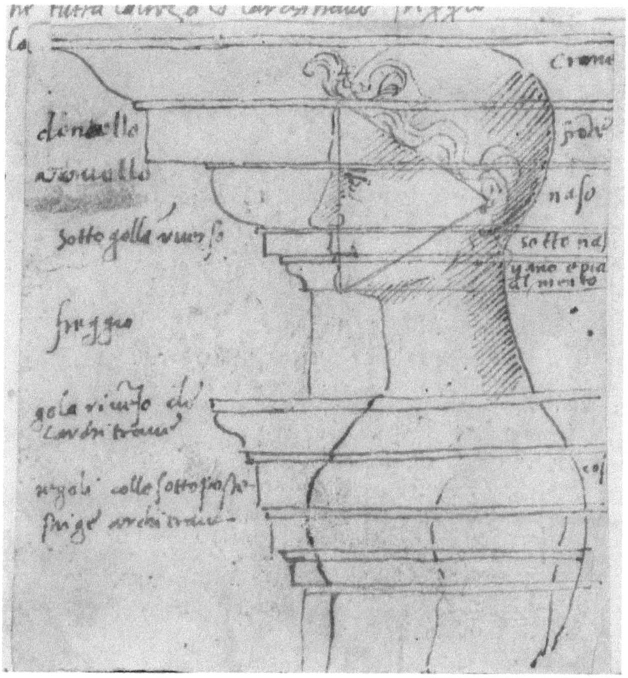

29

Raphael, Garden Loggia, Villa Madama, Rome

The bases and pedestals of the garden loggia are derived from ancient sources, studied and then recombined by the architect. As much sculpture as architecture, the rhythm of convex and concave shapes expresses the weight and compression of the stone as if the building were composed out of organic, living bone and muscle. The loggia was originally open to the garden terrace; the glass was added later.

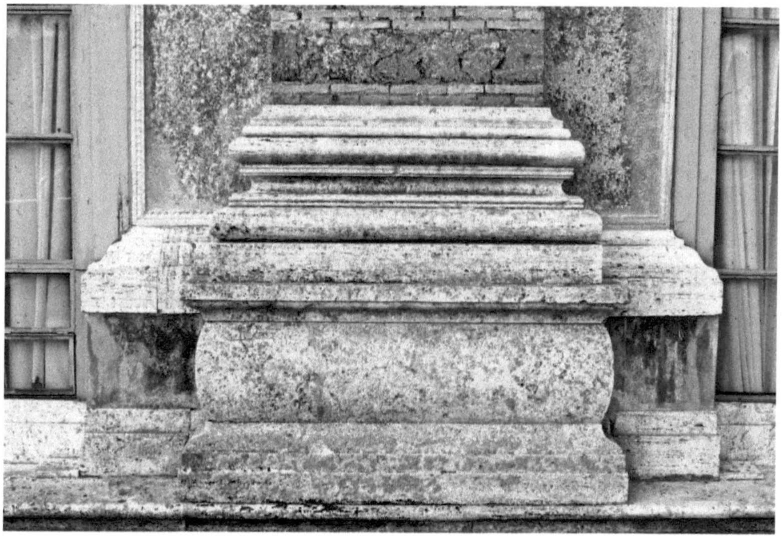

Madama, for example, Raphael used a richly curving pedestal to support the pilasters [**29**]. Their swelling and curved forms, right at the height of someone standing in the loggia, answer the human body, and animate the building and the space surrounding it.

Alberti, following Vitruvius, had described each of the classical orders as individuals, corresponding to a Roman god. By personifying the orders, Alberti ascribes to each architectural system (the column with all of its attendant ornament and proportions) not only a gender, thus a body, but also a personality. Buildings employing certain ornament could then be spoken of not only as appropriate for certain kinds of uses, the form matching the function, but also as active agents, engaging in the world around them. The circle of anthropomorphizing was complete. Buildings were parallel entities to the people that inhabited them, endowed with the same personalities and experiences, participants in the world in which they both shared space.

The Development of the Architectural Treatise

The emergence of the architectural treatise, one of the most important aspects of Renaissance architecture, disseminated ideas about buildings to a wider audience. Through printed books, which could emerge thanks to a highly developed printing press, architects could promote their own designs and advance the ideas about building that they knew from practical experience and study. Treatises allowed for a greater degree of communication between architects and their audience than ever before.

Before the fifteenth century it is difficult to say that a genre of architectural literature existed, distinct from other topics. Architecture was part of a much larger category of books on various related themes: descriptions of buildings in history, geography treatises, technical aspects of architecture in books on machinery, and so on.

When Alberti published his ten books on architecture, he wrote his work in Latin, the language of the educated classes, the international language of the elite. It was also the language of ancient Rome, of course, and Alberti modelled his treatise on the ancient writer Vitruvius' ten books on architecture. Alberti however made a subtle change in the title of his treatise. Instead of *De architectura*, on architecture, Alberti called his book *De re aedificatoria*, on architectural things. That subtle shift reflected Alberti's desire to talk about topics on and related to architecture. The book is as much social and political theory as it is a book about architecture. For Alberti, architecture is the way that societies and communities live together, creating the physical domains that define them as individuals and groups. That these social ties can be defined by an architecture derived from antiquity reflects the importance of ancient civilization in the formation of fifteenth-century ideas, and also a moral choice about what is the best model to be followed.

If Alberti's idea of architecture as a part of a broader humanist culture extended the audience for architecture, then there was an equal interest in the technical aspects of building. Francesco di Giorgio's *Trattati* (written from about 1480 to 1501) exist in two principal versions in manuscript. The summation of his career as fortification designer, engineer, and architect, the treatises demonstrate the level to which architecture in fifteenth-century Italy was understood as a

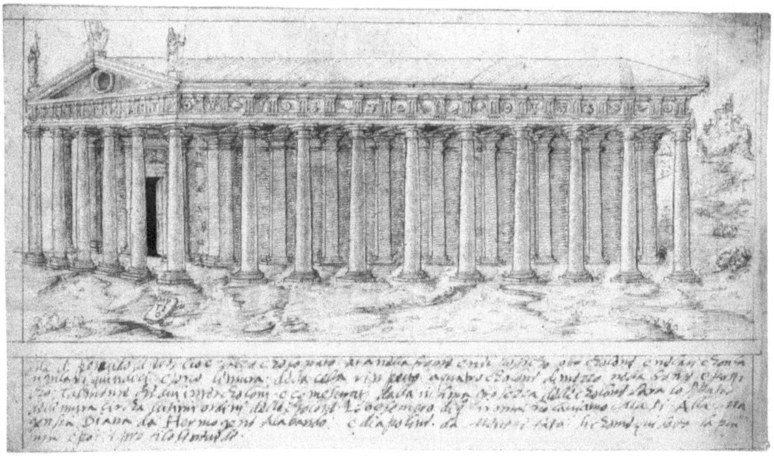

30

Attributed to a member of the Sangallo family, Pseudodipteral temple, *c.*1530–45, pen and dark brown ink

This drawing by a member of the Sangallo family of architects and craftsmen supposedly illustrates a passage from Vitruvius (Bk. III, ch. 2) describing the pseudodipteral temple, with eight columns on the front and back, and fifteen on each side, although the columns in the drawing do not correspond to the text. Vitruvius' text is translated on the sheet into Italian, and the drawing was probably part of a project to produce a new translation of Vitruvius with illustrations that reflect the direct study of ancient ruins in Rome.

technical art, part of the study of machinery and fortress bastions. Each section begins with a review of Vitruvius, but then goes on to present the author's own opinions on the best practices in each area. Although remaining in manuscript and never printed, the treatises had a great influence on later architects, including Leonardo da Vinci and the group of architects working on St Peter's: Giuliano da Sangallo, his brother Antonio da Sangallo, and Baldassare Peruzzi [**30**].[4]

Textual descriptions, as well as actual ancient buildings with great religious importance, served as models for new construction in the Renaissance. Many of these models were centrally planned buildings, and the profusion of this shape in medieval and especially Renaissance buildings recalls and stands in for these sacred predecessors: the Dome of the

Bible as Architectural Treatise

In the Bible, the faithful are builders, constructing God's house on a solid foundation and following God as the first architect of the faith. In his letter to the Corinthians, the apostle Paul wrote that 'By the grace God has given me, I laid a foundation as an expert builder, and someone else is building on it. But each one should be careful how he builds. For no one can lay any foundation other than the one already laid, which is Jesus Christ' (1 Cor. 3: 9–11). If Christ is the cornerstone, then the Church itself rises on that strong foundation (Eph 2: 20–2).

Descriptions of architecture are also presented in a more literal way. According to the Hebrew Bible, the first temple or the Temple of Solomon was built in Jerusalem to house the Ark of the Covenant. King David assembled the materials but it was his son, Solomon, who constructed the building. In the Book of Kings, there is a lengthy description of the size and details of the temple (60 cubits long by 20 cubits wide by 30 cubits high) as well as the costly woods (cedar and olive-wood), bronze, gold, and stone that were used for its construction. The perfectly corresponding measurements and precious materials of the building reinforce the religious and political importance of the structure to the Jews, and its location on the Temple Mount marked that place as one of great significance that it would remain up to the present day.

Rock and the Holy Sepulchre in Jerusalem, the Pantheon and Lateran Baptistery in Rome, and the Mausoleum of Theodoric in Ravenna.[5]

Books and Readers

Treatises implied readers. The expansion in the number of titles, especially those in the vernacular languages, in contrast to the more learned language of Latin, fed a growing market for books on architecture. The audience was as varied as the variety of books. Some titles were intended for craftsmen, eager for new patterns to satisfy clients wanting up-to-date designs. Patrons purchased titles that offered models of villas or palaces that could be adapted to their own needs. Practitioners from allied disciplines, such as military engineers, read the increasing number of titles on fortifications. Classicists and humanists welcomed new editions and commentaries on Vitruvius.

Architects also owned books, and catalogues of their books, included in inventories of their estates, show the many topics they studied. Books on architecture were kept side by side with volumes on history, geography, mathematics and perspective, theological texts, poetry, and plays. In some ways this is a reading list of any educated individual in the Renaissance, although the professional demands of the architect required a more directed reading of topics that were thought to contribute to the practice of architecture in all its dimensions. Fortifications and military arts, for example, were an important area of expertise for Renaissance architects.[6] In this way libraries tell us much about the learned expectations of the architect, fulfilling in practice as well as in theory Vitruvius' prescription that the architect be educated in the full range of the disciplines.[7]

Occasionally the actual books survive from an architect's collection, and marginal annotations give an idea of what the reader thought of the book and the author's ideas. Publishers made a practice of printing marginal references to other books and learned commentaries. By the end of the sixteenth century architects as well as their potential patrons had access to a reading list in common that might include various editions of Vitruvius, books on the orders and ornament, collections of plans for houses, and books on antiquities.

The Professional Architect

A modern ideal of the architect developed in the Renaissance: a trained individual, knowledgeable not only in the craft of building but also in its cultural implications, and, overall, serving as the supervisor of the building project. There are specific master masons whose names are known from the Middle Ages, who functioned in much the same way as this model of the architect, yet we know less about them as individuals and their working method. In fact, Renaissance architecture has been studied, in contrast to that of the medieval period, for example, as a series of great architects working for important patrons. This attention to individual genius has its origins in the period itself. Giorgio Vasari, in his important book on artists and styles, *Le vite de più eccellenti architetti, pittori, et scultori* (Florence, 1550) (*The Lives of the Best Architects, Painters, and Sculptors*), writes about what he understood to be the best in art through a discussion of its most important protagonists. The second edition of that book, published in 1568, contains several additional biographies of architects. Italian artists were predominant but he also included artists from northern Europe, grouping individuals based on geographical proximity. Vasari's influence on the writing of art and architectural history was profound. The focus on individuals as masters of their art, with Michelangelo as the paradigm, who followed the best precepts in the best style (that is, according to Vasari, following the antique), shaped the approach to Renaissance architecture as a history of the solitary, inventive architect. Yet even for those most singular architects, they worked in collaboration with a team of craftsmen, all of whom had some level of control over their work. The architects that Vasari includes in his book came to architecture from a variety of backgrounds. Bramante, Raphael, and Peruzzi were trained as painters. Michelangelo and Jacopo Sansovino (1486–1570) began as sculptors.

In France, Philibert de l'Orme (1514–70) began as a mason (as did Palladio), training first with his father.[8] In *Le Premier Tome de l'architecture* (1567) de l'Orme drew from his practical experience, putting down his opinions on the best methods for building, ornamental preferences, and architectural designs [**31**]. The book was a continuation of his practice of training young craftsmen in the best working methods, which he asserted transformed French architectural practice.

> In addition to all that, have I not provided other services, to wit having brought to France the method of building well, eliminating barbarous methods and coarse joins, showing all and sundry how to observe the right measures in architecture, even training the finest workers of our day, as they themselves acknowledge? Let it be recalled how people worked before I began Sainct Mort [Saint Maur] for Cardinal du Belloy [Bellay]![9]

While it was not only architects who wrote about the art of building, the desire to codify their experience and enter into a public dialogue on architecture, through print, may be one mark of the professional architect in the Renaissance.

Outside the Italian peninsula, where the profession of architect was more readily theorized, there was no hard division between the master mason and the architect. In England, the first use of the term 'architect'

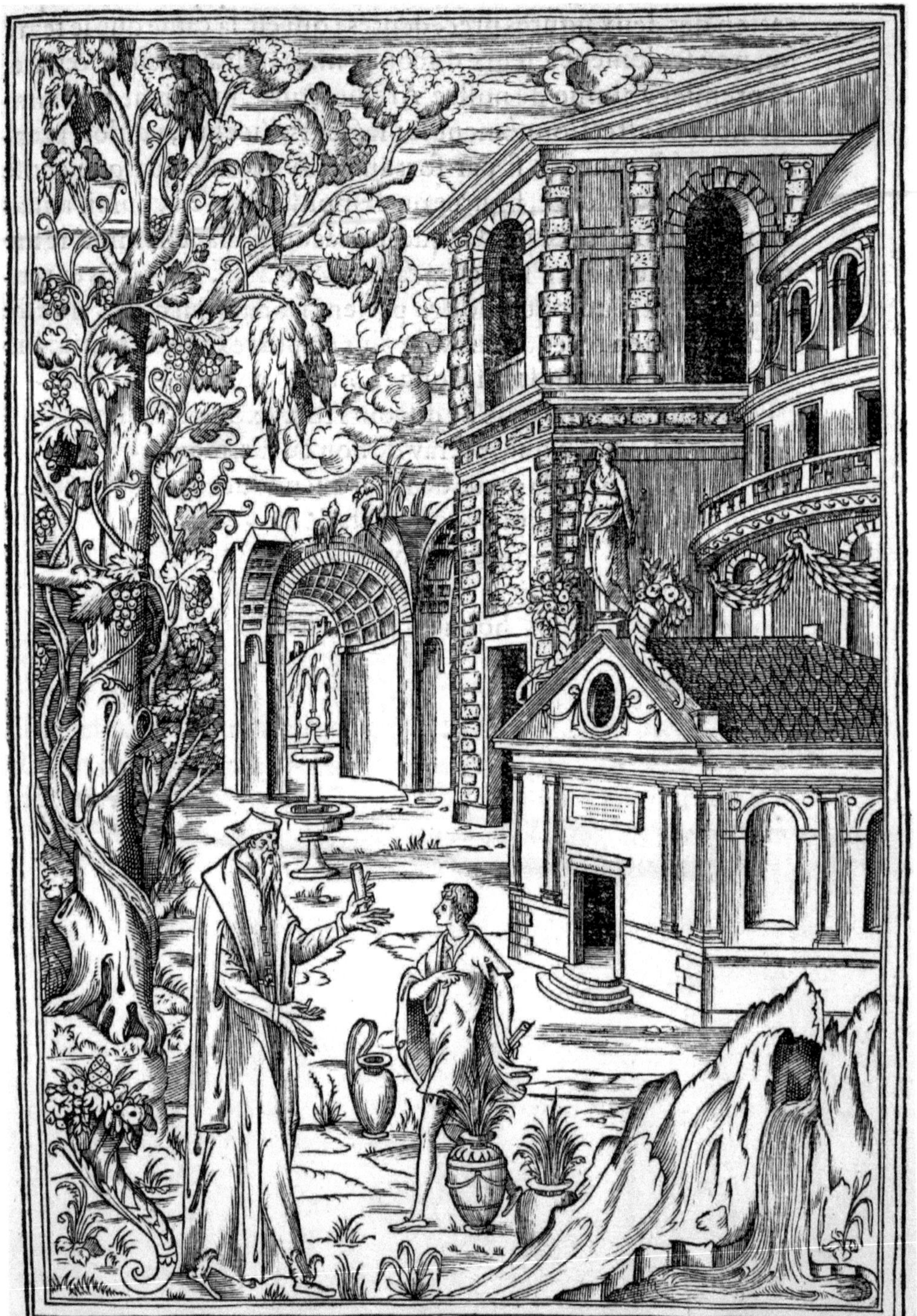

was by John Shute, author of *The First and Chiefe Groundes of Architecture* (1563), in reference to himself. Shute was well versed in the architectural writings of Serlio, Vitruvius, and Philibert de l'Orme, and his book was a synthesis of those writings, adapted for an English audience. Yet, Shute did little architectural designing, and his adoption of the term architect seems more a reference to the breadth of his learning than a comment on his role as the overseer of any building projects. Gradually the term replaced the ancient 'skylled artyfycer'.[10]

One way to distinguish between the roles of architect and master mason may be the ways in which information was communicated between designer and craftsmen. The architect increasingly used drawings as a way to ensure the continuity of a design, especially in large projects such as St Peter's that would go forward long after the lifespan of any one architect. Print and publication allowed architects to disseminate their ideas to a much wider audience. While literacy (of text and drawn image) did not supersede the oral communication of information, part of the work on the building site, it added a further social distinction between those actually working on the building and the architect as overseer. On the building site, masters communicated 'ad personam' to their apprentices, relaying information and directing the work with words as well as with actions.[11]

While some architectural authors such as Alberti argued for a clear separation between the professional domains of the architect and craftsmen, the sculptor and architect Antonio di Pietro Averlino, called Filarete (*c*.1400–*c*.1469), voiced concern that an architect must retain the knowledge of how things were made in order to convey his ideas to his workmen.

> It would [thus] be necessary for him to know how to do so many things that it would be impossible for him. I say that if he does not know how to do them with his own hand, he will never know how to show them or to explain them so they will turn out well. He must be clever and imaginative in making different things and in showing them by his own hand. In addition to these two things, that is, knowing how to do it with his own hand and being inventive, it is also necessary for him to know how to draw.[12]

31

Philibert de l'Orme, Allegory of the Good Architect, *Le Premier Tome de l'architecture*, Paris 1567

Fiercely nationalistic, Philibert de l'Orme studied antiquity in Rome in order to forge a French architectural style and building practice that could rival the ancients or any other contemporary work. His allegory of the good architect shows the mason as teacher, with three hands (for making) and four eyes (for seeing). He and his young apprentice are surrounded by buildings based on ancient models.

Filarete insists upon the hand and the knowledge it confers (making, showing, knowing, inventing, and ultimately drawing) as the determining factor in good architectural practice. Through the hand, Filarete wrote, comes a kind of architectural knowledge that is essential and unique, and accessible only through physical and tactile means. The tacit knowledge held by craftsmen remained an essential part of architectural practice.[13] The ability to judge high-quality materials, determine the necessary amounts, select appropriately for each project, and transform it into architecture: these were all skills traditionally held by the master craftsmen, and developed over years of apprenticeship and practice.

Spolia

Much of the decoration of the early Christian basilica at St Peter's was *spolia*, that is, architectural elements taken from other, older monuments and then incorporated into the fabric of the church. The shafts in the nave of the early Christian building were monoliths, made from one piece of stone, and from a rich selection of stones: red and white granite, and marbles taken from all over the Roman Empire including Africa and Asia Minor. Architects in the Renaissance, such as Baldassare Peruzzi, made a meticulous study of all the columns including their measurements. They valued both the exotic materials of the columns and the richness of their ornament.

Six large twisted columns surrounded the apostle St Peter's tomb [**32**]. Others were included in the church to mark especially important shrines, such as the altar dedicated to St Veronica and the relic of her veil. The columns originally came from an ancient Greek temple, and their twisted vines and naked *putti* suggest that they were connected with a building dedicated to a Dionysian cult, hardly an appropriate source for a shrine and basilica honouring one of the Christian apostles. The origin of the columns was eventually, some time in the twelfth or thirteenth centuries, re-ascribed to the Temple

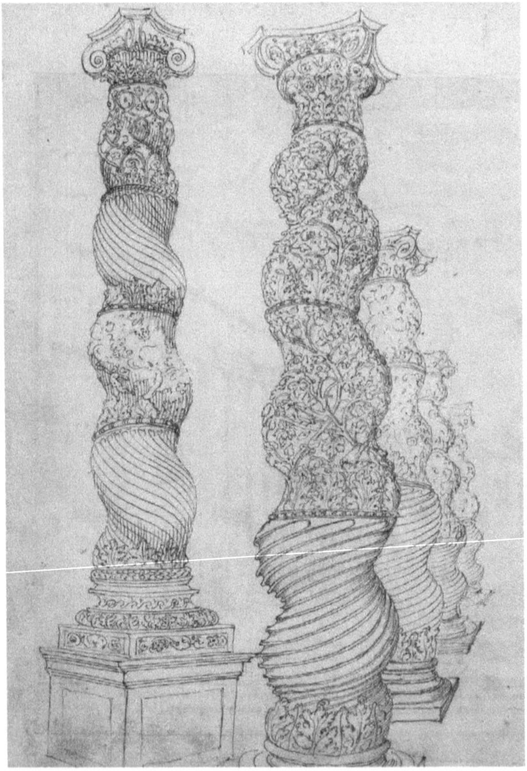

32

Étienne Dupérac, Twisted columns from St Peter's, drawing *c.*1575

There were originally six twisted columns that surrounded the tomb of St Peter's, given in the fourth century; and another six given later in the eighth century. About 4.5 metres high, they had different sorts of decoration, twisted fluting, vines, and naked *putti*. Dupérac records five of the columns in this drawing, showing their animated form and variety of ornament. As objects with an ancient origin, and remarkable materials and workmanship, they were marvels from the earliest stage of the church's history.

of Solomon in Jerusalem. If the columns were thought to be from Solomon's Temple, then it was possible to connect them even more directly with the Jesus Christ who, in John's Gospel, 'was walking in the Temple, in the portico of Solomon' (John 10: 23).

This is the column on which leaned our Lord JESUS CHRIST. He stood against it while he preached to the people and prayed to God the Father in the Temple. Brought in triumph with the other eleven columns here surrounding it from the Temple of Solomon, it was placed in this basilica. It expels demons and restores those afflicted by unclean spirits to freedom, and it performs many miracles daily. Adorned by the most reverend father and lord Cardinal Orsini in the year of our Lord 1438.[14]

This sacred column, believed to be infused with special healing powers, drew more pilgrims to St Peter's than to all other pilgrim churches in Rome.

The Orders

As *spolia*, the columns were the very stuff of the ancient world. They were also examples of the architectural orders, the combination of column shaft, base and pedestal, entablature and capital that served as both support and ornament in architecture. From their reading of Vitruvius, as well as the study of ancient buildings themselves, Renaissance architects and scholars of the ancient culture understood that there were different types of orders. They could be thought of as families or groups, characterized by their proportions, ornament, and use in architecture. Vitruvius had discussed three orders, Doric, Ionic, Corinthian, providing explanations for their origins, ornament, and proper use. Yet any Renaissance reader of Vitruvius' treatise would not only have found the text difficult to understand (there were no illustrated examples of the book that had survived from antiquity or the Middle Ages), the language technical and with no easy translations into the vernacular, but, even worse, not corresponding to what could be observed on the ground. Thus, Vitruvius offered not an explanation of ancient building, but another parallel source, a textual authority that had to be reconciled (and often with difficulty) with the surviving evidence.

Buildings were richer sources of information [**33**]. Roman buildings survived in Rome, of course, but antiquities could also be found in many places that Romans had colonized. Thus there were antiquities to be seen and studied throughout the Italian peninsula, in Istanbul (formerly Constantinople) and the eastern Mediterranean, in France and Spain, and into northern Europe. Scholars and antiquarians studied local Roman remains, such as Jean Poldo d'Albenas's *Discours historial de l'antique et illustre cité de Nismes* (Lyons, 1559);

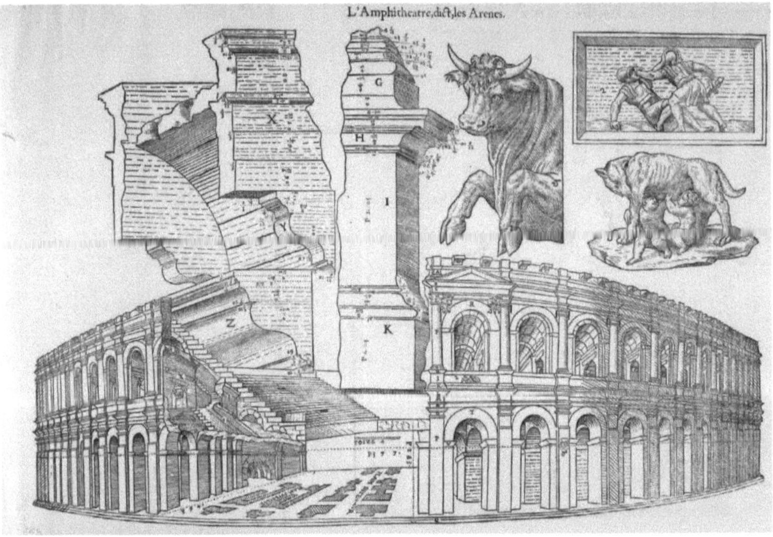

33

Amphitheatre, Nîmes, Jean Poldo d'Albenas, *Discours historial de l'antique et illustre cité de Nismes,* Lyons, 1560

The interest in Roman antiquities became increasingly localized in the 16th century. Jean Poldo d'Albenas published the surviving ancient buildings in his birth city of Nîmes in order to write the history of that place. In addition to the amphitheatre, which was nearly complete, there were several other important buildings including the Maison Carrée. D'Albenas measured the buildings himself, and included the measurements on his extraordinary woodcuts, which showed the buildings in plan, section, and elevation including details of important features. Andrea Palladio, who never went to Nîmes but included the Maison Carrée in his treatise (1570), used d'Albenas as his source of Roman temples in France.

and, when possible, made architectural pilgrimages to Rome to see the largest collection of antiquities easily available.[15] Many architects made their pilgrimages to study antiquities as evidence of their seriousness as scholars and, therefore, evidence of the merit and authenticity of their buildings. Andrea Palladio begins his treatise with a testimony about his trips to Rome in the 1550s. When architects travelled they took time and expense to measure the buildings; it was not enough to simply admire them from afar or sketch them as picturesque ruins. Scaffolding was erected, and measurements taken which could then be added to drawings [**34**]. These drawings and measurements were subsequently a precious resource.

The use of the orders in Renaissance architecture (and later) has been described as the 'hard spine' that runs through the history of Western architecture.[16] The orders give structure and regularity to Renaissance architecture, providing a common language based in antiquity, with a rich library of associated values, cultural references, and authorities. In the history of Renaissance architecture, one could look at the use of the orders as the dominant theme of buildings in many places and times—and certainly in twentieth-century interpretations. As Renaissance scholars took on a more rigorous study of ancient texts, mastering the necessary ancient languages, so too architects began to approach the orders and architectural ornament of the ancients as a language that could be learned and used.[17]

Yet a rigorous classicism was never the dominant architectural language outside of a very small community of architects and scholars working in central Italy. As we have seen, it was incorporated within local architectural idioms and transformed to suit local needs. In the fifteenth century architects interpreted the orders based on local

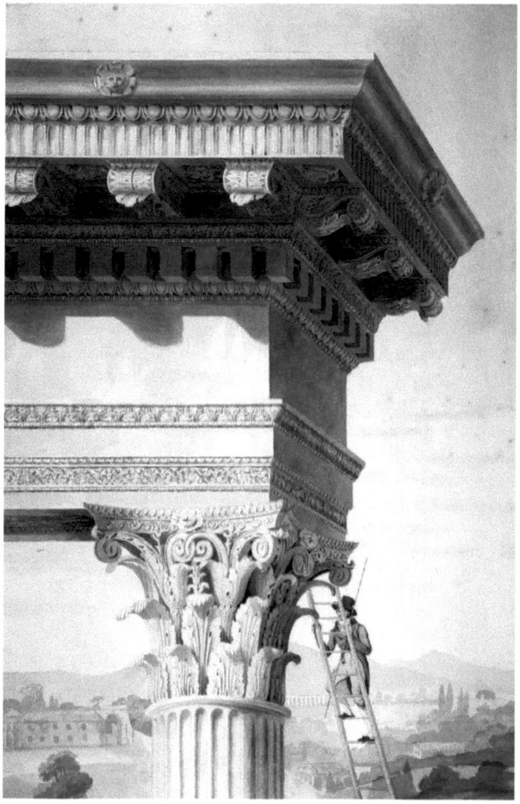

34

Henry Parke, *Student measuring the Temple of Castor and Pollux in Rome*, 1819

The study of ancient Roman buildings was demanding and costly work. Architects and antiquarians needed to pay for the construction of scaffolding to reach the upper levels, including the capitals and entablatures, and then proceed to carefully record not only the form but also the measurements for later reference. In his treatise, Serlio often remarks that he has measured the buildings himself, and apologizes to the reader when he had to rely on the work of others.

precedent and usage. In Florence, therefore, Filippo Brunelleschi looked to local Tuscan buildings as models for the use of the orders in his buildings in Florence. If the orders were equivalent to a language, then they followed the same predilection to local idiom. It was not until the sixteenth century in Sebastiano Serlio's treatise *Regole generali di architettura* (1537) that five Roman orders (Tuscan, Doric, Ionic, Corinthian, and Composite) were presented as a unified system [**35**]. Serlio makes explicit the connection between character and architectural ornament: 'the ancients dedicated buildings to the gods, matching them to their natures, robust or delicate, accordingly: for example, Doric work for Jupiter, Mars and Hercules—these Doric forms taken from a man' (Bk. IV, III^{r}).[18]

For Elizabethan England classicism was a foreign and sometimes highly suspect system of ornament, connected as it was to Catholic countries with its origins in pagan culture. There is no question that architects and craftsmen knew the principles of devising the orders based on books that were recorded in libraries. Yet patrons also valued invented ornament that came from a variety of sources. When in the early seventeenth century an architect such as Inigo Jones desired to differentiate his designs from those of others he advocated a masculine

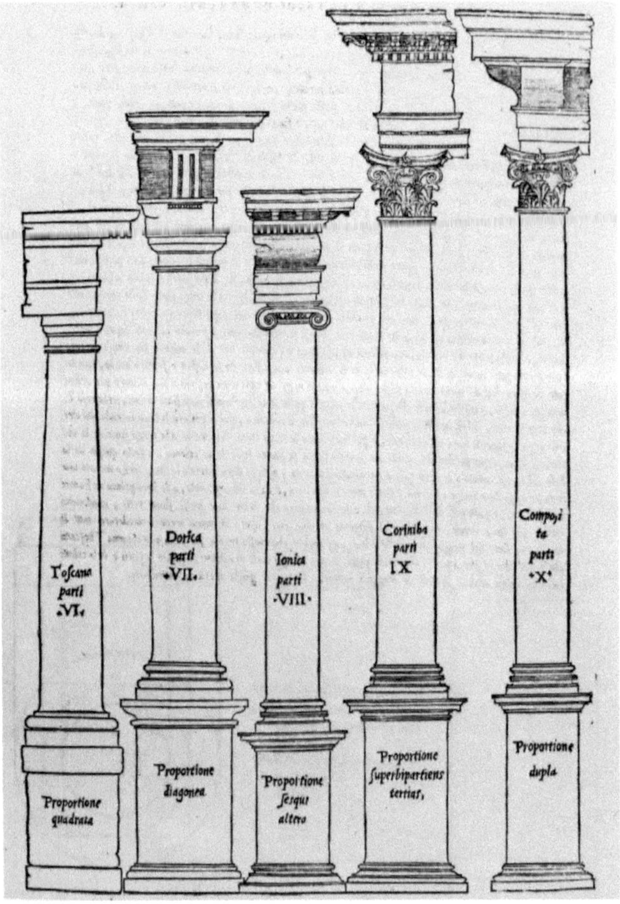

35

Sebastiano Serlio, *Regole generali di architettura* (1537), Bk. IV, 127r

In contrast to earlier authors, and indeed to Vitruvius himself, Serlio tried to formulate more consistent rules for the use of ancient architectural ornament, which he was the first to call 'orders'. Here he shows the five orders, in a logical sequence based on their proportions and characteristics. Serlio assumed, however, that while there could be standards for their use, the orders must be adapted based on the specific conditions of the building and the desires of the architect and patron.

architecture, built according to the rules of the orders. Classicism in England and elsewhere came to be an architecture of authority and *gravitas*, learned against the local building practices that did not have a written theory based on scholarship and scientific principles.

In order to understand the origins and authorities relating to the orders more fully, scholars and architects stepped up the pace of their antiquarian studies throughout the sixteenth century using all of the scholarly methods currently available, including the study of manuscripts, coins, textual analysis, and archaeological study of the ruins themselves. One of the most influential of these author-architects was the French scholar and canon Guillaume Philandrier (1505–65), who published in 1544 his *Annotationes*, an illustrated Latin commentary on Vitruvius.[19] By far the most scholarly writing on architecture to date, his book had a wide audience among those who saw in the use of the orders the opportunity to infuse architecture with even more authority as a cultural and artistic language.

Even in the most rigorous of books on the orders that appeared in the sixteenth century, including the treatise of Giacomo Vignola, the orders were never understood to be a fixed system; they were always open to interpretation. The limits of that interpretation, however, varied greatly depending on local architectural practice and expectations. In England, therefore, while the orders were known somewhat through travel and mostly through drawings and publications, they were used in an English manner as a sign of humanist education and social status [**36**].

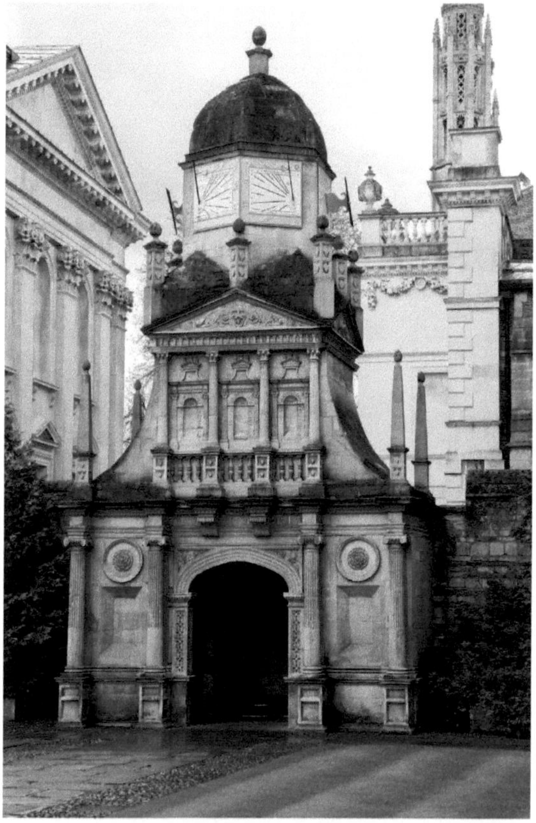

36

Gate of Honour, Gonville and Caius College, Cambridge, England, completed 1575

Reference to ancient architecture was particularly appropriate for buildings connected with colleges and universities. While individual elements of the gate, through which graduates of the college passed, are derived from Italian and French sources, more important was the overall effect of a learned architectural language.

Nature as Model

It is worth remembering that all architects did not universally hold Rome as an architectural and cultural model, and other architects, in other places throughout Europe, looked elsewhere for inspiration. Perhaps as a response to the publication of Alberti's treatise, in 1486 the Regensburg master mason Matthäus Roriczer (1435–95) published a small book on the design of pinnacles and finials. In laying out the method for Gothic building forms, Roriczer was promoting northern (and specifically southern German) architectural traditions. The historian Paul Crossley has suggested that this 'return to the forest' was drawn from Vitruvius' discussion of the origins of architecture from trees tied together in the forest.[20] Some northern European buildings around this time used ribs and vaulting that resembled branches and offered an alternative to classicism that derives from references to nature, not the architecture of the ancients [**37**].

37

Erhard and Ulrich Heydenreich, Church of Our Lady, 1510–20, Ingolstadt

Two systems of vaults are used in a group of chapels added to the church at Ingolstadt. One system of tracery against the shell of the chapel is geometrical and regular, derived from late Gothic traditions. The other set of vaults that hangs below it is derived from plant forms, vines and stripped tree limbs, and offer an alternative view of the origins of architectural form and subsequently of devotional experience that is possible in this space.

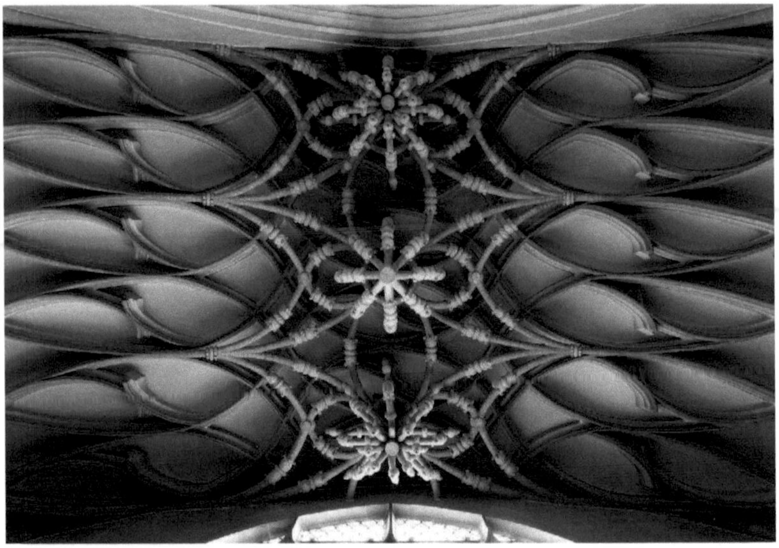

38

Wendel Dietterlin, *Architectura*, Nuremberg, 1598

By the time Dietterlin published his book, there was a lively debate among authors on the best models and canonical forms of the orders. Serlio, Vignola, Hans Blum, Philibert de l'Orme, and Palladio were just a few of the authors writing on the orders; and their books circulated widely and were often translated. Dietterlin, however, does not offer another prototype. His inventive and often fantastic images suggest an approach to design that gives full rein to the creativity of the craftsmen to devise ornament using the orders as a guide.

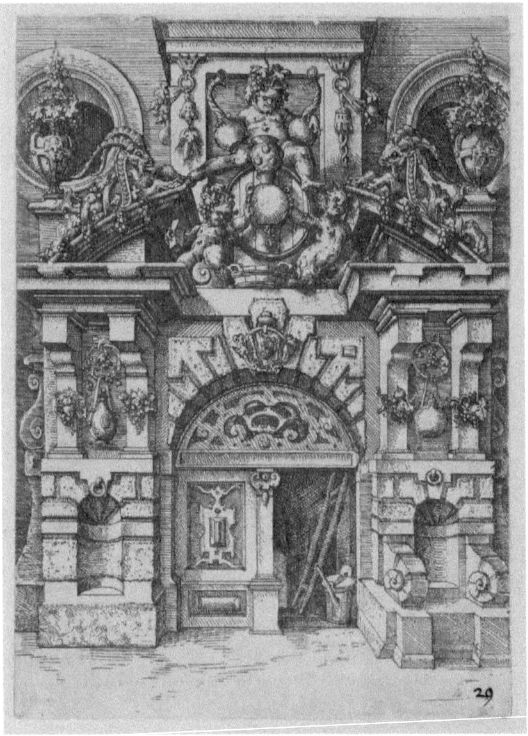

The orders provided an armature of structure that allowed for variation and invention. In his work for the Gonzaga court in Mantua, Giulio Romano (1499?–1546) knew full well the emotional impact of the orders, so closely resembling the human form and so ripe for manipulation [**138**]. In Strasbourg, the painter Wendel Dietterlin

St Peter's Timeline	
AD 64	Apostle Peter buried in the cemetery on north-west side of the Circus of Caligula and Nero
2nd century AD	Shrine to St Peter, Vatican
c.324–after 337	Construction of basilica dedicated to St Peter
8th century AD	Pope Stephen II built first bell tower
	Pope Gregory I built confessio crypt around saint's tomb and fixed main altar over the shrine
847–55	Pope Leo IV encloses Vatican area within wall
1309–78	Popes resident in Avignon
1417–25	Pope Martin V restores St Peter's roof
c.1433–45	Antonio Averlino, called Filarete, makes two bronze doors for central portal; commissioned by Pope Eugene IV
1452–4	Pope Nicholas V begins new construction on the west end of St Peter's including new choir, transepts, and crossing
1470s	Pope Pius II begins new entrance façade [benediction loggia]
18 April 1506	Foundation stone laid for new St Peter's
1513	Julius II dies
1514	Bramante dies; Raphael becomes head architect
1519	South choir ambulatory, pier niches, barrel vaulting built
1520	Raphael dies; Antonio da Sangallo becomes lead architect with Baldassare Peruzzi as second architect
1527	Sack of Rome
1539–46	Antonio da Sangallo builds wooden model
1546	Antonio da Sangallo dies; Michelangelo becomes lead architect
1548–9	Demolition of south ambulatory
1550–1560s	South and north arms of the crossing built
1585–7	Choir demolished in favour of Michelangelo's project
1558–61	Model of dome (Michelangelo)
1564	Pirro Ligorio and Jacopo Vignola become lead architects
1573	Giacomo della Porta becomes lead architect
1578–1601	Clementine Chapel
1585–7	Demolition of choir by Bernardo Rossellino and Bramante
1588–90	Dome constructed according to plans by Giacomo della Porta
After 1590	New confessio and high altar
1603	Lantern completed

(1550–99) published an extraordinary book, *Architectura* (Nuremburg, 1598). In 203 engravings, and almost no text, Dietterlin showed the full range of decorative and psychological possibilities in the use of the orders [**38**]. Although based on the five orders, his architectural inventions are populated by half-human beasts, nature in all its fecundity, and a world where architecture is definitely alive.[21]

St Peter's, Rome

There was no building in the Renaissance more complex in its design process or building history than St Peter's in Rome [**25**]. The ancient church, built in the fourth century to capitalize on the presence of the apostle's tomb and a growing collection of important relics, was by the fifteenth century in desperate need of repair. Some accounts claimed that even a strong wind or a gentle push would topple the basilica. When the papacy returned to Rome in 1377 after its nearly century-long absence in Avignon, the renovation of that church and the Vatican Palace became a priority. The papal court moved their primary residence in Rome from the Lateran to the area on the west of the Tiber, at the edge of the city. The building up of this area as a new power centre removed the papacy from the immediate city life of Rome, and offered the protection of the Castel Sant'Angelo and the defensive walls that had been added by Pope Leo IV in the ninth century.

During the fifteenth and sixteenth centuries, a sequence of popes issued plans to renovate St Peter's and the Vatican Palace. But the complexity of the project combined with the stream of architects working at St Peter's stimulated the development of new methods of communicating their ideas and ensured the continuation of their project long after their tenure as architects to the papal court. For they knew that no one patron, or architect, would ever live to see the project completed.

Nicholas V

Before Pope Nicholas V began his extensive additions to St Peter's in 1452, the church had already had several phases of renovation. But Nicholas took a more comprehensive approach to the thousand-year-old building and planned a greatly enlarged choir and transept arms around a dome over the crossing. At St Peter's this was the western end of the church, which was the liturgical focus; the main door was to the east. The additional space would have enlarged the capacity of the building to welcome pilgrims, increasing the importance of St Peter's as one of the seven pilgrimage churches of Rome. Nicholas planned to add chapels along the aisles in order to shore up the outer walls, but otherwise to keep the five aisles with arches and vaults supported by columns from the existing church. The building project established the two fundamental concerns of all subsequent building at St Peter's: the creation of a structurally sound building that would accommodate large numbers of pilgrims, and the creation of a more imperial church appropriate for an expanding papal court.

The projected work was never completed. Even if Nicholas had lived longer or had had fewer projects under way, the scope of the work at St Peter's was monumental. Nicholas's architectural ambitions, however, set a pattern for all future work at St Peter's. He projected onto the building a vision of new work that was personal and political. He was not content with shoring up the past, but desired to build in order to establish the primacy of the church as the basis for papal power.

39

Basilica of Maxentius, Rome, in Bernardo Gamucci, *Le antichita della città di Roma*, Venice, 1569

Guidebooks offered views and descriptions of the major antique monuments and Christian pilgrimage churches. The mapping of ancient buildings created a cult of monuments that shaped the creation of St Peter's as the rebirth of the pagan city as the centre of the Christian world.

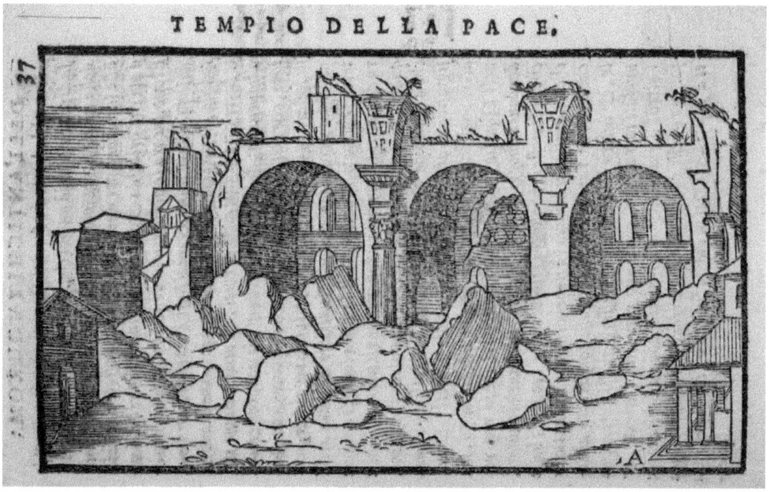

In the same year that construction began at St Peter's, Alberti gave Nicholas the first draft of his treatise *De re aedificatoria*. Yet there is no evidence that Alberti had anything to do with the plans, other than perhaps serving as an outside commentator on the technical difficulties of the building. The Florentine architect Bernardo Rossellino (1409–64) may have been involved, but there is no single name associated with the project.

Julius II

When Giuliano della Rovere became Pope Julius II in 1503, he set a new standard and level of ambition for the rebuilding of St Peter's, and hired Donato Bramante as the papal architect. Bramante had only completed a few buildings by this time in Rome, but his ability to transform ancient architectural models into new imperial uses must have caught the eye of Julius II while he was still cardinal. With Bramante's project we have a completely new vision of what St Peter's might be like, all in keeping with Bramante's earlier projects: a large, spacious, and well-lit building. Julius, however, had his own ideas, based on his previous experience renovating churches to make them more accommodating to the religious orders. He was also quite frugal, and did not want to completely abandon the existing early Christian building or the work that had already been done. From this point forward the debates and discussions over the various projects were often conducted on the level of the drawings and models.

Bramante's design for the new St Peter's consciously imitated ancient buildings in its use of the dome to create a large vaulted space. The Pantheon in Rome (built 118–25) was the best-preserved temple from antiquity, and served as a model and a challenge to both architect and patron to create a greater Christian temple to supersede the pagan

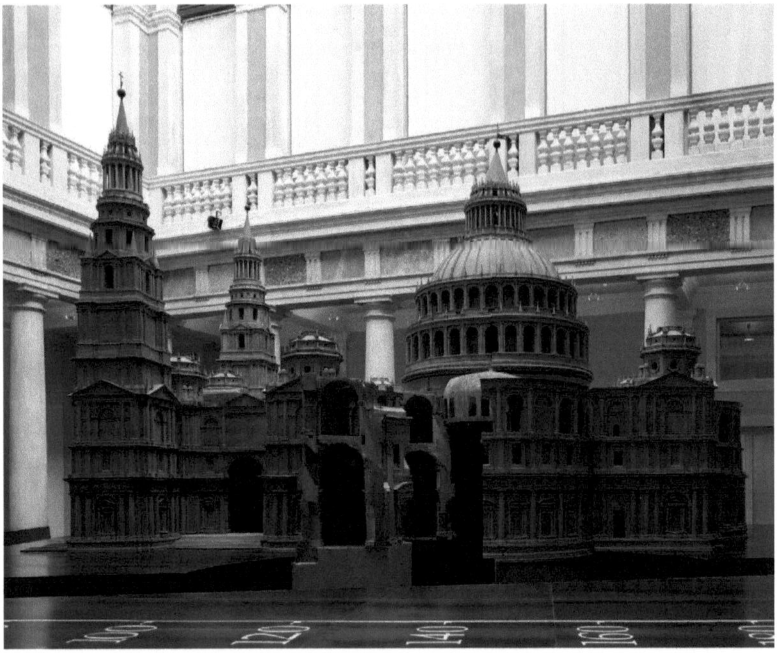

40

Antonio da Sangallo and Antonio Labacco, wooden model for St Peter's, 1539–46

The model was built at a scale of 1:30, and is over 7 metres long and 6 metres wide. The number and variety of craftsmen employed on the model rivalled that for a small building, and indicate the importance given to the creation of a model by both architect and patron. The model was originally painted, and a variety of materials were used to suggest the effect the building would have when built.

monuments of the Roman Empire [**9**]. Bramante is said to have wanted to place the Pantheon on top of the piers and great vaulted spaces of coffered domes and half domes of the Basilica of Maxentius (*c*.307–12). Overlooking the Forum Romanum, the Basilica of Maxentius had collapsed in the Middle Ages, revealing its vast, vaulted interior that had served ancient Rome for civic and judicial functions [**39**]. Both architect and patron conceived of the new St Peter's as the triumph of Christianity presented in the guise of ancient Rome.

Models and Drawings

Only a small amount of visual evidence survives from the changes to St Peter's initiated by Nicholas V. From Julius' pontificate, however, we have numerous models and drawings of the planned renovations. Models of the new building were an important way to visually demonstrate the idea of the project. In fact, we know that models of St Peter's were made for designs by Bramante, Raphael, Peruzzi, Antonio da Sangallo, Michelangelo, Giacomo della Porta, and Maderno throughout the sixteenth century. However, from all of these models that were made, the only ones that survive are two by Michelangelo and one by Antonio da Sangallo.

The Sangallo model, built by Antonio Labacco (1495?–1567), is the largest surviving Renaissance architectural model, and its great size and expense were in keeping with the importance of St Peter's as a project [**40**]. It is large enough to walk into, and gave the viewer a

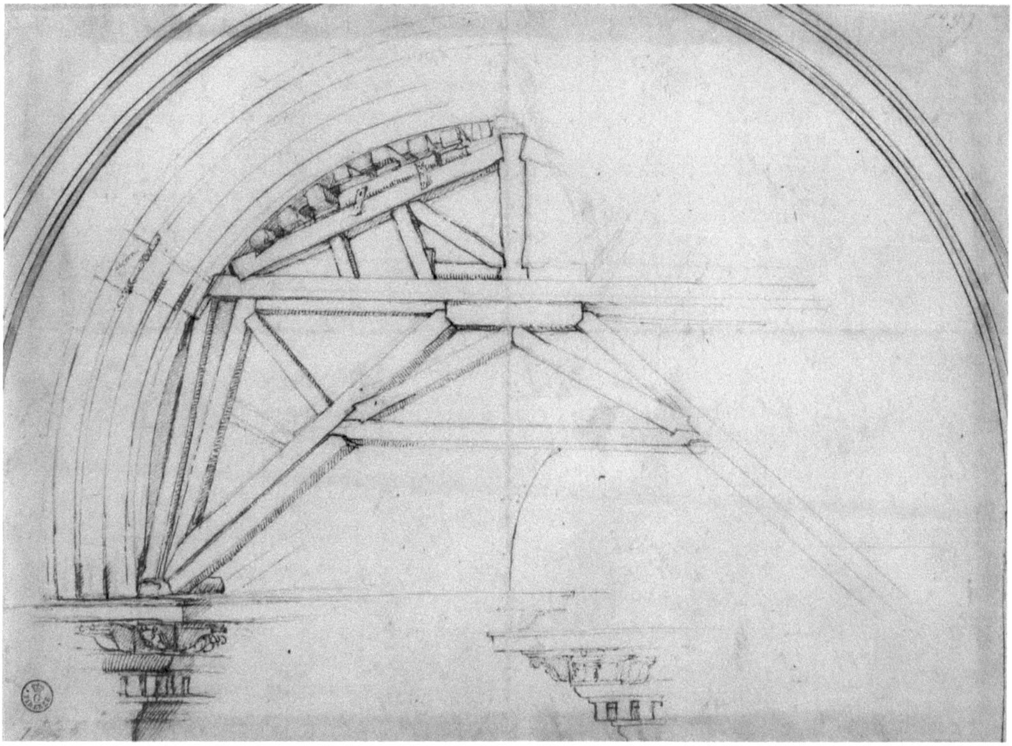

41

Bramante, Project for the centring of pier arches, St Peter's, *c.*1509

One of the few surviving drawings by Bramante, this shows the integration of the scaffolding system and the projecting cornices. The wooden scaffold required the support of the cornice to be effective and allow the masons to insert the keystones to secure the arch.

rich sense of Sangallo's ideas in three-dimensional form. The painted interior of the model and extensive details of the architectural ornament would have given the viewer a sense not only of the space of the building and its external appearance, but also of the experience of entering into the space. The attention to the details of the building was certainly intended to provide the patron, Pope Paul III, with a sense of what the building would have been like when completed, right down to the level of the particular ornament.

Michelangelo did not like Sangallo's plan for St Peter's and criticized it for reducing the light that was central to Bramante's design.

> One cannot deny that Bramante was as skilled in architecture as anyone since the time of the ancients. He it was who laid down the first plan of St. Peter's, not full of confusion, but clear, simple, luminous and detached in such a way that it in no wise impinged upon the Palace. It was held to be a beautiful design, and manifestly still is, so that anyone who has departed from Bramante's arrangement, as Sangallo has done, has departed from the true course; and that this is so can be seen by anyone who looks at his model with unprejudiced eyes.
>
> He, with that outer ambulatory of his, in the first place takes away all the light from Bramante's plan; and not only this, but does so when it has no light of its own, and so many dark lurking places above and below that they afford

ample opportunity for numerous rascalities, such as the hiding of exiles, the coining of base money, the raping of nuns and other rascalities, so that at night, when the said church closes, it would need twenty-five men, to seek out those who remained hidden inside, whom it would be a job to find.[22]

Sangallo's model was made of wood, and carpenters or joiners were hired to construct what were in effect buildings in miniature. Models were also made in clay (Michelangelo for St Peter's) or even in papier-maché (St Maclou in Rouen, France). The choice of material was in keeping with the model's function. For Michelangelo and Brunelleschi, models could serve as guides to workmen. Filippo Brunelleschi had his models left intentionally incomplete, showing primarily the relationship of the walls and other parts of the building. When used as part of the design process, as Leon Battista Alberti advised, models allowed the architect to understand the building in a physical, tangible way.

I will always commend the time-honored custom, practiced by the best builders, of preparing not only drawings and sketches but also models of wood or any other material. These will enable us to weigh up repeatedly and examine, with the advice of experts, the work as a whole and the individual dimensions of all the parts, and, before continuing any farther, to estimate the likely trouble and expense.[23]

Throughout the Renaissance, models were increasingly popular as part of the design process, and although few survive, we know from building accounts that they were made as presentations to patrons, helping the non-architectural expert to envision what the building would be like, and ideally to convince him or her to pay for its construction.

Development of Architectural Drawing

As architectural practice became more developed, and especially at St Peter's, drawings came to play an ever more important role in the design process. Architects employed new forms of architectural drawings, using perspective, **orthogonal** projection, and sketches in order to explore their ideas and record them on paper. Improvements in manufacturing techniques produced a better-quality paper that was more readily available and less expensive.[24] Compared to the expense of a model, drawings were a relatively inexpensive part of the research and design aspect of architect, and allowed the architect to test out his ideas, imagine them in a visual format, and ultimately develop them over time. Not only do a large number of drawings survive from the Renaissance, they offer us an even greater insight into the working methods of the architect and allow us to see design in action.

Medieval architects made drawings as well, of course, and we should not think that drawing was a completely new invention of the

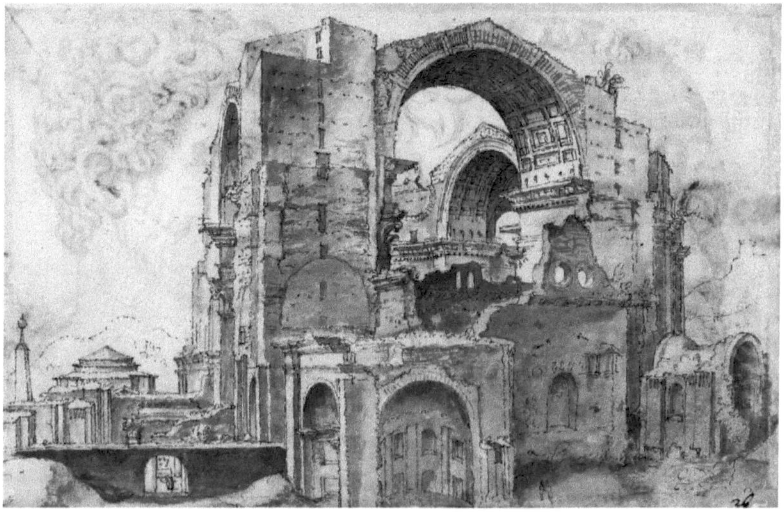

42

Maerten van Heemskerck, St Peter's exterior from the north, 1532/6

One of many drawings by Heemskerck of St Peter's under construction showing the great piers and arches of Bramante's church rising above fragments of the early medieval basilica.

Renaissance. A drawing of the Sansedoni Palace in Siena was made to accompany the building contract of 1340. The full view of the façade of the palace, with its details and dimensions, was part of the legal documents for the construction, and ensured that the builders knew exactly what was expected.[25]

Drawings are part of the architectural process, and as architecture demanded more skills and a greater range of abilities, drawing methods developed in ways that supported the profession of the architect. As antique buildings were seen as a more important part of architects' training, architects increasingly drew after antique monuments. Serlio advised young architects to learn about antiquities by measuring them, and then recording their observations in drawings. The drawings could then serve as a record of the ancient buildings, their measurements and proportions, and be used in conjunction with treatises, prints, and other types of information on antiquity. These kinds of drawings were often gathered together by architects into portfolios, combined with drawings of their own inventions of ornaments or complete buildings. Collections like these were a valuable resource within the workshop or studio and often passed down to sons or apprentices.

In very complex projects, such as the construction of the new St Peter's, the architects used drawings to ensure continuity of design. On a practical level, recording ideas on paper or through a model ensured that the craftsmen understood what was expected and ensured the control of the architect over all aspects of the construction. And for a project that was to take generations, a visual record in conjunction with a contract fixed the idea into the future.[26] Thus the pressures of large building projects can explain the increase in the number of drawings made for St Peter's [**41, 46, 47**]. Yet simple practicality alone

43
Cristofo Foppa Caradosso, Foundation medal for St Peter's, 1505

Bronze or gold medals were struck to commemorate important building commissions. They were placed in the foundation and were also given as gifts. This medal shows Bramante's design for a centralized church, seen from the west, with the large central dome with a colonnaded drum, smaller domes over the entrance and in the corners, and towers.

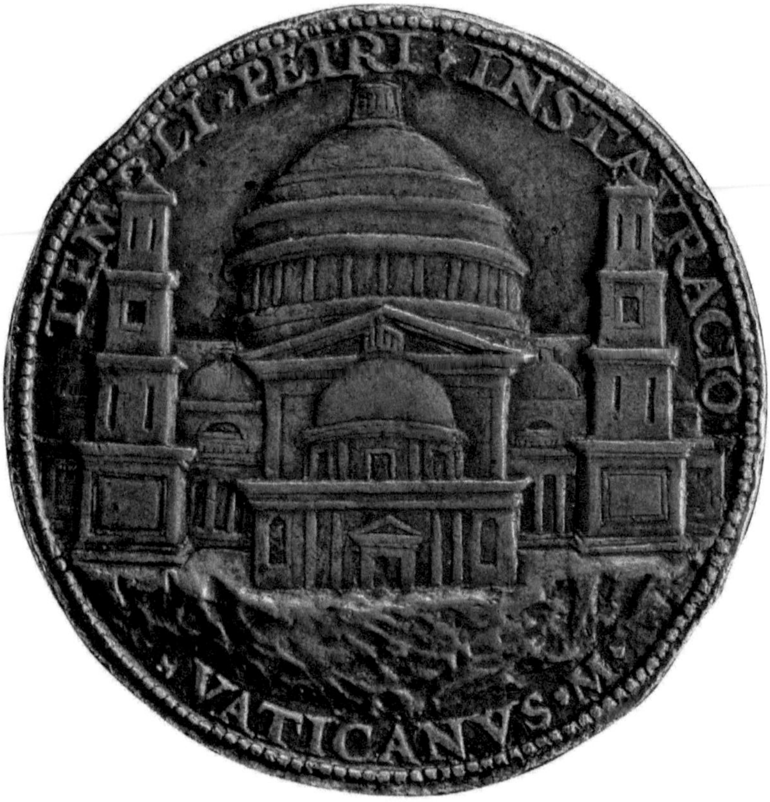

cannot explain the appearance of new types of drawings, especially those that emerged from the *fabbrica* at St Peter's. Drawings by sixteenth-century architectural tourists, studying the buildings of Rome, recorded their experience of seeing these massive piers rising from the rubble of the building site amid the remains of the early Christian basilica [**42**].

What we see over the course of the rebuilding of St Peter's is an increase in the variety of types of drawings. When Donato Bramante began the process of designing the new St Peter's his large drawing of half the ground plan established the intention of creating a centrally planned church with vast and complex piers to support the massive dome. The contrast between this design and the existing longitudinal, early Christian church would have presented a dramatic change to the patron Julius II. A medal struck at the same time showed the proposed building in elevation, with the large central dome with supporting towers and smaller domes [**43**].

The solution for the design of St Peter's—was it to be a centrally planned building or longitudinal?—was debated throughout the history of the project, well into the second half of the sixteenth century when eventually the benefit of a larger, processional space became clear, although the nave was not begun until 1607. The various

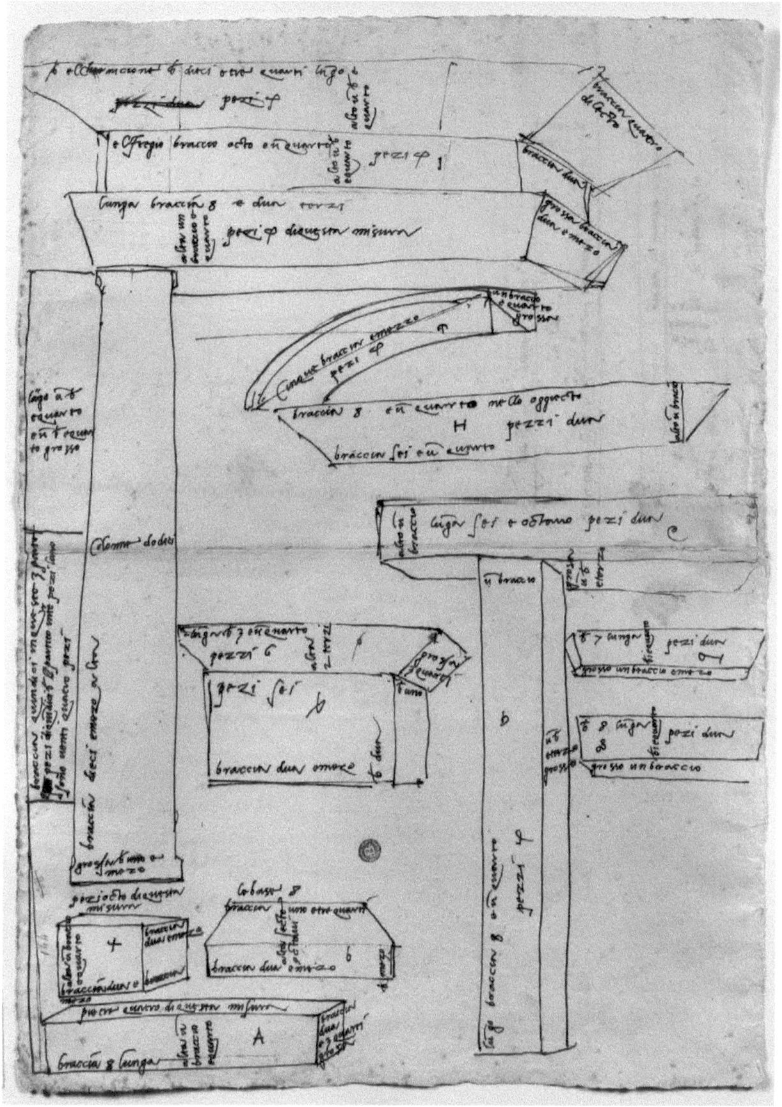

44

Michelangelo, Drawing of blocks for the San Lorenzo façade

As part of his order to the quarry, Michelangelo drew each block needed for the façade of the church of San Lorenzo (Florence). He includes the dimensions of the blocks, and the number needed of each, on the image of the stone, as if he were writing on the thing itself. Architects had to communicate with stonecutters and the craftsmen who would provide the raw materials for their projects.

positions were certainly discussed at length, and there are drawings that give some evidence of the back and forth arguments by various architects. Bramante's centrally planned church, for example, was countered by Giuliano da Sangallo, who advocated a more stable design with reinforced pillars that would have reduced the interior space.

The development in types of architectural drawings responded to a real need to communicate ideas from the architect to the patrons to explain what the finished product would look like, and many drawings survive as a record of the design process. Drawings made by the architect for the quarry or building site were often destroyed in the very

45

Leonardo da Vinci, Embryo in the womb, 1510

Developments in scientific and technical drawing offered architectural draughtsmen new modes of representation. Through the use of section, as Leonardo da Vinci does here, drawings could show interior spaces as they related to exterior structure. Drawings, and book illustrations, allowed architects to communicate their ideas more fully and persuasively to patrons and craftsmen as well as to a wider public.

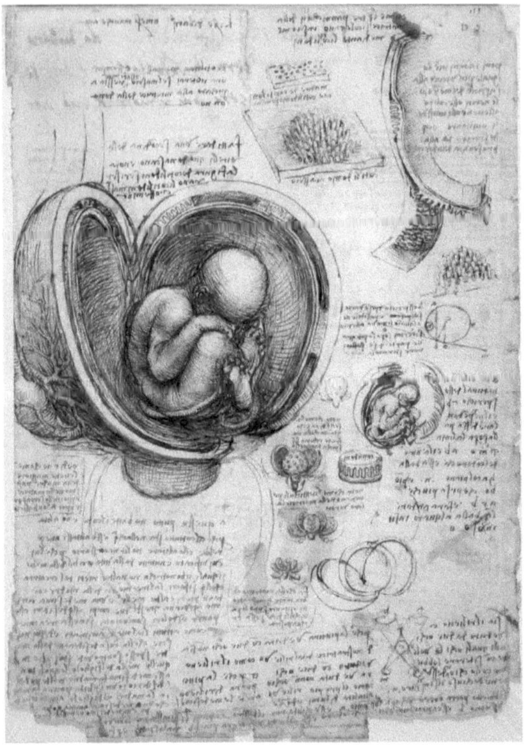

46

Baldessare Peruzzi, Bird's-eye perspective view of project for St Peter's, *c.*1535

When Peruzzi became architect of St Peter's, alongside Antonio da Sangallo, he proposed a new plan for the building. This drawing was probably intended to convince the Pope, then Paul III, of the merits of his design. The elevated view, and ability to understand many aspects of the building at once (plan, elevation, and section), would have allowed the architect to make a convincing argument for his project.

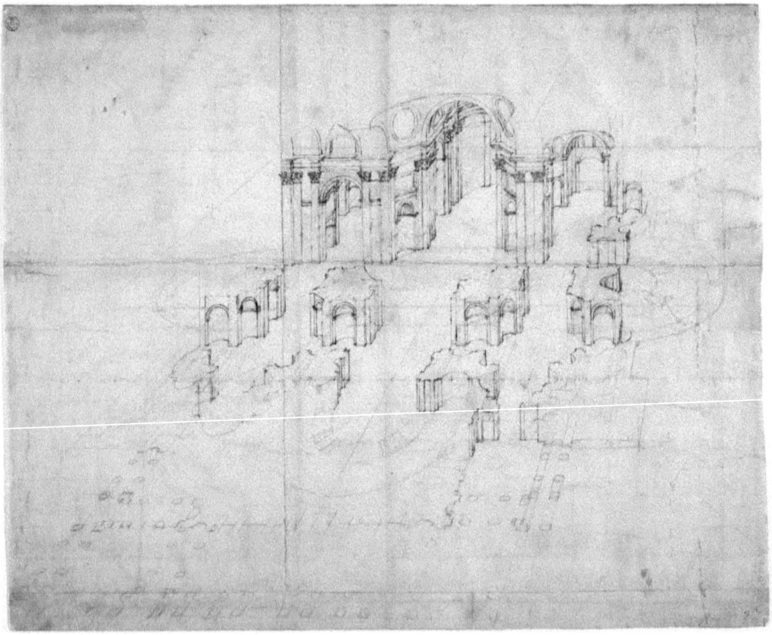

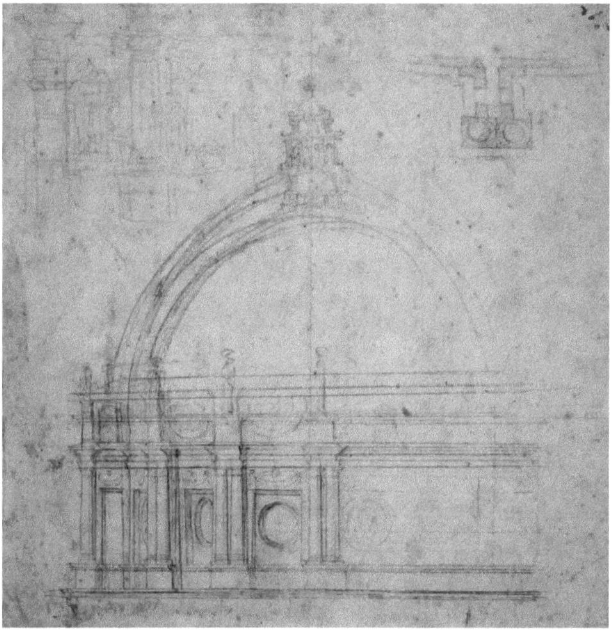

47

Michelangelo, Drawing for dome of St Peter's, probably 1546–7

The design of the drum, dome, and lantern for St Peter's was ongoing, and continued after Michelangelo's death on 18 February 1564. Even fundamental questions such as the profile and shape of the dome had not been settled. Drawings, such as this by Michelangelo for the dome and drum, give some indication of the possible options. Here the architect evaluates the relationship between the dome and the drum if the shape of the inner and outer domes were to change.

process of building [**44**]. Once the project was completed, the drawing, by now often in a tattered state, was thrown away. Other drawings might have been kept by the architect as part of a collection of working tools, as important to him as his pens and instruments.

Drawing techniques developed out of architectural need, as well as from related disciplines. In 1514–15 Raphael wrote a letter to Pope Leo X responding to the Pope's request for a drawing of the antiquities of Rome. Raphael insisted that architects should use three types of drawings: the plan, and views of the exterior and interior walls. The plan shows the building at ground level, while the view of the outside wall, what we now call the elevation of the building, shows the windows, door, and ornament. The view of the interior wall, called the section, shows what would appear if the building could be opened up, and its interior elements displayed to a viewer. The section of a building, like the plan, gives a privileged view, one not easily if ever observable in the normal course of events. The section shared with anatomical drawings, like that of a baby in *utero* by Leonard da Vinci, the sense that the interior was now, miraculously, available for study [**45**]. Each type of architectural view offered different information, and allowed more aspects of a building to be known and compared with its sources of design and other buildings of the same type. The immensity of the project at St Peter's, and the complexity of the design and construction, inspired in their turn numerous drawings.

The architect and painter Baldassare Peruzzi (1481–1536) left his native Siena, and spent much of his career in Rome, paid through the accounts at St Peter's. His great talents as an architect, painter, and fortification designer attest to his broad training and abilities to work on any type of project in order to satisfy the demands of his patrons. What he actually contributed to the building of St Peter's, however, is not clear. Throughout his career, Peruzzi used drawing as a means to study antiquity as a source for new designs, and to develop modes of representation that would express a building's inherent design and visual effect.[27] Onc of the most extraordinary of these drawings is an aerial perspective of the interior of St Peter's [**46**]. The centrally planned design is seen in perspective, as if the viewer were able to hover in the air over one corner. From that plan, Peruzzi has drawn the structure rising up in gradual steps, as if the construction were occurring in real time. Not only does the drawing give a more potent impression of what the new St Peter's would have been like, it adds a drama to the building, anticipating the religious drama that would eventually take place within.

All architectural drawings were made for a purpose. Architects drew to explore design options [**47**] and to relay information to craftsmen. Presentation drawings conveyed the idea to a patron and as a record of an architect's intentions; drawings conveyed his intentions into the future.

The Building Site

Drawings by the Dutch artist Maarten van Heemskerck (1498–1574) in the 1530s give some idea of the scale of the project at St Peter's, and

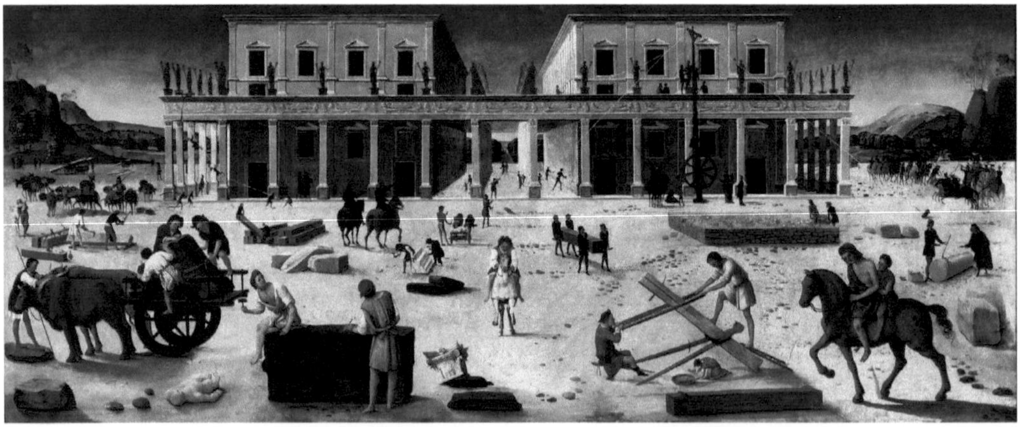

48

Piero di Cosimo, *The Building of a Palace*, *c.*1515–20

In the foreground of this painting is the activity of building. Stone arrives from the quarry, shaped by the masons, and hoisted into place on the building. The building site is where ideas are put into action, a sort of architectural laboratory or classroom, filled with masters and workers of all ages. The many children in the scene at play, or imitating the craftsmen, suggest that architecture is a place of learning.

the state of the building while it was under construction [**42**]. The great arches of the Bramante project can be seen, but the project at this time had been abandoned after the Sack of Rome, the attack on the city in 1527 by the troops of Charles V. The building site appears deserted, with little chance that work will resume soon. Work did begin again under Pope Paul III, with a desire to contain costs and speed building along. For Paul III, Peruzzi crafted a plan that he characterized as 'bella e breve', beautiful and quick to execute. But it too was eventually abandoned in favour of something else.[28] The up and down progress on St Peter's was in some ways not surprising for a building of that size, although efforts were made from the very beginning to establish controls over the process of design and construction.

The complexity of the project at St Peter's existed on every front: the demolition of an ancient church and ancillary structures, repeated periods of design development, and maintaining construction standards, all while papal masses needed to continue. These very practical requirements demanded greater rigour in the building process. Existing structures had to be measured carefully and recorded in drawings. Materials needed to be secured in sufficient quantity and quality.[29]

Out of the chaos of construction, however, also came innovation. Building sites were one of a number of places including libraries, observatories, courts, and arsenals where early modern scholars, practitioners, and patrons came together. This sense of the community of workers at the building site is recorded in numerous images of the ***cantiere*** in fifteenth- and sixteenth-century art. Piero di Cosimo's painting of a double palace sets off the various activities of building including the transportation of materials, the carving of stone, sawing of wood, laying foundations, and so on against a building which is eerily almost complete, as if the work happening in the foreground were in another time zone than the product of its labour in the distance [**48**]. Yet in that disconnect is also this same working out of the two worlds of Renaissance architecture—the labour of the craftsmen which goes on in its own domain, guided by long-established practices and attendant to the materials, and the visionary product of the architect's invention.

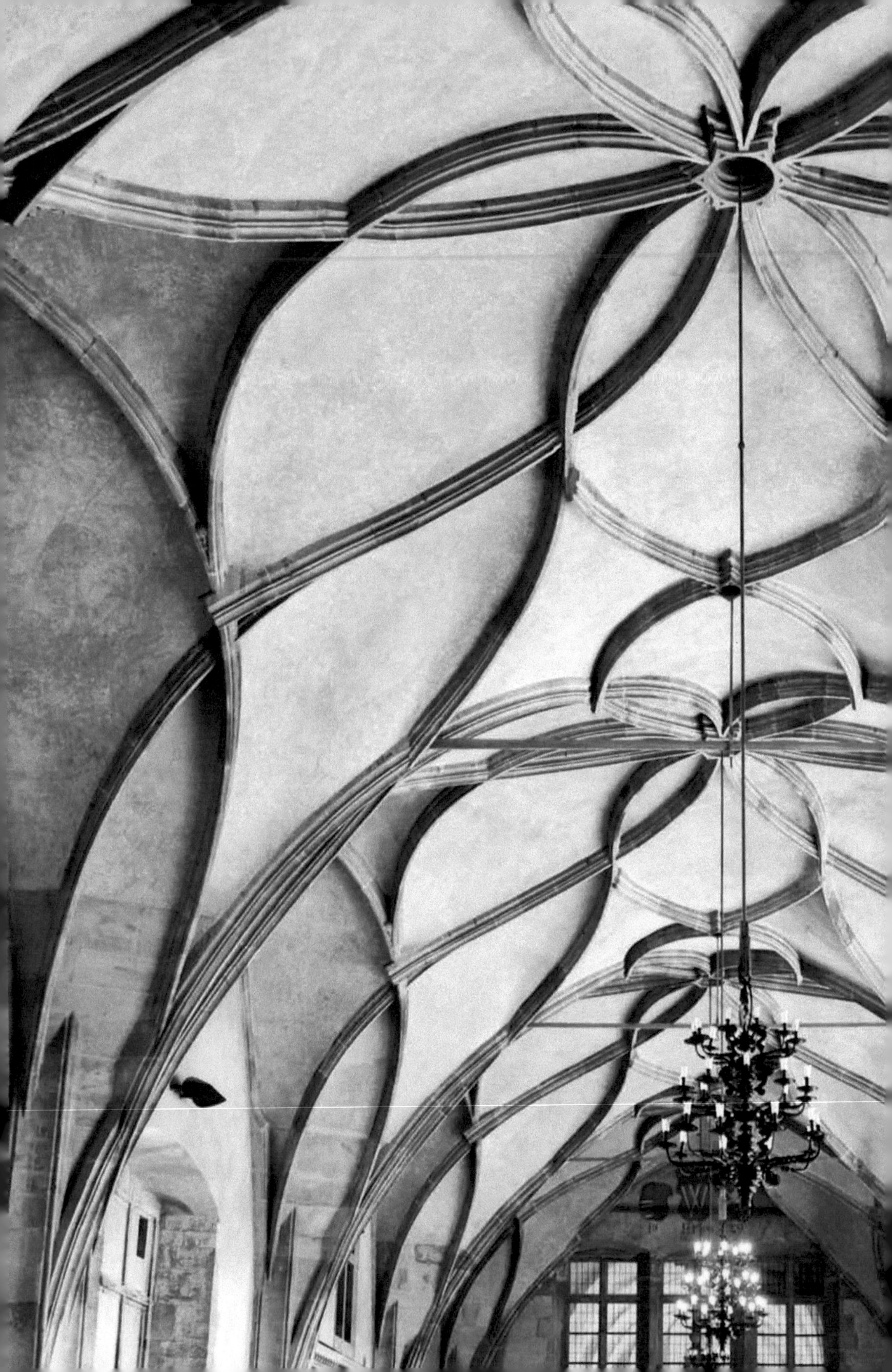

The Architecture of Ascendancy

Buildings and Power

4

Political rule is a spatial reality. For the Renaissance prince, the route to power came through the control of his dominion. Moving out from the body of the monarch, the first concern was the protection of the sovereign; the palace extended his or her presence into the public realm. Cities and fortresses project the authority of the palace even further, and stand as a sign of political power to others. Political historians talk of this embodied authority, and in architectural terms all the buildings of political power are integral to the creation and maintenance of rule. The court was both a political organization as well as an architectural space.[1] Within the court, complex rules of behaviour based on rank, favouritism, and family connections allowed for various levels of intimacy and physical proximity to the ruler. All these conventions and practices shaped the design of architecture, and buildings functioned as a constant reminder to adhere to protocol. We must see architecture in this context as an active participant in political rule, projecting the identity of those in power and standing in for their physical presence.[2]

Ferdinand and Isabella's Spain

When Ferdinand II, King of Aragon and Sicily, married his cousin, Isabella of Castile, in 1469, they forged a political alliance that was also a union of the varied artistic heritages of Spain. Their emphasis on a strengthened monarchy, centralized administration, and religious conformity shaped their artistic patronage as well. Isabella was the more active patron, with a varied court entourage of scholars, artists, and architects from the Iberian peninsula and abroad. Isabella's confessor, Cardinal Francisco Jiménez de Cisneros (1436–1517), shaped the religious conservatism of the Catholic Monarchs. The rigid intolerance toward the Moors and Jews, especially those in the kingdom of Granada that Ferdinand and Isabella ultimately captured in 1492, reflected Cisneros's austere religious policies. The imperial aspirations of Spain in the Americas and Africa were a further aspect of Cisneros's fervour to support an ascendant Spanish monarchy. The court style of Ferdinand and Isabella's architectural patronage was also imperial,

Detail of 64

taking elements from all aspects of the rulers' own ancestry as well as elements from the territories they brought under Spanish rule.

Ferdinand and Isabella's rule was challenged by the claims of Juana la Beltraneja, daughter of the previous King of Castile, Enrique IV. Isabella, Enrique IV's sister, eliminated the challenge when her and Ferdinand's forces defeated the Portuguese King Alfonso at the Battle of Toro (1476). In thanksgiving for the victory, Isabella founded the Franciscan monastery of San Juan de los Reyes in Toledo (1477–1504) that was intended to serve as the royal mausoleum [**49**].[3]

The plain, undecorated walls of the exterior reflect Cardinal Cisneros's own stylistic preferences for austere architecture, with few external flourishes. That restraint, however, is not present in the decoration of the cloister or chapel at San Juan de los Reyes. The church has a wide central nave, with four chapels along each side, shallow transepts, and an octagonal apse. That relatively simple plan provides ample opportunity for the architect, Juan Guas, to glorify the patrons through lavish decoration and royal symbols.

The richest decoration is at the crossing between the nave and shallow transepts, under the lantern vault where the royal tombs would be placed. Throughout the church and cloister the vaulting is of a type that was used throughout Europe, combining Gothic forms in a regular and mathematically composed way. The *cimborio* has vaulting (parallel ribs) like that used at the domes of the great mosque in Cordoba. North and south, the walls of the transept are covered with the royal heraldry, the sheaf of arrows and the yoke, emblems of submission and control. Heraldry spoke a clear language to any visitor,

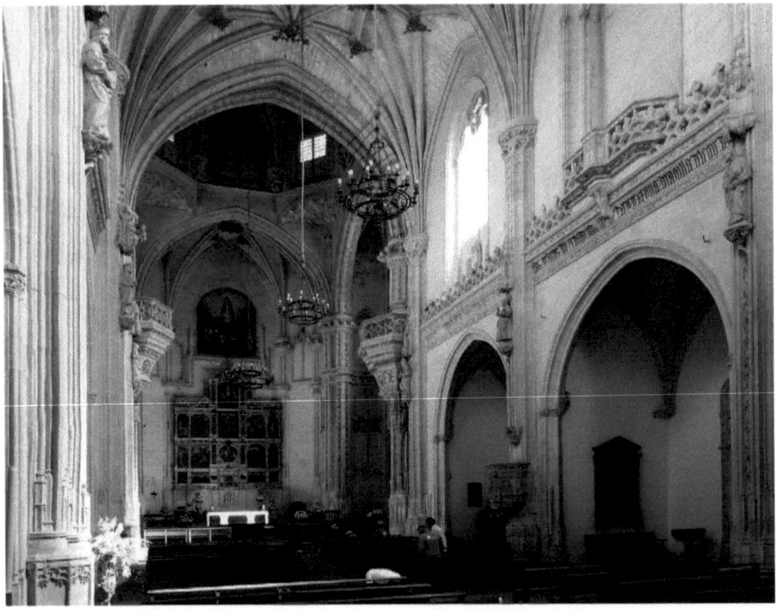

49

Juan Guas, Chapel, San Juan de los Reyes, 1477–1504, Toledo, Spain

The simple, aisle-less church allows the rich carving and sculpture to take centre stage. Gothic tracery, treated as a balustrade, runs along the top of the entablature above the arches. The richest decoration is in the crossing with its very shallow arms. There sculpture including heraldry and inscriptions proclaim the glory and triumphs of Ferdinand and Isabella.

and would have been supervised by a member of Isabella's court. That responsibility may have fallen to the court humanist Antonio de Nebrija, who also composed the Queen's motto *Tanto monta, monta tanto, Isabel como Fernando* ('As much as the one is worth, so is the other'), thus proclaiming that Isabella's power was equal to that of her husband's. Shaping the court image, through architecture, was an important part of politics.

Juan Guas (*c*.1430–1496) was the Master of the Royal Works for Isabella, and principal architect at San Juan de los Reyes. He was born in Brittany (France), the son of a mason, and arrived in Spain at about the age of 10. His training in Spain gave him a first-hand understanding of the crafts of building and the coordination of teams of workers including sculptors, scholars, artists, and craftsmen.

The ornament at San Juan de los Reyes is a combination of forms and techniques from Islamic craftsmen who had been working in Spain even after it had been placed under Christian rule (called *mudéjar*), and Flemish late Gothic architecture, introduced through the strong ties to French culture. This Hispano-Flemish style is uniquely representative of the mix of cultures in Isabella's political and cultural world. Craftsmen brought with them knowledge of building traditions from their own backgrounds, and these were combined in the construction and ornament at San Juan de los Reyes. Thus, the ceiling in the cloister is a traditional Islamic ceiling construction, called *artesonado*, composed of multiple interlocking pieces of wood, here with the emblems of the Catholic Monarchs [**50**]. This combination of traditions in Hispano-Flemish architecture should not be

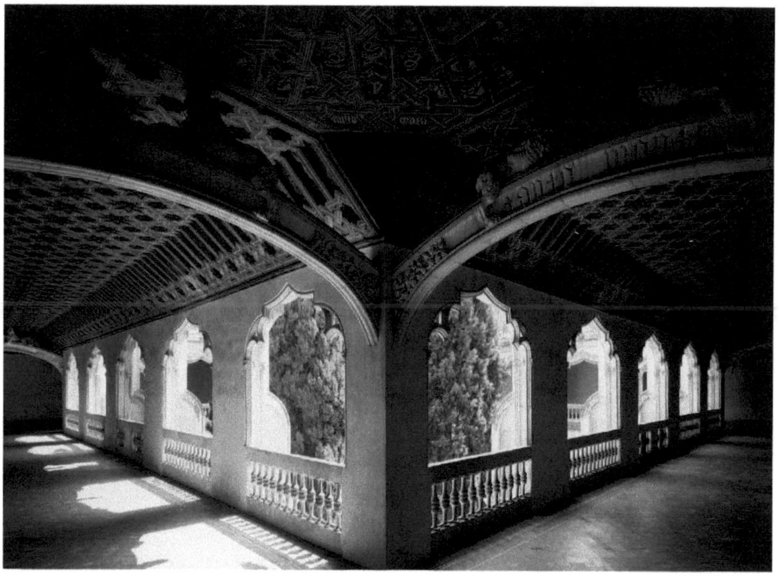

50

Juan Guas, Upper cloister, San Juan de los Reyes, 1477–1504, Toledo, Spain

One of Guas's great skills was his ability to merge architectural traditions and techniques from the various cultures that inhabited the Iberian peninsula. *Artesonado*, a Spanish term for the intricately joined wooden ceilings, derived from North African and Spanish building traditions. In Islamic architecture, *artesonado* ceilings could represent the seven heavens of Islam. The technique continued to be used into the fifteenth and sixteenth centuries, and often incorporated, as here, other decorative elements such as heraldry.

necessarily seen as a sign of tolerance but rather part of Ferdinand and Isabella's policy of imperial assimilation, combining elements from the various cultures and entities under their rule. Much Renaissance court art takes a similar approach in creating a style fused from various sources as a mark of the ruler's power to bring all his people into his domain. Here the combination may have been as part of a harsh political reality, yet the effect preserved the heritage of the Christian and Muslim origins of Ferdinand and Isabella's dominions.

Margaret of Austria

Having survived three marriages, the first to Charles VIII, King of France, when she was just an infant, Margaret of Austria (1480–1530) spent her last years at the centre of her own court of humanists, poets, and artists. She was the daughter of the Holy Roman Emperor, Maximilian I, and as was usual for the children of royal and noble families, had her life planned through a series of political alliances. The marriage to Charles VIII was annulled after only three years, when Margaret was 3, but she was then wed to Juan, heir of Castile and Aragon, son of Ferdinand and Isabella of Spain. Juan's sudden death in 1497 left her free to marry Philibert II, Duke of Savoy, in 1501. By 1504 Margaret was a widow once again. Now, however, Margaret took up her role as Regent of the Netherlands, and began to shape her court and palace at Mechelen.

As with many important female patrons of the Renaissance, Margaret had the political savvy to negotiate a life that allowed her as much freedom as possible within the accepted behaviour for noble women. Books such as *De institutione feminae christianae* by the humanist Juan Luis Vives (1524) prescribed appropriate images of women, aligning their image with that of the Virgin Mary.

In 1506 Margaret chose the city of Mechelen for her permanent residence, where her close relative, Margaret of York (1446–1503) had spent the last thirty years of her life. For the city fathers, the opportunity to welcome Margaret of Austria's entourage encouraged them to support financially the construction of her residence.

The city architect of Mechelen, Anthonis Keldermans I, designed the new palace wings for Margaret incorporating existing houses near the site, and taking into account a hospital and church that were the property of Margaret's father, Maximilian [**51**]. Keldermans was a member of a large family of architects, masons, and artists working in the Burgundian Netherlands.

Brick and stone combined were used for court and noble architecture where stone was at a premium. The distinctive linear patterning that runs across the building unified the separate stages of construction, and marked out the palace as a building of high status through

51

Anthonis Keldermans I, Palace for Margaret of Austria, begun 1506, Mechelen, northern Netherlands

The loggia merged the old and new sections of the palace, and marked out Margaret of Austria's transformation of the existing structure. The antique work, however, was localized by employing regional building materials and techniques as well as the use of stepped gables set against the steeply pitched roof.

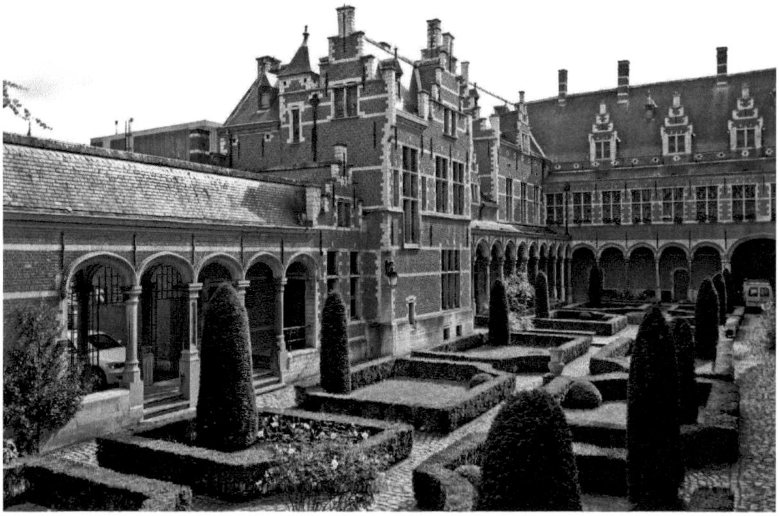

the mixture of materials and the uniformity of its construction. Staessen Le Prince, a member of an important family of stonecutters and stone suppliers, provided the stone components of the loggia at Mechelen.[4]

Rooms devoted to her collections of art and objects distinguish parts of the palace built for Margaret. A thick walled jewellery chamber, deep within the palace, held precious objects, including gold and silver plate. A 'riche cabinet' in Margaret's living quarters contained objects that established her royal lineage and authority to rule, including twenty panel paintings by Juan de Flandres, originally belonging to Margaret's first mother-in-law, Queen Isabella of Castile. Hangings, tables, and chandeliers were marked with Margaret's coat of arms with angels and enamelled daisies. The most extraordinary *wunderkammer*, however, was the coral cabinet, off the garden courtyard. Margaret herself organized the unique and curious objects in the room, including over fifty branches of natural coral, precious stones, religious figurines, and scientific instruments such as astrolabes, games, and mirrors. Many of the objects were adorned with her initials forming an acrostic of the French version of her name, Marguerite.[5]

Here, she used 'anticse werken', or antique work, that is, classical architecture. The loggia in the main courtyard included a type of composite column, four round columns surrounding a square pier, a distinctive invention of the architect, Rombout II Keldermans, and the mason, Staessen Le Prince. This free interpretation of ancient Roman architecture, and modern buildings based on those models, created a distinctive local style that could be identified as the mark of a particular region or patron. But overall, the very use of classical elements, understood by the knowledgeable architectural observer to be derived from antiquity, aligned that building and its patrons with the ideals of ancient culture. Humanist scholars, especially those such as associated with Margaret's court, translated ancient texts into the local language, offering the knowledge of ancient culture as a model for modern life. Architecture based on antiquity did much the same thing, serving as a sign of Margaret's own intellectual prowess and interest in the highest forms of learning and culture.

Classical architecture made sense for Margaret of Austria's palace in Mechelen, as it served as a statement of her educational ideas. At the same time as Margaret was involved in her palace, however, she was also actively directing the construction of her church and tombs in Brou, in the duchy of Savoy, chosen for its connection to Margaret's husband, Philibert [**52**]. There, the choir and tombs for Margaret, her husband Philibert of Savoy, and her mother-in-law Margaret of Bourbon employ lavish Gothic ornament in the tracery, finials, and sculptural decoration. This use of Gothic was thoughtfully modulated by Margaret and her artists, Jan van Roome and Loys van Broghem, both from Brussels. Margaret chose Gothic at Brou only after she had considered other options, including a design more

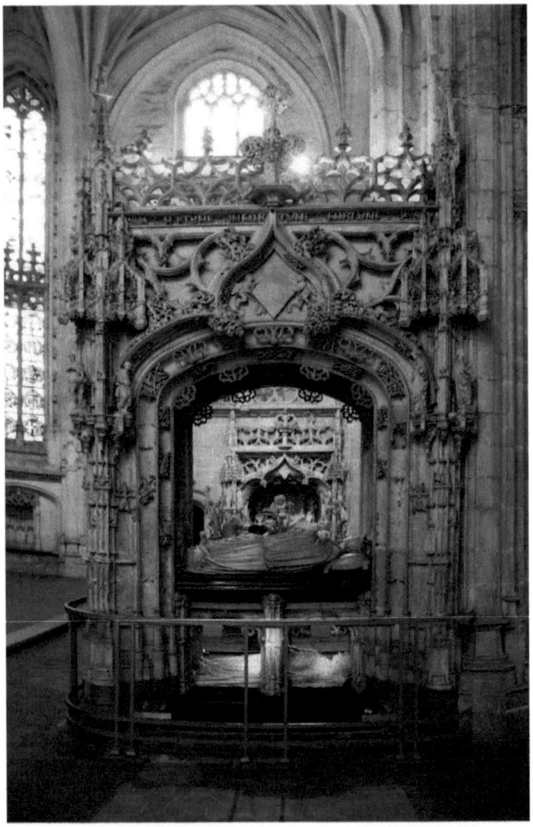

52

Lodewijk van Boghen, Jan van Roome, and Conrat Meyt, Tomb of Margaret of Savoy, 1516–30, Church of St Nicholas, Brou, France

In the sixteenth century Gothic architecture was called 'modern' work to distinguish it from classical architecture, or the antique.

Italianate and based on ancient Roman models. Lavish ornament at Brou is at once a sign of her wealth and a statement of her allegiance to a tradition of royal monuments. Margaret had lived in Spain during her brief marriage to Juan of Castile from 1497 to 1499, and during those years the monastery of San Juan de los Reyes in Toledo was nearly completed. Tracery, vegetal ornament, and use of heraldry in Toledo all offered an important model for Margaret to adopt in her own works.[6]

Hapsburg Patronage and the Control of Classicism

Given the richness of the architecture of Ferdinand and Isabella, the austerity and restraint of the monastery of S. Lorenzo el Real des Escorial (1563–84), built for Philip II, is a radical departure for the architectural traditions of Spain. It had a threefold function: as a monastery for the Hieronymite order; as a church that would serve as a funeral chapel for Philip's father Charles V and the Hapsburg dynasty; and as a palace [**53**]. The very size and dominance of the Escorial signals Philip's less itinerant political policies, especially in contrast to his peripatetic father, who claimed that an emperor needed

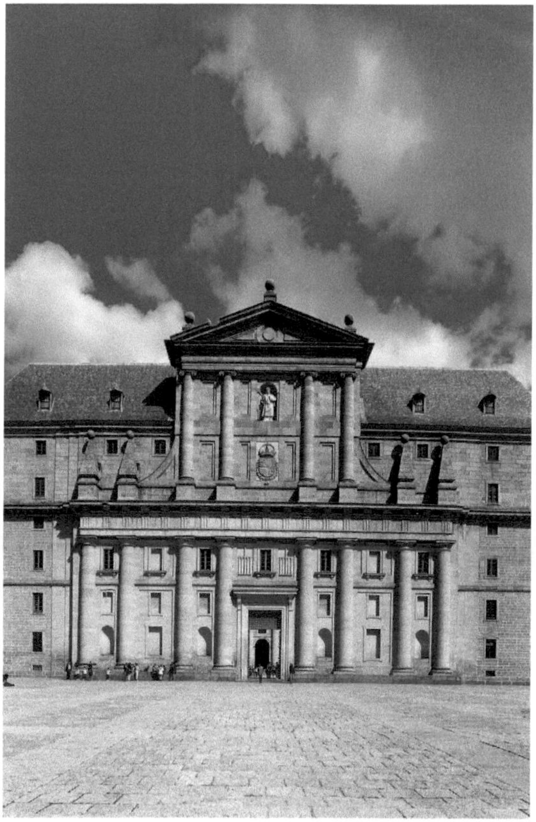

53
Juan Bautista de Toledo and Juan de Herrera, San Lorenzo el Real de Escorial, 1563–84, El Escorial, Spain

Philip II kept close control of the architectural planning and construction. The specific choices of plan and ornament must reflect therefore his approach to building. Overall the building evokes the sort of single-mindedness and clarity that one would expect when the patron is so involved. The temple front on the western façade, seen here, does not lead directly into the church, as one would expect, but into the courtyard, with the church beyond.

54

San Lorenzo el Real de Escorial, 1563–84, El Escorial, Spain

All three sections of the monastery are entered from the western façade: the monastery to the south, church at the centre, and the seminary and *Colegio* to the north. Cross-shaped divisions incorporate patios or courtyards, as seen in this seventeenth-century painting. The palace for Philip II was along the eastern side of the complex, entered through the northern façade. The sequences of rooms for particular groups within this vast building are clearly defined and legible in the plan. Scholars have suggested various interpretations for the plan as the New Jerusalem or Augustine's City of God. The highly reduced classical architecture, however, evokes ideas of a primal Christian building type, derived from ancient models and transformed for modern use.

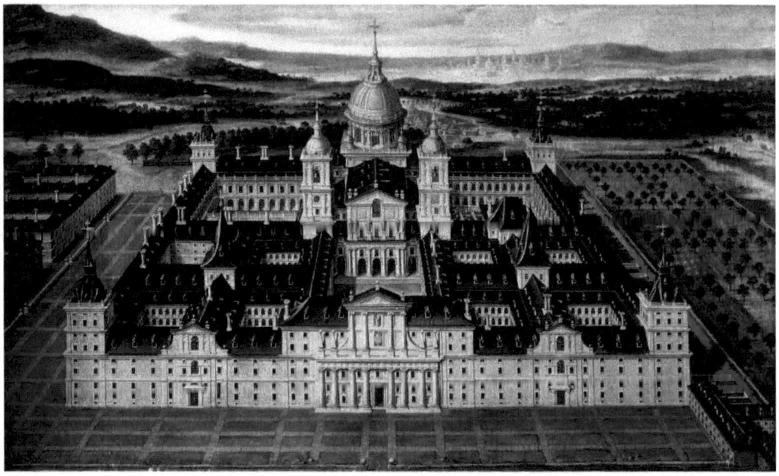

no other residence than his saddle.[7] The church is dedicated to the Spanish saint St Lawrence, martyred in the third century over fire, and the geometrical form of the gridirons appears on the façade of the building and more obliquely in the plan of the complex overall [**54**].

Philip's father, Charles V, had already set a new pattern of building in the construction of a palace within the sprawling layout of the great fourteenth-century palace of the Islamic Nasrid Dynasty, the Alhambra in Granada [**55**]. There the architect Pedro Machuca had devised a plan of a circle within a square, the most constrained of architectural compositions, as a counterpoint to the fluid, experiential spaces of the Alhambra. Whereas the Lion Court and the seemingly

55

Pedro Machuca, Palace for Charles V, 1533–61, Granada, Spain

Machuca spent his early years in Italy, and returned to Spain with a thorough knowledge of art and architecture in Rome at the workshop of Raphael. The strict geometry of Charles V's palace is a radical departure from the fluid design of the Alhambra to which it is attached.

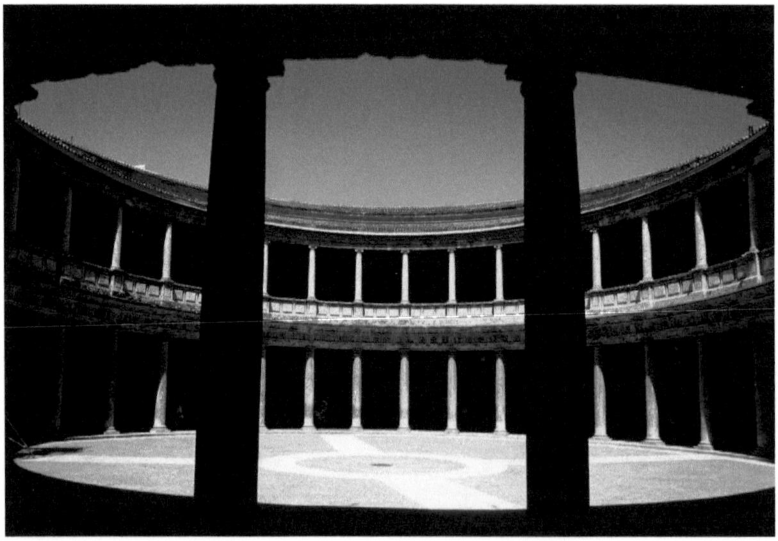

endless sequence of rooms from the earlier Islamic palace have no obvious edges, no beginning and no end, the Palace of Charles V expresses the most overt geometry. A two-storey courtyard is ringed with Doric and Ionic columns, echoing Italian architecture. It is the contrast, however, between the cultural past and the political present that must have compelled Charles and his architect to create this imperial statement of Hapsburg rule, side by side with the Islamic tradition that runs throughout Spanish history and culture.

The Escorial sits in the shadow of the rolling hills outside Madrid, and that undulating landscape makes the rigid geometry of six quadrangles, grid-like and unrelenting, appear even starker. The threefold function of the complex is manifest in the building's plan: the church is at the centre of the complex, with palaces for the family to the right and a palace for the courtiers to the left. The front quadrangle is dedicated to the monastery and university functions.

The first architect was Juan Bautista de Toledo, from Naples, who had worked on St Peter's in Rome as an assistant to Michelangelo. Thus he brought to the design of the Escorial an understanding of the use of the classical orders as a reference to antiquity and as a way to connect new construction to the *gravitas* and solemnity of ancient Roman architecture. As at St Peter's, however, the models from the past were always tempered with new interpretations and local references. Philip began the building of the Escorial after he had returned from a prolonged time in Flanders, and just as San Juan de los Reyes incorporated vegetal ornament from the Gothic tradition, so too did he press for Flemish associations here in the pitched roofs and spires of the corner towers.

After Juan Bautista de Toledo's death in 1567, his assistant Juan de Herrera (1530–97) became the architect in charge. He worked within the general plan laid down by his predecessor yet shaped the ultimate appearance of the building through the choice of ornament, use of architectural materials, and understanding of the goals of his patron, Philip II. Herrera began his career as a member of the army, and his expertise gained there in mathematics, scientific instruments, fortification, and engineering provided valuable expertise to the court. These disciplines were also understood to be an essential part of the training for any architect, based on classical and humanist writings. The shift to architectural design in his role as court architect proved the value of science as a fundamental training for architecture or, in fact, any practical service at court. This background certainly shaped Herrera's approach to the design at the Escorial. The masses of the building are conceived of as geometric solids, punctuated through the use of classical ornament. The size of the building certainly demanded a thorough understanding of construction techniques and engineering. Yet Herrera makes that mathematical process evident in the reduction of ornament to a minimum, and the focus kept on the fundamentals of the architecture's materials and structure.

His architecture continued the classicizing trend initiated by Pacheco and developed under Juan Battista, yet his particular feel for the essence of classicism led him to shape a style of building which subsequently in the nineteenth century came to be called the *estilo desornamentado*, or the unornamented style, a negative term that historians coined to describe what they saw as severe and restricted ornament.[8] The pilasters in the church at the Escorial, or the vaulting in the hallways throughout the palace, typify an architecture which attempts to balance the massing of the structure with an ornamental system with enough strength and clarity to inflect the grey granite used throughout.

Philip II's court historian and librarian, Fray José de Sigüenza (1544–1606), was a witness to the building of the Escorial. Around 1590 he wrote a two-part book about the building, describing first a history of the Hieronymite monastic order based there and second an analysis of the architecture.[9] Sigüenza based his interpretation of the restrained style of the Escorial on his knowledge of St Augustine (354–430), whose works had a special significance as the founding tenets of the Hieronymite order. Using the aesthetic categories described by Augustine, Sigüenza praises the Escorial as an expression of the rule of Philip.

> One of the great beauties of this building is seen in how all its parts imitate one another, and how much the whole is in all the parts. The building which fails to keep this order shows the poor resources and understanding of its architect, in not having bound together or unified the whole body. What we call correspondence is none other than the right reason of art...with the authority not alone of Vitruvius...but that of the divine Augustine, doctor of the church, who, as a man of high genius, wished, among a thousand other matters of learning found in his books, to touch also on this of correspondence in architecture.
>
> As Spain had lost the habits of the fine arts in the savagery and wildness of the war against the Moors...people were astonished to see preserved here [at the Escorial] so much correspondence in architecture, and believed that it was only the taste or inclination of King Philip, or an idle curiosity, that wherever a door or window appeared another should respond to it...Thus we may say that this Prince, as we learn from Saint Augustine, returned us to reason and made us notice that the arts contain reason both in themselves and in the proportion they make with our souls.[10]

A more florid ornamental system, such as that used for Ferdinand and Isabella, would have been totally out of keeping with the austerity desired by Philip II. Classical details at the Escorial are often reduced to such a degree, as in the fluting of a column isolated on a wall or the traces of handrails along the main staircase, that they seem a distant echo of the most avant-garde architecture in Italy or elsewhere. The most current architectural treatises such as Sebastiano Serlio's *Regole generali di architettura sopra le cinque maniere degli edifici* (Venice, 1537–51), translated into Spanish by Francisco de Villalpando (1552), offered architects options in their interpretation of the orders. Yet the innovation seen at the Escorial is a specific response to the wishes of the patron in light of local traditions and the history of architecture in Spain.

The Triumph of Maximilian I

No architectural form better represents royal power than the triumphal arch. In the ancient world, free-standing arches represented the triumph of ancient Rome and her control over a vast empire. Two of the best known arches in the Roman Forum, the arch of Septimius Severus (dedicated in 203) and the Arch of Titus (dedicated in 315), celebrated military victories. Their function, therefore, was celebratory and commemorative, making a permanent urban monument that incorporated the temporary banners of festival architecture. Alberti incorporated the form of the local Roman arch of Augustus (27 BC) in the exterior of the church of San Francesco in Rimini [**56, 57**]. Even for those places that did not have their own Roman arch surviving from the past, the form was well known through prints and publications. A triumphal arch was such a powerful mark of political power and military triumph that its very appearance gave the imprimatur of the royal presence.

The Holy Roman Emperor Maximilian I connected himself to these long-standing traditions through the creation of a triumphal arch laden with his coat of arms, family portraits, genealogical trees, and a display of classical architectural forms. One scene within the arch commemorates Maximilian's rediscovery of a fragment of the robe worn by Christ at the Crucifixion, and long forgotten in the Cathedral of Trier.[11] Devised by the court artist Albrecht Dürer from about 1512 on, the arch was not constructed in any permanent material, but rather composed of 192 woodblock prints and when assembled was over 7 square metres. An edition of 700 was made in 1517–18, and sent to the councils of imperial cities and loyal princes.[12] Its description as an *Ehrenpforte*, or Gate of Honour, reflected both the long traditions of the form and imagery related directly to Maximilian I [**58**].

The Cultural Benefits of War

For Federico da Montefeltro (1422–82) and his wife Battista Sforza the creation of a great court meant the creation of a great city. They

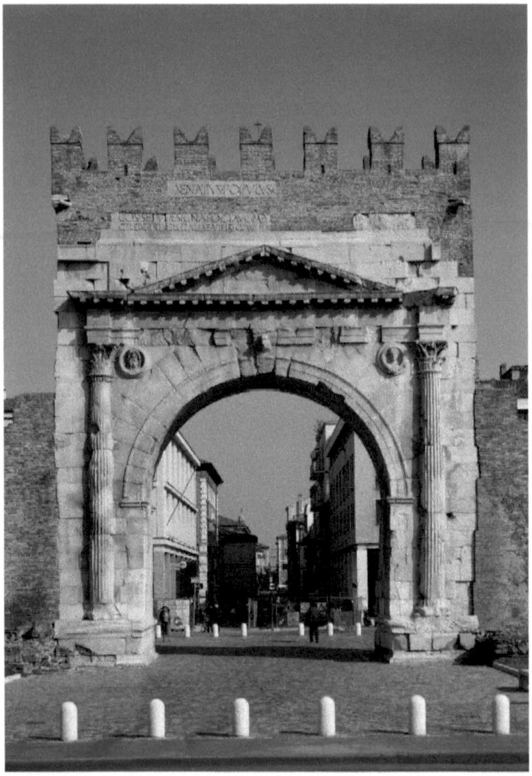

56

Arch of Augustus, 27 BC, Rimini, Italy

Ancient Roman arches commemorated military triumphs and were known by travellers as well as from treatises and guides. The form of the arch, with a large central arch and smaller side arches, became a marker of ancient architecture. Renaissance architects used the a-b-a pattern of the arch as a recognizable rhythm on building façades, as in Bramante's Belvedere. Where there were local examples, as in Rimini, those often served as the models for Renaissance builders.

transformed Urbino, the small town in the hills west of Rimini, into the setting for a magnificent court by building convents, monasteries, and a cathedral. Their patronage confirmed their control of the city through good works and financial support.

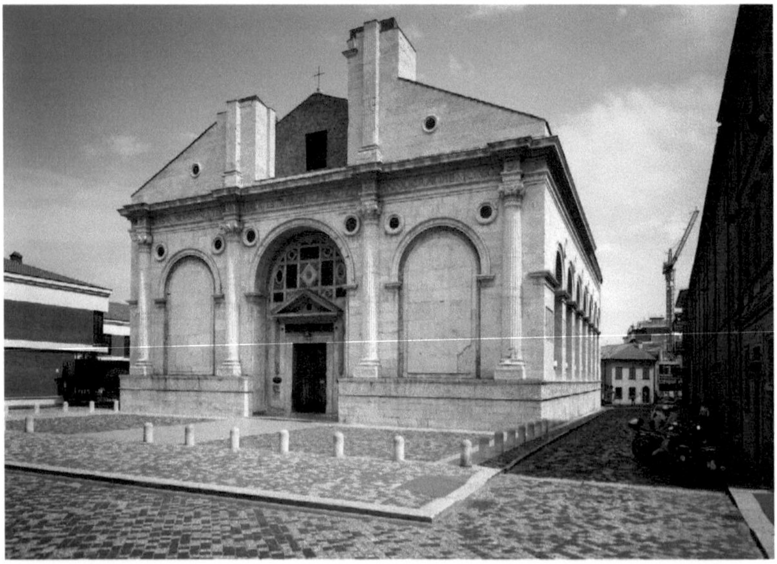

57

Leon Battista Alberti, Church of San Francesco, enlarged 1450–6, Rimini, Italy

Alberti wrapped the earlier 13th-century church, built of brick, in a new shell of white marble. He modelled the arches, attached columns, and roundels on the ancient Arch of Augustus, not far from the church. Sigismondo Malatesta (1417–68), *condottiere* and prince, aimed to create a cultural centre in Rimini through the patronage of scholars and artists, and by positioning himself as the restorer of ancient Roman greatness. The cloak of classical learning and the arts at San Francesco proclaimed Malatesta's cultural ambitions. Alberti's project was never completed, and is known primarily from the survival of a foundation medal that shows the building as if it were completed.

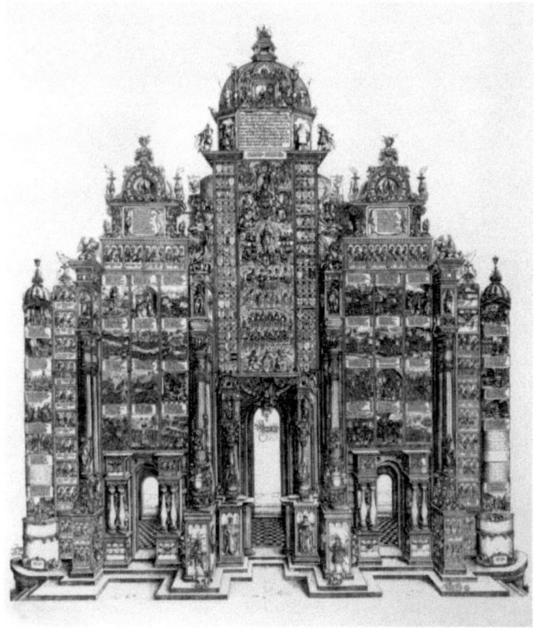

58

Albrecht Dürer, Triumphal Arch of Maximilian I, 1512–18

The invention of movable type print in the mid-fifteenth century, and the expansion of block printing technology, encouraged ambitious projects such as this arch for Maximilian I. It allowed him to control the imagery used for his triumphal entries; he was not dependent upon local guilds or groups to create arches in his honour. Easily erected, and as easily taken down, innovative schemes promoted the royal image in the absence of the ruler himself.

Federico was Count of Urbino from 1444 to 1482, and then given the title Duke of Urbino in 1474 by Pope Sixtus IV, a new honour that rewarded him for his service to the papacy as military commander. Federico had made his wealth through his role as a *condottiere*, providing troops for hire. Military culture therefore dominated all of his building projects, either in the form of fortifications throughout his territory in the Marche region on the northern Adriatic coast of Italy, or as symbolic elements in his own palace in Urbino [**59**]. The court residence's renovation and expansion, beginning in 1450, was attuned to its setting within the city and appearance from afar. Federico had a piazza, or open space, created on the city side of the palace toward the east. Along this façade, doors and windows were to be covered with marble revetments, and framed with classical pilasters and surrounds, although only parts of this side were completed.

The palace on the edge of the city, rising from the sheer cliffs that were the city's setting, was the main sign of Federico's magnificence. Approaching the city from the west, the great walls of the palace appear impenetrable. Yet on this side Federico had also built a tower with a three-storey loggia of classical arches. Impressive from a distance and marking the palace as a princely seat, the arches offered a commanding view across the landscape. This quality of the visible—seeing the palace against city and prospect from palace—reflects the complex way this building both defined the image of the ruler and reinforced his own understanding of his political rule.

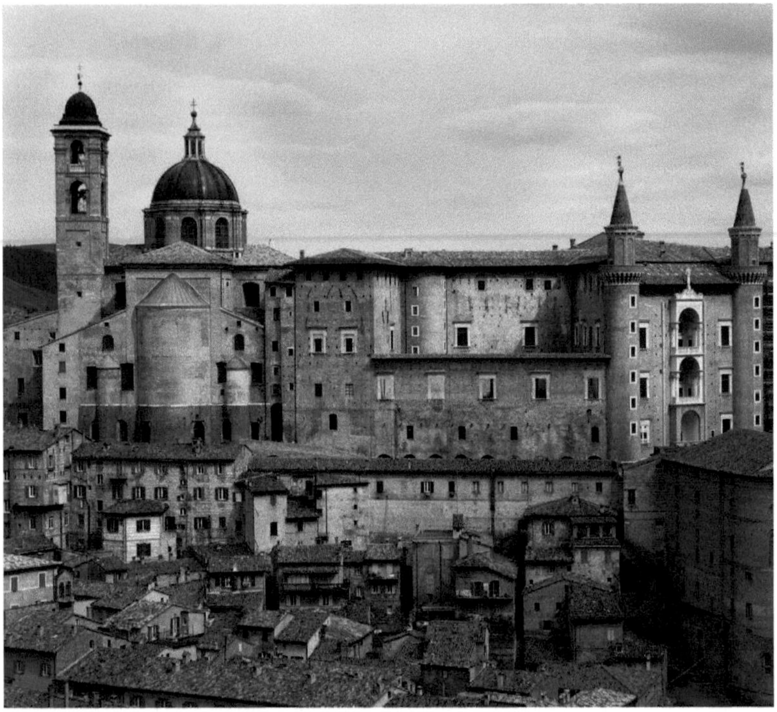

59

Urbino, Italy

The town, and the palace of Federico da Montefeltro that marks its edge, is high on a rocky hill, commanding the valley below. With the architectural advice of Luciano Laurana (from 1468) and later Francesco di Giorgio, Federico began an ambitious programme of renovation and expansion, adding extensive wings and suites of rooms, gardens, towers, and courtyards. The two towers, framing arches, provide views over the countryside and a multi-storeyed triumphal arch, visible to all approaching the town.

The grandeur of Federico's palace, as with many of the great court residences in Europe, resides in control of the movement through the courtyards and rooms. Here, visitors would climb the great height from the city to the palace via a long ramp accessible by horses and on foot. The great courtyard entered first immediately signalled that here was the palace of a cultured soldier [**60**]. Arches on composite columns, a triumphal architectural form, ring the regular space of the courtyard. An inscription in ancient Roman lettering proclaims the glory and culture of the patron. The geometric regularity of the courtyard and choice of ornament suggest how Federico da Montefeltro could control not only his political world but also the shape of its architectural setting.

A wide, dignified staircase rises on an axis from the courtyard, leading to the ceremonial rooms and private apartments on the upper storeys [**61**]. Separate apartments were laid out for the prince and his wife, with the rooms becoming progressively smaller as one moves into the more private spaces. A separate apartment provided for the warmer days of the summer. Battista Sforza's rooms connected with the cathedral next door, offering her direct access to private chapels for her devotional practices and masses. Several sequences of rooms were planned around a *giardino pensile*, or hanging garden, with windows in its outer wall giving views across the landscape. Equally impressive as the spaces above are the vast service areas in the

60

Luciano Laurana and Francesco di Giorgio Martini, Cortile d'Onore, 1467–72, Urbino

The courtyard forms the centre of the palace plan, and all activity radiates out from it. Laurana treated each side of the courtyard as a distinct façade, breaking the continuity of the arcade with strongly articulated piers at the corners. Francesco di Giorgio completed the storey above the arches, and the attic storey was added in the mid-sixteenth century. Laurana was born in Zara, Dalmatia (now Zadar, Croatia), but knew the buildings of Brunelleschi and Alberti. Out of their work he forged a distinctive style and a reputation for refined and modern palaces.

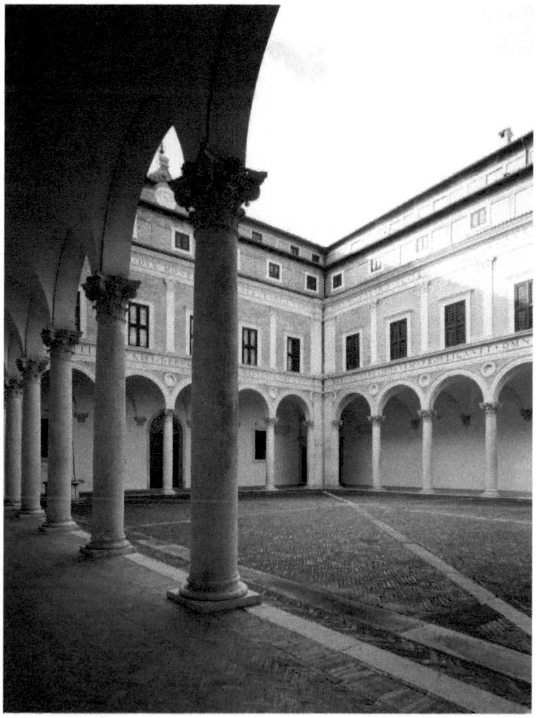

61

Staircase, Urbino

The planning for the staircase probably happened early in the history of the palace. Its position in the main wing of the palace affected many other factors of the design including the location of windows on the exterior. The stairs move up through the building with wide and gracious steps, adding exceptional dignity to the experience of the building on even the most basic level.

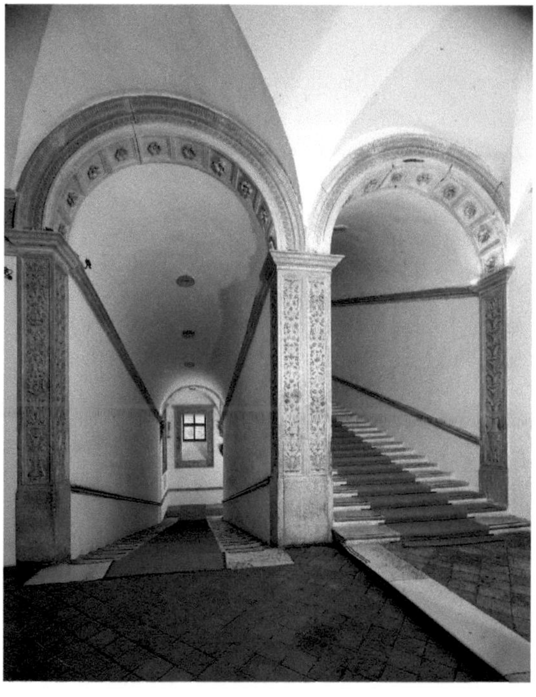

substructure of the building, including stabling for hundreds of horses and storage for the food and supplies needed for the large numbers connected with the court.

Denmark

The Reformation in Denmark and Sweden exacerbated tensions between the King, the clergy, and the nobility. In Denmark the exile of the Catholic King Christian II in 1523 allowed his uncle, Frederick I, to gain control and bring the Lutheran Protestants to the throne. The following decades saw fractious manoeuvring for power between the monarchy and the nobility, with economic and political control finally secured in a hereditary monarchy. For the King to maintain his rule, however, required a steady source of income. A toll, the Sound Dues, levied on all ships passing through the Øresund, the narrow straight between Denmark and Sweden that leads to the Baltic Sea, provided up to two-thirds of the monarch's income in the sixteenth and seventeenth centuries, and remained in effect into the twentieth century. Ships were required to pay up to 2 per cent of the value of their cargo, risking cannon fire from both sides of the strait if they refused to pay. This toll, financially so important, enabled King Frederick II to vastly expand Kronborg, the fifteenth-century fortress in the town of Helsingør, beginning in 1574 [**62**].[13]

Impressive from both land and sea, Kronborg encompassed some of the earlier structures built on the site in the 1420s by King Erik of Pomerania. The castle is situated out on the *krogen*, or hook, extending into the sound, and is set off from the town which was planned and developed in the previous century. Such a position enhanced the visual effect of the castle, discouraging any merchants trying to thwart the King's taxes.

Frederick II's first concern was the redesign of the fortifications that were by the sixteenth century out of date. New bastions and curtain walls provided extra protection and an impenetrable appearance. The Flemish architect Antonis van Obberghen (1543–1611) was brought in to design the fortifications, having extensive experience as a military engineer and designer in Antwerp, Dresden, Wrocław, and other northern cities. Three ranges of the earlier castle were expanded to four around a central courtyard with corner towers, thus creating the largest castle in Scandinavia. The north wing contained the King and Queen's apartments. State events such as the celebration in 1589 of the marriage of Anne of Denmark, sister of King Christian IV, and King James VI of Scotland took place in the Riddersal, or Knight's Hall [**63**]. Although the hall is missing the rich tapestries that would have been hung for any official occasion, the room's great length and luminous interior could not have failed to impress any visitor.

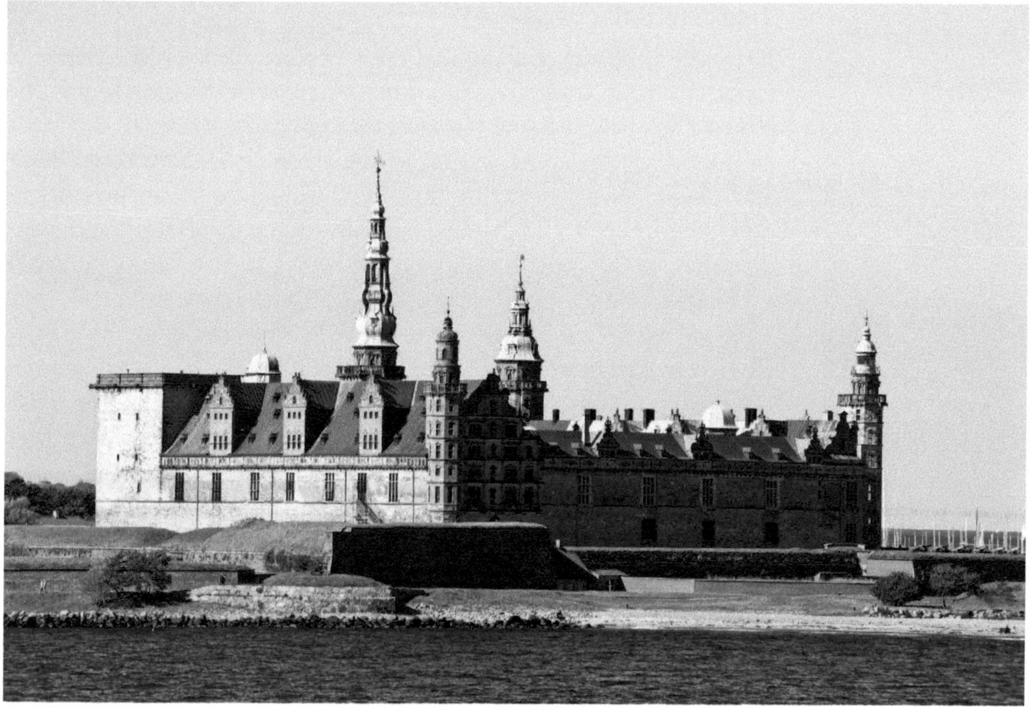

62

Anthonis Obberghen, Kronborg Catle, 1574–85, Helsingør, Denmark

Rebuilding the medieval brick castle began with the fortifications. Frederick II wished to create a great courtly residence, but he also needed to ensure his position by collecting taxes from all ships passing through the narrow sound. He added to each wing of the new palace in turn, adding cannon towers, a chapel (based on the Lutheran model at Torgau), apartments, and grand reception halls. From 1580 the castle was resurfaced with white sandstone, giving the appearance of unity to the building that had been added to gradually and making it a visual presence on its site, overlooking the sea.

63

Riddersal, Kronborg, 1579, Helsingør, Denmark

The south wing was raised another storey to accommodate a new ceremonial hall, or throne room. At 62 metres long by 12 metres wide, it was one of the largest banqueting rooms in Europe. A fire in 1629 destroyed much of the room's original decoration including its wooden ceiling, wall paintings, and fireplaces.

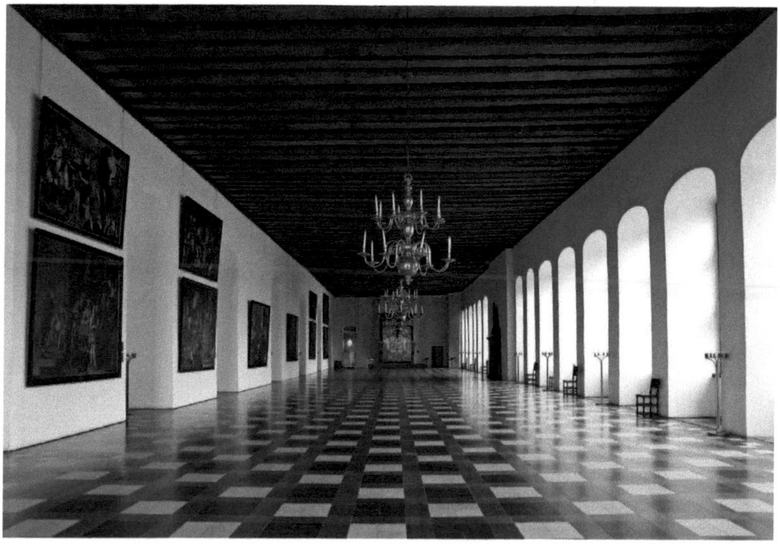

Vladislav Hall, Prague

By about 1500, the Jagiellonian dynasty controlled a vast expanse of central Europe from the Baltic to the Adriatic Sea, eastward into Russia and encompassing Hungary and Bohemia. Vladislav II Jagiełło chose to base his court in Prague, which along with Krakow, Buda, and Prague all had a tradition of humanist culture that included all areas of the arts and letters. Scholars came from Italy and were employed at the court throughout the fifteenth century.

Vladislav's decision to occupy the Hradčany Castle in Prague from 1485 allowed him to associate his rule with the long history of Bohemian kings who had held the castle before. He established a political continuity that ensured the legitimacy of his reign. The architect Benedikt Ried was brought in to add onto the existing structure.

The existing hall was, at the time it was completed, the largest ceremonial hall in central Europe [**64**]. Using walls from the earlier palace, Ried created a vast vaulted space supported on massive piers that reach down into the lower floors. Flame-like vaulting seems to rise in a miraculous way over the floor, creating a royal baldachin where the pageantry of state could be performed. Ried varied the

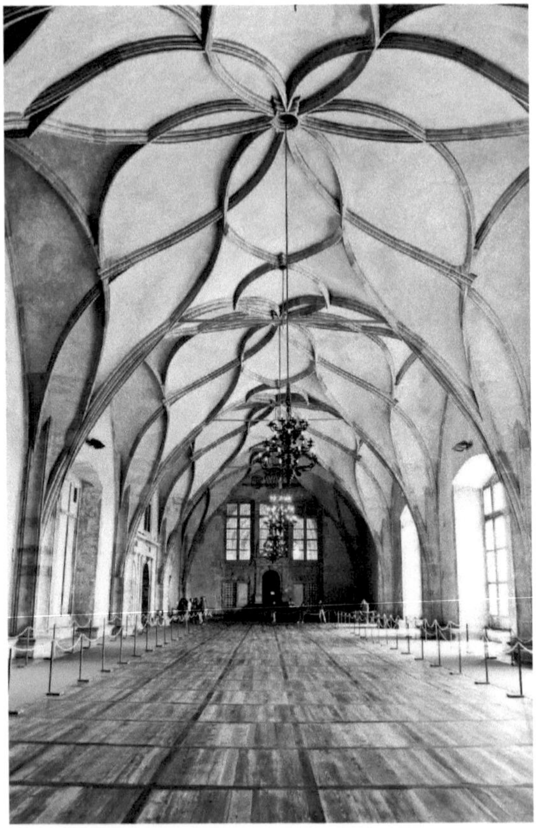

64

Benedikt Ried, Vladislav Hall, finished 1502, Hradčany, Prague

Ried made this vast hall, the largest in Europe at the time, out of three smaller spaces. The vaulting embraces the whole of the space, covering the ceiling and side walls in one large stroke that emphasizes the vastness of the space.

vaulting slightly on the Riders' Staircase that leads to the hall, by which knights on horseback could enter. This vaulting type was an elaboration of the older, traditional ornament used in the Gothic period, and derived from religious architecture. Yet the vaulting goes far beyond any specific Gothic examples. Its technical virtuosity and effect are the mark of a new ruler intent on making a link with the history of Bohemian rulers. In doing so, Vladislav sought to align his own reign with earlier Bohemian kings.[14]

Benedikt Ried, however, worked in two different modes at Hradčany Castle. As if speaking in two languages he adapted classical forms as well as Gothic traditions. Classical architecture, including the full vocabulary of columns, entablatures, and mouldings, had earlier been used by Florentine architects working in Hungary. This architecture was well known by both Ried and his patrons in Prague, and evoked the principles of humanist education that, as we have seen, were part of courtly culture. Alongside the Gothic, this other language of architecture was used for the exterior of the hall, window frames, and entrance doors [**65**].[15]

Both traditional and more modern architectural forms expressed the complex identity of Vladislav's rule: a rightful heir to the tradition of Bohemian rule, and equally fluent with the humanist culture popular in the European courts. Classical architecture, referred to as the modern style, was closely associated with the study of the history, literature, and natural sciences of the ancient world. The analogy of language is useful here. Courts were increasingly international. In addition to foreign visitors, diplomats, and envoys, they offered numerous employment opportunities for the expertise of scholars, scientists and artists. But an interest in humanist culture, as ever, did

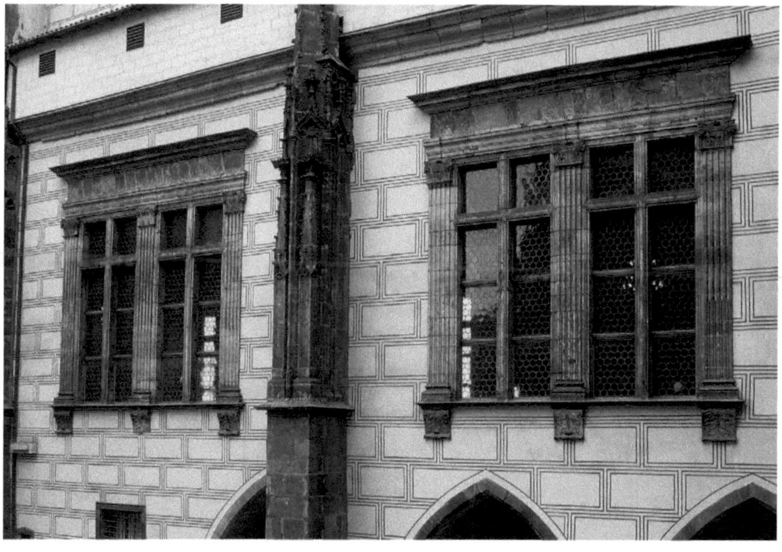

65

Benedikt Ried, Vladislav Hall, finished 1502, Hradčany, Prague

The large rectangular windows of the hall are framed on the exterior with classical window surrounds.

not preclude the importance of local traditions. Vladislav probably requested renovations and additions to the castle in Prague from both conventions. Art, architecture, and other forms of court display were most effective when they spoke to diverse audiences, both in a local dialect and in an international language.

Russian Models, Italian Engineering

Under Grand Duke Ivan III (reg. 1462–1505), Moscow became the capital of the Russian state. Moscow gained a further status as the centre of the Orthodox Church when they broke from western European church leaders after the Council of Florence in 1439. At that meeting the Byzantine and eastern churches joined with the Bishop of Rome in recognizing the power of the Pope and the benefit of joining forces in resisting the threat from the Ottoman Empire. The Russian Church, however, refused to cede their independence to the Roman Church. On both religious and political grounds Moscow was, by the middle of the fifteenth century, an autonomous power and Ivan III initiated a building programme that would provide the appropriate setting for the new capital of the powerful Russian state.

The existing walls of the Kremlin were stone, which had replaced the earlier walls of oak, but by the fifteenth century these were dilapidated and dangerously weak. Ivan III had the walls rebuilt with specially designed bricks that were particularly heavy and strong. Twenty towers marked the vulnerable corners and entrances of the fortifications. Ivan commissioned new palaces and banqueting halls within the Kremlin, all necessary additions for the new capital. For the walls and other new buildings, Ivan hired both Russian architects who knew the regional building traditions as well as foreign architects and engineers who had the latest technical knowledge necessary to solve specific building problems. Pietro Antonio Solari (*c.*1450–1493) of Milan designed several of the towers and the Rusticated Chambers (1487–91), a state reception hall.

Ivan III may have known of the technical expertise of Italian architects from his wife Zoë Palaiologa, a niece of the last Byzantine emperor. She had been raised in Rome as a ward of the Pope after the fall of Constantinople in 1453. In addition to her promotion of Italian building, Italy and Russia had a long history of trade, especially for the luxury goods of furs and hawks that ambassadors to the east brought back to Italian courts.[16]

When Ivan III took power in 1462, the Cathedral of the Dormition in the Kremlin was near to collapse. The church had a special political importance as the site of the crowning of Russian rulers and the burial place of Moscow's princes and metropolitans (the leaders of the Church). Metropolitan Philip, an enthusiastic supporter of Ivan's building programme, began the renovations to the church. He engaged two Russian architects, Ivan Krivtsov and Myshkin, and ordered new stone from a quarry close to Moscow. The cornerstone for the new church was laid on 30 April 1472; by May 1474 the walls and vaulting of the new church were complete and the large central drum for the main dome begun. An earthquake on 19 May, however, weakened the building, which in addition may also have had serious structural faults from the use of poor-quality stone, insufficient mortar between the blocks, and a construction technique of rubble infill in the walls. The building collapsed the next day.[17]

That year Ivan sent an envoy to Italy with a mission to hire an architect capable of rebuilding this important church. Aristotele Fioravanti (1420–85) was known for his work as an engineer designing fortifications, straightening towers, and repairing canals. Beginning in 1475, he rebuilt the church of the Dormition with deeper foundations and limestone walls [**66**]. Fioravanti studied other Russian churches for the design requirements, yet deviated from his predecessors in composing a unified exterior and open, lighter interior space. Tall pilasters and columns serve as buttresses, supporting

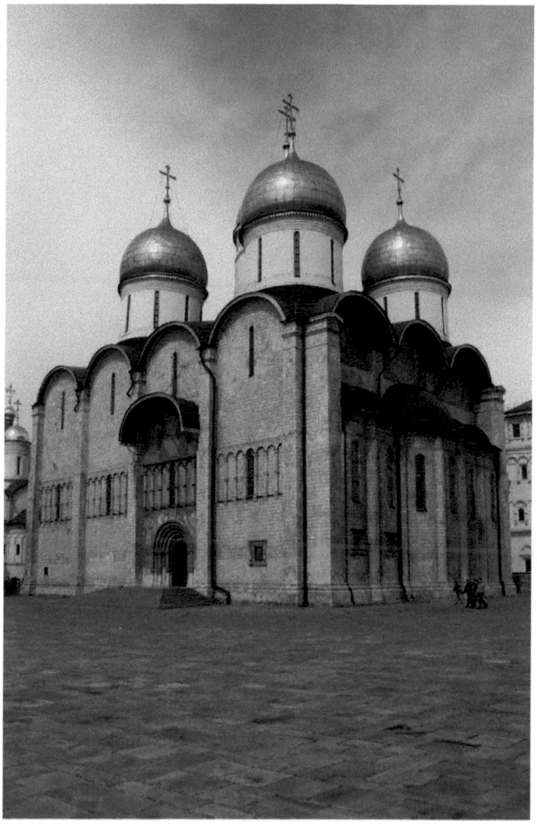

66

Aristotele Fioravanti da Bologna, Cathedral of the Dormition, Kremlin, *c.*1476, Moscow

Italian architects were renowned as great engineers, and Aristotele Fioravanti da Bologna went to Russia in order to shore up the cathedral then being built in the Kremlin. He introduced many structural innovations, including the use of lightweight bricks and deep foundations to prevent further cracking. Although the rebuilt cathedral benefited from Italian engineering, the design and function remained true to Russian ecclesiastical traditions. Aristotele studied buildings in Vladimir and Novgorod in order to understand local traditions for this important church that was used for coronations and imperial ceremonies.

the five domes that are typical of Russian churches. The unified appearance of the church comes from the repetition of the *zakomary* and blind arcades, an Italian composition of traditional Russian elements.

The Italianate interventions in Russian architecture diminished in the next generation of building. After an extensive fire in June 1547, architects working for Ivan IV looked again to Russian models for inspiration. The onion domes and multiple chapels of St Basil's Cathedral (1555–65) recall Russian wooden architecture. The exterior was later painted, and even more domes added over the chapels, further emphasizing the effect of the exterior and the church's appearance at the end of Red Square.

Addicted to Building

For King Francis I, building was a personal passion and a matter of international policy. At the beginning of his reign, he added a new wing at Blois, an ancient chateau that had been earlier renovated by Louis XII. In this new wing a three-storey loggia overlooks the garden, with an impressive open stairway that projects into the main courtyard. Even in this early building project, Francis set the pattern for his later building, incorporating architectural elements from recent Italian building. The loggia at Blois recalled the Vatican loggia designed by Raphael and completed by 1516. The staircase, however, was a grand version of French stairways. Here again a ruler sought an architectural language that incorporated classical building with its authority from ancient sources within the framework of traditional French building traditions.

From 1519, Francis began his grandest building project, the chateau at Chambord [**67**]. Not far from Blois, along the Chasson River, and on the edge of a great forest, the site was excellent for hunting, the land was under royal control, and thus free from any encumbrances from noble landowners. Francis was here free to build a vast house that embodied all the aspirations of his reign.

The general form of Chambord is based on the traditional French *château-fort*, the defensible medieval castle with its corner towers and massive walls. The square keep at Chambord recalls that castle type, as it rises from one side of a walled in courtyard. First impressions are of a vast castle rising out of the lush valley, an image well established with French royal building. On closer inspection, however, the fortified aspects of the chateau function as a backdrop to ornament of pilasters, window frames, and mouldings derived from classical models used in architecture in Italy. The plan of the entire chateau is also more regular and symmetrical than earlier *châteaux-fort*; cross-shaped halls divide the keep into equal quadrants, each holding a separate apartment.

67

Chambord, France

All of the elements used at Chambord can be found in earlier French chateaux (the keep, corner towers, spiral stair). Yet their scale and combination in a centralized, Italianate plan, transform these traditional elements into something new. Francis I spent little time at the chateau; its importance for him transcended any function as a residence. By the end of his reign it had become a monument to him and his rule.

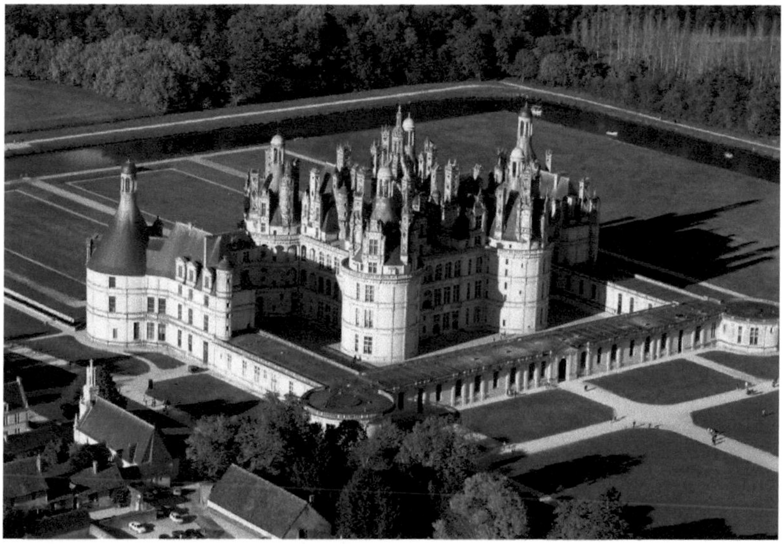

This recalls the experiments by Italian architects with Greek cross plans for church designs, including St Peter's in Rome.

The mix of Italian and French elements appears most dramatically on the roof of the chateau, which seen from a distance looks like a fantasy cityscape of towers and turrets rising from the great mass of the keep [**68**]. A silhouette of spires against the sky was an important part of medieval architecture, and the mass of the medieval *château-fort* was an easily visible sign of seigneurial power in the landscape. At Chambord that tradition is amplified into a thousand facets, as now the roof sprouts chimneys, towers, and dormers along alleys of

68

Roof pavilions, Chambord, France

Roofs were well-used spaces in grand houses. Small pavilions, also called banqueting houses, offered an escape from the formality of the regulated life of the main house. These rooms offered cool air and great views across the landscape and the hunt. In these intimate spaces, diners consumed special confections and exotic meals.

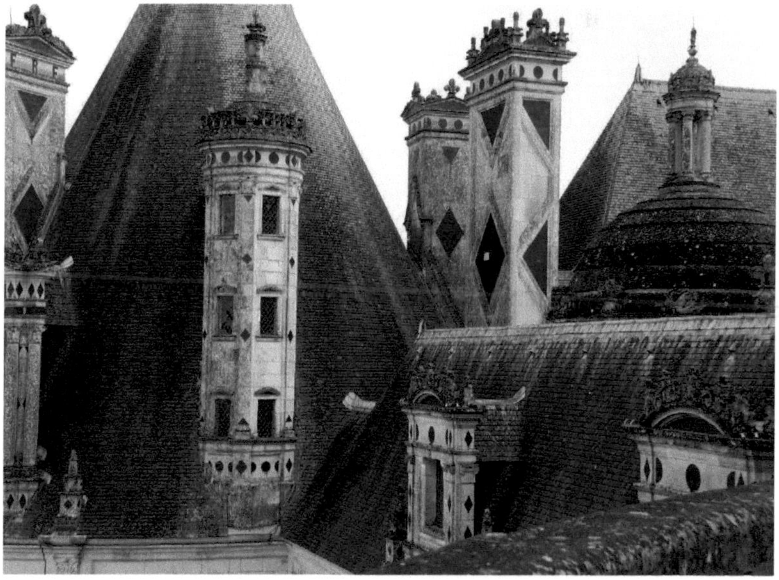

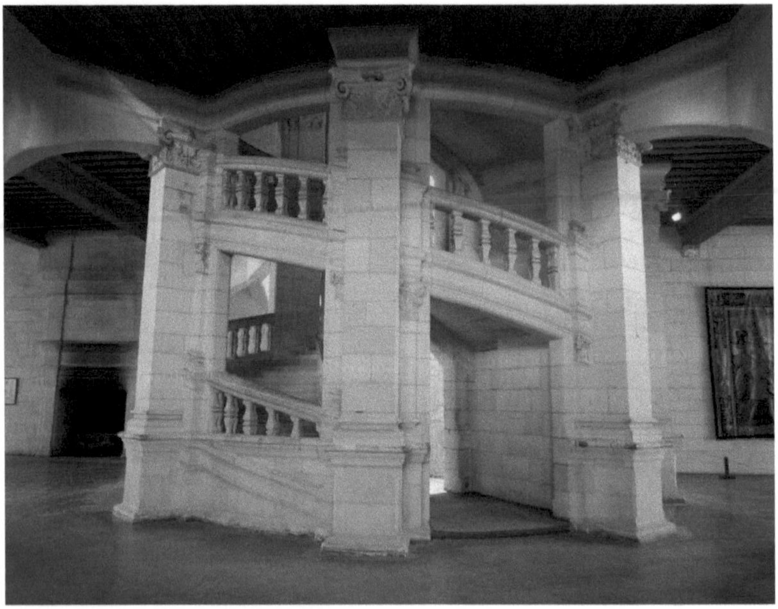

69

Double spiral staircase, Chambord, France

The staircase rises through the centre of the keep. At the centre of the cross-plan it animates the interior of the chateau from its highly visible location. Like other aspects of the chateau, the stair is a French form amplified in its scale and situation.

walkways. Detailing on these miniature buildings is classical. Yet the overall effect is more like the flamboyant decoration of late Gothic design than anything in Italy.

A double spiral staircase is at the centre of the keep, contained within a stone skeleton [**69**]. The twisting form within the building breaks through the roof as a lantern and spire, allowing light down into the core. A model of Chambord shows the stair as straight flights, typical in Italian buildings, perhaps an earlier design suggested by an Italian designer. The French solution, used here, creates a marvellous effect that is experienced only when one is at the centre of the stair. Its twisting form, only partially visible at any time, animates the massive building around its double, entwined spirals. At the top, you enter out into light under a stone frame, filled with glass, emerging into the rooftop pavilions.

Many architects, including Domenico da Fontana and Leonardo da Vinci, have been proposed as the designers at Chambord. Francis himself, given his interest in architecture, was certainly involved on some level in the choices of the site, overall conception, and ultimate effect on his royal visitors. A project this complex would have employed a vast number of designers and craftsmen, both domestic and foreign. A conception based on the *châteaux-fort* provided the framework for countless innovations and modifications.

An interplay between French traditions and Italian planning and ornament perfectly suited Francis I's ambitions on the European political stage. Francis himself, however, spent little time at this rural palace of vast scale. Its function was to express to both French nobles and international rivals his understanding of the ways in which architecture could express political policy.

The Field of the Cloth of Gold

Preparations for a diplomatic meeting in June 1520 between King Francis I of France and King Henry VIII of England began months in advance. They met in a valley in north-west France, in between the towns of Guines and Ardres. For two weeks they held tournaments, jousting and competing in mock battles, to celebrate the Treaty of London, a peace agreement they had signed in 1518. Both sides planned elaborate but temporary buildings for their retinues with all of the luxury of their permanent palaces back home [**70**]. Essentially pavilions, the buildings cost about 200,000 *livres* (worth about £400,000 in today's money) and required thousands of hours of labour.

The French encampment was a group of tents, some as tall as 40 metres, covered in a cloth woven with gold and silver threads, lined with blue velvet, and embellished with the French fleurs-de-lis. The effect of the sun on the metallic fabric must have been extraordinary against the green fields. Tents evoked the temporary buildings used in military campaigns, recalling the chivalric imagery at the heart of Francis I's rule.

The English court held their ceremonial events in temporary Tudor palaces, modelled after the many palaces used by Henry VIII in England. Brick, easily available nearby, was used for the ground floor of the main building. The upper storey was made from wood and plaster, painted to look like brick. Set into these less precious materials were large double windows with individual glass panes shaped like diamonds. The effect of glittering light off the faceted glass rivalled the French tents of gold and silver cloth. If France and England met to celebrate a diplomatic peace, their rivalry continued in the opulence of their architecture.[18]

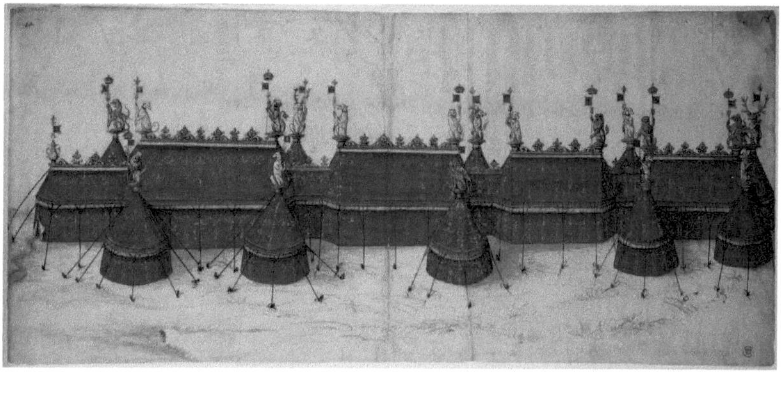

70
Tent design for the Field of the Cloth of Gold, June 1520

Several tents were linked together to create a pavilion. Royal mottoes (DIEU ET MON DROIT and SEMPER VIVAT IN ETERNO), royal 'animals' holding standards, and the repeated image of the Tudor rose decorate the tents. Although temporary structures, the sophistication of the imagery and richness of the materials were equal to any more permanent building.

None of the buildings survives from this diplomatic encounter; storms threatened to pull down the French tents and they lasted only four days. Yet temporary architecture like this, and the arches built elsewhere for triumphal entries, shaped the public perception of a ruling power's political reach and international importance. Paintings and written descriptions recorded the events for an audience far greater than the small group who might have seen the temporary structures in person.

The expense and effort of constructing elaborate temporary structures were an extension of a wider cultural policy pursued by both monarchs of using architecture as part of their political rule. Both were insatiable builders. At the end of his life Henry VIII claimed nearly fifty houses, castles, and lodges throughout England.[19] And with each new building project, Francis I too reaffirmed his power and presence.

Good Advice

On his accession, Duke Albrecht V of Bavaria (1528–79, reg. 1550–79) moved his capital to Munich. He added buildings to the Residenz, transforming it into an appropriate setting for his growing collection of paintings, coins, and ancient sculpture. In his collecting, as well as in the design of the building, Albrecht V sought the advice of Hans Jakob Fugger, a member of the important banking family of Augsburg. Hans Jakob, however, had little interest in the family business and spent much of his time instead cultivating his own knowledge in the arts and supporting painters, sculptors, craftsmen, and architects who were sympathetic to his rarefied tastes. One of Fugger's agents in Europe was the antiquarian and artist Jacopo Strada. Fugger surely recommended Strada to the Duke, and in 1567 Strada was in his native Mantua making measured drawings of the Ducal Palace and the Palazzo Te, both belonging to the Gonzaga family [**138**].[20] The Gonzaga palaces were ideal models for this type of building venture because of the reputation of the court as important patrons of the arts, well known to Strada and thus Fugger as well.

Around this time, the Duke was beginning to make plans for the construction of an Antiquarium, a display room for the collection of antiquities he had bought using Strada as agent [**71**]. In his role as antiquarian to the Duke, Strada offered his knowledge on all aspects of ancient culture and it was probably his idea to make the Antiquarium a long, low room, 69 metres long, under barrel vaults like a Roman ***cryptoporticus***, supporting a library above.[21] The room was more cavern-like than it is now; the floor was lowered at the end of the sixteenth century when the artist Frederick Sustris painted the walls and ceilings with grotesque ornament.

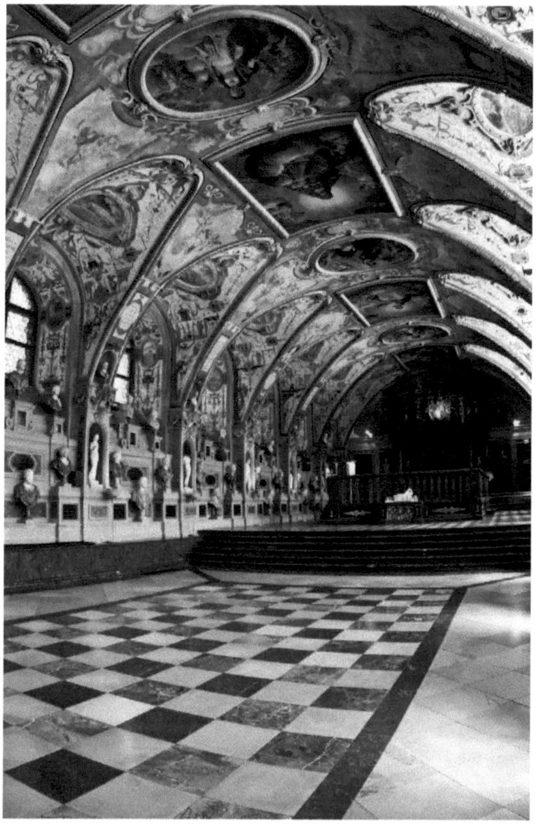

71

Jacopo Strada and Bernhard and Simon Zwitzel, Antiquarium, Residenz, begun 1569, Munich, Germany

The long and low shape of this room derived from an ancient Roman model, the *cryptoporticus*, a covered walkway or passage. The barrel vault shape was meant to provide support to an upper structure, as it does in this case as well. In ancient times the space might have been used for storage. In the Residenz in Munich, the decoration was added later by Frederik Sustris beginning in 1586. The grotesque work, again modelled after ancient Roman rooms, changes the character of the room, making it lighter and less a focus on the ancient sculptures that were the original intention.

Many rulers employed scholars within their court, men able to offer practical advice on culture as well as military tactics, religious practice, and political policy. Strada served Fugger and Duke Albrecht, as well as his other clients, by transforming his scholarly knowledge into useful information. From his base in Vienna, Strada worked on numerous publications, including books based on his own drawings of buildings and the work of artists such as Titian and Raphael, as well as supervising the projects of others. In Lyons in the 1550s Strada had met the architect Sebastiano Serlio and purchased his unpublished manuscript that he later had printed and published. As Imperial Antiquary, Strada was an agent and promoter, supervising projects as diverse as court festivals, silver table services, and artistic programmes for his wealthy and powerful patrons.

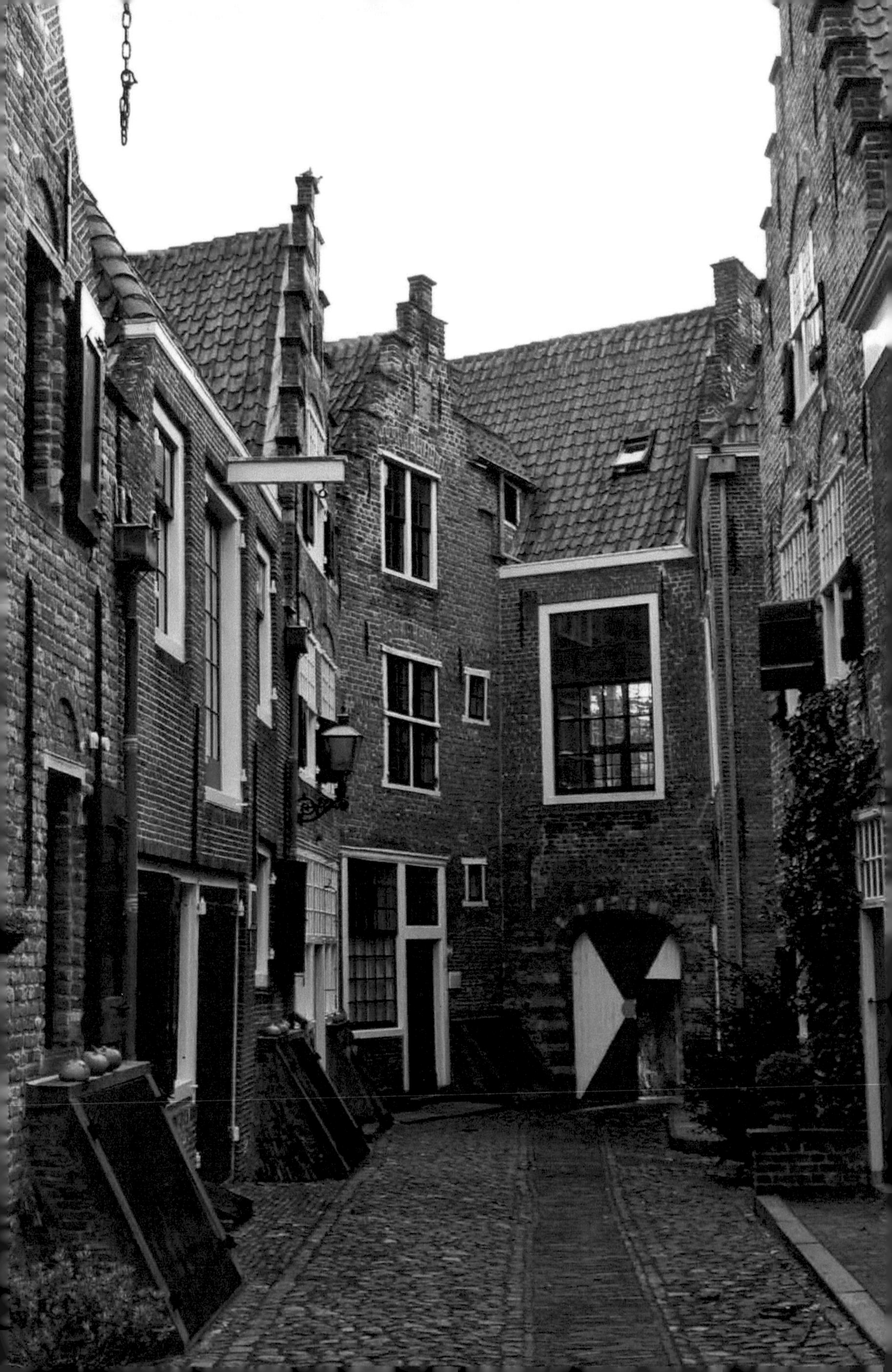

5 Corporate Identity

> May it please God, my devout wish is that the rich burghers, merchants, financiers, and others who enjoy a wealth of property in all affluence and beyond all measure, would sooner give themselves to the founding of hospices or colleges for relief of the poor and public utility, rather than build a mound of superb and magnificent houses that only bring them envy and misfortune, as usually transpires.[1]
>
> (Philibert de L'Orme, *L'Architecture* (Paris, 1567))

One function of architecture in early modern Europe was the creation and presentation of image and identity. Groups such as confraternities, guilds, religious orders, and civic governing bodies often served as architectural patrons commissioning buildings for both functional and propagandistic purposes. In this there was a complex interplay between the projection of the body and the desires of the individual, the expression of collective coherence, and the playing out of social hierarchies. A key aspect of Renaissance studies has been the notion of self-fashioning, the ways in which individual identity was created and displayed, often through visual cues. For the historian Jacob Burckhardt, writing in the nineteenth century, one fundamental characteristic of the Renaissance was the importance and public presence of the individual. According to this view, strongly held by scholars and the general public alike, the Renaissance was a period of great men who through their individual talents rose above the mass of nameless people to produce the great works of the age. However, individuals could also act in groups, working together to create a lasting and potent expression of their aims and aspirations.[2]

Certainly there were people who were recognized in their day as remarkable individuals, though there are several problems with this view. On the simplest level, this approach to the period leaves women and the history of non-European peoples out of the equation; the achievements of men tended to be the only ones recognized. While women did not normally assume a professional role as architect, they

Detail of 77

frequently served as patrons of major building projects, either on their own or continuing projects after their husbands' deaths. Within even the relatively strict confines of monastic life, women were able to shape their spaces to their preferences.

Casting a wider net also takes into account the importance and prevalence of social interaction within society and in its works. Even the most remarkable individuals worked with others, collaborating, interacting, and identifying themselves as members of groups. The architect, as overseer of any building, would also have had to work closely with guilds of craftsmen, and may even have been a member of one of those groups himself. At any given moment one person might have identified with a variety of groups simultaneously. Filippo Brunelleschi, for example, was an architect, a member of the silk guild, an official of the *fabbrica* (office of works) of the church of Santa Maria del Fiore, a citizen of Florence, and the head of his own family. Social historians suggest the importance of these often contradictory and ambiguous identities in understanding social relationships in this period.[3] And as I hope previous chapters have shown, architecture is nothing if not a social art, the product of human interactions, identities, and desires.

Works of Mercy

For the wealthy, taking care of the poor was a benefit in this life and a way of ensuring that after death time in purgatory would be brief. In fifteenth-century England, chantries were created as a benefit to the community in exchange for the saying of the Divine Offices, prayers for the souls of the benefactors. In 1437, William and Alice de la Pole, the Earl and Countess of Suffolk, received permission from King Henry VI to found an almshouse in the village of Ewelme (Oxfordshire) where they had built a grand palace [**72**]. Alice de la Pole was the granddaughter of the poet Geoffrey Chaucer, and inherited property there. The almshouse was to serve two chaplains and thirteen poor men, in exchange for prayers for their patrons. The statutes of the institution, to be called God's House, are explicit in describing the duties of the residents:

> We, William de la Pole, Duke of Suffolk, and Alice my wife, Duchess of Suffolk, desire health in body, grace in soul, and everlasting joy... Because all Christian people, meekly and devoutly considering how, by the upholding and maintaining of Divine Service and by the exercise of works of mercy in the state of this deadly life [shall], in the last dreadful day of Doom, with the mercy of Our Lord, take their part and portion of joy and bliss with them that shall be saved; [therefore all Christians] ought of reason have a great and fervent desire, and a busy charge in mind to uphold and maintain Divine Service, and to exercise, fulfil and do works of mercy before the end of their mortal life.[4]

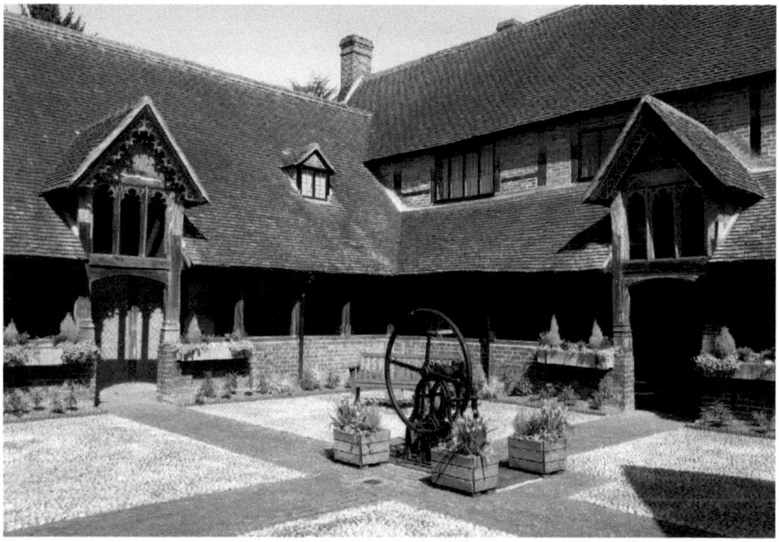

72
Almshouse, 1437, Ewelme, England

As with the Oxford colleges, not far away, which were also descended from monastic institutions, the residents of the almshouse at Ewelme formed a community, centred around the courtyard. The rooms are connected by a covered walkway or cloister. A service wing, adjoining the residences and attached to the school, provided kitchens and communal dining spaces.

The cottages were arranged on a hillside in the village, around a cloister as in a monastery; the pattern of life for the almsmen was regularized by the times of prayer during the day and the demands of communal life. The church of St Mary was also substantially rebuilt by Alice de la Pole and her husband, and is connected to the almshouse by a covered stairway. Although the life was rigorous, the surroundings for the residents were luxurious given the conditions that were usual for the poor in fifteenth-century England. The regularization of the layout and the choice of materials, the unusual use of brick at this time, asserted the high standards provided by the patrons, a fitting counterpart to the wealth of their own manor house nearby.

The almsmen said their prayers in a chapel within the church dedicated to St John that also served as a burial chapel for Alice de la Pole and her parents [**73**]. Texts from the Vulgate edition of the Bible and the Christian monogram 'IHS' were painted on the wall. The main ornament to the space was the tomb of Alice de la Pole, with two figures of the Duchess. On top of the burial chest was an idealized image of her, with all the marks of her favoured royal status. Underneath was another sculpture of the Duchess as she might have appeared after her death, her body withered and shrivelled. The chapel recorded her two physical and spiritual states, much as the almsmen were instructed to pray for her in this life and the next.

Although not mentioned in the original licence, the complex also included a school for the children from Ewelme manor, to be run by one of the priests. Education was often one of the functions of perpetual chantries, and the school at Ewelme may have been inspired by Henry VI's own foundation of college, almshouse, and school at Eton not far away at Windsor.[5] Chantries, such as that at Ewelme, provided

73

Chapel of St John, St Mary the Virgin, 1437, Ewelme, England

Alice de la Pole is entombed in a separate chapel dedicated to St John the Baptist. Her alabaster tomb, surrounded by weeping figures holding coats of arms, lies between the chapel and the chancel.

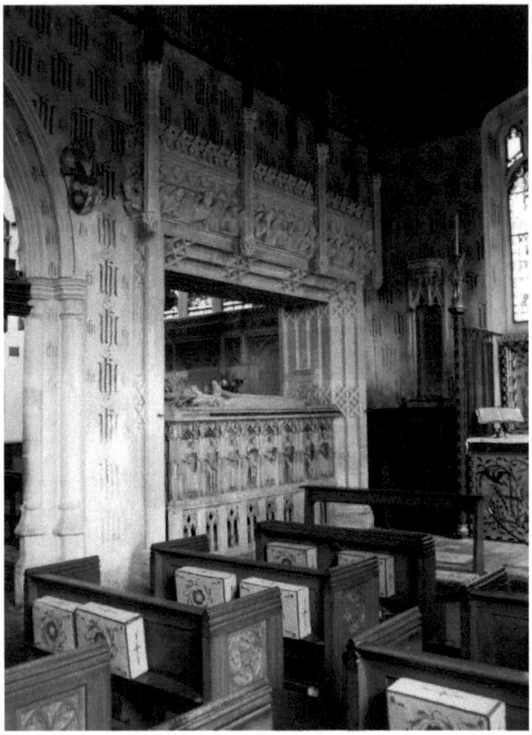

a single setting for the everyday physical, social, and spiritual care of the poor and the young—and, of course, for the eternal spiritual welfare of the rich.

Grammar Schools

Before the Reformation in England, schools were, as at Ewelme, under the control of chantry foundations or monasteries. After Henry VIII broke with the Church of Rome, local communities took more immediate control over the education of the young in their immediate area. Political loyalty and religious conformity could be shaped through education, and there was a growing need for well-trained young men from the gentry classes who could enter into government and public service. Local schools took over the responsibility for shaping children as useful members of their society and class. As a part of the town, there was thought given to how the post-Reformation school should be laid out and organized. In his treatise on education, *Positions* (1581), Richard Mulcaster advised locating schools on the edges of towns:

> ... neare to the fields ... there might not be much want of room ... To have a faire schoole house above with freedome of aire for the tongues, and an other beneath for other pointes of learning, and perfiting or continuing the Elementarie entrancres, which will hardly be kept, if they be posted over to

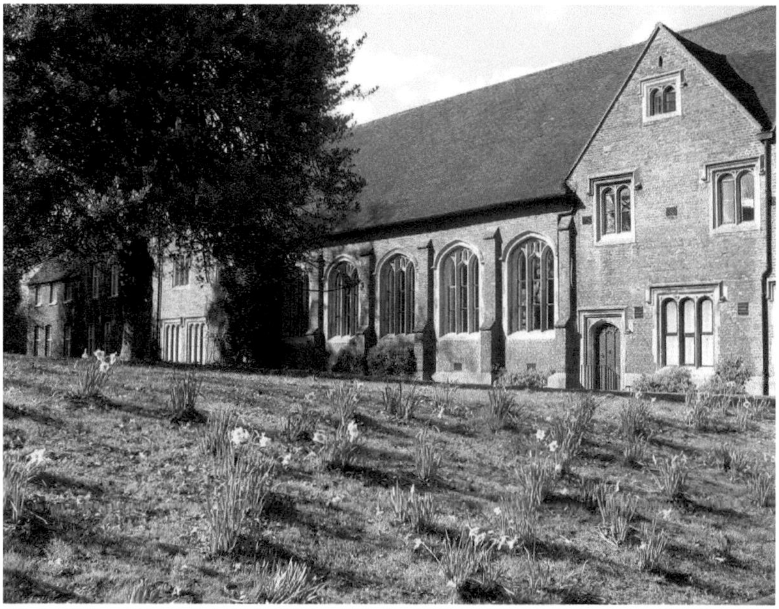

74
Old Hall, Berkhamsted School, begun *c.*1544, Hertfordshire, England
The various functions of the school building, hall and residence, are distinguished in the exterior.

private practicing at home: to have the maister and his familie though of some good number conveniently well lodged: to have a pretie close adioyning to the schoole walled round about, and one quarter if no more covered above cloisture like, for the children's exercise in the raine weather, as it will require a good minde and no mean purse.[6]

The grammar school in Berkhamsted (begun *c.*1544) represented a new model of school as community incubator, with lodgings provided for the schoolmaster and usher as part of the extended school buildings [**74**].

Housing 'Like Sorts'

Like the Medici of Florence, the Fugger family of Augsburg amassed great wealth that they used not only to glorify their own family but also to benefit the residents of their native city. Jakob Fugger II (1459–1525) developed the family's cloth business into banking and mining through privileges granted by the Holy Roman emperors. He spent time in Rome and Venice in 1477–8, managing the family's interests there. In Augsburg, he commissioned a burial chapel (1509–13) in the monastic church of St Anna with sculpture by Albrecht Dürer, Sebastian Loscher (*fl.* 1510–48), and Hans Daucher that incorporated classical ornament in combination with exuberant Gothic vaulting [**75**]. In addition to studying the stylistic work in Italy, Jakob Fugger may also have seen urban developments in Venice, including the housing built in 1395 for old and disabled shipbuilders, the Marinarezza.[7] Communal housing offered patrons the opportunity to benefit their

75

Attr. Sebastian Loscher, Drawing for Fuggerkapelle (consecrated 1518), St Anna, Augsburg, 1509–10?

The Fuggers' Catholic artistic patronage took many forms. At their chapel in Augsburg, they brought together artists working in both Italianate styles and regional modes. The drawing, perhaps by Loscher (one of the sculptors working in the chapel), shows the Gothic foliate vaulting as well as the classical triumphal arch wall arrangement and *all'antica* carving on the pilasters.

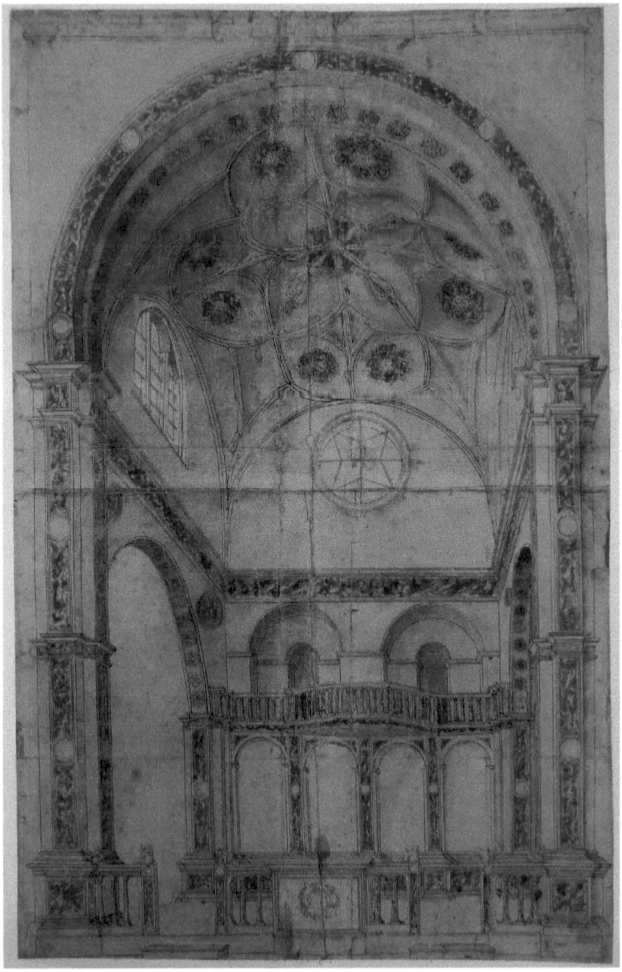

city, contributing to the financial and social security of the citizens, while also doing good works in their family's name.

In 1517 Fugger began a social housing project in Augsburg, the Fuggerei, planned by Thomas Krebs (*fl.* 1513–23), the most important builder in Augsburg [**76**]. There were fifty-two houses in the first phase of the construction, completed in 1523, each with their own kitchen and garden, as well as streets and wells. The entire complex was walled with three gates, making it an enclave within the larger urban setting. The Fuggerei was intended for working families, and continues to function in that role today. The rent was prescribed by Jakob Fugger as one Rhenish guilder per year (currently, a bit less than one Euro), and was never to increase.

In contrast to perpetual chantries, public housing complexes were more socially prescriptive and aimed their beneficence at specific

76

Thomas Krebs, Fuggerei, 1517–23, Augsburg, Germany

Jakob Fugger first acquired property for his public housing project in 1514, and further land in 1516. That year he also received permission from the city to begin building, and a favourable judgement reducing his taxes on the land. More than simply housing, the Fuggerei was a complete urban development with regularized streets, gardens for the residents, and a chapel and infirmary added later in the century. Modern, twentieth-century, architects have long admired the houses for their rational, unornamented architecture that derives from functional concerns. Similar projects were built throughout Europe, including the new living quarters for the navy in the Nyboder in Copenhagen (1631).

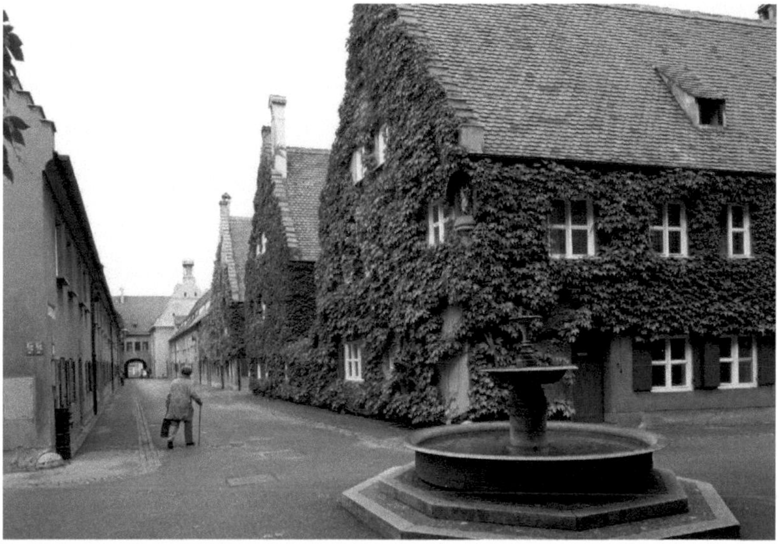

groups of society, and were often associated with a guild. In Middelburg (the Netherlands), a small street near the harbour was built as housing and workshops for the city's coopers. The Kuiperspoort (from the mid-sixteenth century) consolidated the power of the guild in that particular area of the city [77]. The tall, narrow houses solidified group

77

Kuiperspoort, Middelburg, Holland

This type of narrow street lined with workshops on the ground storey with housing above can still be found in many cities. Workers of similar professions tended to reside in close proximity, facilitating what were often communal aspects of their individual businesses. Guilds, such as the coopers here, may have regulated business practices in each area, including apprentice programmes and trade, even if the houses were individually owned.

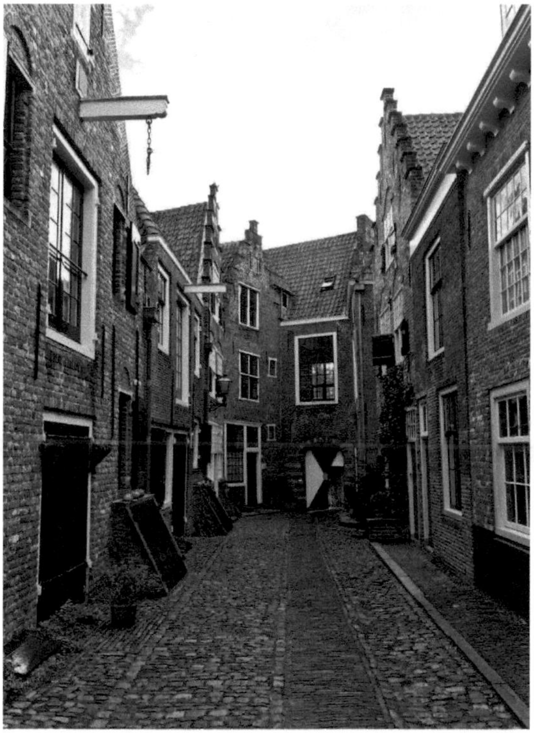

identity and provided additional economic strength for that group within the complex city structure. A remarkable number of social housing experiments, including those discussed here, are still occupied and functioning as their donors intended. These architectural experiments, motivated through faith and a desire to ensure salvation, attest to the public benefit of communal architectural projects.

Higher Learning

The number of universities expanded in the Renaissance, with some, like Paris and Bologna, attracting students from throughout Europe. The range of studies during this time was essentially unchanged, with theology, law, and medicine as the main areas of the curriculum, increasingly shaped by rhetorical practices adapted from classical texts. While a career in the clergy was the usual end for most students, increasingly university education was understood to be a route to public life, in addition to whatever family responsibility was demanded for young men from the upper classes. While some universities had an international student membership, wars and eventually religious dissent closed that option for many. The Anglo-French Wars, for example, of the late twelfth century spurred the development of the university at Oxford, which slowly shifted its architectural planning away from monastic-based halls toward a new system of colleges.

In the late Middle Ages, Oxford University was a loose organization of colleges and halls, with some common facilities and buildings. The many monastic foundations around the city attracted students who wished to study law, the main topic of study in the thirteenth century. As the university grew and the number of students increased, academic halls (usually owned by the monasteries) provided room and board for students. The halls were transformed into versions of what are now colleges, supported by benefactors in part as perpetual chantries for the saying of mass for the patron's soul. The earliest colleges (Merton, Balliol, and University) evolved organically, with buildings added or converted to new use as needed. While some accommodations were made for the needs of scholars, most of these early plans followed the monastic prototype of the open quadrangle or cloister from which the college descended.[8]

While all the elements were already there in embryonic form, the foundation of New College by William Wykeham in 1379 established the type of the Oxford college from which all others emerged. Planned on the site of fifty-one deserted tenements on the edge of the city, the college was created as a coherent architectural whole with a hall, kitchen, chapel, chambers for fellows, and residences for the head of the college [**78**]. The single, great quadrangle had residences on three sides, and the chapel and hall on the fourth side. The

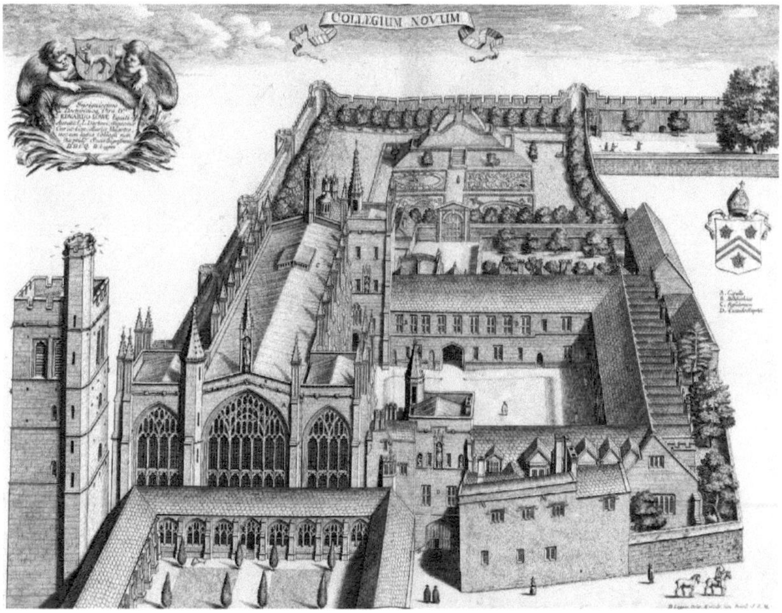

78

New College, 1379–86, Oxford, England, in David Loggan, *Oxonia illustrata* (1675)

The site for the new college was long and irregular, and bordered the city walls on the north; see on the left-hand side of Loggan's engraving. A gatetower on the west led into the quadrangle, similar in plan to a courtyard house or castle. The residential ranges are to the south and east, with little decoration or differentiation. To the north, however (seen on the left in the print), is the cloister with the chapel beyond. The hall extended from the chapel but has a different type of window to distinguish it from the other parts of the college. The garden quadrangle (at the top of the print) was added in the 17th century.

codification of all the elements required for a university college added dignity and grandeur to the everyday elements of academic life.

The impetus to build a new divinity school began around 1423 with a long process of fundraising. Land in the centre of the city had been given by Balliol College; and the college wrote to bishops, deans, and

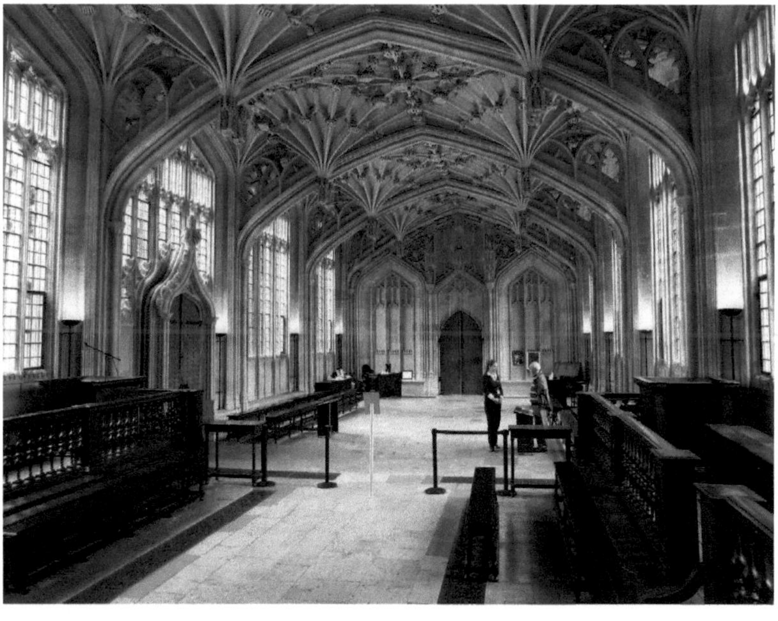

79

William Orchard, Divinity School, begun 1420, continued 1480–3, Oxford, England

The two dominant features in the Divinity School are the elaborate but regular vaulting, and the absence of almost any wall structure. The effect therefore is of an architecture devoid of weight and dissolved into pattern and light from the vast windows that run along both long sides of the building. The single space, encased in repeated patterns of vaulting, is marked by the hanging pendants from the ceiling and the ribs that span from wall to wall.

chapters across England soliciting funds to begin building. Progress on the building was slow, due both to the lack of financial support and the elaborate work by the first mason, Richard Winchcombe [**79**]. He had been appointed in August 1430 and remains of his work shows his preference for rich and complex ornament, especially in the mouldings, all of which added to the cost of the project. When Thomas Elkyn was later appointed, he was told to simplify the ornamentation as a cost-saving measure.

By 1440 the building had only reached a few feet off the ground on the south side. However, a large gift of books and money in 1444 by Humphrey, Duke of Gloucester, gave new energy to the project in order to make it a showpiece of the university buildings. The elaborate **lierne** vault of the ceiling was probably the work of the architect William Orchard, who also worked on Magdalen College, Oxford, from 1468. Numerous extra ribs create a net-like pattern of lines across the ceiling, subsuming the structural vaulting system in a virtuosic flourish. The vaulting spreads out over the roof, providing a dramatic counterpart to the side walls that are almost entirely filled with glass. Armorial details and monograms at the intersections of the ribs record the many donors to the building, whose presence is now permanently a part of the building.[9]

Pilgrims, Plagues, and Children

Hospitals in the Renaissance provided a range of services, all deriving from the ancient notion of offering shelter to guests (*hospes*). Ferdinand and Isabella funded the construction of a hospital to house pilgrims on the main square in Santiago de Compostela [**80**]. Many

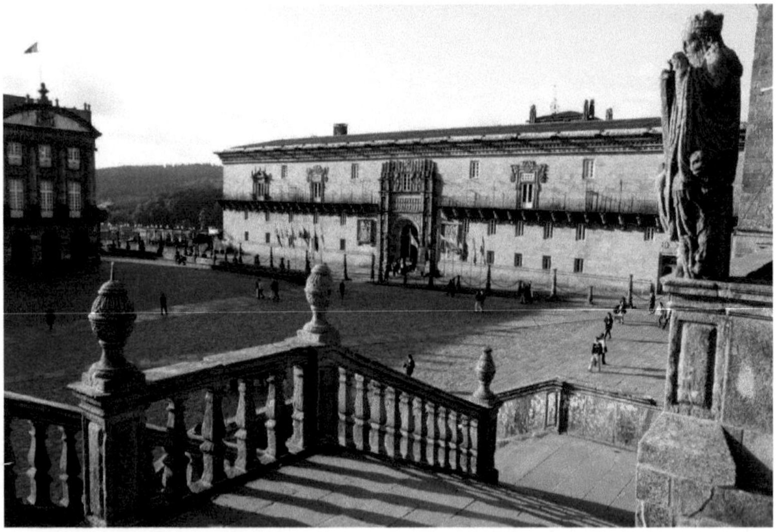

80

Antón and Enrique Egas, Hospital Real, 1501–11, Santiago de Compostela, Spain

The pilgrimage to Santiago ends at the cathedral on the main square. Next to the church is the hostel, built around four courtyards. Fountains provided clean water for residents, and a chapel at the centre allowed for the required prayers of all residents.

almshouses gave refuge for the poor and homeless. Hospitals directed at specific physical infirmities increasingly explored ways of providing better care for all aspects of illness.[10]

Caring for the sick meant not only attending to their physical infirmities but also worrying about the health of the soul. Thus, from the Middle Ages, wards were connected to chapels so that the patients could see, or at least hear, the saying of the mass and the daily prayers. Specific spaces for the ill were included in many medieval monasteries, such as at Cluny Abbey (twelfth century), where the multi-chambered infirmary was located near to the church apse.

When Nicholas Rolin and Guigone de Salins founded their hospital, the Hôtel de Dieu, in Beaune, France (1443), there were several important examples not far away [**81**]. The hospital at Tonnerre, for example (built at the end of the thirteenth century), was a large and important institution connected to a monastic order. There was no specific religious order involved in the construction at Beaune, however. This may have been an incentive for Rolin to found his hospital where he might shape the new buildings and their institutional connection as he wished. The city was also at a major crossroads, so the hospital would be very visible and Rolin's generosity well known. The income was ensured through the donation of land and vineyards that provided wine that could be sold under the hospital's name. The exterior of the building was plain, though built of the very finest and well-crafted ashlar masonry. From the courtyard, the magnificence of the building was clear in its size, vast pitched roofs, and quality materials. In order to provide fresh water, and a sanitary system of waste disposal, the Bouzaise River was diverted from its usual course to run under the building.[11]

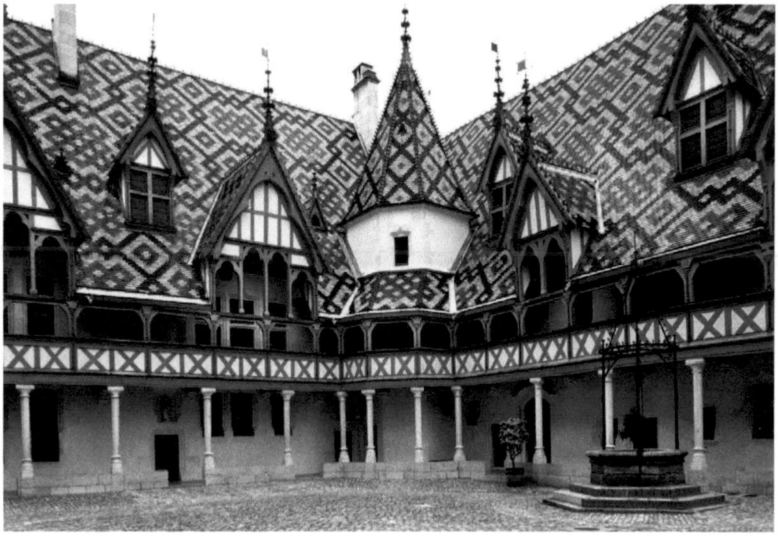

81

Hôtel de Dieu, 1443–51, Beaune, France

In his forty years as Chancellor to Duke Philip the Good, Rolin amassed vast properties and great wealth. The building turns inward; there is almost no sense from the street of the multi-gabled courtyard with timber walkways connecting the rooms for the sick and service areas.

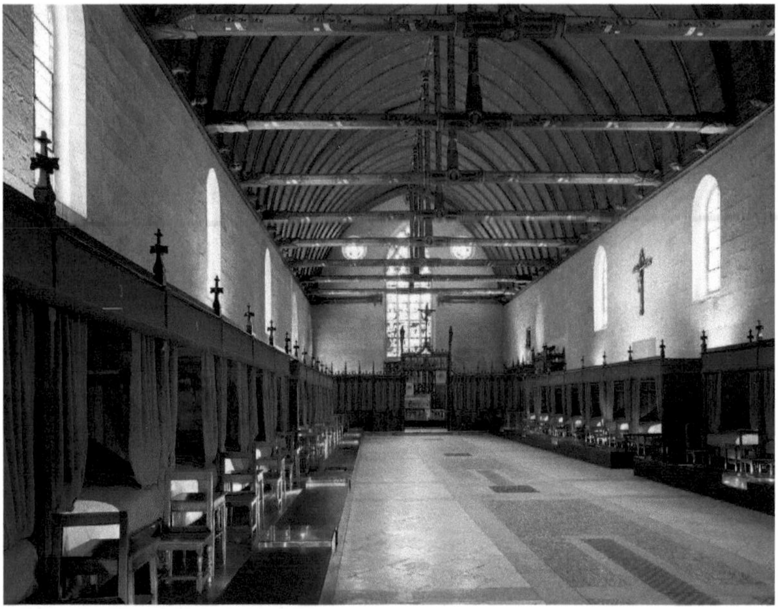

82
Grande Salle de Pauvres, Hôtel de Dieu, 1443–51, Beaune, France

The vast vaulted room, modelled on earlier examples including the 13th-century hospital at Byloke in Ghent, allowed for the circulation of air. The long space, culminating in a chapel at the end, was church-like, satisfying both the devotional and health needs of the patients.

The centre of the hospital was a large courtyard, protected from the city by the high walls and rooms that ring the perimeter of the building. Covered loggias around the courtyard connected the rooms on the various floors. Opening directly onto the courtyard, however, was the main room for the patients, a large room, the Grande Salle des Pauvres, with a high barrel-vaulted roof including a system of openings along the top to provide fresh air [**82**]. Originally tables down the centre were for the stronger patients to take their meals, and all beds faced the chapel at the far end. The best local craftsmen were hired to work on the hospital and all its fittings, including the furniture, chests, tapestries, and the ornamentation of the chapel.

There were two main innovations in the design of hospitals during the Renaissance: the portico along the street, and the cruciform plan. The covered portico space offered a protected place on the street, and contributed to the magnificence of the building by providing a public amenity. As public works, paid for by civic groups or private benefactors, hospitals had a broader audience than just those housed inside their walls. The Ospedale degli Innocenti, or the Foundling Hospital, designed by Filippo Brunelleschi and funded by his guild, included a graceful and majestic portico along the side of the Piazza SS Annunziata in Florence [**83**].[12] The plan of the complex was established by 1419–24 with a new symmetry and regularity, all expressed in the public spaces by the relationship of the building to the street. Earlier buildings, including a medieval hospital not far from Florence, had previously incorporated porticos in the design, but Brunelleschi revised the local tradition through his use of a classical

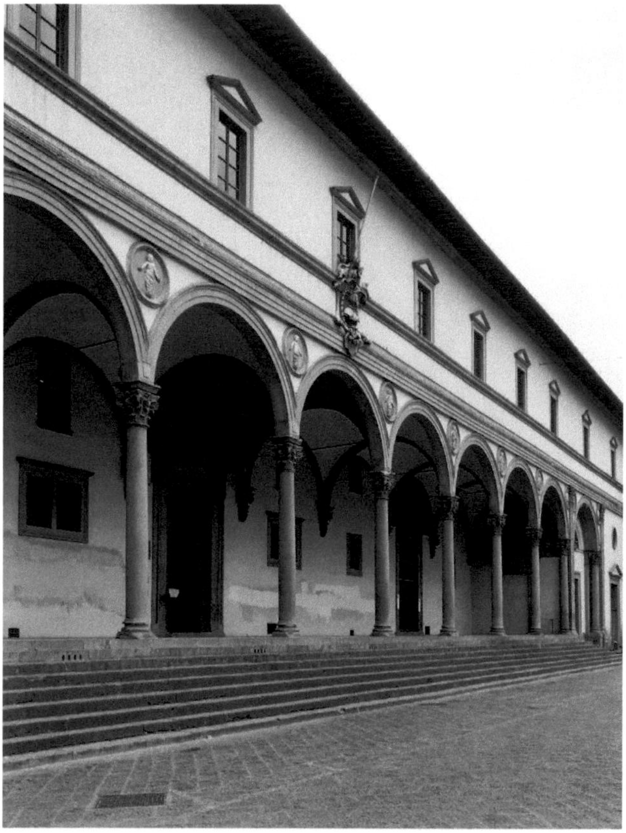

83

Filippo Brunelleschi, Ospedale degli Innocenti, 1419–24, Florence, Italy

Brunelleschi expanded and refined the plan for hospitals in Tuscany with an open loggia along the façade, and courtyards within. His decorative solution of columns supporting arches for a loggia of shallow domes was widely imitated for buildings of all types. As with all of his architecture, he transformed the building type through careful optical and functional adjustments in design and plan.

vocabulary of ornament. Corinthian columns supported semicircular arches and deep entablatures. Instead of medieval vaults, Brunelleschi used shallow domed or sail vaults. **Roundels** in the **spandrels** of the arches had terracotta relief sculptures of babies in swaddling, giving an explicit identification of the building's function in the public arena. The Ospedale spoke both to local traditions and the most current interest in the vocabulary of ancient building, all in a calm and dignified voice.

Renaissance plans for hospitals follow the theory, and often the practice, for domestic space.[13] Alberti had described the hospital as a great private palace shaped by ideas of social order, gender, and class relations. The plan of the Ospedale Maggiore in Milan by Antonio di Pietro Averlino, called Filarete (1400–69), for Duke Francesco Sforza and Duchess Bianca Maria Sforza incorporated many structural innovations including a complex system of wastewater removal and ventilation [**84**]. Only part of the hospital was ever constructed as disagreements between the architect and hospital administrators led to a stalemate. Had the entire complex been built, the careful

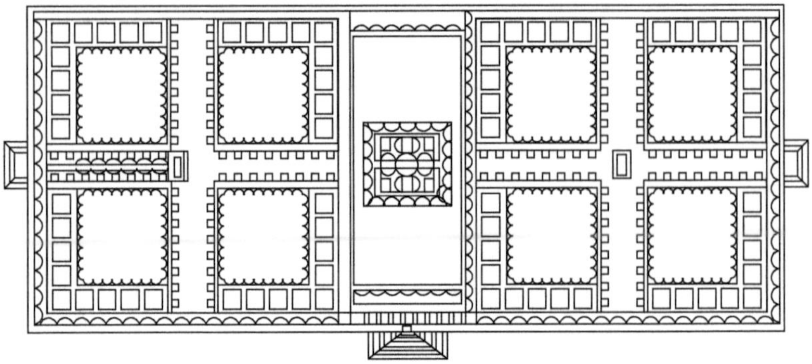

84
Antonio di Pietro Averlino called Filarete, Ospedale Maggiore, 1456–65, Milan, Italy

Filarete adopted Brunelleschi's scheme of columns on arches in his design for the hospital for his patron in Milan, Duke Francesco Sforza, now much altered. The project for the Ospedale Maggiore, however, derived from the architect's careful study of earlier hospital buildings. He rationalized the plan around two parallel cruciform wards, integrated with sanitation systems and the needs of the patients depending on their age and illness.

segregation of the sexes into separate wings and the codification of functions would have constituted a new prototype for the hospital that would have attended to all the perceived illnesses of the corporate body and its social condition.

Like-minded Souls

Throughout Europe, groups of Catholic laypersons came together for spiritual practice, good works, social kinship, and civic pride. Known variously as guilds, companies, *scuole*, or confraternities, they offered members an organized spiritual life through communal activities such as civic processions, public penitence, good works, and artistic patronage. Some were intended for foreigners within a city, others for members of a specific trade or profession, still others were connected with new religious orders such as the Theatines or the Jesuits. As organized groups they had a strong public presence, with an overt political influence, and their religious focus made them an important factor in the everyday devotional life of many.[14] In the face of pressures from Protestant reform groups, they reaffirmed the central tenets of Catholic faith, acting, as Francesco Sansovino wrote in 1580, much like 'an Academy or in public schools, where one learns and practises Christian deeds, to the benefit of the souls of the brethren, both alive and departed [and] they are of great benefit to the poor, and to the glory of God'.[15] Artistic and architectural patronage was a suitable and effective form of public expression, and ensured a permanent home for group activities. The architecture could take various forms. In England, guilds often funded parish churches and elaborate open spaces, such as the Merchant Adventurers Hall in York (begun 1357), that were used for meetings and social occasions [**85**].

By the end of the fifteenth century in Venice, there were five *scuole grandi* that built elaborate buildings adjoining monastic houses, as the lay counterpart to the religious orders. All classes of citizens could become members of the *scuole*, mediating between the government

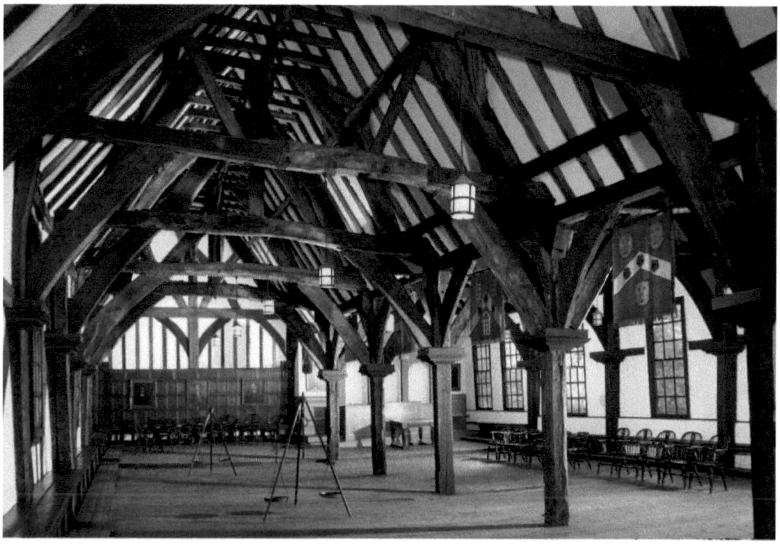

85

Great Hall, Merchant Adventurers Hall, 1357–61, York, England

The vaulted hall gave a newly formed group of mercers in York a dedicated room to meet and conduct their business. Architecture helped to establish their autonomy and status within the vibrant mercantile centre of York.

structure and the ordinary citizens. Because the *scuole* mirrored civic institutions, it is not surprising that they aspired to buildings that would have as strong a public presence as the palatine chapel of San Marco or the Doge's Palace. The Scuola Grande di San Marco was dedicated to the national patron, San Marco, giving it prestige by association and necessitating an important site [**86**].

Within the building were a series of halls used for meetings of the members, and an especially ornate room on the first storey, the *albergo*, where the governing board met. But the main attention at the Scuola di San Marco was on the façade design, which would set a standard

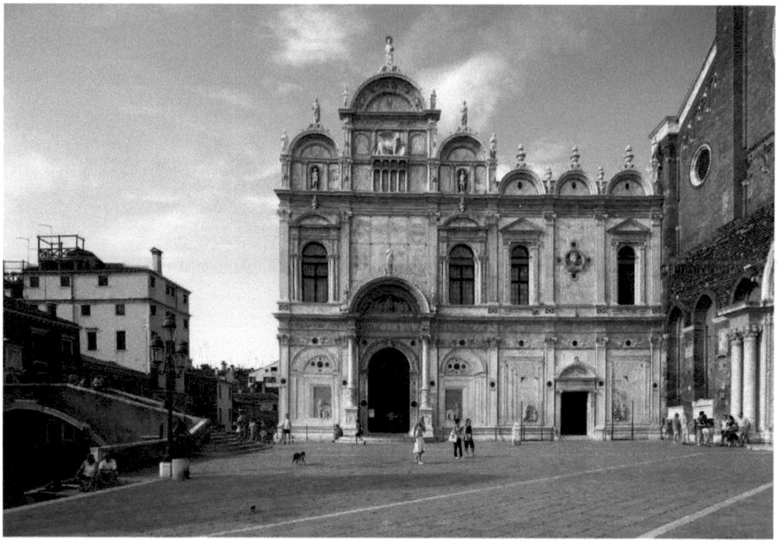

86

Pietro and Tullio Lombardo and Giovanni di Antonio Buora, Antonio Rizzo, and Mauro Codussi, Scuola di San Marco,1489– , Venice, Italy

A fire in 1485 offered the confraternity the opportunity to rebuild on a larger and more ornate scale on the same site. A few sculptures could be saved from the earlier building, but the new building offered the opportunity to invent new forms and especially new decorative schemes. Pietro Lombardo's son Tullio carved the panels at ground level. On either side of the door are low relief sculptures of the Lion of St Mark, posed within perspectival frames that relate to the hall one is just about to enter. The two panels to the right are of St Mark Healing Anianus and St Mark Baptizing Anianus. The building is now the public entrance to the city hospital of Venice.

for lavish and inventive architecture for other *scuole*. It was begun by Pietro Lombardo and Giovannni Buora in 1489, with Mauro Codussi continuing the work after 1490. San Marco provided the model for the **lunettes** along the upper storey and the rich use of marble in pictorial and decorative patterns. The façade was really in two sections. To the west, on the left, was the taller three-bay section, with the large *salone* or hall on the ground floor. To the right was another three-bay section, though lower, that contained the *albergo*, or governing board meeting room, in its upper storey. The sections were treated as related though distinct parts of one building (something made necessary by the complexity of the site, the multiple functions of the building, and the various changes in designers), yet still managed to emphasize the singleness of purpose of the building as a whole.

The great effect of the façade as a backdrop to the *campo*, or open square, on which it sat was the multiple and distinctive voices of its decoration. It was not an expression of a single idea but rather an expression of the range of possible solutions available in Venice at that time. On the ground storey, the ornate carving, marble inlays, and two sets of perspective scenes on either side of the doorway were executed by Pietro Lombardo's son Tullio. Codussi probably changed the tenor of the decoration on the first and upper floors, with the local reference to San Marco in the **lunettes** and the contrasting references to ancient architecture in the triangular and segmental arches over the windows on the first storey.[16]

The experience within the building was equally remarkable through the design of a double-branched staircase that leads up to the *salone*. This innovative internal staircase (when most stairs in Venice were still on the exterior of buildings) would have added a further grandeur to the activities of the *scuole*, and contributed to the ritual importance of the group's events.

'The Common Convenience of the Learned'

The increased importance of humanist education in the Renaissance made the storage of manuscripts, and later printed books, a concern for both individuals and groups such as monasteries and universities entrusted with their care. Those with small collections might have been fine keeping them in trunks. However, as the number of items went into the thousands, more permanent and organized spaces were required. Even private libraries had a public dimension and individuals were often allowed limited access to the collections. The function of the Vatican Library was expanded in 1450 when Pope Nicholas V established a library 'for the common convenience of the learned'. A scholar, Bartolomeo Sacchi (called Platina), became the first librarian at the Vatican at the end of the fifteenth century. Pope Sixtus V commissioned his architect Domenico Fontana to build a great wing as the library in 1585–90, where it still remains, bisecting Donato Bramante's Belvedere courtyard.

Questions about the plan and appearance of the library were an ongoing concern and the type evolved as thinking about the use of the library changed. Michelozzo's long twelve-bay, three-aisle library at the Florentine monastery of San Marco (after 1438) established a model that later architects adapted. The Ionic columns support cross vaults in the side aisles that open through arches into the barrel-vaulted main space [**87**].

San Marco was a project of the Medici in Florence, and they supported another library commission in the early sixteenth century as the repository for their own collection. The sheer number of manuscripts meant that the library could not be located on the same site as their urban palace. Moreover, it was also important that the building be located somewhere with easy public access, thus reinforcing the family's status as benefactors of scholars. A new library was planned by Medici Pope Clement VII, and correspondence between him and his architect, Michelangelo, began in 1524. The Laurentian Library was to be built as the second floor

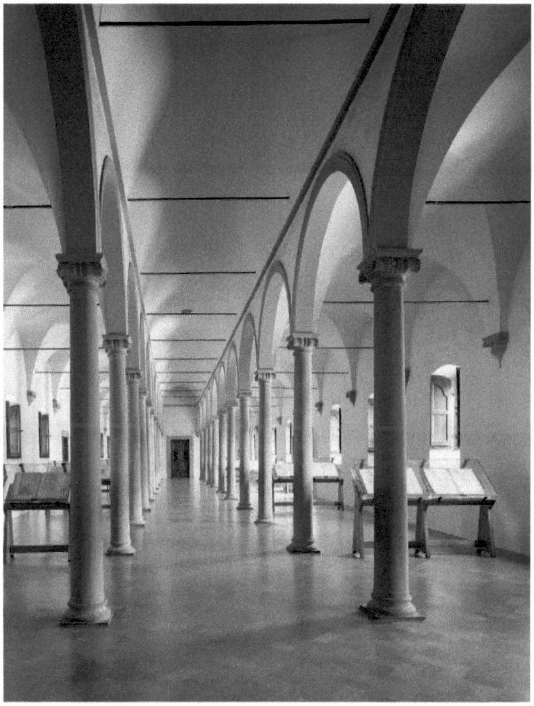

87

Michelozzo di Bartolomeo, Library, after 1438, Monastery of San Marco, Florence

The long, three-aisled space is divided by delicate Ionic columns. The two side spaces have groin vaults that end in ornamental brackets high on the wall; the central space is undivided and covered by a barrel vault. These subtle differences add to the stillness of the space, appropriate for the study of manuscripts kept here. This first purposely designed library was understood to contribute to the activities of the monastery and the devotions of the Dominican brothers.

on top of the existing monastic buildings at the church of San Lorenzo, Florence. This followed the scheme of the second-floor monastic library at San Marco by Michelozzo, and established a link with the earlier Medici project as well as simply repeating a practical solution to keeping books close at hand yet away from the damp, and providing good light for readers. The lower-storey walls were not to be reinforced in any significant way, and thus the upper storey with the library had to be as light as possible. The reading room, over 46 metres in length, went through numerous design changes by Michelangelo, eventually arriving at a system where the bays created by the pilasters on the side walls were repeated in the ceiling panels [**88**]. The entire ornamental system in the reading room emphasized the planes and flatness of the walls, and the lightness of the structure. The reading desks, designed by Michelangelo, projected at right angles from the wall, serving as a support, a visual buttress, to the long and unrelenting wall and window openings. As was typical in medieval and Renaissance libraries, the books were chained to the desk for security. Everything in the room is thus held in check, giving it the quiet atmosphere necessary for study.

The vestibule to the library was as unnerving as the reading room was calm [**89**]. Changes to the project increased the height of the room to over 14 metres, nearly twice that of the reading room. From early designs, Michelangelo had always conceived of the room as being shaped by groups of columns set in between

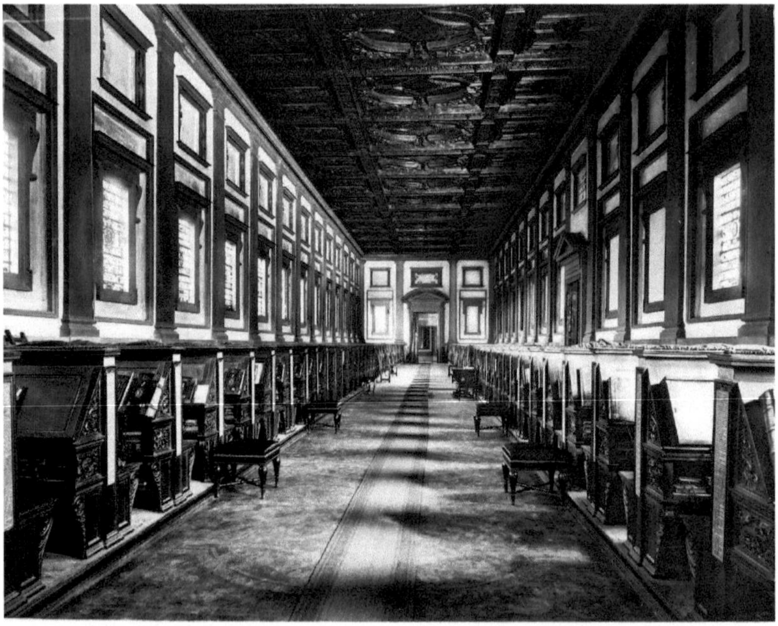

88

Michelangelo Buonarroti, Reading Room, Laurentian Library, 1525, San Lorenzo, Florence

The use of the classical orders to define the space was done earlier [**87**], but the subtle modulations of the pilasters on the side walls, framing inset windows, create a more powerful effect. The windows are high on the wall and frequent down the length of the room, lighting the desks for optimal study conditions. Each element of the interior reverberates with the others. The pilasters on the short end walls, used in a triumphal arch rhythm, continue in the divisions of the ceiling. The architectural elements of the side walls, the pilasters and window panels, begin just above the height of the desk, integrating furniture and ornament within the same system.

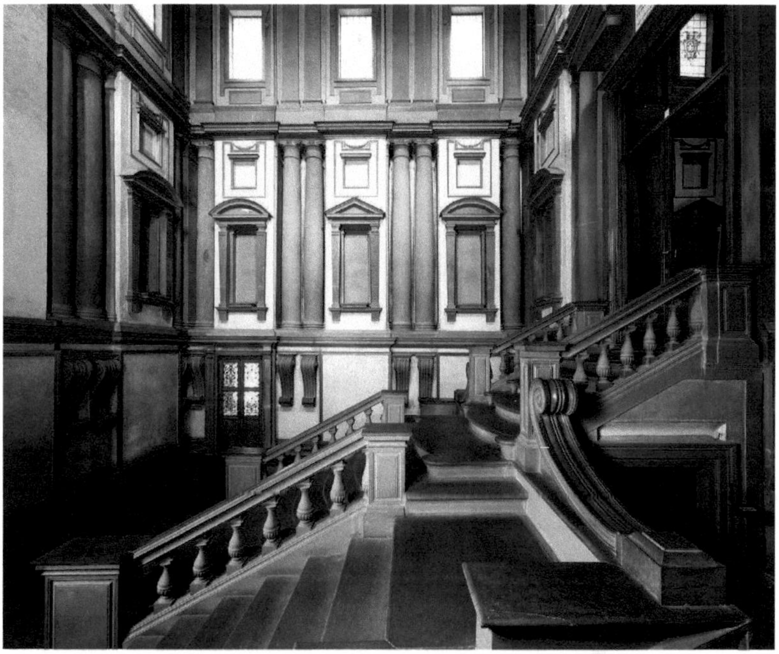

89

Michelangelo Buonarroti, Entrance vestibule and stair, Laurentian Library, begun 1533–4, San Lorenzo, Florence, Italy

The patron, Pope Clement VII, urged Michelangelo to find 'some new idea' for the design of the library. Almost every aspect of the vestibule is unexpected and surprising. The stairs rise up in three flights, and join at the first landing. The contrast between the oval shapes of the centre and the rectilinear side flights reinforces the uneasy junction between other elements of the room. Dark, monolith columns are entombed in tight recesses along the wall. Heavy frames surround blank aedicules, beneath linear frames on the wall just above. The effect is compelling but strange, all composed of elements well known from other, earlier buildings but never composed in this way before.

tabernacles on all walls, above head height upon entering. As the project developed, however, the technical limitations of the building, i.e. its relatively thin foundations, did not allow the columns to be set in front of the wall, as was typical in a Renaissance building. Rather Michelangelo inset the columns into recessions in the wall, as if they were embedded within the structure and only partly revealed. From a technical standpoint, this allowed Michelangelo to use the monolithic stone columns as structural components of the building, much as Gothic piers were not ornamental but part of the structural system.[17] This went against expected Renaissance architectural practice, as did almost every other aspect of the vestibule. Although derived from a variety of ancient and modern sources, the details were used in an unexpected way.[18] Everything conspired to set the visitor on edge, to prick his attention and mark off this space as a zone of transition between the world outside and the serene space of the reading room beyond.

The reading room was three metres above the floor level of the vestibule, and stairs were needed to make that transition [**90**]. An early idea by Michelangelo was to have the stairs follow the walls, leaving the centre of the space open. The solution, designed by Michelangelo though executed after his death by Bartolomeo Ammanati (1511–92), was for a free-standing stairway. The central flight flowed out from the stairs in curvilinear forms, in contrast to the side flights that were all straight angles. The viewer was left to traverse this variety of experi-

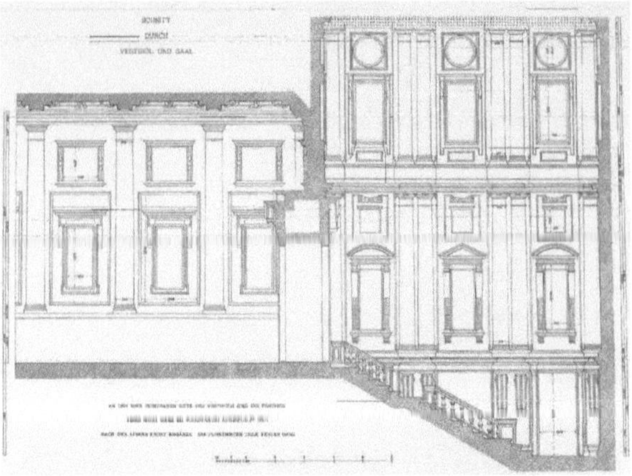

90

Section, Laurentian Library, San Lorenzo, Florence, Italy

The library is located on a level above the cloister of the monastery, and a first set of stairs brings you to the vestibule. The effect, however, is that one is entering from underground: the main storey of the vestibule, with the embedded columns, is above you when you enter. Even the climb up Michelangelo's unusual stairs does not allow you to access the upper storey of the vestibule, visible yet out of reach. That sense of arrival, yet thwarted, is achieved in Michelangelo's design through both spatial and ornamental means.

ences with care, much as they negotiated the stairs, which do not have side railings, with caution.

All of the visual interest in Michelangelo's library was on the interior spaces, and the sequence of experiences for the viewer between the vestibule as he entered the reading room. Jacopo Sansovino's design for a library in Venice was, in contrast, a very public and urban expression of the wish of the Procuracy of St Mark's to glorify the main public space through the construction of a great repository of learning [**91**].[19] The project for the library, the building of which was begun in 1537, started a half-century earlier

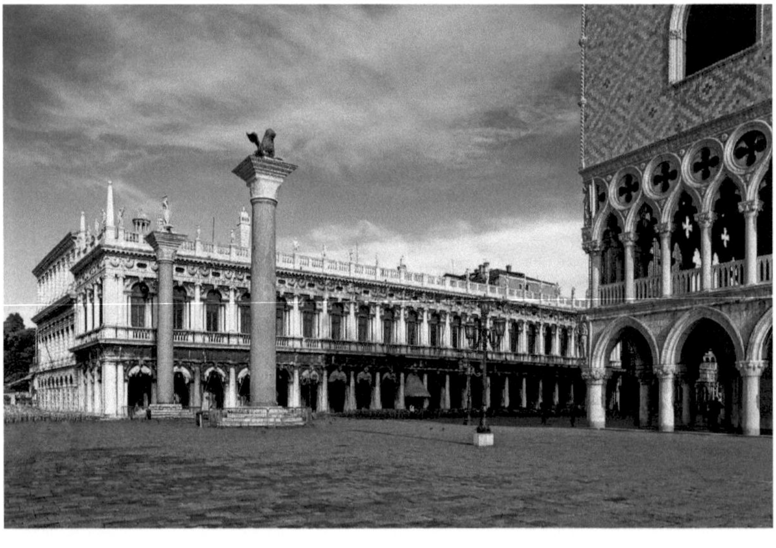

91

Jacopo Sansovino, Library San Marco, begun 1537, Venice, Italy

Building began at the end closest to the piazza, and was set back from the Campanile, thereby opening up the square. Sixteen bays were completed first, with shops on the ground floor and civic offices and the library above. Sansovino's rich façade, based on motifs of Serlio and Sansovino's own sculptural ability, created a classical façade that could resonate with the Byzantine Gothic details of the Doge's Palace across the *piazzetta*. The festive details of the library proclaimed its important place on the public square.

with the gift of a great collection of Greek and Latin manuscripts by Cardinal Bessarion in 1468. The collection languished, mostly in its original crates in rooms in the Doge's Palace, while an appropriate site was selected and acquired near to San Marco as stipulated in Bessarion's bequest. The sixteenth-century librarian and historian Cardinal Pietro Bembo urged the project forward with his concern for the state of the books and desire to further promote classical learning. Part of the project was the incorporation of a school for the sons of the nobility in the vestibule of the library, drawing on the rich holdings contained there.

The richness of the interior decoration, drawing directly on ancient descriptions of libraries as covered in stucco and gilding, with columns and lavish ceiling ornament, was also projected into the public space of the *piazzetta* onto which the building faces. The exterior was a two-storey façade, eventually completed with twenty-one bays. The Doric columns on the ground storey and Ionic on the upper level competed with ancient models of libraries with hundreds of columns, built as great demonstrations of public beneficence and magnificence. Bessarion intended that the library and its collections would be open to any reader, and that sense of communal benefit was projected not only through the actual contents of its collections but also through the ancient architecture of its façade on the public square.

Religious Camps

The monastery is a form of religious military camp, where a number of men (such as those who dedicate their lives to religion, and who take the holy vow of chastity) may come together for a life of piety and virtue. (Leon Battista Alberti, *De re aedificatoria*, Bk. V: *Works of Individuals*, 127)

Once monastic communities were established in the early Middle Ages, the pattern of buildings and related functions changed little into the Renaissance period. A collection of buildings dedicated to prayer and communal living allowed like-minded individuals the opportunity to pursue their religious goals drawing strength from shared ideals and practices. The idealized plan of a monastery made for the Benedictine monastery of St Gall, probably in the ninth century, showed the number and complexity that would be necessary. In addition to the central abbey church were cloisters, residences, refectories, hospitals, gardens, lavatories, rooms for visitors, and a full range of subsidiary buildings that allowed the residents to function as a nearly autonomous community. There were inevitable variations between the different religious orders, but the monastic buildings represented ideas of a city in miniature.

Monasteries continued to be built and renovated in the Renaissance, although new religious pressures directly affected their planning and viability. The Council of Trent (1545–63) reinstated early medieval regulations governing monasteries and convents in an effort to increase the spiritual atmosphere of the communities. The concern that monastic houses were too worldly, and independent of the central authority of the Church, was part of broader concerns about splinter religious groups and the effects of reform movements. The increased controls had only limited effect. If the Council of Trent wanted to strengthen the notion of *clausura*, a separation from the world, especially for female religious organizations, members of those religious houses found various ways to assert their own authority. Nuns might have an active role in selecting their own imagery. They also advocated spaces best suited to their religious and personal practices, such as private chapels, separate apartments, and visiting spaces for family members.[20]

On 7 July 1497, shortly before departing on his voyage around the Cape, Vasco da Gama stopped to pray at Santa Maria de Belém, Our Lady, Star of the Sea, a church at the port on the outskirts of Lisbon in Restelo. Prince Henry the Navigator had recently ordered that the church should be enlarged and dedicated to the needs of sailors. The Hieronymite order was responsible for the new foundation and construction began on the Feast of the Epiphany, 6 January 1501 or 1502, the day commemorating the arrival of the Three Kings bringing riches from afar. The connection between Vasco da Gama's stop at Belém, and the discovery of the sea route to India which brought increased wealth to Portugal, was intertwined in the history of the monastery.

The vast and lavish building was the very physical and visible presence of Portugal's success in trade to India. Niches in the walls of the church were intended, according to the programme for the church written in 1510, to contain imagery directly related to Portugal's explorations and discoveries in India, references to the ships that left from the port, Restelo, 'which put to sea with the Cross of Christ on their sails . . . borne by angels, with the name of each vessel on the side'.[21]

The complex, with its cloister, church, and dormitories, was laid out by Diogo Boitaca, and construction continued under his direction to around 1517. During this first phase great quantities of dressed white and black stone arrived on site, workers made progress on the cloister, and several of the exterior walls were built, though not yet decorated at this stage. In 1517, the project took a different turn under the direction of João de Castilho. More workers were employed, including foreign carvers specifically brought in to work on the important south portal to the church. Castilho was a master at managing the scale of the project and the teams of craftsmen working on each aspect of the building. In the church, the ceiling has elaborate and innovative vaulting that rises above the almost cubic space [**92**].

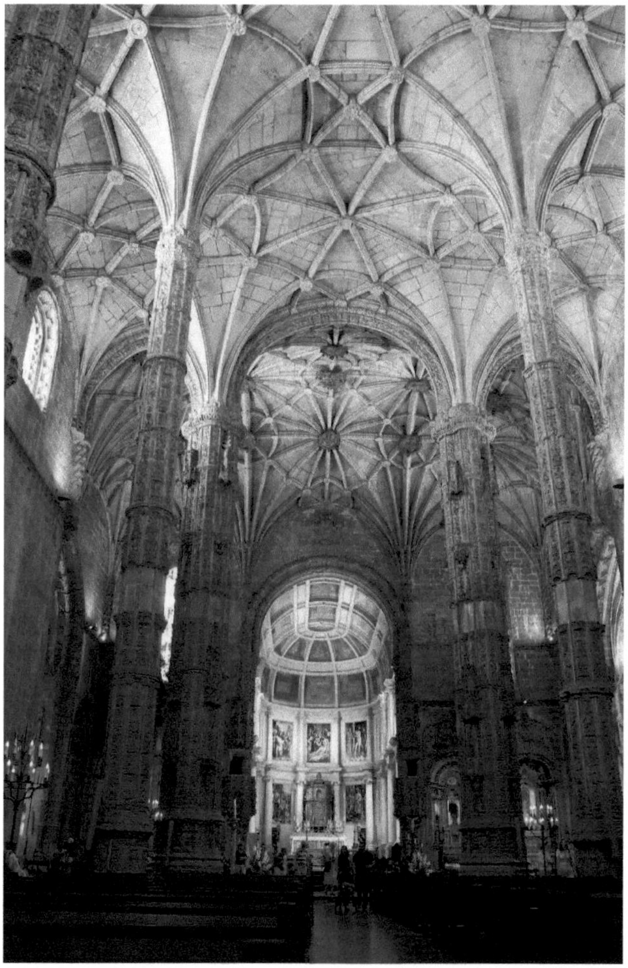

92

Diogo Boitaca and João de Castilho, S. Maria de Belém, Jerónimos Abbey, 1501–22, Belém, Portugal

Six octagonal piers support the vaulted roof that covers the nave and aisles of this hall church. The piers are the starting point for the rib vaulting system, emerging from the tops of the columns in a net-like system that gives the greatest unity to the space below. The smooth surface of the walls beneath the clerestory windows is only broken by the twelve doors of the confessionals that are embedded into the walls and entered by the priests from the cloister. In light of pre-Reformation ecclesiastical policy, a unified space would unite the congregation in their devotional practice. The large congregation, entering the church as individuals, would worship as one corporate body, awed by the grandeur of the space.

The Jerónimos Abbey is an extraordinary example of the combination of political and religious imagery, fused in the creation of an architectural complex for the benefit of a corporate group. The cloisters, the product of both Boitaca and Castilho, are rich in Manueline ornament (so called because it is associated with work completed during the reign of King Manuel I, Prince Henry's successor) [**93**].

In some countries the power of religious communities rivalled that of the state, in their control of land and resources, and the architecture of large monasteries also rivalled palaces in their size and grandeur. In England, King Henry VIII dissolved all monastic communities in 1536 as part of his break with the Church of Rome and the establishment of the Church of England.[22] The dissolution of hundreds of monastic houses changed the nature of communal religious practice

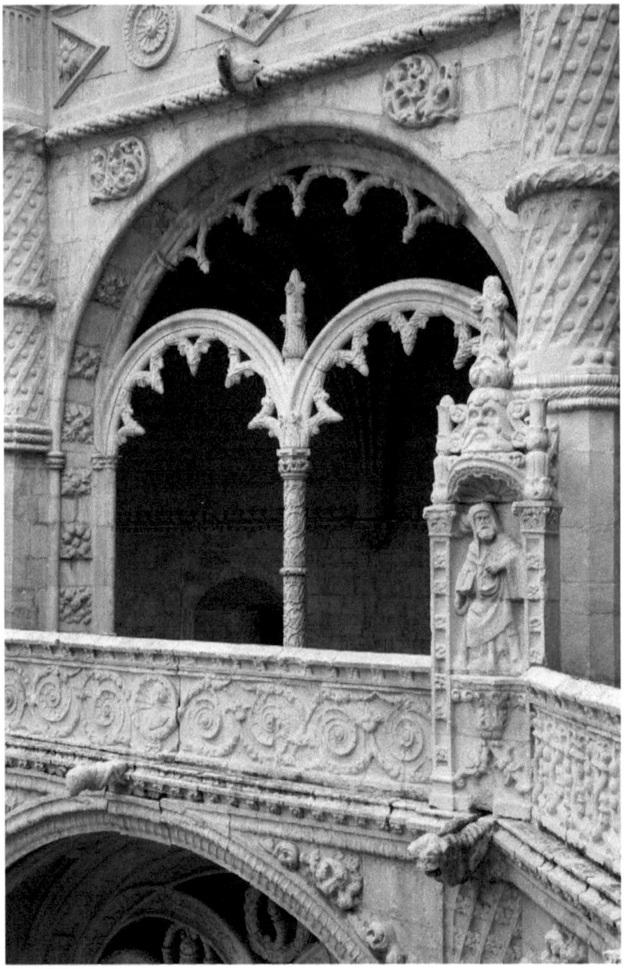

93

Diogo Boitaca and João de Castilho, Cloister, Jerónimos Abbey, 1501–22, Belém, Portugal

When Castilho took over the design of the cloisters in 1517, he transformed the project already under way. He changed the shape of the lower supports, creating piers where Boitaca had cylindrical supports, and, more significantly, adding a dense layer of sculpted images throughout the cloister. In addition to symbols of the reign of King Manuel I (his coats of arms, cipher, emblems of the armillary sphere), images centred on the life of Christ are integrated into the cloister on both levels. Cloisters were traditionally spaces for quiet contemplation. In pre-Reformation Portugal, and especially within court circles, the practice of the *devotio moderna* encouraged meditation on the suffering of Christ. Images as in the cloister at Belém could serve as mnemonic devices, reminding the viewer of texts read earlier and recalled in the course of gentle walking and religious practice.

and released a vast amount of buildings and building materials for private use. Henry VIII bestowed the monastic properties on his nobles in order to further ensure their loyalty. The monastic buildings then became like quarries for their recipients, disassembled to varying degrees and reused in the construction of some of the great country houses of the Tudor period.

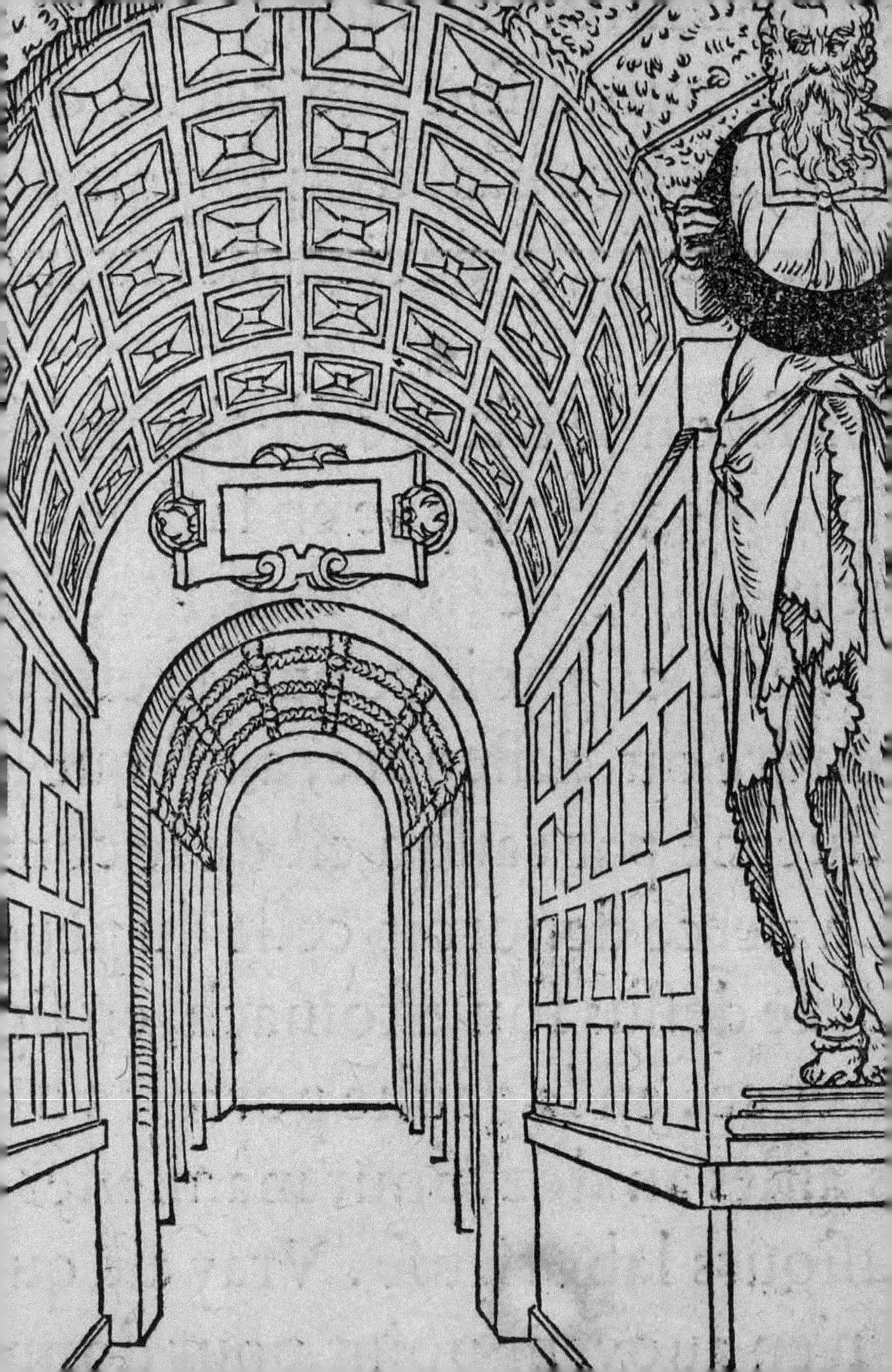

6

Shaping the Renaissance City

Some cities grew up organically during the Middle Ages with buildings added as populations grew, taking up any available open space within the city and expanding outside the protection of the walls when necessary. The street pattern emerged as the city expanded, and into the Renaissance proved remarkably resistant to change. It is not surprising that this was so. Property owners had little incentive to sell buildings in order to accommodate a prince's wish to regularize the city plan, which was understood by both the general populace and the city groups to provide the ruler with an easier time controlling crowds. The winding streets favoured the very local population in each quarter of the city, cities within cities, who maintained a great deal of autonomy over their local domain.

At the same time, the survival of Roman street layouts, as in Autun (France), provided a model for the shaping of new cities as well. New towns in southern France, *bastides*, established trade centres for rival lords in the thirteenth and fourteenth centuries.[1] New towns in the territory controlled by Florence were organized around central squares and built to strict regulations. Buildings within the city followed hierarchical standards, larger houses along the main street and lesser buildings behind.[2]

Private houses were built out over the street on upper levels, taking advantage of every possible opportunity to create more usable (and rentable) space. The ground floor of artisan and merchant houses might include a shop front onto the street, opened up with the simple lifting of a large window that created a shelf for the display of goods [**94**]. Religious images were embedded into the fabric of buildings throughout the city reinforcing the everyday, and everywhere, presence of the divine. Although many cities today, such as Bruges, Siena, Venice, York, and Talinn, retain the essential footprint of their medieval origins, it is more difficult for the modern visitor to capture the fluidity of experience that the early modern city offered, where there was no clear division between public and private, sacred and secular, commerce and culture.

Detail of 104

94

Brunetto Latini, *Le Livre du trésor*, 1450–75

In this manuscript the ground floor of houses opens to the street, with wide shelves that could accommodate the display of goods. The upper storeys were usually the residence of the artisans shown in their shopfront. It is in this urban setting of goods and exchange that the women perform their good works and engage in their devotional practices.

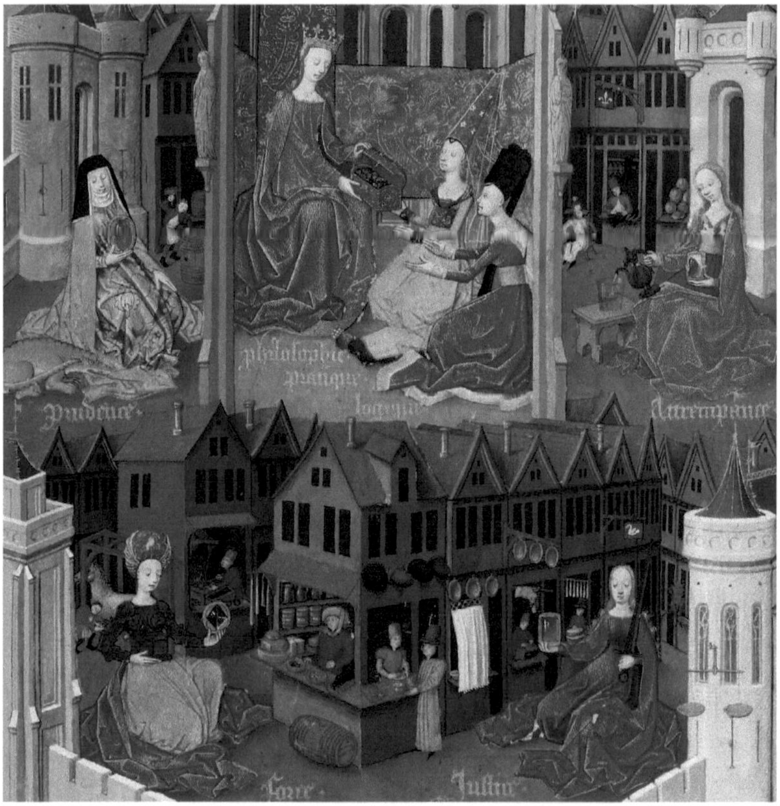

One approach to cities in the early modern period sees them as primarily centres of trade and commerce, growing and changing as economic conditions shifted. Therefore, the consolidation of squares in the sixteenth century that we see in many cities, Venice, Seville, and London to name just a few, emerged from trade conditions rather than any abstract notion of perfect architectural form. Although writers such as Francesco di Giorgio and Filarete proposed ideal city plans, they proved almost impossible to implement in any existing city.

New World Cities

When John White, an Elizabethan gentleman, travelled to North America around 1580 he found a world rich with natural resources and inhabited by people with exotic habits. He tried to make sense of what he saw: the customs of dress and family life, the ways of hunting and agriculture, and even the curious habit of preserving the deceased elders of the community as part of their spiritual practice. In the architecture and villages of the Algonquian, he tried to reconcile their way of living with what he knew from his own experience. His drawings of the Algonquians in what is now North Carolina included views of two of the towns along Pamlico Sound, Secotan and Pomeiooc [**95**]. White showed how buildings were made of bark or reed mats, with rounded, arched roofs that gave the buildings stability. Although there were similarities to the layout of English villages, including the connection of the houses to the agricultural land around them, White seemed equally interested in showing how the houses were connected to the rituals of the people. Although the Algonquians were certainly thought to be exotic, he depicted their civic life in a way that would resonate for his audience with English customs.

The longhouses, a type common to the North American native peoples, all face into the centre, and were organized into two concentric circles. White showed the houses with some of the end walls removed in order to give a view into the interiors with their sleeping benches. The houses were organized around a central open space where White showed people gathered around a fire. Thus the orientation of the houses, differentiated according to their function or the status of the inhabitants, depended upon shared rituals. Fire was also the explanation the ancient writer Vitruvius had given for the origins of architecture. Whether or not White knew that text, he recognized

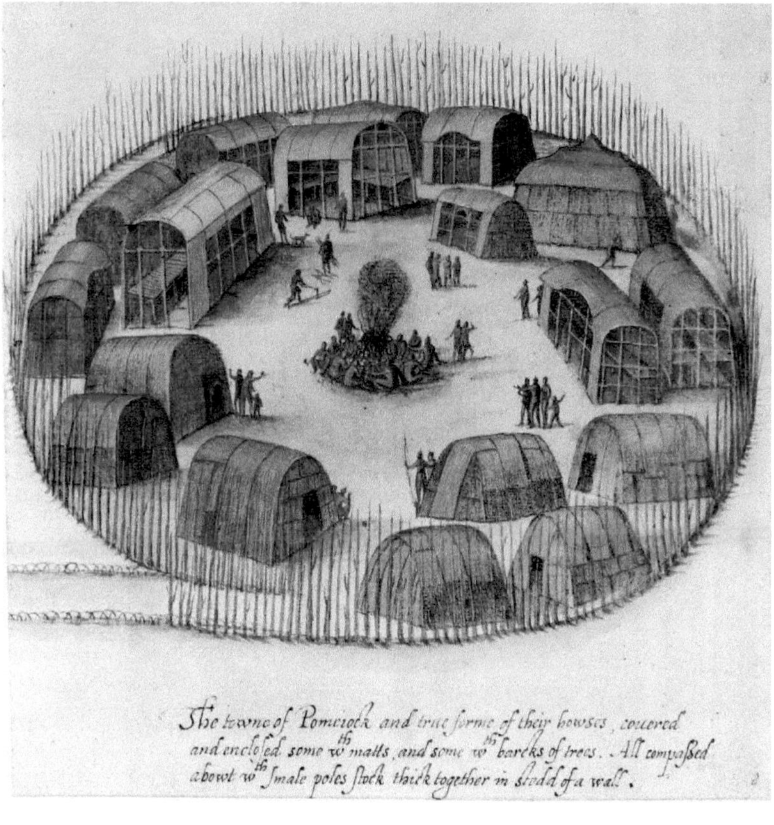

95

John White, *Town of Pomeiooc*, 1585

Pomeiooc, inhabited either by members of the Secotan or Roanoke tribes, was a palisaded village. In the inscription White records that the houses are 'covered and enclosed some with mats, and some with barks of trees. All [en]compassed about with small poles stuck thick together instead of a wall.'

what could be some common elements between the native organization of civic space, and what he knew back at home.

The houses were also ringed 'about with small poles stuck thick together instead of a wall'. That is, the communal life and its buildings were protected by a stockade, much as a town in England or Europe would be encircled with a protective wall and fortifications.

Walls and Enclosures

For Europeans seeing native settlements for the first time, the wooden stockade fence was comparable to what they knew at home from city walls yet seemingly primitive compared to the new stone walls in European cities, designed to withstand the force of modern warfare. Cities varied greatly in size, but nearly all had walls that defined the boundaries of the city and protected its inhabitants. Although native settlements were vastly different from the stone-built architecture of Europe, the common currency of cities was the desire to distinguish the built space from the world outside and to offer protection from invaders.

It was walls, in fact, that defined a city, no matter its size. The town secretary of Eisenach (Thuringia) wrote in 1399 that 'what has a wall around it, that we call a city'.[3] The construction of walls was the most expensive public project for any city, and often took many decades or even centuries to complete. Civic leaders and courtly princes believed walls to be essential to a city's existence, and therefore worthy of the time and expense. Massive stone walls discouraged attacks, and offered the city's inhabitants a sense of security. Movement of people, goods, and potentially disease could be controlled, to some extent, through city gates. And walls defined the area of a city, limiting growth and creating an urban density that was important to both safety and commerce [**96**]. Venice is the exception that proves the rule. The Republic's great navy protected the city from attack from the sea, and the long span of open loggias across the Ducal Palace asserted a confidence that attack was unlikely across the expanse of water.

In the sixteenth and seventeenth centuries, the population of cities grew as trade and economic wealth increased. For some cities such as Paris and Florence, this growth required new walls that expanded the perimeter. In London, the two distinct centres of the city, Westminster as the court capital to the west, and London to the east, merged as growth filled in the open fields between them. Walls also remained even when populations shrank. In Rome, the ancient walls enclosed large tracts of empty land in the medieval era and into the sixteenth century as the popes worked to re-establish the size and magnificence of the city.

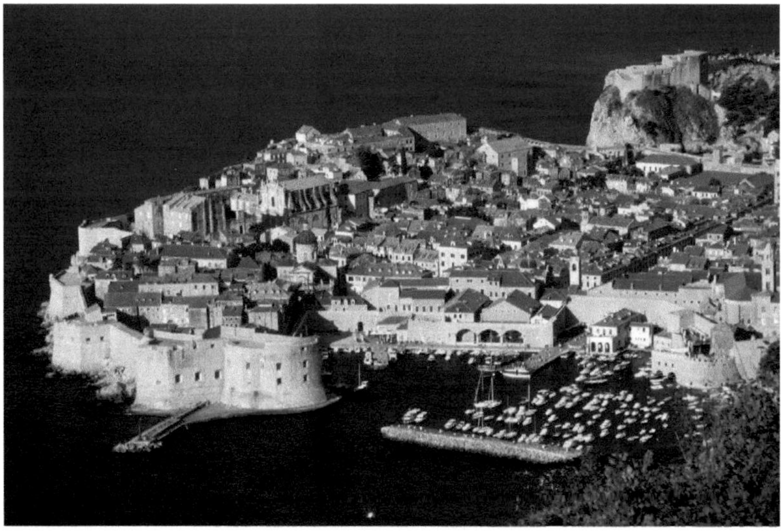

96
Dubrovnik, Croatia

The walls and bastions around Dubrovnik were extended in two campaigns during the Renaissance. Michelozzo di Bartolomeo and Giorgio da Sebenico designed the fortifications on the land side of the city in 1464–5 in response to the Turkish capture of Bosnia in 1463. New fortifications were added along the sea throughout the 16th century in anticipation of an attack by the Venetians.

In many cities walls are now destroyed or hidden behind buildings that give no hint of their importance. Medieval and early modern city walls were no match for modern warfare. And where they do survive, the suburbs have expanded and made the walls only an outmoded artefact that no longer carries the symbolic weight or civic function it once did.

City Gates

Walls were the main form of protection for cities. Gates allowed for controlled access in and out of the city centre. From the Middle Ages they were often designed with complex twists and turns, over a series of ramps and bridges that were intended to prevent anyone (human or animal) sneaking through the gate undetected. This didn't always work, of course. Walls and gates were highly permeable membranes that permitted a flow of people and goods, in and out.

Gates were an important part of urban control but they were equally signs of a city's status and independence in their imposing size and symbolic decoration. The great Holstentor in Lübeck (1464–78) marked the western flank of the city [**97**]. It is the only surviving part of a complex gate system that was begun in the thirteenth century and extended by additional gate structures to increase the security leading into the city. The various interior spaces in the gates provided rooms for the toll collector and the city official in charge of the streets and fortifications. The desire for an impressive entrance became more important as Lübeck's role in the Hanseatic League increased. The Holstentor has different façades to the interior and exterior, as did many city gates. The side toward the fields had few

97

Holstentor, 1464–78, Lübeck, Germany

By the end of the Middle Ages, brick rivalled stone in its status as a building material in northern Germany. Lübeck, along with other cities controlled by the Hanseatic League, was developed in the 12th and 13th centuries with the construction of important religious and civic buildings in the local brick, finished with various glazes. The Holstentor incorporated the stepped gable façade used elsewhere in the city between twin towers and steep conical roofs, a Baltic version of the triumphal arch as gateway.

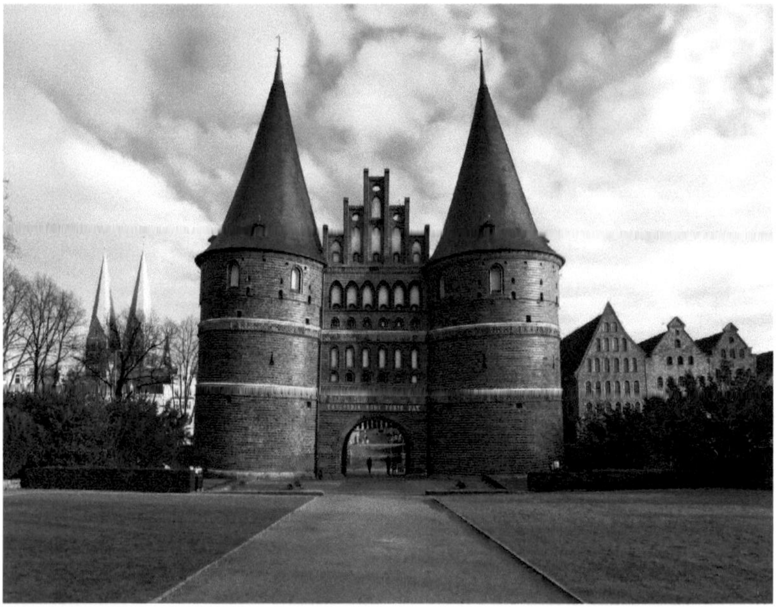

windows whereas the city side had rows of windows that link the two towers. The brick construction, conical roofs, and stepped gable in the centre were all distinctive to architecture along the Baltic generally, and typical of the buildings in Lübeck. The gate was thus a sign of civic and regional identity, immediately recognizable to anyone entering the city.

The importance of gates as a symbolic gesture in the city increased as new forms of urban protection were developed. In the sixteenth century, fortification design began to favour earthen ramparts, protected behind deep ditches. Walls, therefore, became a less important sign of civic status and authority and gates took on that role. The Porta Nuova in Verona (begun 1533), designed by Michele Sanmicheli (1487–1559), was an interpretation of an ancient Roman triumphal arch applied to a fortified gate [**98**]. The central opening had engaged Doric columns supporting a pediment, with classical ornament and Venetian coat of arms that spoke to the city's identity as a modern version of ancient Roman ideals. The structure itself, however, was a fully realized defensive structure, strong enough to support guns on the roof.[4]

Pienza

Soon after he was elevated to the papacy, Pope Pius II returned to his native town of Corsignano in Tuscany, about 30 miles south-east of Siena. Most of the residents of the small town made their living from agriculture, farming the rich landscape in the valleys below the town

98

Michele Sanmicheli, Porta Nuova, 1533, Verona, Italy

In addition to the technical innovations, Sanmicheli also introduced rustication and the simple Doric order as appropriate forms and ornament for civic fortifications. Both ancient and modern in inspiration, all of the details of the gate are carefully calculated to reinforce both the image of impenetrability and dignity appropriate for this building.

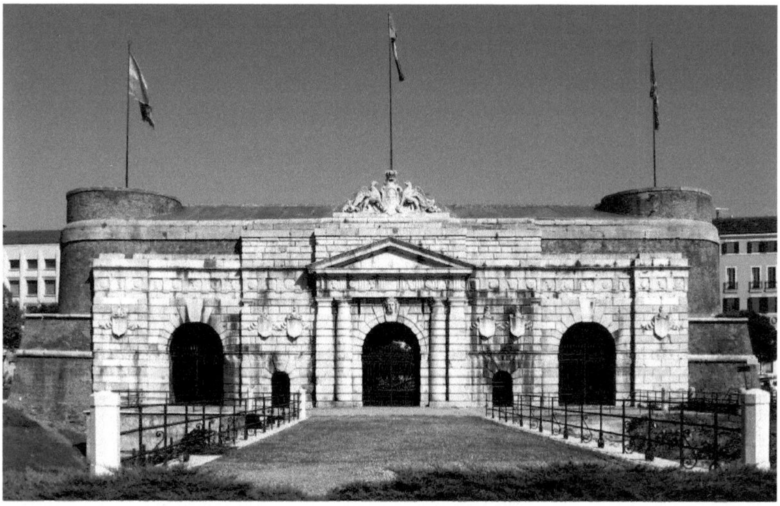

centre. When Pius II returned there in 1459, the ageing population and modest buildings evoked his own sense of time passing. By transforming Corsignano into his namesake Pienza, the town's most famous native son could establish a lasting monument to his own cultural ideas and to the fame of his family.

99

Pienza, Italy

The cathedral and the Palazzo Piccolomini, seen here, were largely completed by 1462 when Pope Pius II returned to Pienza. He then ordered additional buildings added to the square: a bishop's palace, a town hall (through whose arches this photo is taken), housing for the canons, and housing for the poor. Each building was designed according to designs appropriate for its type. Together, however, they create a total architectural experience of variety within a defined architectural language of classical forms. The layout of the piazza, opening out toward the view behind the cathedral, creates a dynamic space that sets off each individual building.

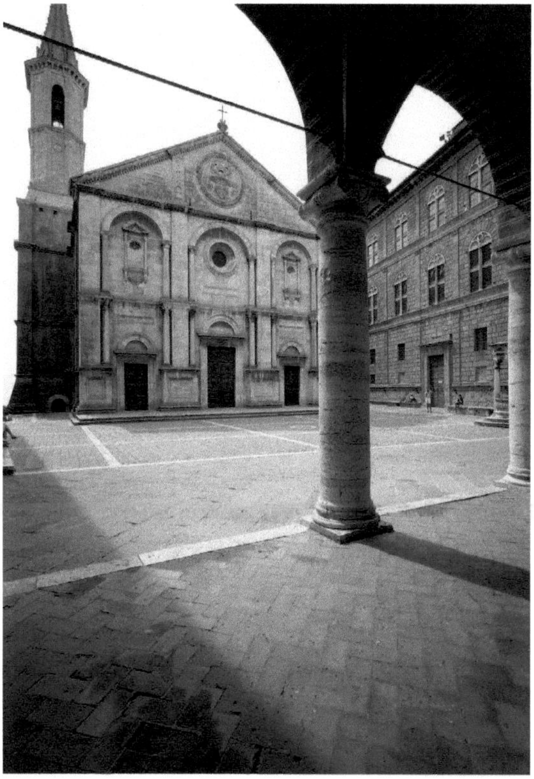

Through his architect, Bernardo Rossellino (1409–63), Pius II created an open space in front of the cathedral, flanked by the family palace, episcopal palace, and communal palace [**99**]. Designed in a language that reflected the most current experiments by architects in Florence including Filippo Brunelleschi and Leon Battista Alberti, the buildings formed a unified whole that was greater than each of the individual parts. A single extraordinary building added into the urban fabric would not have had the same effect as the aggregate, whose effect seems to radiate out through the town.

Pius II elevated Pienza into a bishopric, vastly increasing its importance for him and his family, the Piccolomini. The transformation of Corsignano into Pienza was part of a much larger campaign to promote the family's status through architectural projects, including numerous new palaces, loggias, and piazzas in nearby Siena. For the residents of Pienza, however, the transformation of the city into a cult centre honouring the Pope was far from painless. In three large buying campaigns from 1459 to 1464, the Pope and his associates acquired 12 per cent of the city's property. Many residents did not want to sell, and had no hope of finding alternative residences in the built-up town. The effect of the rapid and massive urban gentrification was an economic and cultural shock to the stable pattern of life in Pienza. The ideal urban centre, as it was conceived by Pius II, required a brutal intervention, now subsumed in the clarity and elegance of what remains.[5]

The City of God

In a fifteenth-century painting from Bruges, the Virgin and Child sit in a rose garden, surrounded by female saints [**100**]. Behind them is a walled city, and beyond that mountains that echo the shape of the city's towers, extending into the distance. The city is unmistakably Bruges, identified by the church spire on the left belonging to the Cathedral of Notre-Dame and the bell tower of the Halle on the right where boats were unloaded containing the goods that made the city rich in the Middle Ages. Both the city and the garden are perfectly enclosed spaces, holy places in a religious and perhaps also in a worldly sense, echoing themes explored in Augustine's *City of God* (started 410).

At the end of the Middle Ages Bruges was indeed a blessed city in economic terms, enjoying all the advantages of wealth from foreign trade. Nearly a third of the city's income was spent on civic infrastructure including walls, paved streets, water systems, and public buildings. The first bourse, or public trading market, in Europe was built in Bruges to corral and consolidate the great influx of merchants into the city.

By the time this painting was made, probably around 1485, Bruges had passed her economic and political prime. The Zwin, the river that

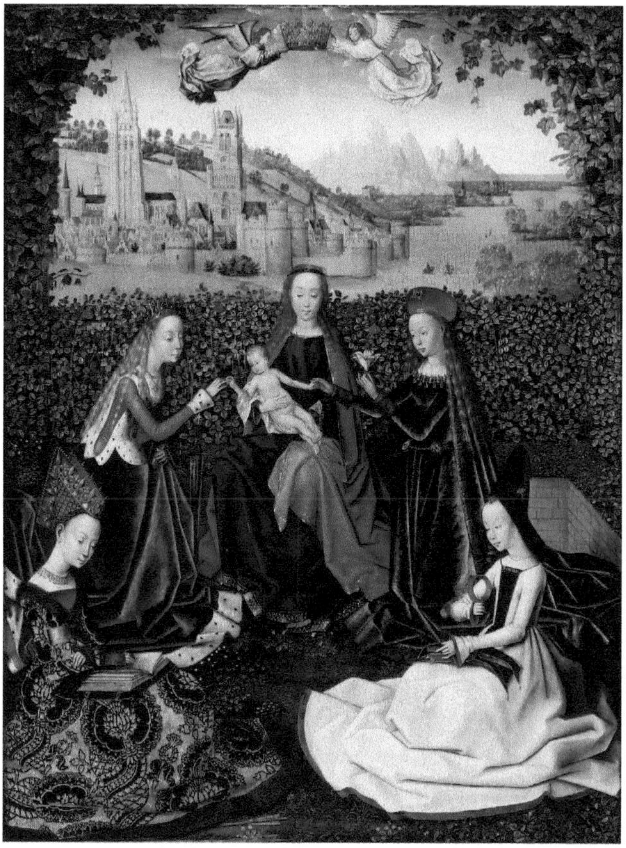

100

Master of the St Lucy Legend, *Virgin of the Rose Garden*, 1475/80

Although clearly identifiable as Bruges, the view of the city was not an objective image of the city but an idealized rendering—much as the saints are depicted in the foreground. The specificity of the city also served as a type of proof of authenticity for the painting, a mark of its origins from a city renowned for the quality of its artistic production. The city of Jan van Eyck and other great early Flemish painters from the beginning of the century, the association with Bruges validates the artistic value of this painting.

allowed ships to come into Bruges, bringing goods from all over Europe and beyond, had begun to silt up. By 1460 the deep-water port of Sluys, near to Bruges, was no longer open to ships. The natural threats to the city were compounded by the political pressures exerted by Emperor Maximilian I. The independence of Bruges was a challenge to his authority and in 1488 Maximilian gave incentives for foreign merchants to move their business and trade to Antwerp.

Yet the painting gives no indication of any of those problems. The city is the mirror of the holy scene in the foreground, as timeless as the female saints in their walled garden. All of the attributes that make Bruges recognizable, including the cathedral tower and belfry, identify the city as unchanging even though everything in its recent history told a very different story.

In this painting Bruges appears like a model, placed in a diorama. City models were in fact made in order to represent a specific place, often for a royal patron. The craftsman Jakob Sandtner (*fl.* 1561–74) made a group of city models for Duke Albrecht V of Bavaria (1528–79) [**101**].[6] Carved from limewood, the same material used to make religious sculpture, and painted to convey the sense that

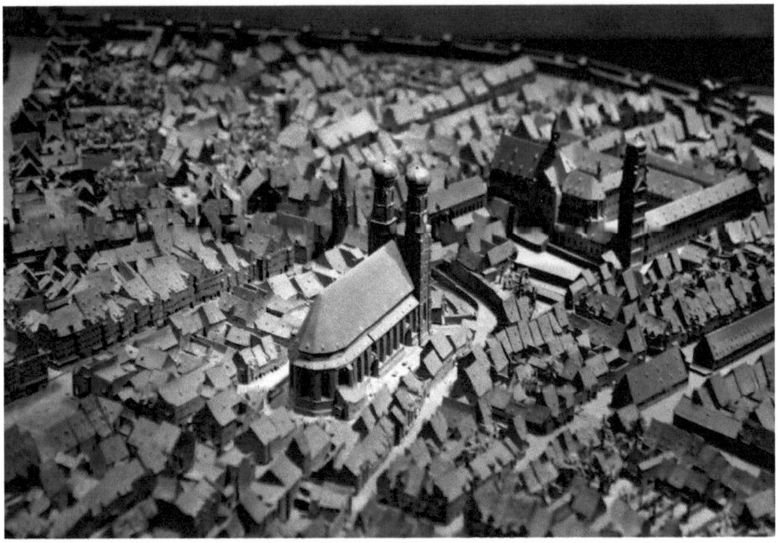

101
Jakob Sandtner, Model of the city of Munich, 1570

Models offered Duke Albrecht V of Bavaria a bird's-eye view of the cities under his control. Crafted out of limewood, and painted to enhance the realistic effect, these models allowed for effective military strategizing. Many of these cities had newly built fortifications, prominently displayed in the models. As immediately useful as these models may have been, they also offered a unique and god-like view of the Duke's territories that reinforced his sense of political and military control.

here was the city in miniature, the models offered a unique view into the city space. Reproductions of the streets and buildings, enclosed within the fortified walls, allowed the Duke to view his Residenzstädte, or seats of government, from within his palace in Munich. The models were part of his collection of marvels. The perfectly ordered model cities affirmed his quixotic sense of complete political power.

City views could give less idealized views, historical snapshots, in an age before the camera, of distant and exotic urban environments known only through travellers' accounts. Prints and even paintings were transportable. Images of the Holy Land were a specific type of these images, often including important pilgrimage sites such as the Holy Sepulchre in Jerusalem that few would have seen in person.

City Halls

As a city grew in wealth and importance, there was a need for an architectural presence that would serve the political and judicial needs of the city as well as marking, in a permanent way, the city's increasing status. The origin of town halls owes much to the rising strength of the guilds in towns after the thirteenth century. While some town halls, especially in the north, may have included an open loggia on the ground floor to be used as a market, as trade increased and greater space was needed for government and trade, city officials as well as guilds separated these functions out into different structures.

New town halls, or major renovations to existing ones, seem to have spawned in clusters. There was competition between neighbouring towns for the most richly decorated exterior, with the grandest interior

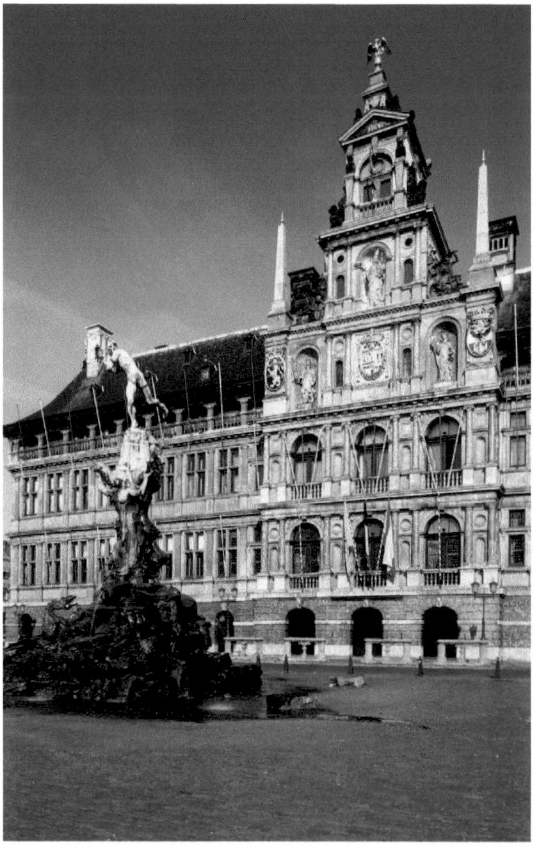

102
Cornelis Floris and Willem Paludanus, Town Hall, 1561–5, Antwerp

As Antwerp grew in population, wealth, and importance in the 16th century, there was a clear need for a new town hall. One attempt was made to build in the 1540s, but that was delayed and the materials used for new city fortifications. The sculptors Floris and Paludanus worked on the design of the façade, formulating the design that had been agreed upon by a committee convened for the purpose. Classical architectural forms, *anticse wercken*, are annexed onto a relatively traditional form. The specific details of the orders come from the recent translation (1539) of Sebastiano Serlio's Book IV on the architectural orders from Italian into Flemish by Pieter Coecke van Aelst.

meeting rooms. And it is because of these inevitable rivalries that groups of extraordinary town halls, all built around the same period, are found in cities of the southern Netherlands, for example, with lavish buildings in Leuven, Brussels, Ghent, and Middelburg. This series of buildings culminates in the Antwerp Town Hall (1561–5), designed by Cornelis Floris and Willem Paludanus, which dwarfs the surrounding houses of the square [**102**]. As with many town halls, throughout Europe, there was a desire to incorporate lavish decoration with traditional and regional aspects. In Antwerp, there was a classical frontispiece at the centre, breaking up the long façade along one side of the square, with classical columns. The use of antique ornament, recognizable by the educated elite of the city as a reference to widely held humanist cultural ideals, was juxtaposed with the steep roof and tall, rectangular windows characteristic of the local Flemish architecture.

The Flow of Goods

The wealth from goods, flowing in and out of cities, or transformed from raw goods into marketable products, shaped the urban space. In

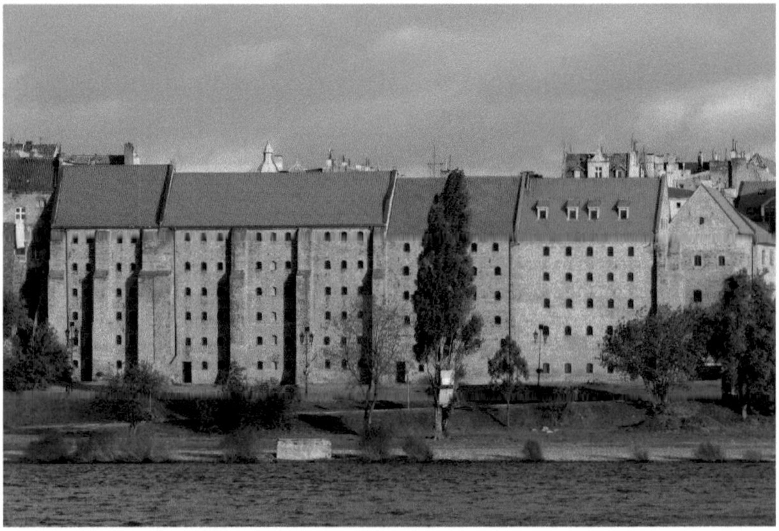

103

Granaries, 15th–18th centuries, Grudziądz, Poland

These granaries are built into the high embankment alongside the Vistula River. From the city side they are two or three storeys high. From the river, they project an image of the city that is both prosperous and secure, serving as protective defences and evidence of the city's role as a centre of trade.

a desire to regulate and control market activities, some cities constructed more grand and permanent buildings to house trade. The Royal Exchange in London (begun 1565) and the Cloth Hall in Ypres (completed 1304) are just two examples of monumental buildings that brought merchants and their customers together in an architectural space that could be better regulated.

The vast quantity of goods could require buildings to store them until they went to market, or were transported on to their final destination. In Venice, a series of *fondaci*, or warehouses, were operated by various trade groups within the city. These large, often regularly built structures were placed close by the market, and with ease of access to transport. Towns along the Vistula River in Poland grew from the grain trade as it was shipped by boat northward towards the port at Gdańsk. Granaries in the town of Grudziądz rise up from the river to the town centre, high on the bank [**103**]. In Venice, the warehouses to hold the salt stores adjoined the Piazza San Marco and are along the Giudecca Canal. Such functional, semi-industrial buildings are often overlooked in the attention on the palaces of the wealthy, the civic monuments, or the towering church spires. Yet these buildings defined cities as centres of wealth and prosperity, and with an importance that extended far beyond their own borders.

The triumphant city

Almost all of the buildings that survive from the pre-modern era were intended to be permanent structures, built out of solid materials. But we must also imagine the city as a changing landscape, periodically transformed by temporary buildings erected for festivals and pageants.

Saints' days and the ecclesiastical calendar dictated religious celebrations which often included the erection of banners, display of relics, and the decoration of buildings which transformed the city with a new costume of religious garb. Religious plays, enacted in public squares and in front of major public buildings, recast those sacred dramas in the everyday space of the city. What was unremarkable became extraordinary when the story of Christ's Passion came to life in the same space as the market or the city hall.

When rulers visited cities within their domain, their arrival was described in the printed accounts as 'joyous', though the imagery was closer to that of a military triumph. Civic groups erected temporary arches made of painted canvas at important points along the parade route. These temporary arches recalled ancient Roman arches and marked a political fealty of the city to a ruler. King Henry II (1519–59) and his wife Marie de' Medici (1519–89) entered Paris on 16 June 1549 as one part of an elaborate celebration that included the coronation of his wife as queen, a mock naval battle on the Seine, and a tournament. The events and decoration were recorded in a book that included woodcuts of the temporary architecture [**104**]. For Henry II's entry into Paris (and a year later into Rouen), the temporary arches were decorated with classical figures representing the King as wise, the nobility blessed by his patronage, and the people loyal to his power.

Most festival architecture was never intended to be permanent. Accounts for payment to craftsmen include details about the installation and removal of the object after the event ended. If the event lived on in the descriptions and woodcuts of publications, the actual materials were recycled whenever possible. The lumber could be reused and the canvas cut up and distributed to artists for another festival or purpose. Festivals did have a lasting effect though on the design of more permanent buildings. Not only were the designers often the very best architects and artists of the day. Almost every architect of note in the Renaissance was involved in the festivals for their court patrons and their native cities. Temporary architecture offered the opportunity to invent decorative schemes and visual effects that were perhaps too unconventional, impractical, or simply extravagant to be made out of more permanent materials. Festivals were thus a kind of experimental laboratory for art, architecture, and craftsmen that moved projects from the drawing board to the urban theatre.

Triumphal entries were also the opportunity to embellish existing buildings, and transform them for the event as well as an urban benefit. An existing fountain in Paris at the corner of the rue Saint Denis and the rue aux Fers had already served as an important focus for processions through the city. When the sculptor Jean Goujon collaborated with the architect Pierre Lescot, they transformed the Fontaine

104

Arch of the Saint-Denis Gate for the entry of Henry II and Catherine de' Medici into Paris: *C'est l'ordre qui a este tenu a la nouvelle et ioyeuse entrée, que... le roy treschrestien Henry deuxieme de ce nom, a faicte en sa bonne ville [et] cité de Paris* (Paris, 1549)

Most temporary decorations for triumphal entries have been lost; they were intended to be destroyed after the event. However, this remarkable small book is one of a handful of printed and published records of the arches and fountains for a royal entry. The sculptor Jean Goujon designed this arch, and its classical form and details reflect the style of the new buildings at the Louvre, just being built at this time. The designer of this plate for the book, possibly Goujon himself, also shows how the arch would have appeared *in situ*, set against the existing and well-worn wall.

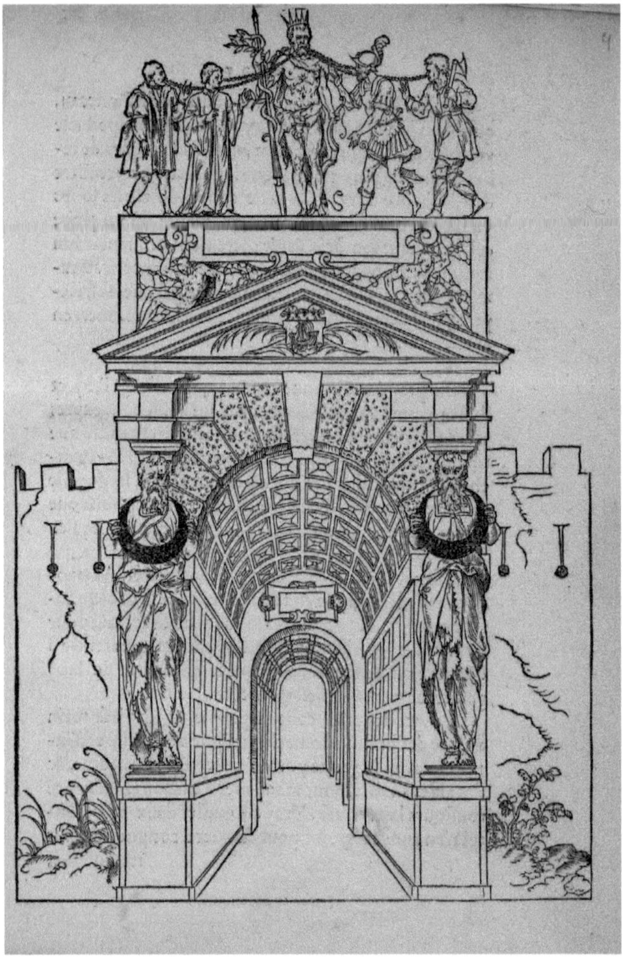

des Innocents into a celebration of the city. The water emerged from the ground level of the pavilion; the upper storey was an open loggia where the Parisian elite could watch the procession as it passed through the city and be watched by the citizens and royalty alike [**105**]. Goujon's low-relief sculptures of water nymphs, dressed in ancient costume, reinforce the allegorical theme of the fountain as a mark of the city's bounty and sanctification. As the historian Henri Zerner suggests, however, given Paris's paltry supply of water, the theme of water was a hopeful one for the citizens.

The Fontaine des Innocents was also as much a work of urbanism and architecture as it was of sculpture.[7] The platform at ground level, with the loggia above, articulated an important intersection in the city. Lescot framed Goujon's sinuous sculpture with a composition of finely wrought classical architecture, making the ornament

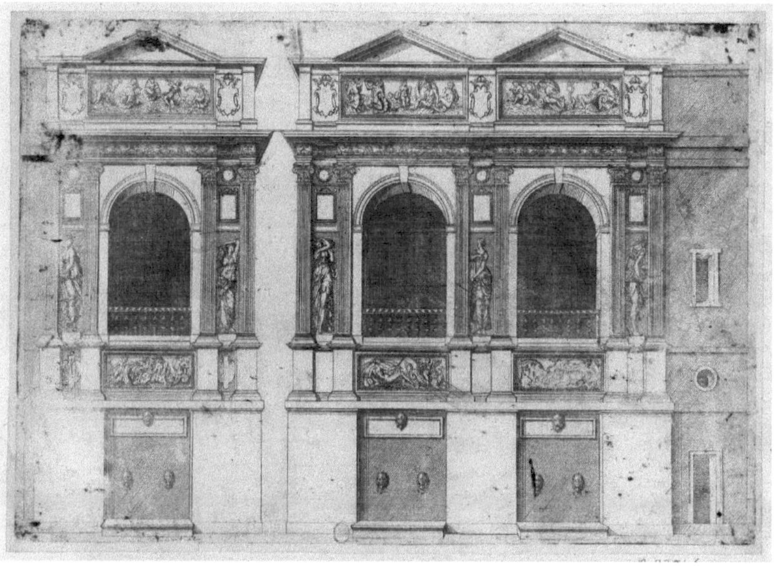

105

Jacques Androuet du Cerceau, *Fontaine des Innocents*, 1550–75

The fountain was added to an existing building; one can see how Lescot connected the mouldings into the adjacent building. From the elevated viewing platform, in the open arcades, the privileged spectators could view the royal procession as well as the city that served as the all-important backdrop for the event. The fountain no longer exists though some of Goujon's sculptural panels have been preserved in the Louvre Museum.

usually reserved for temporary architecture a permanent part of the urban scene.

Towers

Landmarks from afar, and marvels close up, the great spires of churches announced the wealth of urban centres. If other buildings such as markets, town halls, and walls served a growing population, spires were not the product of an immediate spatial or functional need. Churches could get by with shorter or less ornate towers. Yet the tallest and most ornate spires expressed the ambitions of a city in the impossibility of their construction, the sheer excess of labour, resources, and skill in attempting so much.

The view of Strasbourg by Hartmann Schedel in the *Liber chronicarum* (1493) is dominated by the north tower of the cathedral, rising far above the rest of the church and the city [**106**].[8] The cathedral was begun in the twelfth century, and the tower completed up to the platform level in 1399. A master mason from Ulm, Ulrich von Ensingen, moved to Strasbourg to complete the tower. His design was remarkable for its octagon shape and interlaced vaults, and the corner stair turrets that run up the full length of the first storey of the tower. After Ulrich von Ensingen's death in 1419, the mason's lodge was put under the control of the Cologne mason Johannes Hultz. The pinnacle and spire, in the shape of a pyramid, were covered with fifty-six smaller towers. By drawing on a sequence of earlier, late medieval, towers, and condensing them into a strict geometrical regularity, the

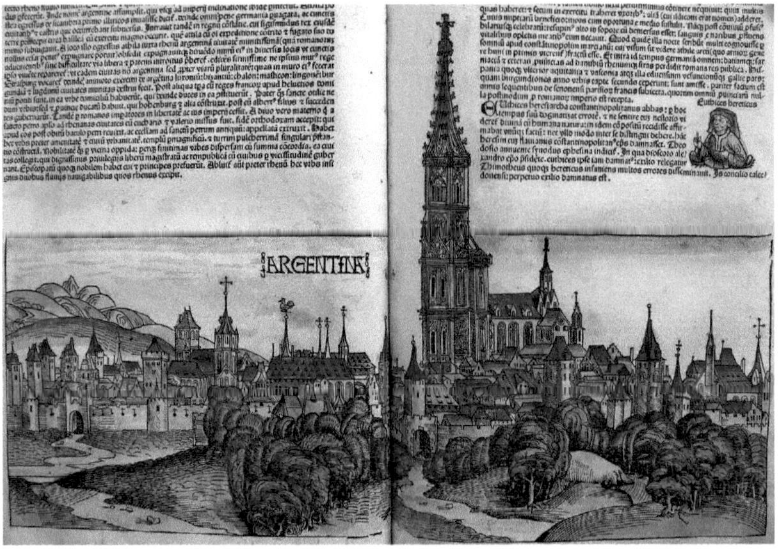

106

Strasbourg from Hartmann Schedel, *Liber chronicarum*, 1493

Rising high above the body of the church and projecting even into the block of the text, the spire of the Strasbourg's cathedral was the city's dominant feature in the woodcut for Schedel's *Nuremberg Chronicle*. This chronicle of the world combined religious history as a part of a comprehensive history played out in specific locations. Strasbourg is just one of the modern cities included alongside biblical sites. The interest in city views, of known and exotic locations, was part of a wider fascination in cosmography and geography.

masons at Strasbourg created a tower that is both a fitting completion to the church below and a sculptural object in its own right. The tower at Strasbourg was the tallest masonry structure of its time, and remained so for several hundred years.

Like the churches and public buildings they rose above, great spires were the ultimate sign of a local identity.[9] They marked the specificity of a place, identifying its uniqueness in an age increasingly fascinated by the knowledge of distant worlds.

Cleanliness

The experience of the early modern city engaged all the senses. Massive stones, rough to the touch, marked out the towers of the important family. Bells ringing from the local church measured out the day in the hours of prayer. Statues of the Virgin embraced by small shrines on many street corners reinforced the presence of the sacred in public space. Location, time of day, identity: these were all aspects of the city that residents understood with all of their senses.

Smell was one of the most profound experiences, and Alberti advised where artisans should be located within the city depending on the nature of their craft.

The charm of a city will be very much enhanced if the various workshops are allocated distinct and well-chosen zones. The silversmiths, painters, and jewellers should be on the forum, then next to them, spice shops, clothes shops, and, in short, all those that might be thought more respectable. Anything foul or offensive (especially the stinking tanners) should be kept well away in the outskirts to the north, as the wind rarely blows from that direction, and when it does, it gusts so strongly as to clear smells away, rather than carry them along. (Alberti, VII, 1, p. 192)

Early industries polluted the air, just as did the everyday waste products of human and animal habitation. Manure from the night was often emptied into the street, and could make just walking a dangerous proposition. But not all cities took this approach. When Leonardo Bruni praised Florence in his *Laudatio Florentinae urbis* (1404) he began with a lengthy description of the city's cleanliness. 'Now what is more marvellous in a populous city than never to have to worry about filth in the street?'[10] The streets had adequate drainage, Bruni goes on, and your feet never got wet, even after a great rainstorm. The streets and squares of Florence were equal to the rooms of great palaces in other cities, and the first evidence of the city's magnificence and importance. Bruni's account of Florentine sanitation was also a metaphor for a praiseworthy civic culture. Cleanliness is essential for urban harmony, Bruni states, and one part of the Florentine political system that brings all members of the society together for the greater good. Clean streets are also a sign for Bruni of the high standards of Florentine language, the norms of self-presentation of her citizens, and the cultural supremacy that Bruni felt defined Florentine citizens.

If Florence was praised for her cleanliness, other cities did not fare as well. The Venetian ambassador Francesco Guicciardini condemned Spain, writing that her cities are not only filled with ugly buildings, but also full of 'mud and filth' ('di fango e di bruttura').[11] Spanish cities may have been just as clean as those in Italy, and Guicciardini's comments may well therefore reflect more his dislike of the foreignness of Spanish culture and the different customs and appearances he found there. What is not familiar feels unclean, an assault upon the senses.

Political Theatre

In the warm climate of Italy, citizens spent a great deal of their time out of doors in the open piazzas or squares that served as the communal spaces for cities and towns. In any city of size, there might be several squares, some devoted more to markets, some connected with an adjoining church. In Florence, the Piazza della Signoria offered the citizens ample opportunity to gather in the shadow of the city's great town hall. The Palazzo della Signoria loomed over the square; her great rusticated stone façade and tower were a dominant presence of the civic authority and political force that shaped the life of Florence's citizens. In contrast to the dominant architecture, however, the square was inherently a less controlled arena where citizens

107

Loggia della Signoria, 1374–82, Florence

The covered space of the loggia offered an appropriately dignified location for the governing body of Florence, or the Signoria, to welcome visiting dignitaries and perform ceremonial functions.

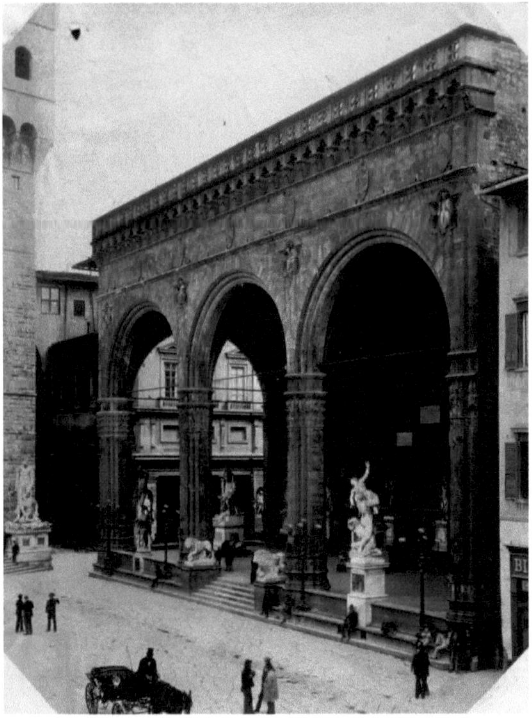

might meet. In the fourteenth and fifteenth centuries, the Florentine government was eager to show its increasing openness and even-handed treatment of its citizens. As with other moments of political change, these transformations appeared in aspects of the urban design. The construction of the Loggia della Signoria (1374–82) offered one such protected space within the square for the enactment of public ceremonies such as inaugurations and the reception of dignitaries [**107**].

Benches around the loggia offered citizens a place to sit and watch proceedings.[12] In the fifteenth century civic authorities also added three tiers of benches in the piazza itself, recalling the seating of both council halls and theatres. The seating in the Florentine piazza was the most extensive of any city on the Italian peninsula, perhaps reflecting the government's desire to make a public acknowledgment of the importance of this square in the political life of the city.

Loggias in Venice, Verona, and other cities in and outside Italy offered a discrete space that was both public yet semi-removed from the general space of the square. The Florentine government found that as the political mood shifted in the fifteenth and sixteenth centuries, the freedom of the piazza and the ability of the city's citizens to gather could also result in a very public display of dissent that could not easily be controlled.

108
Michelozzo di Bartolomeo, Palazzo Medici, 1444, Florence

The arches at the corner of the Palazzo Medici were originally open and offered a loggia onto the street. Michelangelo designed the windows that were added to the palace in the sixteenth century. Unlike many other palaces of the time, the Palazzo Medici does not have shops on the ground storey to provide additional income for the family to offset the cost of building or upkeep.

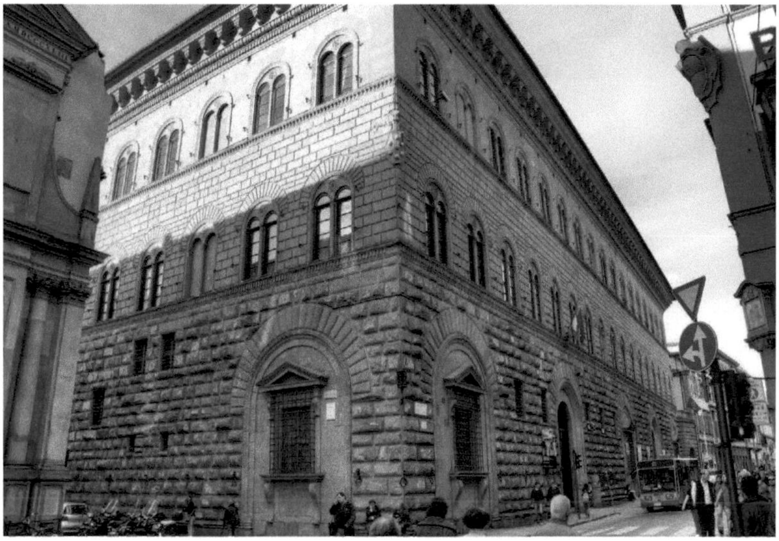

When the Medici created a new palace that would affirm their status within the political sphere of Florence, their architect Michelozzo di Bartolomeo (1396–1472) appropriated the language of public architecture [**108**]. Massive blocks of stone recall the rustication of the Palazzo della Signoria, and benches along the Via Larga created seating along the streets. The great innovation at the Medici Palace was Michelozzo's appropriation of aspects of civic architecture into a palace for a private family.

The Benefits of Luxury Trades

As cities came to take on an ever-greater role as the engines of economic wealth in the Renaissance, their prosperity often came from trade. Merchants increased in status as their financial power grew, and that income could then be used on the tangible signs of their status: clothing, household goods, civic patronage, religious endowments, and architecture. Soon after the French merchant Jacques Cœur was elevated to the ranks of the nobility in 1441, he began a series of architectural projects in his hometown of Bourges. In addition to the purchase of chateaux and the embellishment of churches, he began a great house that would also serve as the centre for his business [**109**].

Jacques Cœur made his wealth through trade, adding to the reputation of Bourges as a European centre of luxury goods.[13] At the height of his company's power, Cœur had six galleys that transported rugs from Persia, silk and porcelain from China, pearls from Ceylon, and spices from Sumatra. His knowledge of the Mediterranean, and

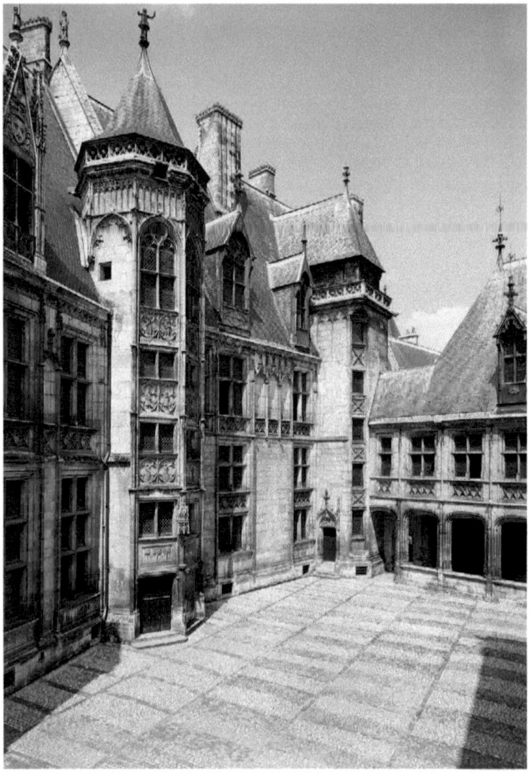

109

Courtyard, House of Jacques Cœur, 1443–51, Bourges, France

The tower with its blind arcades and tall dormer windows recalls a medieval chateau, including the castle of Mehun-sur-Yèvre (destroyed) that the Duc owned nearby. Staircases, in the tall narrow towers that project into the courtyard, connect the main public rooms on the ground storey, and the suites of personal chambers on the upper floors. Although the courtyard façade seems irregular, there is a careful alignment of the vertical elements in the window bays and in the horizontal mouldings that tie together each range of rooms.

personal wealth, encouraged King Charles VII to appoint him finance minister in 1434, adding further to his stature.

His house in Bourges was both innovative in plan and conservative in imagery.[14] The turrets, pinnacles, trefoil panelling, and irregular elevation recalled the late medieval chateaux of the area, especially those owned by Jean, Duc de Berry, the great noble of the previous generation. The aura of an ancient castle was consciously incorporated into Jacques Cœur's house, built in one concerted building campaign from 1443 to 1451. His economic resources allowed him to build such a grand house so quickly; even nobles with more status than money usually had to build bit by bit, giving their houses the piecemeal look that Jacques Cœur consciously built into his new house.

The house sits atop the ancient Gallo-Roman wall that encloses the city, and bends in the middle to follow the existing street. The entrance to the house, on the city side, is through a large double door under a canopy where a statue of the King once sat (now destroyed). On the upper storey of the square entrance block is the chapel marked off by a large window with Gothic stone tracery. The ornament, sequence of windows, and tower turrets all create a public face, which firmly connects Jacques Cœur to the architectural ancestry of local French nobility. Throughout the interior Cœur pays homage to the King by

110

Plan, House of Jacques Cœur

The house was built into the city walls of Bourges, seen to the left of the plan, along the west. The round towers are incorporated into the house plan, and the main rooms are placed along this curve of the wall and entered through the courtyard. Access to the rooms is from the stair turrets, along narrow passageways. The experience, therefore, of the house plays off surprise and controlled movement from place to place. The main entrance to the house, from the city and under the main tower, offers a wider passage for horses and a narrower door for foot traffic.

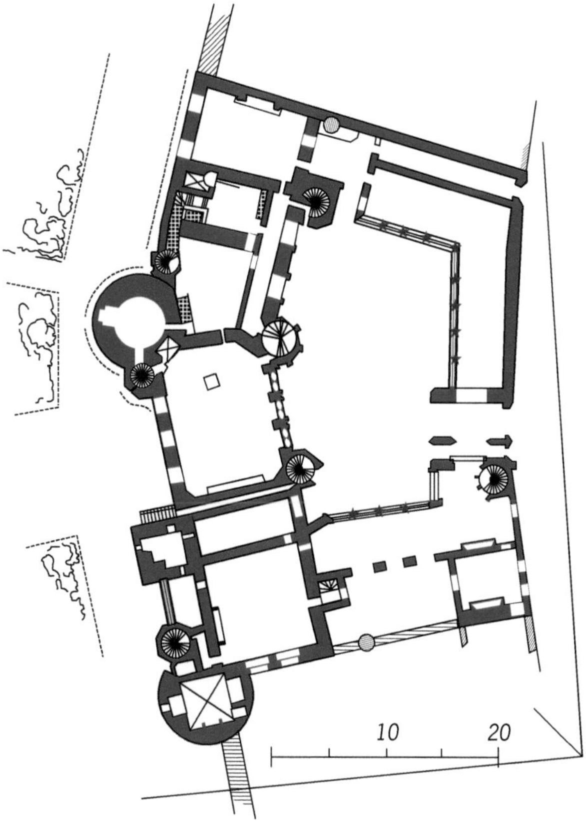

including elements from the royal coat of arms, including fleurs-de-lis and hearts. Equally prominent are the marks of Cœur himself, his wife, his agents, and close friends and family. In this way the house was a sign of political connections, family fealty, and economic resources.

Although the imagery of the palace recalled the great chateau of Jacques Cœur's predecessor, Jean, Duc de Berry, the plan and scheme of the palace included several innovations [**110**]. The galleries, which were usually just passages from one suite of rooms to the next, became prominent rooms in their own right. Cœur, and his masons, gave more attention to these transitional rooms in the house, adding elaborate vaulting and fireplaces, which in later French architecture would take on a major role as spaces appropriate for decoration and ritual. The private apartments were set at the back of the house and accessible only through a series of antechambers (*garde-robes*) and up half-hidden stairs and passageways, offering an additional separation of public and private spaces in an urban palace.

Jacques Cœur's profitable trade throughout Europe and the East provided the capital to finance his grand house in his hometown. For

111

Donato Bramante, Palazzo Caprini, 1510, Rome

This sketch, by an anonymous 16th-century draughtsman, shows the bold rustication of the ground floor and the Doric columns of the main level of the residence. Bramante's design established a new type of palace façade, rich and sculptural, using the orders and ornament to project an image of the owner. The ground floor included spaces for shops, framed by rusticated voussoirs, and storage in the mezzanines for the shopkeepers' goods. The palace was destroyed, and is known from drawings like this by architects who studied its design.

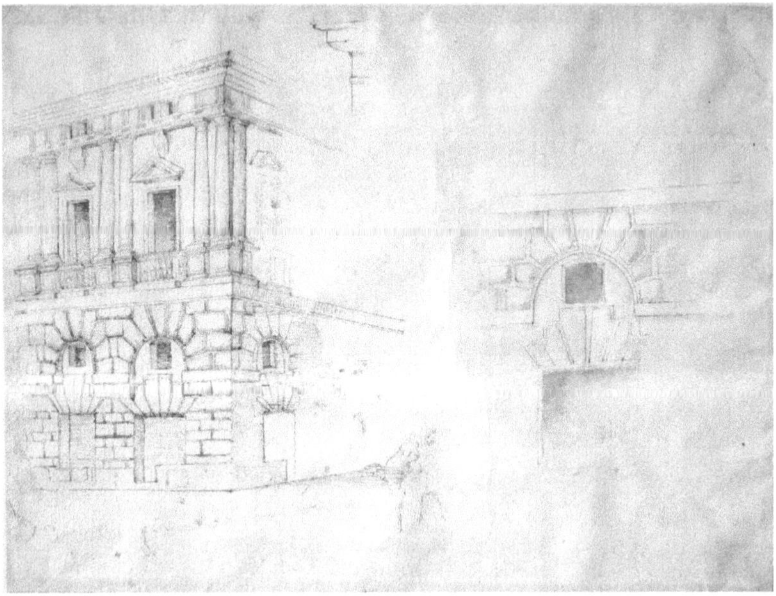

others, wishing to build grandly, their houses might have been financed through the lease of shops at street level. The Palazzo Caprini in Rome (completed 1510), designed by Donato Bramante for Adriano Caprini, the Bishop of Viterbo, incorporated an innovative design that used rustication on the ground floor and paired Doric columns for the residence level [**111**]. The palace, now destroyed and at one time the residence of the artist Raphael, sat on the busy via Alessandrina that led to St Peter's Basilica. Palaces in Italian cities often included shops when their location offered enough traffic to ensure a steady flow of business.[15] The lease from the shops supported the construction of the palace and ensured the family a steady income for its support.

Merchant Housing

The economist and sociologist Max Weber (1864–1920) observed that cities are mostly composed of the residences of their citizens.[16] Weber certainly wasn't thinking about the grand palaces that dominate by size though not in number. Most residences in the early modern city were those of the workers, merchants, and artisans. In all cities these houses varied greatly in size and comfort, though in each place they tended to follow local traditions [**112**]. The most important factor that determined their appearance was the available materials as well as locally established techniques and practices. These buildings reflected economic choices, but also the desire to identify with a place. Social and economic security grew out of the power of the group. Permission

112
Sebastiano Serlio, City dwellings for artisans in the Italian and French manner

This page from Serlio's book on domestic architecture shows houses for a 'better-off' artisan (the upper two examples) and those for a rich artisan or good merchant, below. On the left are houses appropriate for Italy, with smaller windows for the warm climate, hipped roofs, and loggia as a respite from the heat of the day. On the right are houses in the French manner, for colder and darker climates, with steep roofs and large windows.

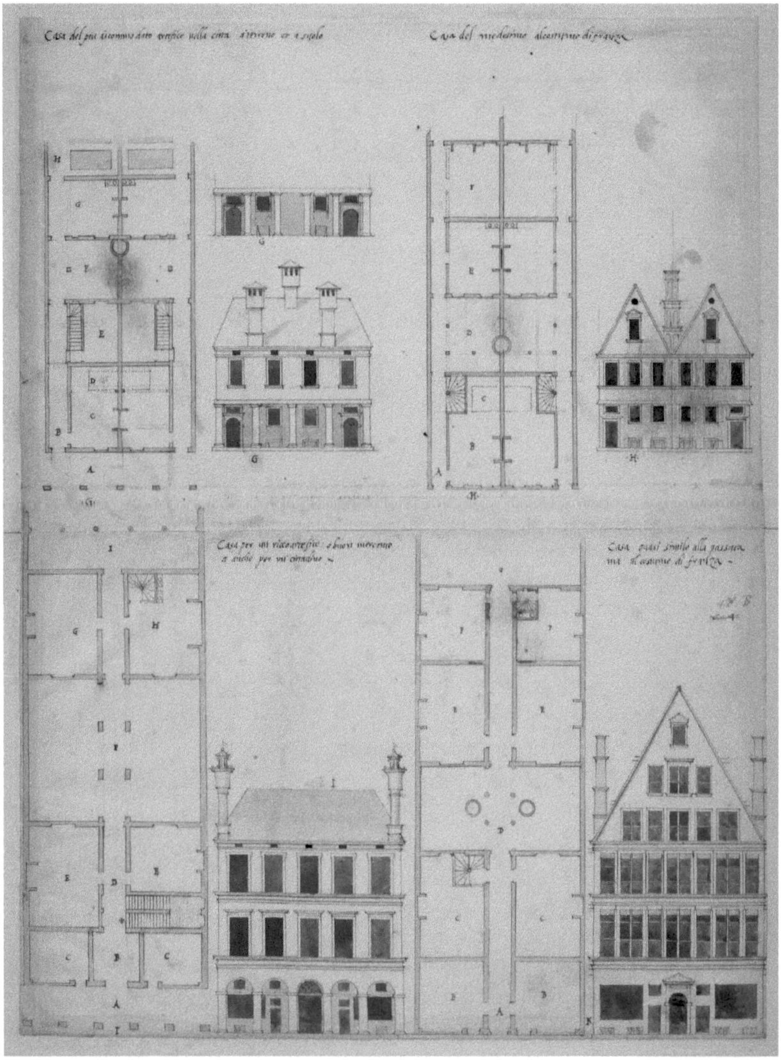

to work as a craftsman, for example, was contingent upon acceptance into the appropriate guild after years of training and loyalty to the group. That same sense of group identity was present in the choice of architecture that aligned, more or less, with the common practice in any city.

In Lower Saxony, for example, one is struck by the continuity of materials: many of the fifteenth- and sixteenth-century houses in that area of Germany are made using half-timbering, or *fachwerk*. Wood was easily available in the nearby Harz Mountain forests and local craftsmen developed expertise in transforming materials based on patrons' economic wherewithal and preferences. The Latin School in Alfeld, for example, is an elaborate example of the local type, built from wood but decorated with a highly elaborate series of images of the Christian

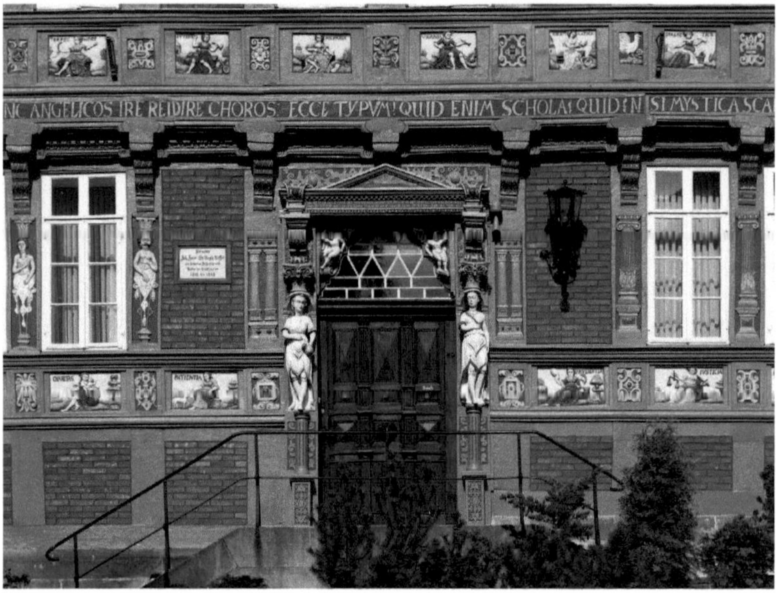

113
Latin School, 1610, Alfeld-an-der-Leine (Germany)

The *fachwerk* on this school building is combined with brick. On each level, the polychrome panels are carved with scenes that were meant to be instructive to the students: scenes of the virtues, arts, and senses along with evangelists and saints from the Bible and modern times. The inscription that runs in between the first and second floors refers to the story of Jacob's ladder (Genesis 28) but also asks for God's blessing on this school, built by the town but with the Church's support.

virtues. As with painted façades, common in Trento (Italy), for example, *fachwerk* allowed builders to easily incorporate figural imagery and text into the building's decoration [**113**]. Entire streets survive of *fachwerk* houses in Einbeck, especially along the Tiedexerstrasse, where most of the houses were made in the years around 1540–60. Wood, painted to emphasize the geometric carved patterns, allowed for variety on all levels of social and economic status.

Houses must be appropriate to their owners, according to Andrea Palladio in his architectural treatise *I quattro libri dell'architettura* (*The Four Books of Architecture*; Venice, 1570). Architects should take special care to build a house that is suitable (*commodo*) to the patrons, choosing the form and ornament that best represents the 'status of the person who will have to live in it and of which the parts will correspond to the whole and to each other'. Houses represent their owners in the public domain, and are therefore active agents in projecting their builders' wishes and desires. The power of architecture to shape public perception, building grandly to appear grand, is a dangerous proposition and one which the architect would do well to avoid yet may be powerless to stop. For as Palladio writes, 'the architect is frequently obliged to accommodate himself to the wishes of those who are paying rather than attending to what he should'.[17]

Meat and Fish

As cities grew in size and population, officials sought to control the display and sale of foodstuffs.[18] One concern was hygiene and cleanliness.

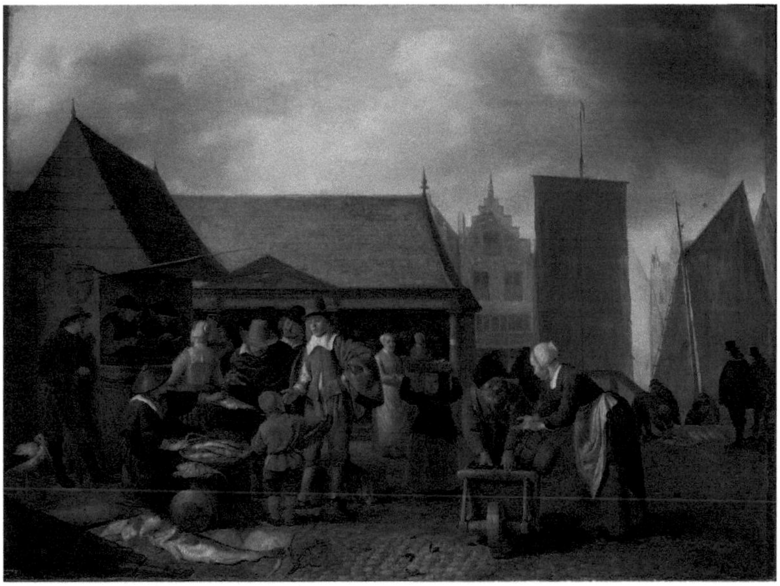

114

Hendrick Martensz. Sorgh, *De Vismarkt*, *c.*1650

Fish markets were often outside to minimize odours. Some cities even kept domesticated storks with clipped wings in order to clean the market spaces after they closed for the day. One stork can be seen at the far left in this painting of an open-air fish market.

The sale of fish in particular was organized into open areas, with limited days and times for the market to be in operation. In the Low Countries, where fish was an important staple of the diet of all social classes because of its ready availability, market areas were under open porticos or temporary stalls that could serve a large number of people and allow for easy cleaning after the market closed [**114**]. Markets for meat required a cool and dark location to preserve the freshness as long as possible. Butchers could slaughter the animals on their own property but the division of the meat into smaller, retail-size

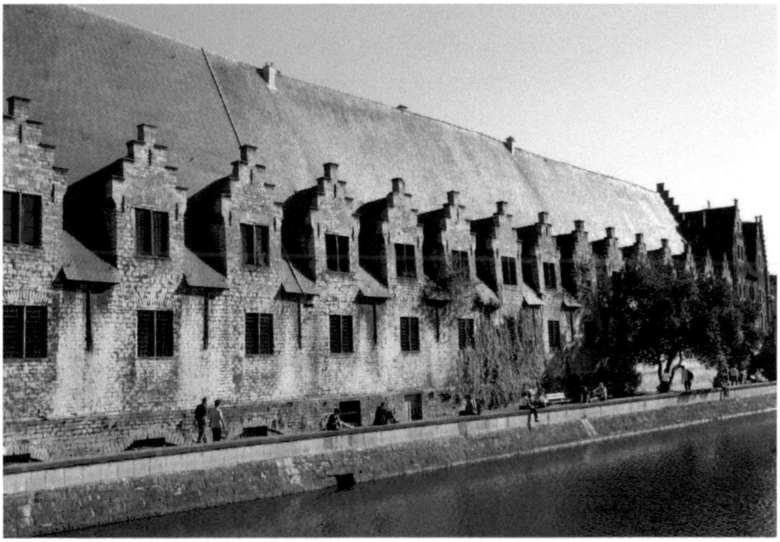

115

Groot Vleeshuis, 1409, Ghent

As guilds and towns sought to regulate trade, they built large and prominent halls. The control of foodstuffs was especially important, given their role in the peaceful functioning of the city.

portions had to be done under the control of the butcher guild and in a centralized place. Butchers could rent a board in the meat hall, where only beef or mutton were sold. Pig was considered unclean and sold elsewhere. Meat halls in the Low Countries were often part of a multifunctional guildhall, as in Bruges where the vast Halle was an economic centre for a variety of civic and merchant purposes.

The availability of high-quality meat was an important marker of a prosperous city, however, and buildings devoted to that purpose testified to the prestige of a city and its people. The Groot Vleeshuis (Great Meat Hall) in Ghent was begun in 1409, one of the several new guild houses built during this period [**115**]. Its central location, stone façade, and great open wooden hall all marked its civic and economic status in the city.[19]

Regulating Trade

Uncontrolled trade could threaten the authority of a city. In major ports like Venice, Antwerp, London, Gdańsk, and Dubrovnik, urban authorities sought to regulate trade to ensure a fair and orderly market. New buildings were designed to oversee trade by collecting tariffs, regulating goods, and ensuring standard weights and measures.

Dubrovnik's political independence, political stability, and strategic location promoted its role as an important trading centre in the Adriatic.[20] In 1516, the Senate there accepted the design by Paskoje Miličević for a new customs house. The rectangular building included galleries around the interior courtyard, recalling the ***fondouks*** of Ottoman architecture, one of their major trading partners [**116**].[21] Around the central open space were offices for the collection of duties for goods transported through the city as well as the mint, treasury, and weigh hall that verified standard units of measurement for the Republic. This centralized all these activities in one civic building, prominently located within the city and with an elaborately decorated façade onto the square.

As with many buildings in Dubrovnik, Miličević combined Gothic and classical ornament in the design of the Divona Palace. Round-headed arches resting on composite columns formed the loggia on the ground storey, but the windows on the ***piano nobile*** had pointed arches with **quatrefoil** tracery in the central, three-light opening. The upper storey had square-headed windows with a pedimented **aedicule** holding a statue of St Blaise, the patron saint of the city.[22]

Ghetto Nuovo

As goods came in and went out of the city, they travelled with their agents, the merchants, ambassadors, pilgrims, and soldiers from places

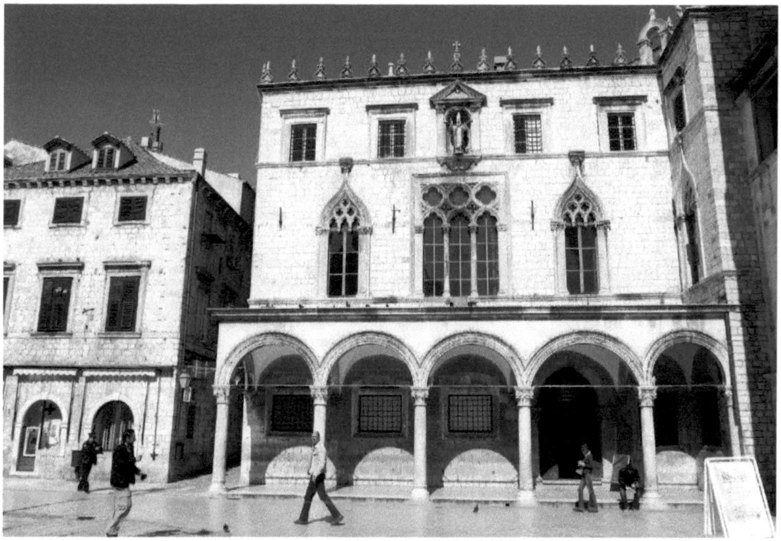

116

Paskoje Miličević and Nikola and Josip Andrijić, Sponza Palace, 1516–21, Dubrovnik, Croatia

At the centre of the city, the Sponza Palace served as the customs house, and an inscription on an inner courtyard attests to the accuracy of the city's measurements ('Our weights do not permit cheating or being cheated. When I measure goods the Lord measures with me'). Stylistically, the palace is a combination of Venetian Gothic designs, in the windows of the second floor, and classical forms in the ground-floor loggia and upper storey. This combination was typical in Croatia, as in many places throughout Europe, and spoke to the varied international community present in this important city.

as close by as the world outside the walls and as distant as the other side of the earth. The density of the early modern city placed these diverse people side by side with the more permanent residents and fellow travellers. As in modern times, to speak of the inhabitants of Paris one must include not only native 'Parisians' but also all those who were in Paris for a brief or lengthy visit [**117**].[23]

Inevitably, the close proximity was at times uneasy as much as it was inevitable. In the twelfth century, the Catholic Church had decreed that Jews should live alongside Christians, although in practice few local authorities made legislation that enforced that ruling. Specific circumstances, however, forced governments to act. When the War of the League of Cambrai threatened Jews who were living on the mainland of the Veneto, they fled to the city of Venice to seek refuge. In 1516 the Senate required them to live together, on a separate island, called the *Ghetto Nuovo*. The term *ghetto*, which came to be more widely used, referred specifically to the nearby copper foundry (*gettare* means to pour or cast). Yet the reality of a specific, restrictive area where Jews were required to live was expanded in the wake of the Counter-Reformation.[24]

The sense that Jews were imprisoned, under surveillance, is confirmed by the description of the ghetto by Zaccaria Dolfin in 1515:

Send them all to live in the Ghetto Nuovo which is like a castle, and to make drawbridges and close it with a wall; they should have only one gate, which would enclose them there and they would stay there, and two boats of the Council of Ten would go and stay there at night, at their expense, for their greater security.[25]

117

Houses of foreign merchants, Bruges, from A. Sanderus, *Flandria illustrata*, 1641

Foreign merchants were usually well organized, seeking connections with local religious groups or civic organizations in order to facilitate their trading activities. Bruges was one of the most important trading cities in the north, and merchants from Italy, Spain and Portugal, England and France, Germany, Turkey, and Armenia all operated there. While many foreign traders stayed in inns, some nations had designated houses, such as these facing onto the central bourse, or market. The two houses marked out here belonged to the delegations from Genoa and Florence.

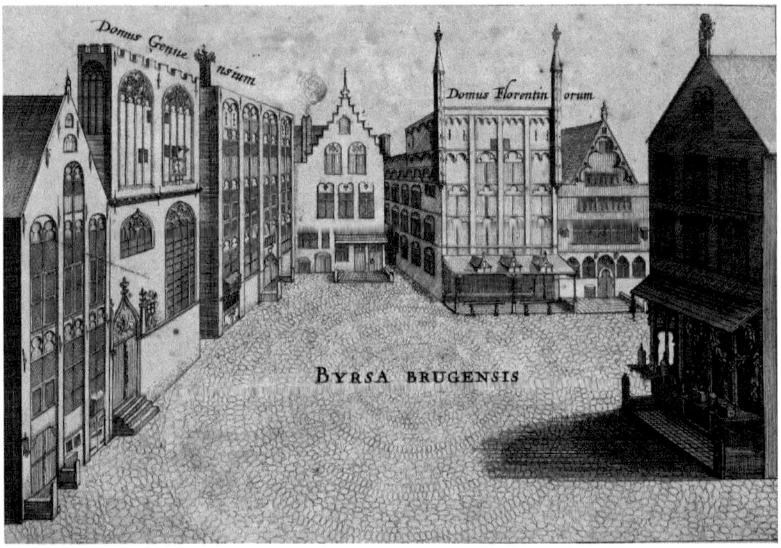

In Venice about 700 Jews were moved into the *Ghetto* in 1516, enclosed on the island by drawbridges, and restricted from leaving the area at night. Windows facing out from the island were shut up, and balconies on the exterior side of houses removed.

Urban Interventions

In his treatise, Filarete describes Sforzinda, an ideal city laid out within strict geometrical lines and designed for Francesco Sforza, the lord of Milan. Each aspect of city function was represented in the design, including churches, royal palaces, markets, and merchants' shops. The design represented a tenuous balancing of civic and political powers, each given a precise designation within the urban landscape. Filarete's scheme laid out the problem of urban design that would occupy theorists and builders into the modern age: how to reconcile urban experience with the possibility of urban reform. Ideal urban schemes appear in numerous architectural writings throughout the sixteenth century. The absolute quality of Sforzinda and the geometrical exercises by Francesco di Giorgio would eventually inspire a burgeoning industry in the design of cities that incorporate the latest in defensible design and military architecture [**118**].

Few new cities were built in the fifteenth or sixteenth century. Yet the desire to improve existing cities did take place. The older, medieval part of Ferrara stretches along the banks of the Po River in northern Italy. Ferrara was a court city, ruled by the Este family. The city reached a political and artistic height in the fifteenth century, expanding its residences in the Palazzo del Corte (begun 1242) and the

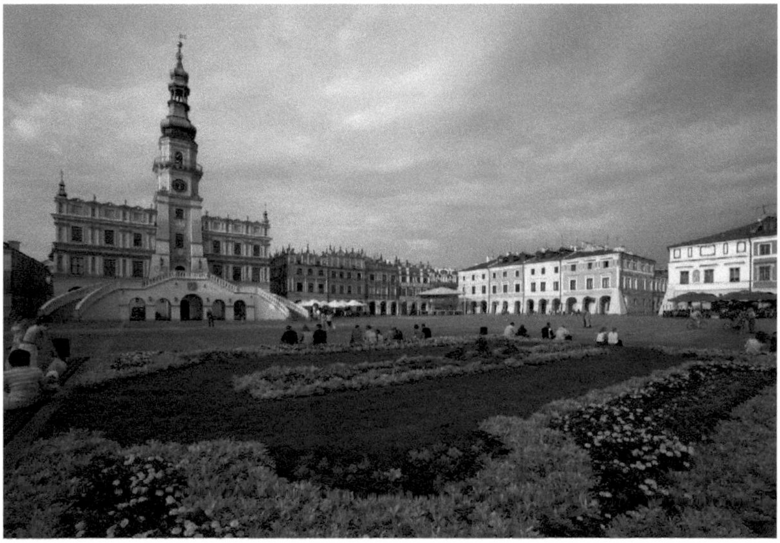

118

Zamosc, founded 1580, Poland

Located on the important trade route between L'viv and Lublin, Zamosc was intended to capitalize on the movement of goods and people through the eastern regions of the Polish empire. Jan Zamoyski (1542–1605) engaged the Italian architect Bernardo Morando in developing the design, based on city plans known in treatises and widely recognized as optimal plans for defence and commerce. As Royal Secretary and Chancellor, Zamoyski envisioned the new city as a benefit to the King and a personal triumph in honouring his own name and reputation. The grid of streets extended out from the central square (planned to be 100 m × 100 m), all protected with the latest developments in fortifications.

moated castle in the city centre. It was the city itself, however, that received the most important additions by the Este. Borso d'Este (1413–71) enclosed open land to the east, along the river, in 1451. His brother Duke Ercole I (1435–1505, reg. 1471–1505) transformed Ferrara beginning in 1492 by more than doubling its area, adding new walls designed to resist the latest in military attacks [**119**]. Streets were added across the enclosed lands that extended the medieval city to the edge of the walls. The Este castle, originally on the northern boundary, was now in the centre of the city and streets were planned to radiate out from its place in the realigned urban fabric. The Corso Ercole I, running north from the castle, and the Corso Porta

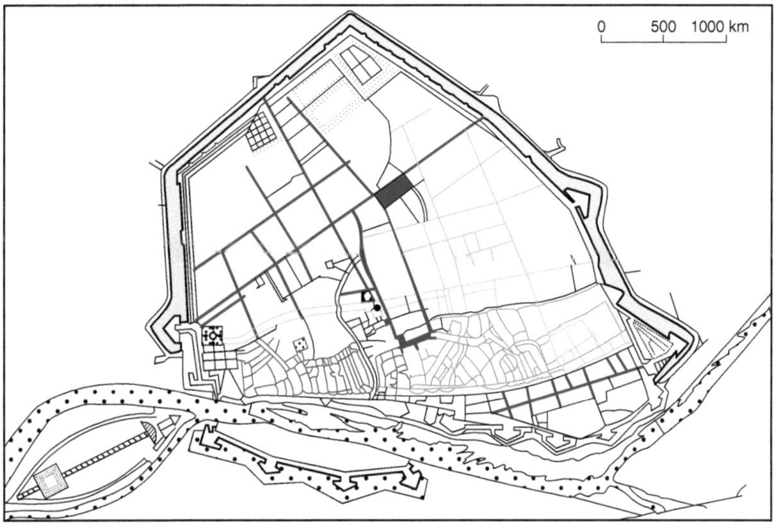

119

Plan, Ercole additions, Ferrara

The darker lines show the additions to Ferrara by Borso d'Este in 1451 (to the lower right, along the river) and by Ercole d'Este (beginning in 1492) to the north. Ercole's additions included major streets that linked up with the existing roads, and extended the residential quarters of the city to the new city walls.

Po met at almost right angles. Ercole, in consultation with his architect, Biagio Rossetti (1447–1516), included a new open space just to the east. The Piazza Nuova (now Piazza Ariostea) created a new urban focus in the 'addition' around which new houses would be built and public space given over to markets and shops.

Visually, the Addizione Ercole achieves much of its effect because of the contrast with the earlier part of the city [**120**]. The wide, open streets of the new section give an uninterrupted vista out to the walls, making the city seem even larger than it is. Movement feels unimpeded and nearly aristocratic. Walking through this part of the city has the aura of a procession, as if the princely characteristics of court life were extruded out into the public sphere.

The new architecture continued Ferrarese building traditions. Brick was the dominant material for the two- to three-storey houses. Ornament was mostly moulded terracotta friezes. The colour of the city overall, therefore, is a warm red-brown, repeated in the small-scale buildings and used throughout in the consistent pattern of decoration. Rossetti embraced the dominant local style in planning the 'addition', using that vernacular building practice as the backdrop against which

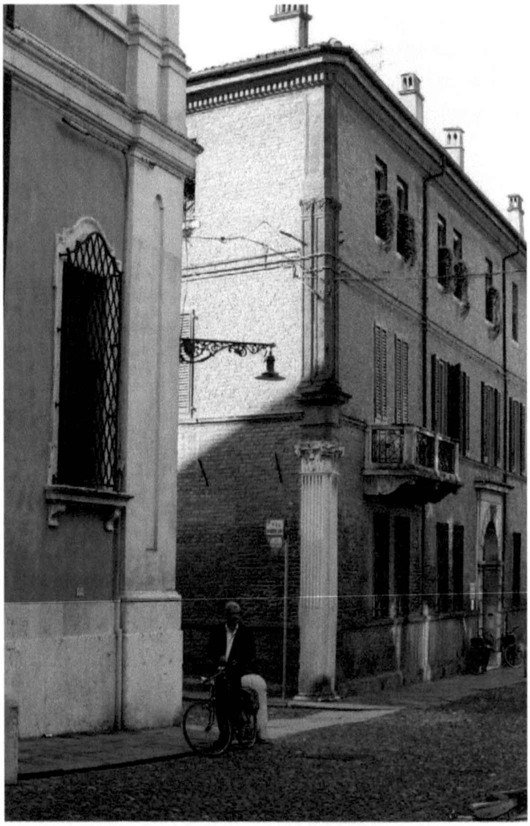

120

Corso Ercole I, 1492, Ferrara

This main street moves out into the new sections of the city from the d'Este castle. Although most buildings are brick and terracotta, the architect Biagio Rossetti included finely carved marble pilasters at important intersections. These white, refined details are elegant moments in the streetscape, and tie the disparate buildings together, creating a common language which is based on local precedent and classical architectural forms.

to craft a new urban language of accent and emphasis. At the intersection of minor streets, for example, are white Istrian stone pilasters, with classical flutings and capitals at street level. As a practical matter, the stone pilasters protected the more fragile brick from damage from carts. As part of the urban experience, however, the white stone serves as a form of punctuation in the long straight streets. They mark out the edges of the urban grid, relieving the repetition of the brick façades, and add a dignity to the city that was to embody the refinement of the Este court.

Along with the new square, churches, and the wall embracing the subsumed land, important palaces were planned in significant places. Four related palaces were to have been placed at the major road junction. Only the Palazzo Diamanti was completed to any extent [**121**]. In stone, not brick, the faceted masonry blocks recall glittering gemstones as much as they do fortified military architecture. Classical grotesque images on the corner pilasters on both levels of the palace, and the projecting balcony, all address the palaces on the other three corners of the intersection that were planned but only ever partially completed.

Much of the urban 'addition' in Ferrara remained empty at the end of the sixteenth century. Not all streets had been built out to the plan enacted by Ercole d'Este and his architect. In contrast to the urban schemes of Filarate and Francesco di Giorgio, Ferrara was planned as a flexible and open-ended solution to a specific urban condition. It derived from existing building traditions, amplified and

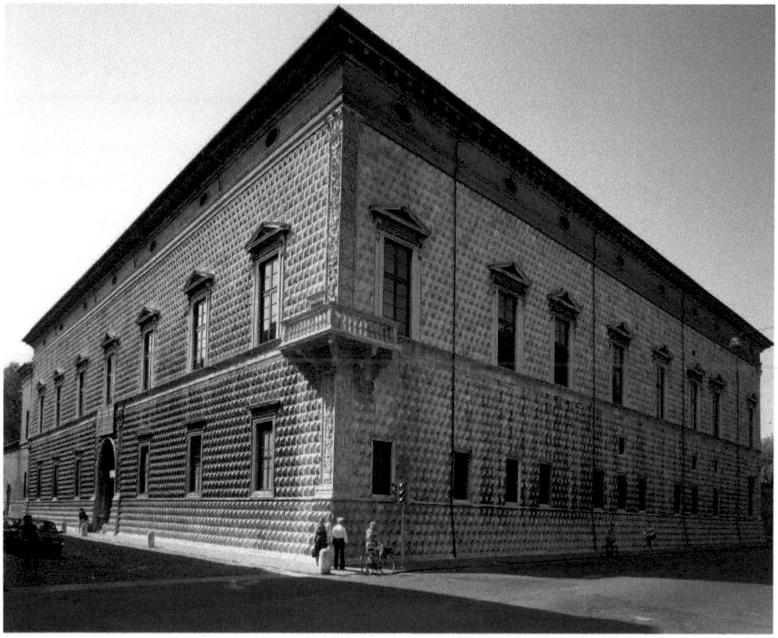

121

Biagio Rossetti, Palazzo Diamanti, begun 1493, Ferrara

Built for Sigismondo d'Este, the Palazzo Diamanti was intended to work with palaces on the other corners in order to mark this important intersection within the city. The faceted stonework and delicately carved corner pilasters, and even the overhanging balcony on the upper floor, all contribute to the scenographic effect on the street.

reinvented in order to create a new city built on the principles of existing practice.

Genoa and the Strada Nuova

In sixteenth-century Genoa, on the Ligurian coast, a group of old patrician families put away their long standing rivalries, and joined together to develop a street of palaces.[26] Genoa was a famously feudal city-state, with each of the major families holding onto areas within the walls, marked out by towers and palace groups. In the late Middle Ages, new noble families and middle-class merchants had challenged the political power of the more established families. Under the leadership of Andrea Doria (1466–1560), the older families once again asserted their dominance in the city. Their decision to create a new residential enclave of palaces presented a unified front in architectural terms [**122**].

They petitioned the Senate of the Republic to clear land for a monumental street on the north edge of the city. The location was significant. High on the Valletta di Soziglia, directly over the port, the

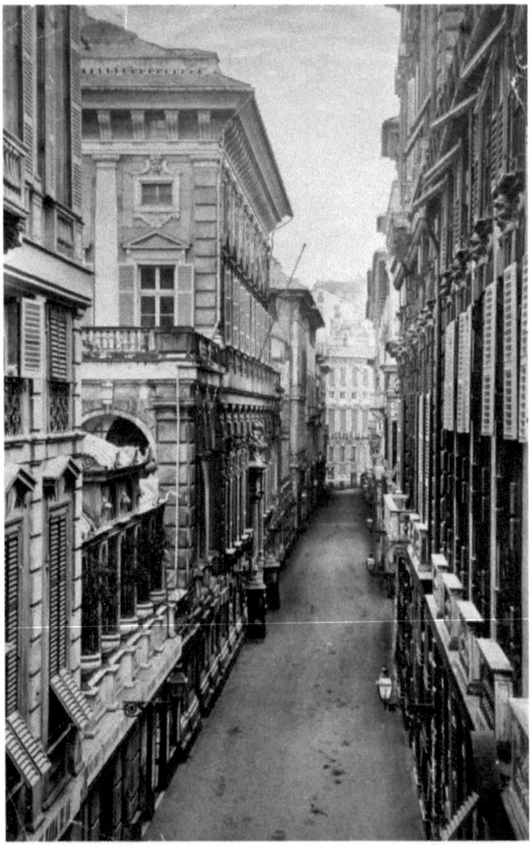

122
Strada Nuova, 1550–8, Genoa

The transformation of the Castelletto, an area of Genoa with important historical significance, gentrified a disreputable part of the city into a fashionable urban enclave. The regular street is lined with palaces, several by Galeazzo Alessi (Perugia, 1512–72), whose restrained designs captured the sentiments of his prominent patrons.

Castelletto area was visible throughout the city. It was also the site of a ruined twelfth-century fortress that was associated for the Genoese with domination by French troops, overthrown by a revolt led by Andrea Doria in September 1528. A new street, planned and occupied by the ancient families of Genoa, was to be a political statement of the city's liberty and independence. By the middle of the sixteenth century, a street lined with classical palaces, all of a type, was also understood by its patrons to be a type of urban stage, a theatre on which to enact their own sense of seniority and ancestry. Ideal city views, sometimes presented as stage sets as in Sebastiano Serlio's *L'architettura*, equated scenery appropriate for different types of theatre with varying architectural styles [**123**]. Classical architecture was tied to tragic drama that made for 'great personages'. Originally the Strada Nuova was a closed-off street, reinforcing the residents' desire to create a distinct neighbourhood, a district for the city's nobility. From the moment they were completed, the palaces along the street served as the setting for both private opulence and public ceremony. Architects responsible for the individual palaces looked back to traditional, medieval Genovese palace types, adapting them within a very narrow band of variety. While individual differences are clear in each palace, they used a similar vocabulary of classical ornament and layout that identify them with local traditions. In the seventeenth century, urban entrepreneurs and princes would go on to shape the city by developing areas for particular social groups, as in Paris at the Place Royale for the French aristocracy (1612) and in London at Covent Garden for merchants and rural gentry (1630s).

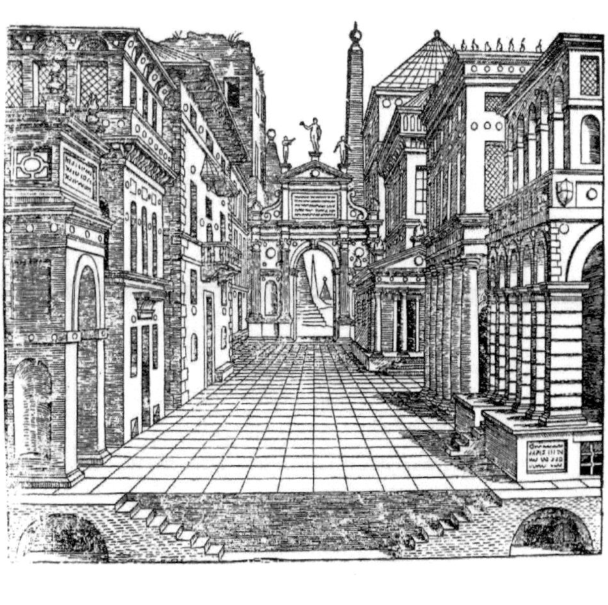

123

Sebastiano Serlio, Tragic Stage Set, from his *De perspective: Il secondo libro di prospettiva*, Paris, 1545

The ancient Roman writer Vitruvius had described three different types of stage sets: comic, tragic, and satiric. Serlio included illustrations of these in his book on perspective. Serlio's teacher, Baldessare Peruzzi (1481–1536), created stage sets for festivals in Rome, recorded in his drawings. In the Tragic Stage Set, Serlio shows a street in perspective lined with a variety of classical buildings. Obelisks and gates like triumphal arches further define the space. If architecture modelled on antiquity was appropriate for historic drama, it was also thought to be fitting for noble patrons and heads of state.

Clean, Fresh Water

All cities needed a regular supply of clean water. Their growth was dependent upon it. If the supply to the cities was destroyed, as happened in Rome when Goths attacked the aqueduct system in 537, the populace could not survive. Businesses such as tanneries and potteries required a steady supply of water for their production. And the cleanliness and sanitation of the city depended upon water for washing and waste removal. For a millennium, from 537 until the middle of the sixteenth century, Romans used the Tiber River as the major source of water. But the river flooded regularly, and was overused and subsequently seriously polluted. A few natural springs provided better drinking water but most of the fountains and collecting pools in the city had been destroyed by centuries of neglect and war.

The restoration of Rome to her former glory of antiquity required the restoration of the water supply. Pope Pius V (reg. 1566–72) continued the renovation begun by Pope Nicholas V in 1453 of the aqueduct called the Aqua Virgo (now called the Acqua Vergine) in 1570 to bring water to the Campus Martius in the centre of the city. He established the *Congregazione cardinilizia super viis pontibus fontibus*, the Congregation of cardinals in charge of streets, bridges, and fountains, to supervise the enormous project, with the city architect, Giacomo della Porta, as technical adviser.[27]

The restoration of the Acqua Felice (in ancient times called the Aqua Alessandrina, restored in 1587) and the Acqua Paola (1612) brought water to the hills of the city, and supported the rapid urban growth sought by the Vatican as part of its programme to consolidate power in Rome. Water moved from the springs in the Roman countryside along the raised stone aqueducts, a marvel of engineering. From the hills the water flowed into fountains that were built or restored as central distribution points [**124**]. Water was a commodity in the city, as important as food, and more difficult to provide in sufficient measure. If in Rome the popes initiated the restoration of the ancient aqueduct system, this also stimulated economic entrepreneurship further down the economic ladder. Watersellers, in Italy called *acquaroli*, were licensed to collect water from the newly built fountains to sell door to door.

The availability of water in Rome spearheaded urban development. Pope Sixtus V followed the restoration of the aqueducts with the establishment of new thoroughfares throughout Rome. The Via Felice, opened in 1585, linked the church of Sta Maria Maggiore with the church of Trinitá dei Monti, and marked the important intersections of streets with obelisks. This was just one of a series of new routes through the city that created a practical and visual order in the urban landscape.

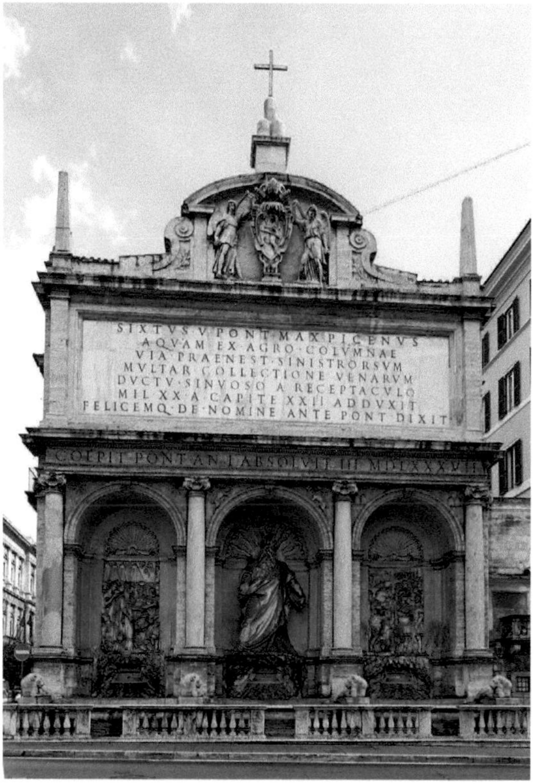

124
Domenico Fontana, Fontana dell'Acqua Felice, 1587, Rome

As papal architect to Sixtus V, Fontana took on the full range of urban projects including work at the Vatican and throughout the city of Rome. The extraordinary feat of moving obelisks to mark new street junctures and the piazza in front of St Peter's was recorded in Fontana's books *Della trasportatione dell'obelisco vaticano* (1590 and 1604). Equally important in his career, however, were his works in consolidating the urban infrastructure of Rome, encouraging new residents to reside in less desirable areas and setting out what would become the modern city.

Abundant, pure water was a sign of a city's prosperity and greatness; and rulers understood the public and personal benefits of promoting urban infrastructure projects. In the epic poem *The Lusiad* (1572), the Portuguese poet Luís de Camões (*c.*1524–1580) praised the Água de Prata (Aqueduct of Silver Water) in Évora for 'Two hundred arches, stretch'd in length, sustain | The marble duct, where, glist'ning to the sun, | Of silver hue the shining waters run' (Bk. III). The aqueduct in Évora was ancient in origin, built when Rome founded the city, and just one of several important Roman monuments that testified to the city's ancient and noble past. King João III restored the aqueduct in 1531–7, employing the military architect Francisco de Arruda who had built the Belém Tower at the mouth of the Tagus River, at the entrance to the harbour in Lisbon, and near to the Monastery of the Jerónimos [**92, 93, 145, 148**].

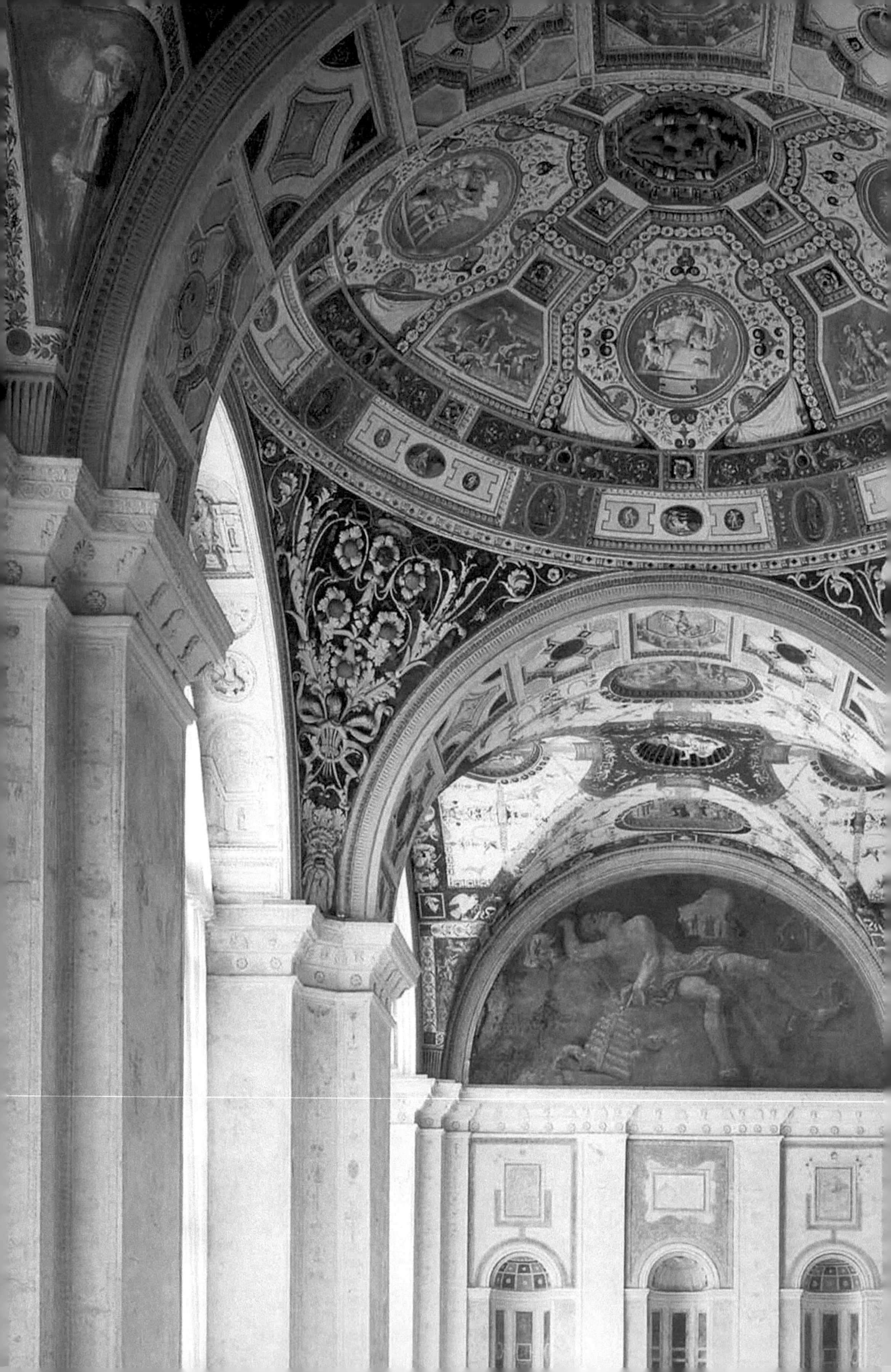

Architecture in the Natural World

7

Who would want to live anywhere out of the country? Here we have complete peace, real freedom, tranquil security and sweet repose. We can enjoy pure air, shady trees with their abundant fruit, clear water, lovely valleys; we can make use of the fertile farmland and the productive vines, as well as appreciating the mountains and hills for the view, the woods for their charm, the fields for their spaciousness and the gardens for their beauty.

Another source of enjoyment is being able to watch the hard work of the farmers and the obedience of their teams, as they skilfully plow and sow the fields, and then the crops growing well and being harvested; and also to hear the songs of the peasants, the pipes of the shepherds, the rustic bagpipes of the cowherds, and the sweet singing of the birds.

(Agostino Gallo, *A discussion between the noble gentlemen Messer Giovanni Battista Avogadro and Messer Cornelio Duccio in the month of May 1553 on the delights of the villa and how it is better to reside there than in the city* (Venice, 1566))[1]

For the Renaissance patron, building in the country satisfied multiple desires. A significant house established land ownership and projected a seigneurial presence in the region. Landownership provided financial security, escape from the health risks of the city, political advantage, and the pleasure of nature. Life in the country offers pleasures in every domain, says Messer Avogadro: clean air, fertile agriculture, beautiful sights, and the labouring peasantry.

Rural residences usually consisted of a number of buildings, some for the habitation of the owners, others for animals and the storage of equipment, others for the collection of the agricultural products that provided wealth to the patron and employment to his labourers. If the countryside was rich with wildlife, life in the country offered the pleasures of hunting and an escape from the demands of city living. With a great house and fertile land, the owner could entertain for the pleasure of their company and the possibility of political profit if the guests were members of the royal court or powerful families.

Detail of 134

As a building type, the country house responded to the social, political, and economic changes in the fifteenth and sixteenth centuries. If protection was no longer as central a concern with the end to some local struggles, then houses could open to the landscape with larger windows and fewer of the defensive moats and walls needed in an earlier time. Yet, traces of architectural elements such as towers continued to be popular elements of even newly built houses as a sign of a noble past and family ancestry.

If the fortified house or castle was one precedent for country houses the agricultural farm offered a local model. Simple rural houses were often cubic in shape and enlarged or rebuilt as the needs of the owners changed. These types of buildings changed slowly, often imperceptibly, over many centuries. Their construction and appearance evolved out of local circumstance, and availability of regional materials. This core of building tradition coexisted with other aspects of rural crafts and meshed with the rural economy of production and use. Builders and craftsmen were often the owners themselves. The continuity of rural building tradition, on the one hand, resisted change when none was needed or expected. When patrons and architects had the financial resources and the desire to build afresh, building in the country offered the opportunity to innovate in ways that urban density did not allow.[2]

Perhaps the most significant change in the history of the country house was the increasing desire by owners of property to live there. As Agostino Gallo writes in the passage that began this chapter, rural life could be filled with pleasurable activities that the city did not offer. Part literary fantasy, part cultural shift, the ideology of the country life captured the contemporary interest in the natural world and the pleasures of leisure. The specific look of rural houses, and the activities that took place there, varied based on local traditions, conditions, and especially the climate. In Scotland, leisure pursuits tended to involve much more activity to counter the cold than in the hot climates of Spain or Italy.[3]

There is in the fifteenth and sixteenth centuries a new attitude toward life in the country. The creation of a Renaissance villa ideology, or set of beliefs about the pleasures and benefits of country living, shaped the perception of even the most traditional of structures. Building in the country was as old as architecture itself, and Vitruvius says that architecture began when people huddled by a fire and built shelters [**125**]. Rural life continued in the same ways as it had essentially before, yet as with the urban palace, Renaissance patrons and architects believed that architecture could project the ideals and aspirations of the owners. The country house was an extension of the individual and the family out into the world.

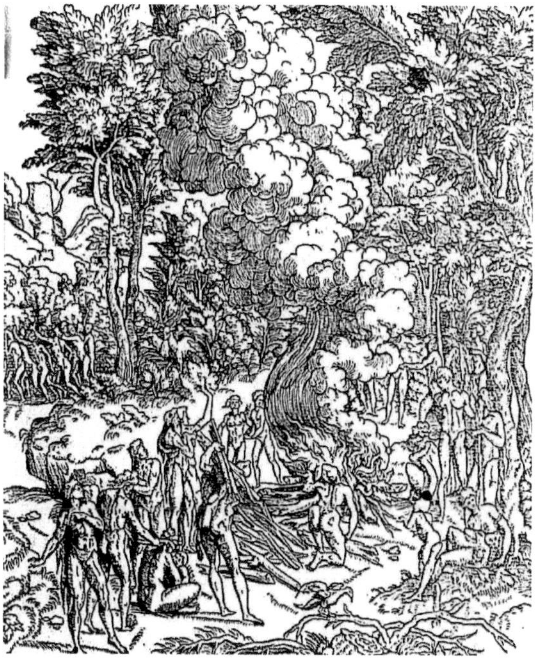

125
Vitruvius, origins of building from Jean Martin, *Architecture, ou Art de bien bastir de Marc Vitruve Pollion Autheur* (Paris, 1547)

Jean Martin (d. 1553) translated the *Hypnerotomachia Poliphili* (1499) and the treatises of Sebastiano Serlio, Leon Battista Alberti, and Vitruvius into French. Singlehandedly, he made the seminal works of architectural classicism available to a wide audience in France. Many interested in ancient culture and humanist learning praised Martin's careful and scholarly translations. In the second half of the sixteenth century, however, others, including Philibert de l'Orme, argued for a more national style, derived from French precedents and attuned to native forms. The sculptor Jean Goujon provided many of the illustrations to Martin's text, freely interpreting the text in order to provide a more pictorial commentary on Vitruvius' work.

Protection and the Castle

At the start of the fifteenth century, country houses for nobles were geared toward protecting the owners and an extended household, and establishing claims to property and agricultural land. The medieval houses of the ruling classes were primarily designed as places of protection that established their authority over the land. Within feudal society landowners needed to protect their family, dependants, and property from the attack of other landowners seeking to expand their holding, or the invasions of foreign powers. Thus the early history of castles, up to the fifteenth century, is directly connected with the history of feudalism that bound vassals to their lords through primarily military service. As the residence for the lords, castles were the locus of their power and prestige. The defensive quality of castles in the medieval era was a fundamental aspect to their design, but they were also private residences of the lord.

The fifteenth century marks a turning point in the history of rural building as patrons became increasingly interested in the comforts of their life as well as the protection of their assets. When Sir Edward Dalyngrigge built Bodiam Castle (East Sussex, England, 1386–8) he had returned from fighting in the Hundred Years War against France [**126**]. Many of the features of Bodiam Castle reflected his experience in France such as the towers which recall the French donjon, or castle house.

126
Bodiam Castle, 1386–8, Sussex, England

By the end of the 14th century, fortified castles already evoked a military past that was no longer relevant. Bodiam Castle still has all the elements of a true fortified house in the towers and protective moat. Yet the attention to a powerful and unforgettable visual effect was equally important in its design and construction.

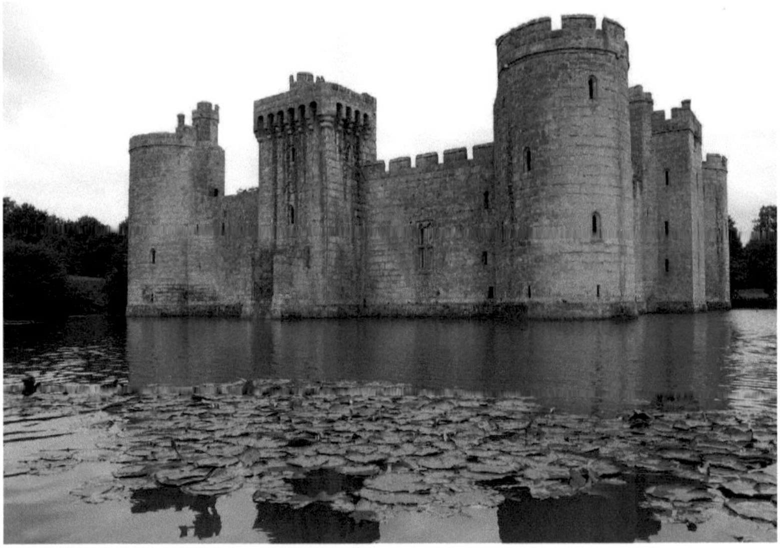

The square castle, impressively high, sited in the middle of a protective moat, makes any assault on the building more difficult while also amplifying the size and importance of the building against the gentle landscape of Sussex. A single road leads to the entrance gate, and controls access to the castle's interior. A rhythm of round corner towers, bastion walls, and rectangular towers is reminiscent of the great walls surrounding many cities, including the medieval walls around Constantinople or even London.

Dalyngrigge received permission 'to crenellate' his house from King Richard II, that is, to add the symbolic and functional battlements along the roofline in order that the castle might serve 'in defense of the adjacent country and for resistance against our enemies'. Like earlier medieval castles, the towers tie this building in with the tradition of tower houses used as protective fortresses by individual families in the English countryside. Dalyngrigge incorporated many of the latest inventions in defensive architecture used by other patrons, and developed during the long period of war in the previous century.

Bodiam was a city unto itself, and was intended to accommodate the large company of family and friends that made up the extended household. Dalyngrigge gave special attention to his own accommodations and those of his servants and retainers. Separate suites of rooms were included for men of standing and class, as well as the service rooms across from the gatehouse needed to feed and entertain the flow of people in the castle. Kitchen, pantry, and buttery served the needs of the hall in the towers and gatehouses. Landowners were required to provide appropriate levels of hospitality for important visitors to the castles as well as the families who worked the lands attached to the castle.

Dalyngrigge built Bodiam to satisfy his desire for a house that would reflect his status and serve his social and political needs after his retirement from war. The need for protection went hand in hand with the desire to appear fortified (through features such as a tall profile, multiple towers, crenellations along the wall, and the moat), which served both to reinforce the patron's desire to be identified with his military occupation and the ideals of chivalry.

Throughout the fifteenth and sixteenth centuries builders continued to use the architectural language associated with military architecture in houses for which there was no immediate defensive purpose. The architecture of chivalry represented the aspirations and noble genealogy of the patrons through the familiar forms and ornament of fortifications. Battlements, towers, and even moats were incorporated into country houses throughout Europe even when the function of those houses was now more directed toward the enjoyment of country life or the agricultural and economic production of land and its resources.

Good Air

Plagues began in the cities, and country life provided an escape from the fetid air that was thought to carry disease. Health, from a Renaissance perspective, was understood to be a careful balance of the four humours: blood, yellow bile, phlegm, and black bile. If any were present in too strong a concentration, then the health of the individual would be compromised. In a Renaissance context, the circulation of air was understood as part of a larger concept of the *pneuma*, an ancient Greek term that encompassed ideas of health and breathing, the energetic matter of the universe, and the spirit. Simply moving out of the city, with its overcrowded streets, poor hygiene, and damp air, could be enough to improve one's health. Fresh air countered the dangers of excessive dampness, and thus disease. In the country the air could circulate freely both outside and within the house, preventing disease from entering the body.

In the cities there was little opportunity to change the location of buildings. In the country, however, patrons could select the best site for a new house. Alberti advised 'a gentleman [to choose a site] somewhere dignified, rather than in a particularly fertile stretch of land, where it could enjoy all the benefit and delight of breeze, sun and view'.[4] A beautiful view, so often praised in architectural writings on the villa and the landscape, was an aesthetic pleasure that ensured a healthy location for living. Builders should thus avoid swampy land, or building close to a river or pond. Among their other skills, architects needed to know the local geography and the patterns of the seasons. When did the land flood? What were the prevailing winds?

Land reclamation projects, including the draining of swamps and fens, increased the usable acreage for cultivation and made it healthier for habitation. In his treatise on *The Art of Living Long* (*Discorsi della vita sobria*, 1558), Alvise Cornaro describes his own villa outside of Venice.

[I]t is, indeed, a very different place than what it was formerly, having once been marshy and of unwholesome atmosphere—a home fit rather for snakes than for human beings. But, after I had drained off the waters, the air became healthful and people flocked thither from every direction; the number of the inhabitants began to multiply exceedingly; and the country was brought to the perfect condition in which it is today.[5]

In the organization of rooms, the planning of the villa could also mitigate the threat of cold and dampness. Rooms with windows on more than one wall allowed for better circulation, and deep porticos shielded the interior from the heat of the summer sun [**127**]. The Villa Capra, one of Palladio's most studied villas, has porticos on the four sides and a large room at the centre under a domed ceiling. Hot air rises toward the dome, and out through the opening at the top (now covered over). Air can circulate freely through the four porches, and into the rooms off the central space.

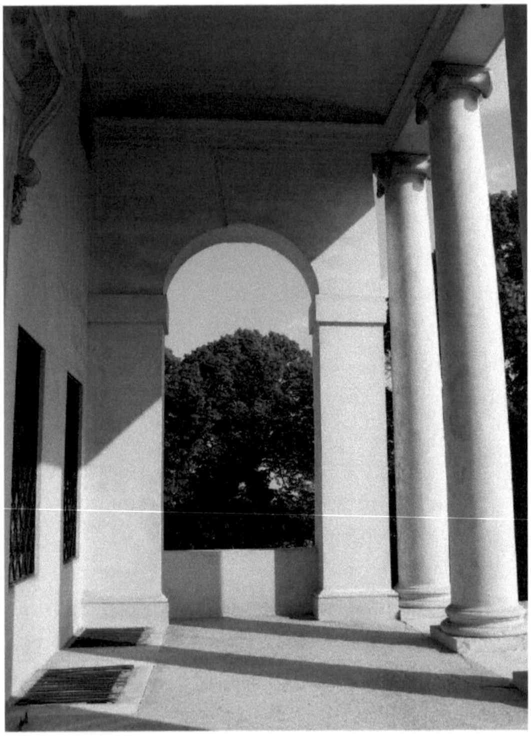

127

Andrea Palladio, Villa Capra, begun 1565, Vicenza, Italy

The Ionic columns of the porch are enclosed by walls pierced with tall narrow arches. This combination of column and wall recalls a type of ancient temple *in antis*. This detail, typical of Palladio's adaptation of an ancient motif to a contemporary use, accentuates the geometrical clarity of the four temple fronts and their simultaneous connection with the main body of the building and their relationship to the landscape.

Palladio's Villa Capra

Palladio's Villa Capra (begun *c.*1565–6) was a *villa suburbana*, built just on the outskirts of the city of Vicenza for Paolo Almerico, a papal envoy who returned to his native city after a career in Rome. The house is on the edge of the hills, overlooking open fields, and within easy walking distance of the city centre [**128**]. The plan is the most closely controlled of any of Palladio's villas, with four porches arranged on the cardinal axes [**149**]. Each porch is a temple front, reached by wide stairs that lead to a landing and entrance into the central domed space. In terms of function, Palladio does not include it among the villas as it is so close to the city, and it served a different function from other country residences. It also comments most directly on the landscape through the four porticos. It is not subservient to the landscape, but takes and moulds it, addressing it through its rigorous geometry and monumental dome. The building is self-consciously architectural in the face of nature.

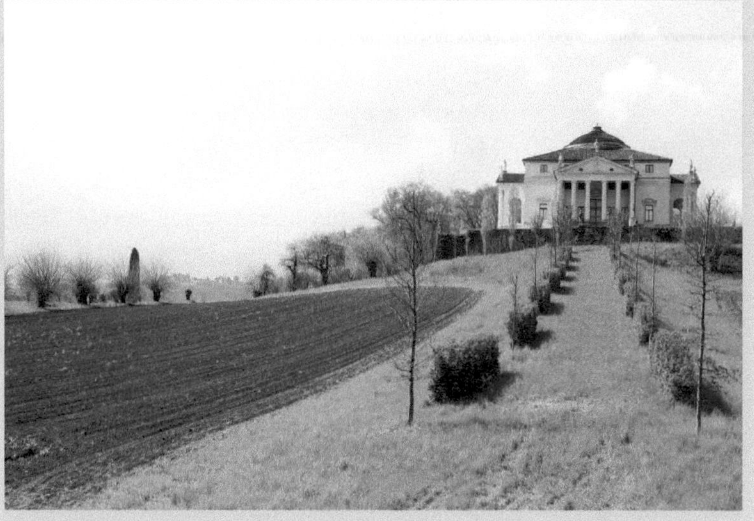

128
Andrea Palladio, Villa Capra, begun 1565, Vicenza, Italy

The main entrance to the Villa Capra was originally along this axis from the road. This view shows how the house articulates the rise of the hill in the form of the dome.

Houses for Different Sorts

Throughout the Italian architect and writer's Sebastiano Serlio's long life (Bologna 1475–France 1553/5) his multi-volume treatise reflected his changing architectural ideas and the fortunes of his career. Each book of the treatise appeared individually, and the whole project was probably intended to include seven books covering all necessary topics for the practising architect including geometry and perspective, antiquity, the orders, temples, and unusual circumstances in building. His attention to the unplanned aspect of building, that is the realities of architecture, reflects Serlio's own work as an architect, though few of his actual projects survive. His greatest legacy is certainly his treatise, which was widely read and translated.

Not all of his ideas made it into print. Book VI, known only through two manuscript copies, showed domestic architecture in the city and country [**112**]. Serlio began it around 1541, soon after he and his family, including his wife and several children, moved to France to work at the court of King Francis I, and it is dedicated to Henry II, son of Francis I. It reflects both his background and initial training in Rome, central Italy, and Venice, and his growing knowledge of French architectural practice and styles. He includes existing buildings, though often modified, and other more general schemes. In the service of the French royal court, Serlio was responsible for work on the palace at Fontainebleau and there built a palace for the Cardinal of Ferrara (built 1544–6), which he included in Book VI. The Château of Ancy-le-Franc (designed from *c*.1541, Burgundy, France), the best surviving building by Serlio, is represented in the book as a 'House of the Illustrious Prince in the Style of a Fortress'. Built for Comte Antoine de Clermont-Tonnerre, the four wings surround a courtyard, and, along with the corner towers, retain the air of the fortified house [**129**]. Classical pilasters on the exterior and in the courtyard were, according to Serlio, the desire of the patron, although in the drawing for the book Serlio shows the ground floor of the exterior with the rough stones of rustication (see the discussion of rustication later in this chapter) as surrounds for the door and window. In praising the patron on the one hand for his 'three qualities: knowledge, will, power' he also disowns some of the aspects of the building as built, for the use of columns was 'in part made according to the wishes of the patron'.[6]

Although Ancy-le-Franc incorporates pilasters over the surface of the exterior, in more ways the building reflects French architectural

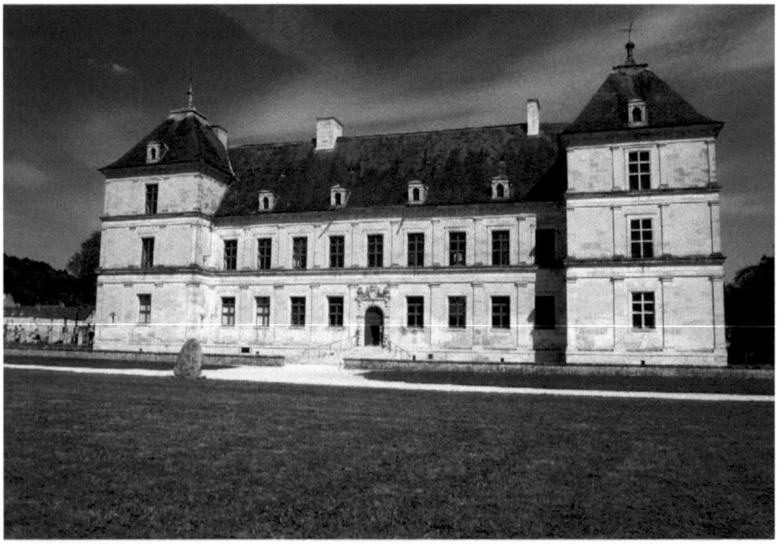

129

Sebastiano Serlio, Ancy-le-Franc, 1544–50, near Tonnerre, France

The pilasters on the exterior of the chateau mark out two different rhythms, one on the main range of rooms, the other on the two towers on the corners. The overall effect is of aesthetic restraint, with the use of a limited palette of ornament and materials and subtle gradations of shadow and the contrast of the white stone against the dark roof. In the courtyard Serlio used a greater variety of ornament and materials, perhaps at the insistence of his patron.

practice in plan, form, and style. The steep roofs are appropriate for the northern climate. A sequence of rooms with minor apartments on one wing and staterooms on the other is consistent with French planning, which Serlio particularly admired. And even the pilasters, the most obvious sign of central Italian architecture, were redistributed on the façade in a French manner. The pilasters for example in the corner towers are brought in close to the windows, giving a more vertical appearance in those blocks rather than the more horizontal distribution of the orders on a comparable Italian building. In his treatise, as well as in his practice, Serlio shows options for both city and country architecture based on national differences.

The most innovative aspect of Book VI, however, may be Serlio's presentation of domestic building as a progression from the simplest architecture for the poorest workers to castles suitable for kings and tyrants.[7] His country architecture, in particular, shows a one-room house, with a basic porch with column supports, as appropriate for rural workers. Italianate villas included rich references to classical architecture, both ancient and modern. The sequence of architectural options shows Serlio exploring the relationship between building type and national distinctions as well as social and economic difference.

Antiquity

The remains of ancient villas outside Rome fed a Renaissance interest in the houses of the ancients. Poggio Bracciolini, a fifteenth-century historian, described what could be seen of the ruins.

> There are many pools and reservoirs ... there are aqueducts ... there are broken columns and various kinds of marble scattered through the fields; also stones visible in huge piles leave intimations of great things in our minds. There still exist very large remains of quite a few villas filled with various bits of ornaments and fragments of statues; there are arches and vaults of subterranean passages and cellars so large that some of them stretch for more than a stadium ... there are also some promenades, beautifully built and still whole.[8]

These elements of ancient buildings, evocative though they were, did not produce a template for Renaissance architects or patrons but rather a group of features that evoked a past way of life.

It was in the literary descriptions in ancient texts that Renaissance readers had a vision of ancient rural life, tempting in its descriptions and maddeningly vague in its architectural details. Pliny the Younger (AD 61–112) described in his letters the leisurely life he enjoyed away from the demands of the city.

> For besides the attractions of the place which I have mentioned the greatest is the relaxation and carefree luxury of the place—there is no need for a toga, the neighbors do not come to call, it is always quiet and peaceful—advantages

as great as the healthful situation and limpid air. I always feel energetic and fit for anything at my Tuscan villa, both mentally and physically. I exercise my mind by study, my body by hunting. My household too flourishes better here than elsewhere: I have never lost a retainer, none of those I brought up with me.[9]

Poggio a Caiano

Both patrons and architects shared an interest in ancient villas which affected the design of new buildings. Giuliano da Sangallo (*c.*1445–1516) won a competition to design a villa for Lorenzo de' Medici (1449–92) on property he had recently acquired [**130**]. The land, about 20 km west of Florence, was a financial investment made by Lorenzo in order to diversify family holdings away from banking and toward real property. However, the purchase also allowed Lorenzo to build anew, working closely with the architect on the design and planning of the villa and its property.

The basic shape of the villa is a simple cubic form, reminiscent of local Tuscan farmhouses. Here the block-like form is amplified and like Bodiam placed against the landscape, raised on a podium evoking the great substructures of ancient villas as described by Bracciolini. This building was calculated to be seen, and to see from—a place to look out over the landscape and to impose on the landscape.

On the main façade, which originally would have been approached by two straight stairs, is the main entrance, marked by a *vestibulum*, an entrance hallway, set off by a loggia with classical columns and a

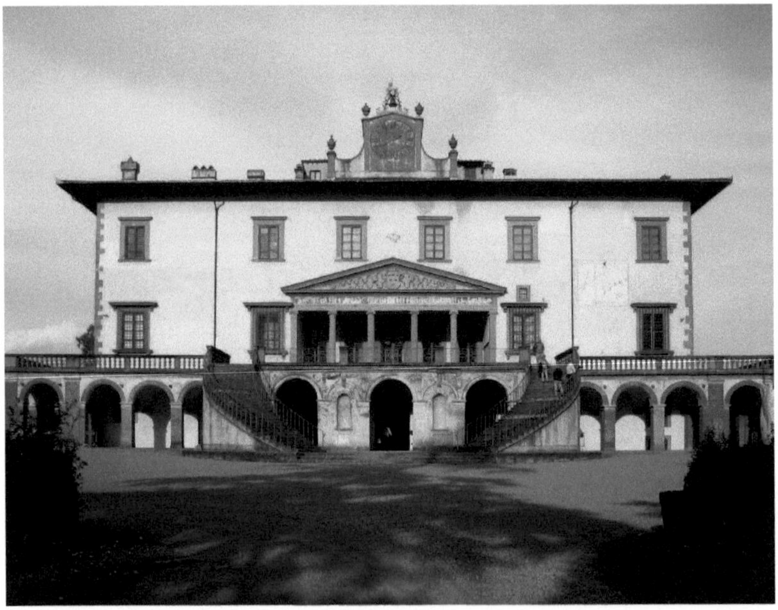

130

Giuliano da Sangallo, Poggio a Caiano, begun 1485, near Prato, Italy

Lorenzo de Medici intended his new villa to be a modern interpretation of the villas of the ancients, and express his own interests in humanist learning. At the end of the fifteenth century, Poggio a Caiano marked a turning point in the design of rural residences in central Italy after decades of experimentation. The practical concerns of land ownership, agricultural economy, and traditional building practices remained the most important concerns of patrons and architects alike; and most builders eschewed innovative design in favour of time-tested formula.

pediment above. In ancient buildings, these elements would have been used on Roman temples; that is religious buildings, a completely different type of building from a villa. Yet a pediment served as a mark of ancient Rome, easily transferable from one building type to another. It conferred upon the building a sign of antiquity, and thus an aura of scholarship that could be associated with the patron. Yet there is no attempt to make an easy transition from the rest of the building to the pediment; the windows are crowded in on the left side, and the pediment surprisingly seems an afterthought, an addition meant to appear distinct. This first use of the pediment in a secular building would become a powerful sign of the owner's status, much like the family coat of arms in the pediment or the general theme of the villa's frieze, which suggested the cyclical return of time and the beneficent rule of the Medici.

Planning of the Ancients

In the last years of his life, Raphael was working on plans for a villa on Monte Mario in Rome for Cardinal Giulio de' Medici (1478–1534), later Pope Clement VII. Close to the Vatican Palace and the dense city centre, the Villa Madama was placed on the side of a hill, with views across the city [**131**].

Superintendent of works was the architect Antonio da Sangallo (*c.*1460–1534), brother of Giuliano da Sangallo. The centre of the villa was to be a large round courtyard off which were the main rooms. A vast complex, it may have been intended as a great reception residence for foreign dignitaries coming into the city for the theatre. Stabling for 200 horses, and a hippodrome with gardens, provided amenities for the great retinues expected [**132**]. From the south a

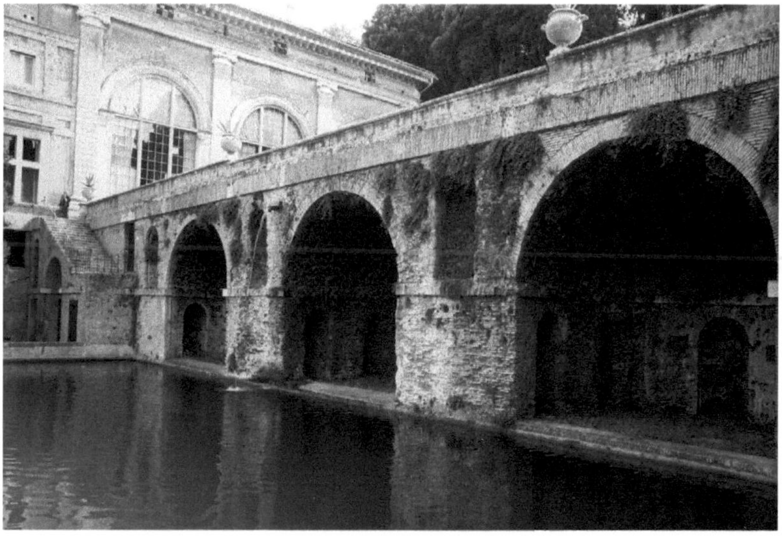

131

Raphael, Antonio da Sangallo, Giulio Romano, and others, Villa Madama, from 1517, Rome

A vaulted substructure supports the upper terrace of the garden, reminiscent of ancient remains visible in Rome and the surrounding landscape. Springs from the hillside collected in fishponds on the lower level.

132

Villa Madama, plan

Only a small part of the villa was built but a surviving plan by Antonio da Sangallo (redrawn here) shows the sequence of rooms and planned outdoor spaces. The axial plan, running alongside the length of the hill, opens and closes into larger and smaller spaces, creating an unfolding experience that cannot be anticipated from one room to another.

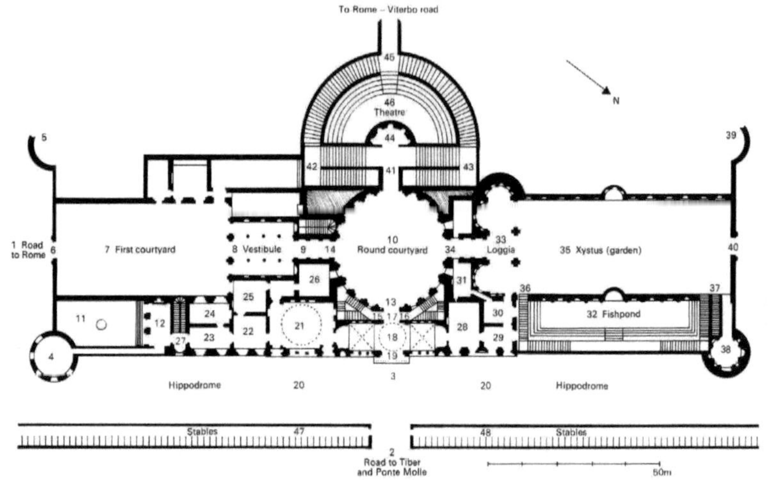

great open stairway was planned, leading up from the Vatican and connecting the building with the city. The building was never finished, and what was constructed was damaged during the Sack of Rome (1527), and only recently has it been renovated. Its present name was acquired when the villa passed into the hands of Margaret of Parma, the daughter of Charles V, in 1536.

There were both ancient precedents and modern examples of this kind of villa planning that fused architecture and natural forms. Ancient Roman villas had often, as here, been built into the sides of hills with arched substructures to support the building. And the recently completed Belvedere by Donato Bramante incorporated vast terraces running across the hill to connect the Vatican Palace to existing buildings on the Mons Vaticanus [**133**].

133

Donato Bramante, Cortile del Belvedere, begun 1505, Vatican

A vast building project, on the scale of the work of the ancients, the Cortile del Belvedere connected the Vatican Palace with the Belvedere of Innocent VIII (elected pope in 1484) with its newly completed sculpture garden (completed 1506). From the papal apartments in the Vatican Palace, the Belvedere offered an unparalleled view of the performances and pageants that were also viewed from the terraces that lined the garden on both sides. Bramante carefully considered the movement from level to level, arranging ramps and stairs to take advantage of the change in height and view.

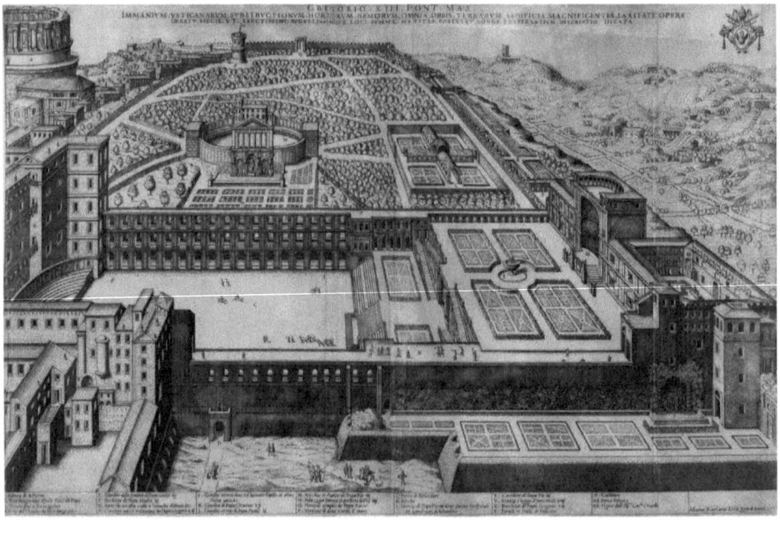

The complex bears witness to a desire to recover not only the forms but also the planning of ancient villas. For symmetry does not order the villa plan, as it had in the quattrocento villas for the Medici; or as the Belvedere had so grandly attempted to make order and sense out of the existing structures on the Vatican. The Villa Madama was laid out on the axes of a cross, each arm of the plan independent in its adaptation to the site and terrain. Thus the proposed theatre was to be built into the hill and only seen when one arrived at it, not to be a part of a whole scenic perspective, as in the Belvedere which relies on a strong visual perspective. Nor is it a building to be taken in at one glance, like the compact cubic forms of Tuscan villas, as at Poggio a Caiano. Instead the Villa Madama is experienced as a sequence of spaces and rooms. Architecture here takes a turn toward a different kind of spatial experience, a potent idea about architectural space and its emotional and psychological possibilities, as Pliny himself had described his villas as a succession of varied rooms, views, and experiences.[10] This seems to propose a relationship of architecture and nature, in which nature makes architecture into a series of disjunctive moments disrupting the boundaries between the natural and the man-made world [**29**].

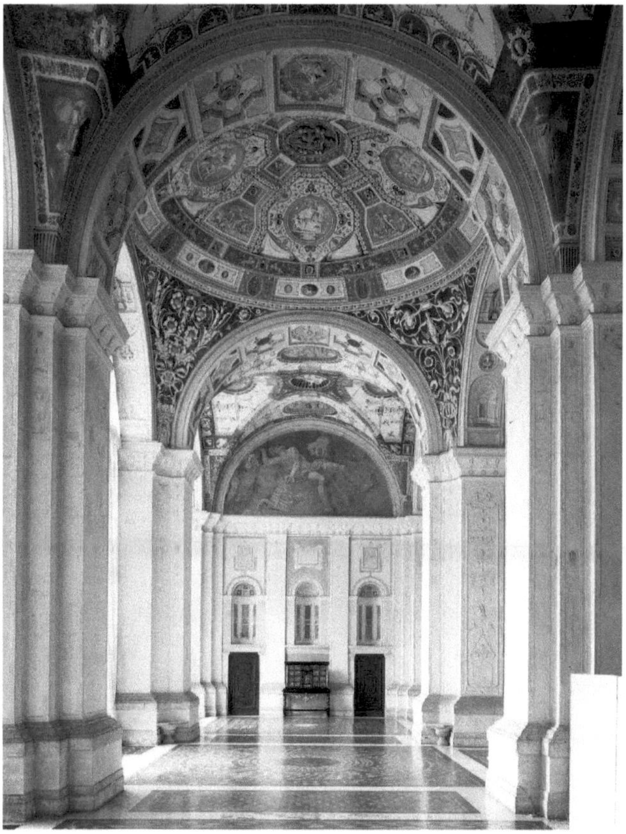

134

Raphael, Antonio da Sangallo, Giulio Romano, and others, Garden Loggia, Villa Madama, from 1517, Rome

When Raphael died in 1520, much of the villa remained without decoration and the project was left to Giovanni da Udine and Giulio Romano. The ornament on the walls and vaults imitated what Renaissance artists had seen in the remains of ancient buildings, and called *alla grottesca* for its appearance in underground grottoes. The scenes incorporate the Cardinal's coats of arms in a range of mythological motifs. The work was done in stucco, a revival of an ancient technique that allowed for a rich, sculptural decoration that could be moulded over less precious building materials such as brick.

The terrace gardens demonstrate this [**131**]. Water from springs on the hillside collects in three niches hollowed out of the retaining wall of the main terrace, and then runs down into fishponds on the lower terrace. The grouping of arches and niches follows a triumphal arch pattern. As architecture and nature were to be united in the villa, so too were all the arts to be present in the decoration and design of the villa. In the garden loggia, the boundary space between inside and outside, the decoration closely reproduced the decoration of ancient Roman building in the grotesque work [**134**].

The Politics of Proximity

Very often villas are grouped together, one family building near another in the same area (suggesting the almost tribal nature of country house building). This is true in the Veneto where families from Vicenza, Verona, and Venice moved into the *terra firma*, reclaiming land through drainage and other technological improvements, and establishing rural residences there. The need to be close enough to travel back into the city or town where business was conducted dictated a certain relative distance between city house and country residence. However, the connection to other families, the need to maintain ties to the same group as in the city, was important for economic and political reasons.

Ideas from Italy, known from the publication of villas as in Andrea Palladio's *I quattro libri dell'architettura* (1570) and travellers' accounts, offered new models to patrons and their architects throughout Europe, yet the importance of these books should not be overstated. Smaller country houses, in contrast to the royal examples, remained fiercely loyal to local precedents. Within the framework of the smaller house, economics dictated that builders use predominantly local materials, and rely on local talent. Moreover, within a particular region, houses were in dialogue with one another. As reflections of their owners, houses were understood to be both part of a social network yet marking out their individuality from that same group. Patrons looked to other houses nearby as models to emulate, and surpass.

Architects who worked for a family in the city were also hired to build their country estates, and often worked for a group of families. This phenomenon is well known in the Veneto, but was also an important part of the concentration of country houses in areas such as the Loire Valley of France, prized by Francis I and his ministers for the excellent hunting, the Weser River Valley (Germany), or the county of Northamptonshire in England. There was often competitiveness between families, a desire to outdo the other in elaborate houses.

Proportionality

Of all the architects who designed country houses, Andrea Palladio (1508–80) is certainly the best known, and the most studied by later architects and patrons. His reputation spread quickly in his own lifetime, based on the quality of his building as well as through the publication of his own designs in his treatise. His buildings were already a destination for visitors to the Veneto soon after they were built. In the early seventeenth century, Thomas Coryat describes the elegance of their decoration and construction. And in 1613–14, the English architect Inigo Jones made a careful study of his architecture with Palladio's own treatise as a guide to his visits [**149**].[11] Architects to the present day have continued a fascination with Palladio's buildings, especially his villas, finding them rich and compelling models that reward careful study. The characteristics that attract architects and visitors to Palladio's buildings—they are among the most visited buildings in the Veneto—may stem from their elegant classical details, used with restraint and unity. It may also be the careful attention Palladio gave to the buildings' location: aligned axially to fields, set against a vista of hills, alongside the canal or river. Many of Palladio's villas are lavishly decorated in the interior, a contrast with the self-possession of the exterior ornamentation. It is also, certainly, that a visit to more than one of his buildings brings a sensation of a repeated theme, heard again but with subtle changes and variations.

The unique quality of Palladio's architecture, difficult to pinpoint even if it is possible to pick out particular features, has been described by scholars as Palladio's attention to proportion. Rudolf Wittkower in a detailed analysis of Palladio's use of mathematical proportion in all aspects of his buildings (plan, elevation, ornamental details) ascribes to Palladio a highly refined use of proportional relationships in his buildings, a characteristic that Wittkower thought gave them a universal aesthetic appeal.

> Once [Palladio] had found the basic geometric pattern for the problem 'villa,' he adapted it as clearly and as simply as possible to the special requirements of each commission. He reconciled the task at hand with the 'certain truth' of mathematics which is final and unchangeable. The geometrical keynote is, subconsciously rather than consciously, perceptible to everyone who visits Palladio's villas and it is this that gives his buildings their convincing quality.[12]

For Wittkower, number was a Platonic truth that emerged through the rigour of Renaissance scholarship. Palladio's use of mathematical proportions in his buildings was evidence of his intellectual sophistication applied to the problem of building, a demonstration of theory applied to practice. The popularity of Wittkower's ideas in the context of twentieth-century architectural modernism, which most likely stimulated his own ideas, has since been challenged. Few, if any, of Palladio's buildings follow any rigorous mathematical systems.[13]

However, if Wittkower held to a fundamental belief in the role of numbers in the creation of a universal architecture that we now find too rigid, it is still possible to see Palladio's interest in number and proportion as an essential part of his architecture. For numbers do, as Wittkower suggests, lie at the heart of Palladio's architecture. Throughout the treatise, Palladio takes special care to insert numbers into the illustrations so that the careful reader can see not only the overall effect of the design but also its relative parts. For example, villa plans are marked with their dimensions, so that readers could transpose that design into their own local system of measurement. Yet to stop at this level does not take Palladio's understanding of the implications of number far enough. If number does exist on the semi-conscious level as Wittkower suggests, then it surely is also present in the very real and immediate demands of architecture as it mediates between people, places, and things.[14] Let us take one of Palladio's villas as an example.

Villa Emo in the village of Fanzolo belonged to Leonardo Emo, a Venetian noble whose family had owned property here since the fifteenth century [**135**]. There was an older house on the property, and the land still shows traces of its ancient Roman heritage in the layout of the fields and the presence of a Roman road. Palladio sites his villa, and its adjoining buildings, to take full advantage of this agricultural heritage, aligning the main entrance to the house along a dominant axis through the fields and elevating the entrance one storey

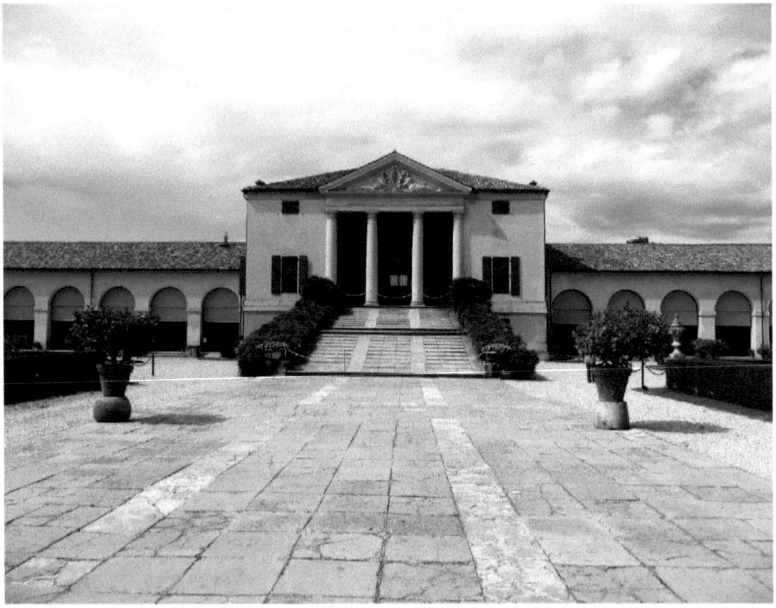

135

Andrea Palladio, Villa Emo, begun 1559, Fanzolo di Vedelago, Italy

The residence is connected to the farm buildings yet distinguished by its raised elevation and classical temple front. The service buildings to the side have simpler arches wide enough to accommodate a farm cart. The deep porch provides shade, and thus cooler air to circulate into the living quarters.

above ground level. Leonardo Emo commissioned Palladio in conjunction with major land reclamation work on the property, draining fields in order to farm grain in the area.

The agricultural function of the building is clear: the main house, the *casa di villa*, is attached to the *barchesse* or service buildings by arcades which stretch out like arms toward the landscape [**136**]. The covered portico not only serves to aesthetically tie the house to the farm buildings, but also to provide further storage area for the farm with a protected area for equipment, produce, and animals. The ramp that goes from ground level to the main entrance to the house most likely served as an area for threshing the grain, close to the barns and storage areas.

If mathematical number is at the heart of the Villa Emo it is expressed in the lucid way Palladio attends to the mass of the building and its ornamentation. The main block of the building is almost entirely devoid of ornament (there are not even any cornices or mouldings around the windows) except for the Doric portico. The pure wall of the house makes the classical elements all the more striking, and serves to demarcate the elevated status of the house over the more functional buildings at the sides. While rigorous in its simplicity, and therefore mathematical by implication, the architecture of the villa should also be appreciated for its corporeal qualities.

Finally, the interior of the villa is surprising in its rich painted decoration that interacts and responds to the building. The artist Battista Zelotti executed the paintings as he had done for other villas, an aspect of the building that Palladio did not attempt to dictate, and

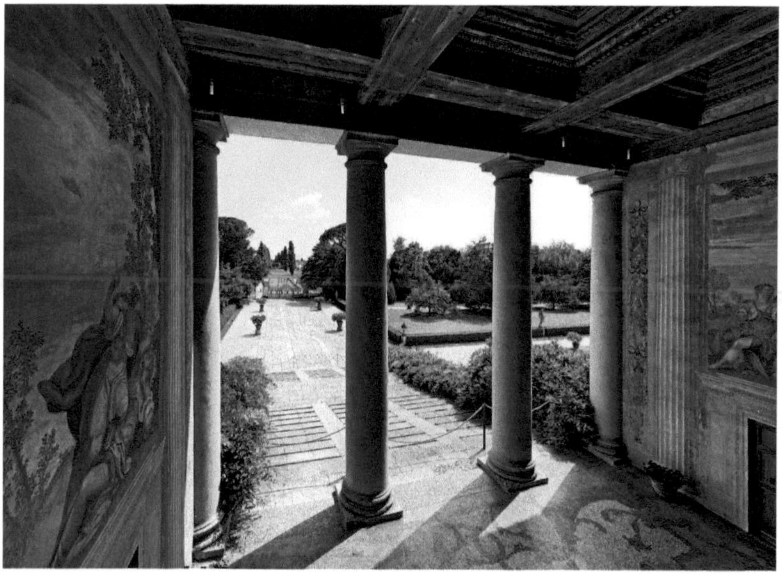

136

View through loggia toward fields, Andrea Palladio, Villa Emo, begun 1559, Fanzolo di Vedelago, Italy

The columns of the porch frame the long vista through the fields. The painted decoration by Battista Zelotti extends the structural beams of the ceiling, and creates a rich and imagined landscape.

Rustication

In villas and gardens the most successful architecture, according to the principles developed in the Renaissance, responded to its setting in the landscape. Nature was a potent force, a living presence that shaped the experience as well as the form of building. Not only were the materials understood as the product of organic processes that must be cultivated and shaped before they could be incorporated into a building, ornament itself might reflect that same fecundity of the earth. Rustication, a term derived from the Latin 'rus' meaning 'country', was rough stones that may in fact have been carved to look that way, allowing architects to express the vital character of the natural world in buildings themselves. The Grotte du Jardin des Pins (1541–3) at Fontainebleau has arches with unhewn stone serving as the voussoirs and Atlantids, mythical giants embedded in the rock [**137**].

Rustication was a mode of building, according to the writer Serlio, and was most often used in combination with either the Doric or Tuscan, the simplest of the classical orders. It had a powerful effect when used in combination with more refined masonry, playing off the finish of the capitals and mouldings against the rough stones. At the Palazzo Te, a villa *suburbana* on the edge of the city of Mantua (begun in the mid-1520s), Giulio Romano exploited the full expressive potential of rustication [**138**] Rough stones appear almost to grow out from the surface of the building or break through the pediments over doorways. The visual puns work because they play on the expectations of the viewer who might expect a more regular and sedate use of the orders, with no surprises.

Serlio wrote that rustication agreed with the character of a soldier or 'a scholar or a merchant with a robust life' (Bk. IV, p. 332) and was particularly appropriate for the architecture of a fortress. Rustication may have been no more impenetrable than regular stone, and in fact would be easily damaged by cannon fire, but its character evoked strength. This quality of protection made rustication perennially popular for any building that was to appear fortified. In Florence, rustication was used on the façade of the Palazzo Medici (1444) and the Palazzo Pitti (from 1457), continuing a local tradition in Tuscany, though updated in combining smooth and rough surfaces in a play on the medieval precedents.

By the sixteenth century, as architects and theorists sought ancient Roman precedents for current practice, models in the perimeter wall of the Forum of Augustus (dedicated in 2 BC) and temples from the time of the Emperor Claudius (10 BC–AD 54) were cited as authorities that justified the growing interest in the evocative and emotional power of architectural forms.

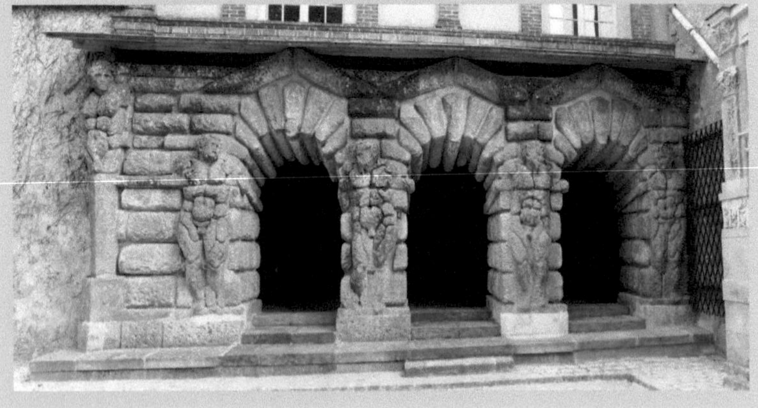

137

Grotte des Jardins des Pins, 1541–3, Fontainebleau, France

This rusticated arch leads into a grotto, originally inlaid with shells and crystals and decorated with mythological paintings. That play with nature and artifice is still present in the exterior arches, with stones consciously carved in rough blocks. Male figures form part of the architecture, their well-developed muscles appropriately formed by rocks still replete with all their natural vitality. The Grotte des Jardins des Pins is variously ascribed to Francesco Primaticcio (1504/5–1570) and Sebastiano Serlio. Both worked at Fontainebleau and designed architectural works with a rich vocabulary of the orders and rustication.

138

Giulio Romano, Palazzo Te, from 1524, Mantua, Italy

In his work for the Gonzaga in Mantua, Giulio Romano served as court architect and artistic adviser. He developed a highly personal use of the orders and especially rustication, adopting an architectural vocabulary based on the nature of the building and its intended audience. For Federico Gonzaga (1500–40), Giulio Romano renovated and expanded the Palazzo Te on the edge of the city. The building amazed and delighted its owner and his guests. Each room offers a different architectural experience, painted with wild banquets of the ancients or portraits of the Duke's beloved horses. The rustication on the exterior and along the walls of the courtyard is unexpected and sophisticated.

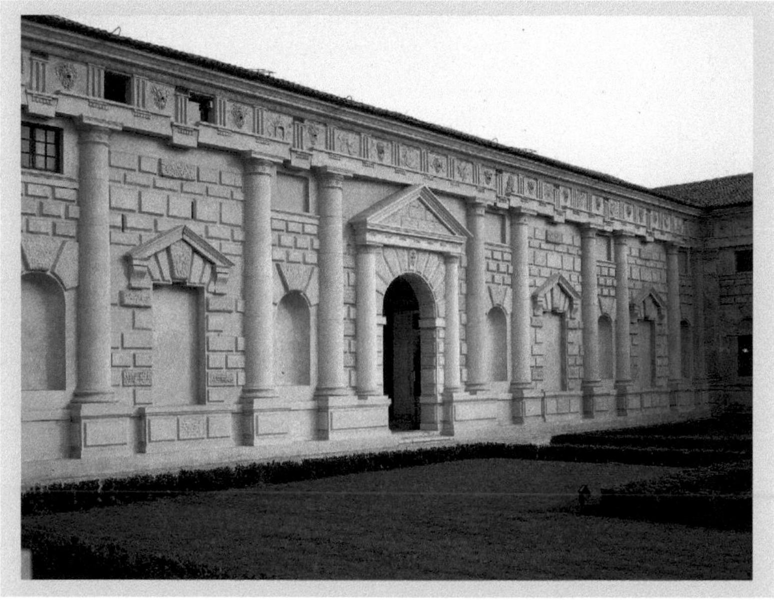

it is again the contrast between the parts—exterior to interior—that provides the effect for both owner and visitor.

One way we might think about proportion in Palladio's architecture is not to see it as a covert aspect of the architecture, waiting to be revealed through complex and erudite texts or the explication of architect and patron. Rather, proportion is an aspect of building that sees elements in relation to one another, this is to that, as one would parse out the mathematical ration of, say, 2 : 3. That ratio may define the dimensions of a room, or the diameter of a column to its height. Ratios are also shorthand for describing objects in dialogue with one another. Silvio Belli, a contemporary of Palladio who was a fellow member of the Accademia Olimpica in Vicenza, published a book, *On Proportions and Proportionality*, in 1573 where he described proportion as a fundamental property 'of beauty and of health'.[15]

If we look again at Palladio's villas we can see how that idea of objects in dialogue can apply to elements of the architecture in the relationship of the building to the landscape, the house to the barns, the ornament to the structure, and the book to the building. Decorum, a central issue in Palladio's architectural approach, dictates the suitability of a house to its owner, and places the building in an active role between patron and architect.

Remarkable Women, Remarkable Builders

Women played an important role as the direct or indirect patrons of architecture. If the male head of the family, having commissioned a building, dies before its completion, the widow may push on with the project, as often happened with Palladio's patrons. Palaces built for female royalty, as in the palace at Mechelen for Margaret of Austria, can be directed to reflect her wishes, within certain limits of court protocol. There are, however, cases where women are able to take the lead, conceiving of a project from its start through to the end, working with the architect, asserting their own personality directly into the project as constructed. Often, this sort of direct architectural involvement, for both male and female patrons, took place with architecture in the country. Away from the limits (social and spatial) of the city, rural building offered patron and architect more freedom to invent new solutions for traditional problems. How much of these innovative buildings can be ascribed to the dynamics of gender is difficult to determine, though it can be seen where the issues of imagery and inventive planning come to the fore. This section will look at two remarkable women and their remarkable buildings: the chateau at Anet by Philibert de l'Orme for Diane de Poitiers, the mistress of Henry II (1547–53); and Hardwick Hall, the great house by Robert Smythson for Elizabeth Shrewsbury (1590).

Diana, the Hunter

The country houses of Francis I and Henry VIII were primarily hunting lodges, built on an extremely grand scale. They were designed to take advantage of the rich reserves of game in the woods and valleys of the Loire Valley or the southern counties of England. In an age when the skills of hunting came ever more to define masculine status, in part as a replacement for the military tests on the battlefield, the houses were the setting for display of masculine identity, now codified through 'new' medieval castles and grand lodges. Yet, the taste for the hunt was not restricted to men.

For Diane de Poitiers (1499–1566), widow of Louis de Brézé (d. 1531) and mistress of Henry II, Philibert de l'Orme designed an extraordinary chateau at Anet, about 75 km west of Paris [**139**]. Like the great parks owned by Francis I, the woods at Anet were excellent for hunting, a passion shared by Diane de Poitiers. What had been a modest house, created under an earlier architect, was now expanded into a multi-courtyard residence that projected Diane de Poitiers's elevated status once Henry II ascended to the throne in 1547. Each element of the chateau, of which only a part remains after much was destroyed in the French Revolution (1798–1811), reveals de l'Orme's interest in creating an architecture which is innovative in its projection of a French style, perfectly suited to his royal client. In the invention of the ***trompe***, the richness of the décor, or the complexity of the chapel's dome, each element of the chateau was a tour-de-force, a gem that reflected the talent of the architect and the prestige of the patron.

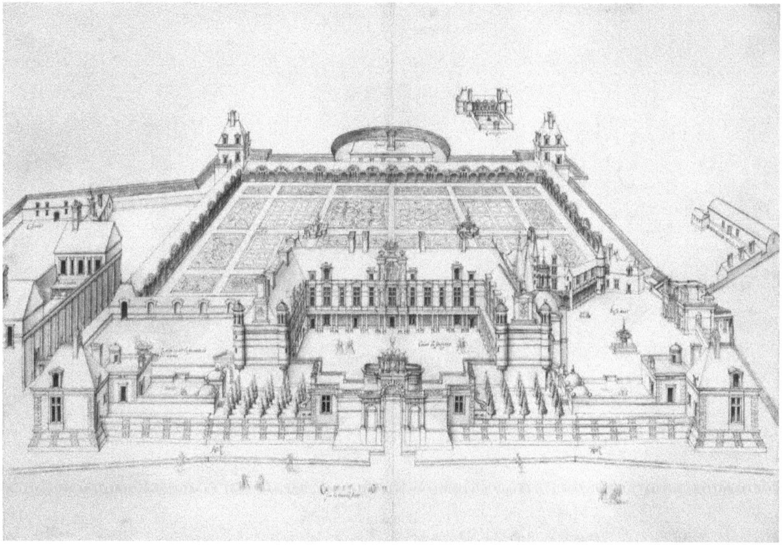

139

Drawing by Jacques Androuet du Cerceau, Chateau of Anet, before 1576

This drawing was ultimately engraved and included in Androuet du Cerceau's book of houses, *Les Plus Excellents Bastiments de France* (1576–9), a celebration of national style and the influence of French patrons and architects. The birds-eye view shows the buildings of Anet with its protective walls and enclosed gardens. The corner towers, prominent in Androuet du Cerceau's drawing, recall earlier French chateaux, an aspect of the building that reinforced its historic ties. The symmetry of the design, an aspect of the overall planning by Philibert de l'Orme, is evident from the alignment of the entrance gate with the three-storey frontispiece in the main courtyard. Anet evoked both new Italianate tastes and the importance of building within the national traditions.

In the entrance gate to the chateau, de l'Orme engages every available aspect of architectural and ornamental language to create a French building that explicitly represents his patron [**140**]. While the gate has the form of a triumphal arch, along with the attention to material consistent with classical building (regular blocks, flat and finely finished ashlar masonry), there are few explicit classical details. Only the Doric columns on either side of the entrance derive from a classical vocabulary. At the same time, the architect brings in architectural citations from older French buildings: the curved wings recalling the turrets of fortified houses and the pierced parapets that were common on Gothic houses. Yet the smooth surface of the stonework with its regular stringcourse and the geometrical patterns of the balustrades have the feel of architecture derived from a classical source. In the tympanum is a bronze sculpture by Benvenuto Cellini. The over-life-size plaque, created for the chateau of Fontainebleau but never installed there, was given to Diane by Henry II. The reclining nude, with one arm draped over the neck of a stag, in this context becomes Diana, the huntress. The explicit imagery of the sculpture projects the patron, in her allegorical identity, crafted as with the architecture from sources both classical and French.

Bess of Hardwick

Through a series of four strategic marriages and great political savvy, Elizabeth, Countess of Shrewsbury (1521–1608), became the second most powerful woman in England (after Queen Elizabeth I). Although the Queen descended from a lineage of great builders (her father Henry VIII had over fifty country estates), Elizabeth herself built little. In order to ensure the loyalty of her nobles and solidify her

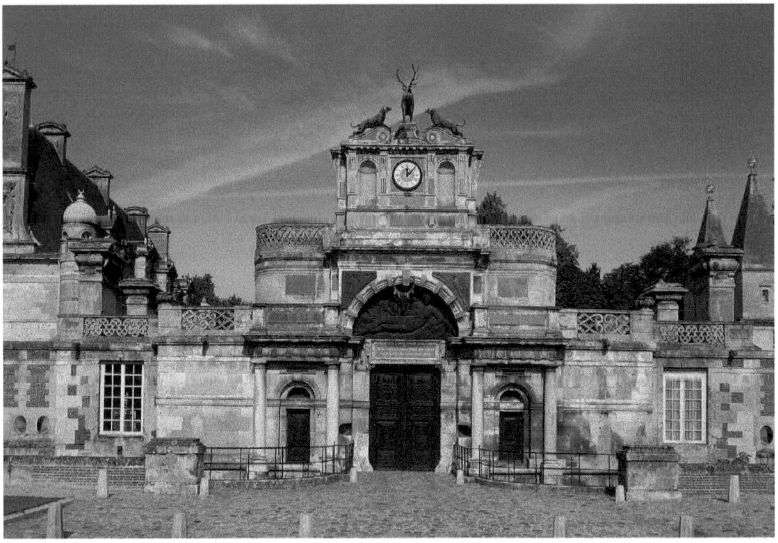

140

Philibert de l'Orme, Gate, Chateau d'Anet, 1552, Eure-et-Loire, France

The architect imagined the gate like the entrance façade of a Romanesque cathedral, an architectural type that prepared the viewer for the full experience of the building through a consistent narrative. The story here is not religious but mythological and personal: Diana as huntress. Each aspect of the building can be read as referring to her and an aspect of her life story. The sum of all the architectural parts is the residence for a member of royalty, but the details lay out a biography connected only to Diane de Poitiers.

political power, she encouraged her courtiers to build grandly in anticipation of a royal visit. These royal progresses required vast estates to house the Queen and her retinue in grand style.

Elizabeth Hardwick employed the most important architect of the era, Robert Smythson (1534–1614), to design her new house.[16] She purchased Hardwick, her ancestral home, around 1583. Although she spent time having the existing house restored 1587–65, after the death of her fourth husband, George Talbot, 6th Earl of Shrewsbury (?1528–90), she employed Robert Smythson to design a new house [**141**]. The new Hardwick Hall was nearly adjacent to the old hall, and the side-by-side juxtaposition of family home and new home was a practical decision that reinforced her own family heritage.

Four corner towers recall English fortified castles. Yet the house is nothing like English medieval houses. Much of the surface of the house is windows, increasing in size on the upper floors. The amount of glass, originally set in faceted, undulating patterns that would have caught the light, dematerializes the façade and asserts the patron's wealth in her use of such a costly material. The patron's initials and coat of arms, prominently displayed along the roofline, identify the house as Elizabeth's alone.

Both Smythson and Elizabeth Shrewsbury owned architectural books, including Palladio's recently published treatise (*I quattro libri dell'architettura*, 1570). The plan at Hardwick is symmetrical, following the general schemes in Palladio, with a large hall at the centre [**142, 149, 151**]. Halls were a traditional part of an English country house, the space where hospitality was given to guests and

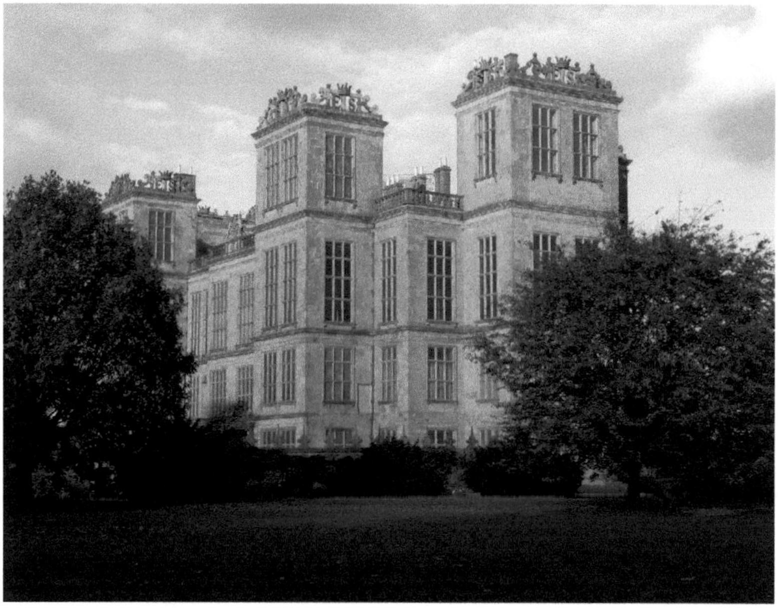

141
Robert Smythson, Hardwick Hall, 1590–7, Derbyshire, England

Set against smooth ashlar walls, the windows at Hardwick Hall increase in height on the upper floors. The experience of moving through the house, therefore, is a passage from darkness into light as the rooms increase in importance and grandeur. Cresting and Elizabeth Shrewsbury's initials appear along the roofline, a variation on the medieval tradition of the pierced parapet. Robert Smythson was well aware of developments in continental architecture, including the work of Palladio, Serlio, and Philibert de l'Orme, and the theory and practice of the orders. Yet the orders only appear here in carefully prescribed locations: at the entrance and on the hall screen in the hall.

the extended household. In the hall, as in the enclosed courtyard of an earlier castle, visitors were received and the family was on display.[17] At Hardwick, however, the plan was designed so that the traditional longitudinal hall, found in great houses like Penshurst Place (dating from the fourteenth century) or even the nearly contemporary Wollaton Hall, was now turned to go across the plan, a cross-hall plan. This allowed Elizabeth to direct and observe the events of the household from the bridge on the upper floors that linked her bedroom to the adjacent chamber. In this way she was able to be present and keep a watch over the house, while being separate from it.[18]

The upper floor is the grandest in the house, with the fewest and largest rooms, all intended to impress the Queen should she visit the house. The great upper chamber was designed to hold a set of tapestries purchased for the house. The long gallery, one of the largest in England at the time, provided a place to exercise in inclement weather, and a room with tremendous views over the land controlled by Elizabeth Shrewsbury [**143**].[19] It also held portraits of both Elizabeth, other members of her family, and the Queen, who never visited the house and was here only in her image.

Garden, Landscape, Territory

Houses in the country always interact with nature, but the garden was a formal construction that tempered nature to particular ends. In this way, gardens are a close relative to agricultural land and the hunting

142

Plan, Hardwick Hall

The plan is loosely symmetrical around the central hall, and the rooms increase in size and importance on the upper floors.

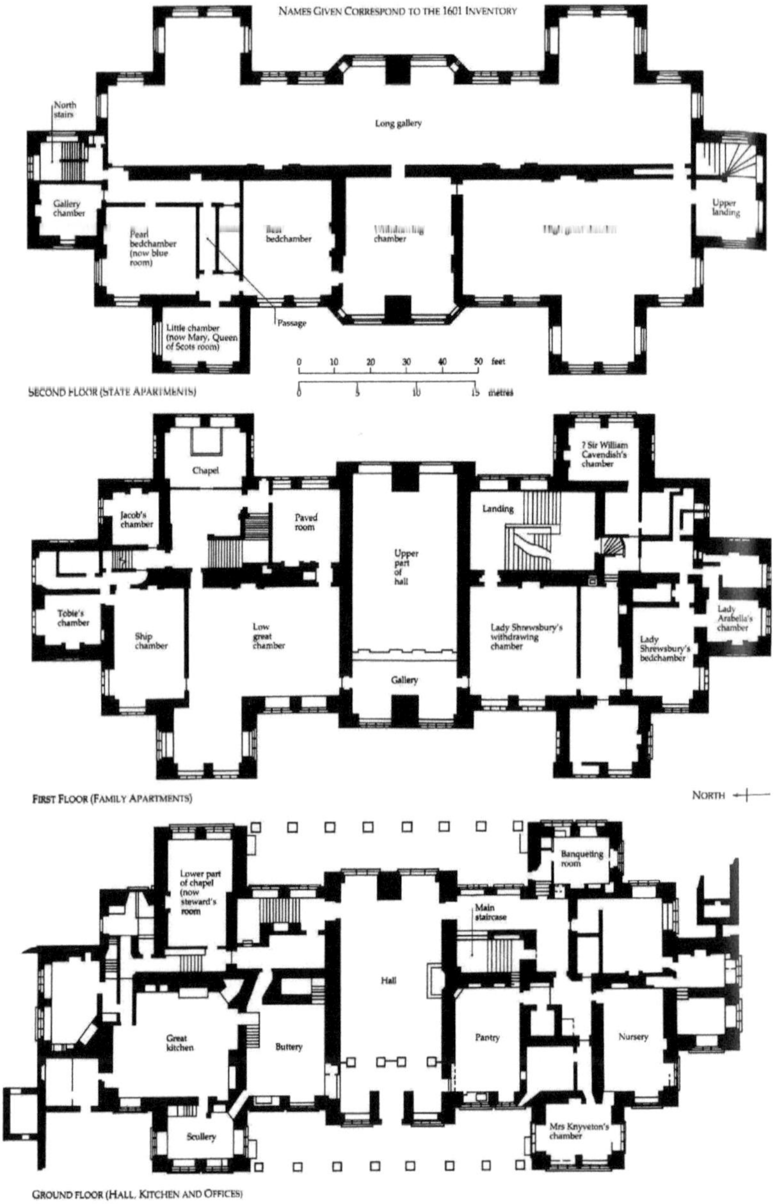

park. Yet the garden existed, like architecture itself, both in the world and in the mind of its beholders. In addition to kitchen gardens, medieval houses had other gardens, walled in, and symbolically connected with the biblical garden of Eden or the Holy Jerusalem as a sacred site. From its medieval sources, the Renaissance garden was already endowed with a functional role and a symbolic potential [**100**]. Contemporary with changes in rural architecture, the Renaissance

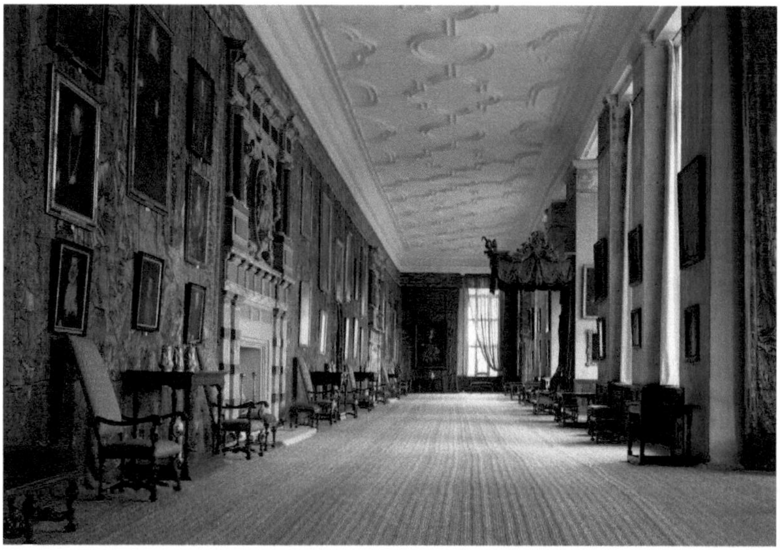

143

Long Gallery, Hardwick Hall, 1590–7, Derbyshire, England

The gallery extended the full length of the house, with views out over the landscape from the tall windows along the eastern wall. This was a space for movement, important in a cold climate where it is better to keep active even indoors, and a highly social space. There was ample opportunity for conversation while walking, and time to admire the work of the full-height fireplaces, carved out of rich materials and displaying the owner's coat of arms.

garden could evoke ideas of ancient gardens, known from Roman texts by Pliny the Younger, Cicero, and Varro. These classical associations, however, were at heart yet another route for Renaissance patrons to promote their own power and erudition.

Descriptions of gardens in ancient writings and religious books offered a context for a symbolic reading of the garden. The garden itself, however, might include sculpture, inscriptions, and statues that linked it to well-known mythological stories and ancient precedents. In its narrative and images, Francesco Colonna's *Hypnerotomachia Poliphili* (1499) [**5**] presented a garden populated by fantastic creatures, half-living, half-sculpture. Nature and artifice coexist there, and the garden is a major character in Colonna's story of longing, adventure, and delight.

The design of gardens went in tandem with a study of nature in all its diversity and wonder. Not all gardens depended upon a deep knowledge of exotic varieties of plants, though some did, but gardens were one site of knowledge, much like the library or the laboratory in the early modern period.[20] Plants were traded and collected, and received as diplomatic gifts.

The use of symbolism in gardens might be explicit. When Philibert de l'Orme created the chateau at Anet for Diane de Poitiers, the design included extensive gardens to the north of the moated house [**139**]. Twenty-four parterres are planted in patterns that depict the patron's initials and emblems. The garden continued the strong central axis from the gateway and through the house.

The labour expended upon gardens, in their creation and maintenance, rivalled that of architecture for it was often on a larger scale and demanded greater resources to see it through to completion. When Donato Bramante planned the Cortile del Belvedere at the Vatican Palace, he was transforming the landscape into a defined outdoor space that would rival ancient constructions in Rome [**133**]. The Belvedere served later sixteenth-century architects as a model for the architectural garden, shaped through man-made structures into a vast earthworks that extended control out into the landscape. Raphael's Villa Madama, built not far from the Vatican, was a similar type of garden, using the steep hillside as an important feature of its design [**29, 131, 132**].

The view over the landscape was a sign of ownership. In the early seventeenth century, Sir Henry Wotton described a 'royaltie of sight...[a] ranging, and imperious, and...usurping Sense, [that] can endure no narrow circumscription; but must be fed, both with extent and variety'.[21] The roof terraces at the chateau of Chambord (1519–50) [**68**] offered a view into the wood and hunting park, and extended the royal prerogative out into the distance. The development of theories of perspective offered scientific theories for this control of nature (and the urban landscape) through rationalized vision.[22]

Palladio's use of the temple front on his rural houses identified the residence of the villa with appropriate dignity. The elevated platform and columns framed the view of the agricultural lands that surrounded the house. In that way, the order of the architecture repeated, as at the Villa Emo, the regularity of the fields and created a dialogue between architecture and nature [**136**].

The history of the garden at Castello, just north-west of Florence, is typical of many rural estates of the sixteenth century. It was purchased in the late fifteenth century by the Medici, and inherited by Cosimo de' Medici in the early sixteenth century. At the time, there were a range of agricultural features including vineyards, farmlands, olive orchards, and a residence referred to as a 'palace'.[23] Niccolò Tribolo designed the garden that extends beyond the house, though not initially on a direct axis with the building. Situated on a slight hill, backed up to Monte Morello and overlooking the basin of the River Arno, the house and garden could be seen from the distance and reinforced the position of the Medici as the rulers of this territory. In contrast to the earlier Medici villas and gardens, Tribolo included sculpture that referred to the local geography of the mountains and rivers, tamed and brought under the control of Medici rule [**144**].

In the grotto, carved into the hill of Monte Morello, barrel-vaulted niches frame basins over which are sculptures of animals. The walls and ceiling drip with stalactites carved from sandstone. Much of this decoration was supervised by Giorgio Vasari, working at Castello

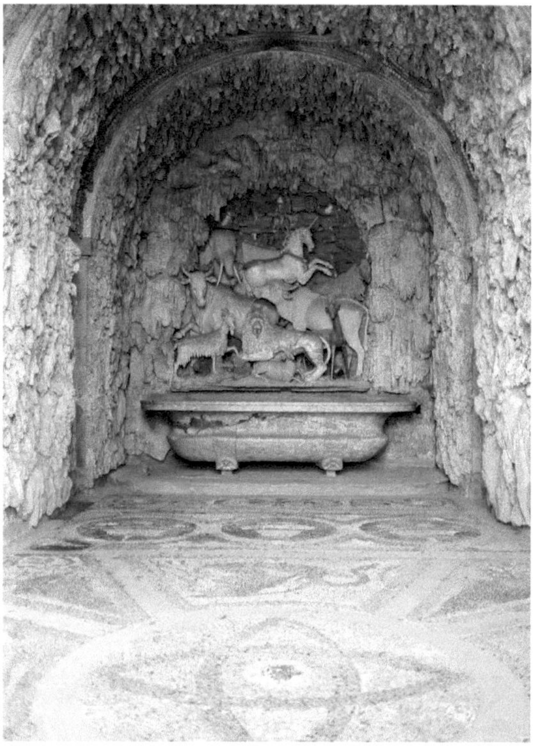

144

Niccolò Tribolo and Giorgio Vasari, Grotto of the Animals, Villa Medici, 1538, Castello, Italy

The grotto at Castello was covered with stalactites from the hill of Monte Morello nearby, recreating nature in this carefully controlled environment. Stones like this, rough and unfinished, were described as 'congealed water' and were evidence of the fluidity and fecundity of the natural world. Water was an important part of the design of the gardens at Castello for Duke Cosimo de' Medici. The fountains and plantings allude to the mythological and ancient origins of the city of Florence nearby. The animals in the grotto, along with the riches of stones and minerals used in its decoration and the startling effect of water that could be sprayed from the floor, were evidence of the vastness of nature brought together and tamed in this garden.

1565–72, and the extraordinary decoration of inset marble, shells, and cut stones was his design. All known animals are here in the grotto, some recalling exotic gifts given to the Medici, others native species, and still others newly discovered in explorations to the New World. Here, they all live in the bounty of natural harmony, a mirror of the world in the arrangement of the garden.[24]

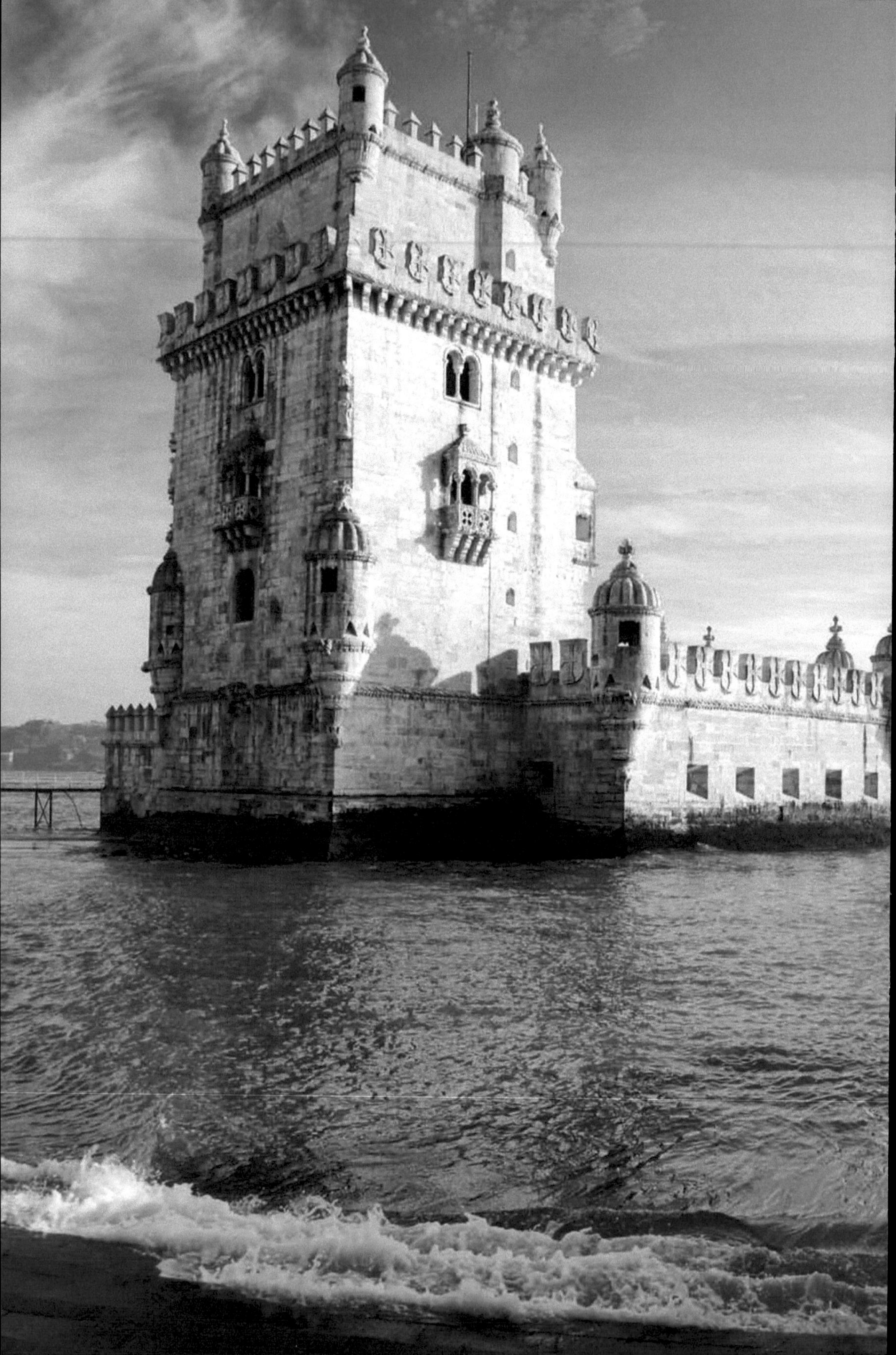

Distant Shores

8

One theme of this book has been the variety of European architecture, the power of national difference and local custom in the creation of not one style of Renaissance architecture but a series of Renaissance practices. Yet this is not enough. What is needed now is a book that encompasses the study of the Renaissance across the globe and looks at building as one product of a series of exchanges between cultures in and out of Europe. That book would need to take account not just of the buildings in China, for example, that were constructed at the same time as the Medici were building in Florence. But rather it would see these distant and different art and architectural cultures as they relate to one another.

I have touched on the close connection between Venice and the Ottoman Empire in the sixteenth century, showing how Palladio and Sinan built similar religious structures that solved similar problems, yet doing so within the scope of their own religious and architectural traditions. In the tradition of Fernand Braudel's work on the Mediterranean as a region, architectural historians have studied how architectural ideas travelled much as other goods did as objects of exchange of knowledge and power.[1] Architecture was a commodity, both in its material requirements for the raw goods out of which it was made, and as the product of increasing wealth. New buildings appear along many of the same routes as other goods, and can be traced, for example, in the towns along the Vistula River in Poland, in cities made rich by the grain trade.[2] The Baltic Sea is another such region, and the importance of the Hanseatic League as a conduit for architectural ideas and as an impetus for building has not yet been fully studied. Given its long reach into Asia and Africa, and across the Atlantic, the architecture of Portugal in connection with those trading partners and ultimate colonies is a powerful example of the two-way exchange between European and other building traditions [**145**].

Looking beyond Europe in a more concerted fashion, and with an attention to the routes of cultural exchange, offers an opportunity to see what identified architecture as regionally specific. For example, when

Detail of 145

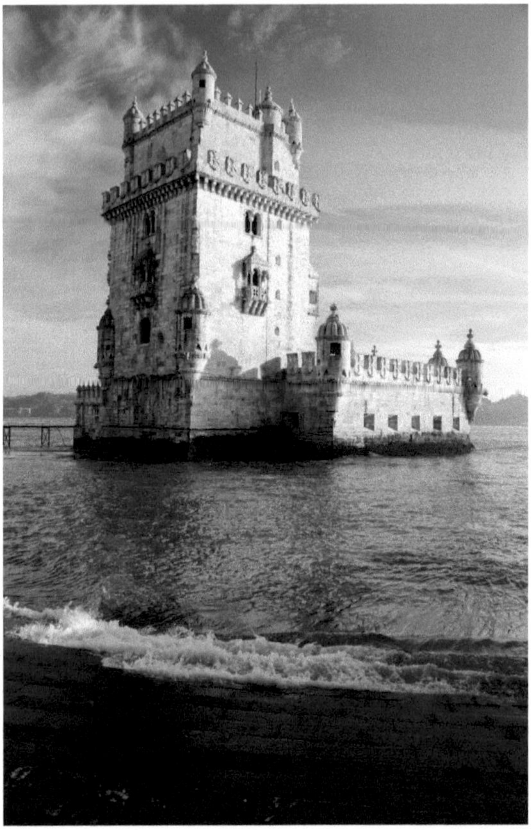

145
Francisco de Arruda, Tower, 1514–21, Belém, Portugal

The tower at Belém marks the entrance to the city of Lisbon from the sea. Here ships would depart to India, Africa, and the New World. The architect, Francisco de Arruda (1480–1537), had designed bastions in North Africa, and at Belém he incorporated innovations in fortifications to resist attack from more powerful artillery. In addition to the technical innovations, Arruda created a monument to Portuguese exploration and trade. The lobed domes over the small corner turrets are an Islamic motif, known to Arruda from his work there. Ornament on the tower includes shields with the cross of the Order of Christ and a loggia with column capitals in the form of turbans. The tower is near to the Jerónimos Monastery, built with the wealth from Portuguese voyages and dedicated to prayers for Portuguese sailors and ships.

ships left Spain and travelled to the New World in the sixteenth and early seventeenth centuries, they often brought with them crates (sometimes numbering in the hundreds) of tiles produced in the workshops of Triana, a suburb of Seville [**146, 147**]. The tiles were then incorporated into buildings in Santo Domingo, Lima, Cuba, and Mexico. Even when tiles could be produced in the New World, and would be a reasonable facsimile for those produced in Spain, priests and local governors insisted upon tiles produced in the Seville workshops.[3] Was it an aesthetic quality that they preferred? Or was it a belief in the authenticity of that architectural material and its local manner of manufacture that gave Triana tiles a special authority as being Spanish?

The turn toward global interpretations has certainly been inspired by our current age with the excitement and simultaneous anxiety over a world whose parts are increasingly interdependent. Our current situation leads us to use that lens to view the past. While there are certainly similarities, it is also true that the period from the fifteenth to the eighteenth centuries was profoundly different from today, and nowhere do we see that more than in attitudes toward architecture. Renaissance viewers, those lovers of architecture that I mentioned in the Introduction, brought to architecture expectations that we no longer have.

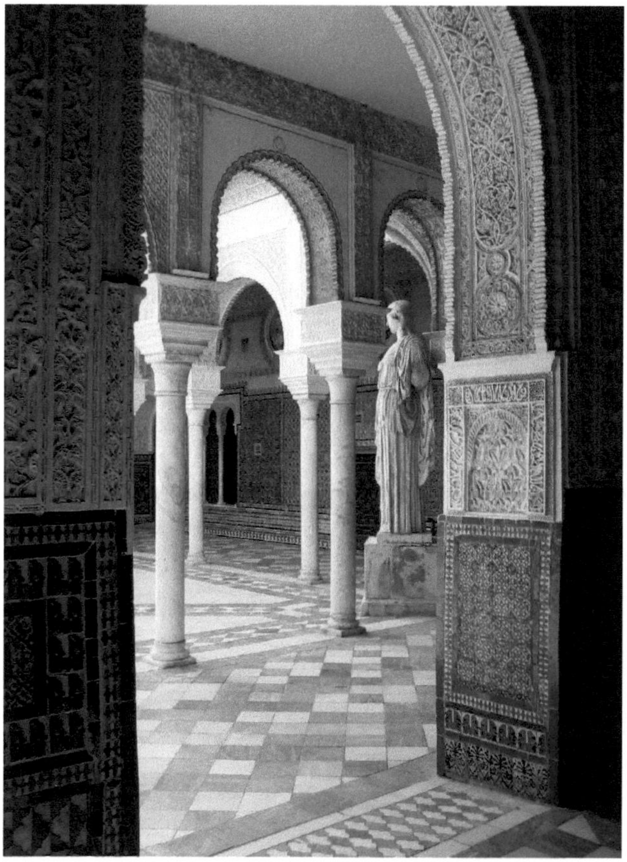

146
Casa de las Pilatos, rebuilt from 1509, Seville

Don Fadrique Enríquez de Ribera began renovations to his family's palace in Seville soon after he returned from a pilgrimage to Jerusalem in 1520. The house became the beginning of a processional route that recreated the *Via Dolorosa* in the Holy Land, based on Don Fadrique's careful study of the monuments he saw there. On his journey, however, he also spent several months in Italy. When the religious procession in Seville, called the Via Crucis, became so popular that the participants could no longer be accommodated in the palace chapel, Don Fadrique commissioned a sculptor from Genoa to create a new doorway to the palace as the starting point for the local pilgrims and columns for the courtyard. Work continued on the house up to Don Fadrique's death in 1539, combining Isabelline ornament from the older building, local *mudéjar* traditions in the plaster, woodwork, and tile, and elements from Italian architecture that he saw on his travels.

Nationalism and Restoration Practices

Because architecture, for the most part, exists in the world far longer than the time span of its makers, it stands to reason that the interpretation of buildings would evolve and change, as the world changes around it. We see this in the changing fortunes of interpretation in the scholarly literature and the public perception as well as in patterns of historic preservation. Manueline architecture produced in Portugal during the reign of King Manuel I (1495–1521) is an interesting case [**148**]. The term has been used to define a national Portuguese style of ornament that combines multiple traditions (Moorish, Islamic, Gothic, classical) into a rich decorative language. Yet, the term 'Manueline' was invented in the nineteenth century by Francisco Adolfo Varnhagen, writing a short history of the Hieronymite Monastery in Belém (see Chapter 5). His book, *Notícia histórica e descriptiva do mosteiro de Belém* ('Historical and Descriptive Notes on the Monastery of Belém'), appeared in 1842.[4] Varnhagen listed the major characteristics of what he defined as the Manueline style, including ornate, flower-like ornament, avoidance of simple repetition, and absence of straight mouldings. The term fed into a period of

147

Tiles from Casa de las Pilatos, Seville

As Don Fadrique Enríquez de Ribera rebuilt the house that came to be called Casa de Pilatos (after Pilate's House in Jerusalem, supposedly a model for the gateway added in the 1520s) he employed numerous craftsmen to embellish the rooms with wood panelling, stucco, paint, gilt, and, especially, tiles. Many rooms in the house, including the courtyard and stairway, have tile dados up to a height of 5.3 metres, in a range of patterns. The master tile maker Polido signed a contract on 1 October 1538 agreeing to provide 2,000 tiles a week. A new technique, *cuenca* (meaning 'hollow'), allowed for a richer vocabulary of images on the tiles, including the incorporation of Moresque, Isabelline, and Italian classical motifs.

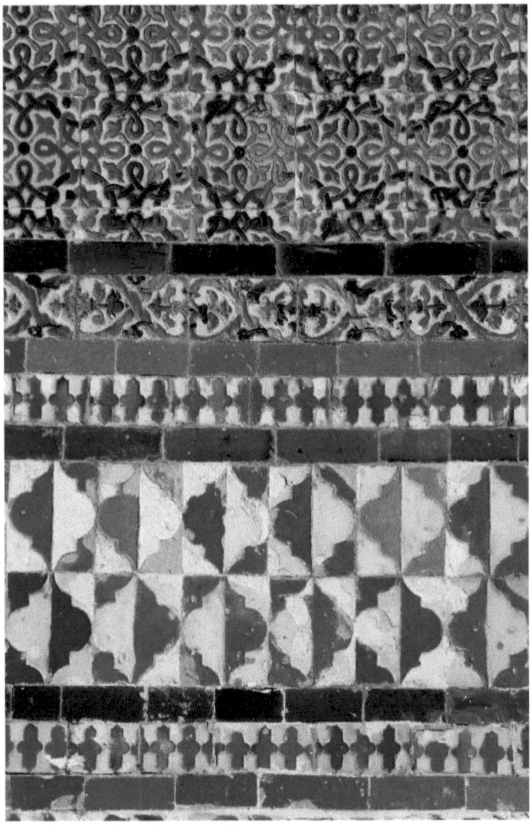

148

Detail: Cloister, Jerónimos Monastery, Belém

Sculptures of ships and exotic animals reinforce the association of the Jerónimos Monastery with the triumphs of Portuguese trade and exploration in the Renaissance. Technical analysis and conservation of the stonework, however, has shown that many of these details were added during a nineteenth-century renovation.

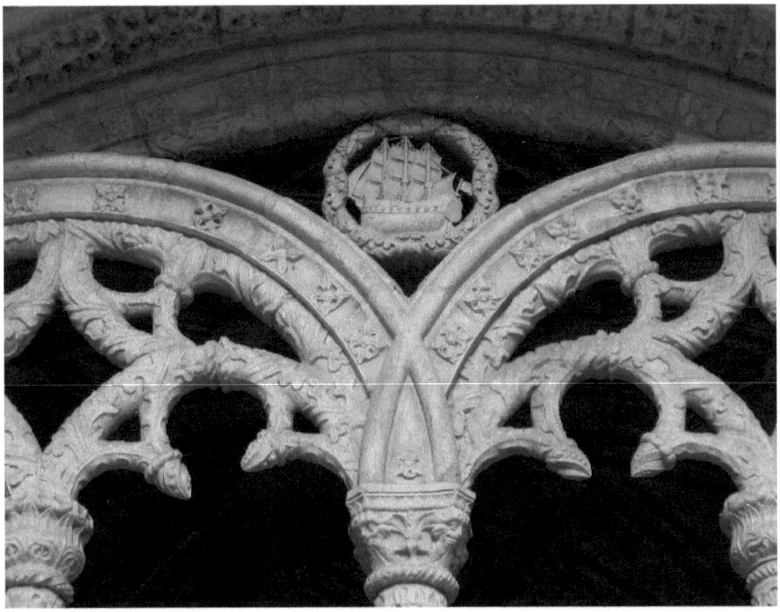

Romantic nationalism in the nineteenth century, and inspired an interpretation that associated that architecture with the great age of maritime exploration. The lizards and twining foliage, twisted mouldings, and invented classical forms were then seen as images of this golden age of Portugal's past, made manifest in architectural ornament. In 1857, a French historian, Edgar Quinet, gave his impressions of Portuguese architecture.

> This is God's house, but it is adorned like a ship about to set sail. On entering the church, one sees the fruits and plants of newly discovered continents, harvested and gathered together in bas-reliefs... Here, Gothic sirens swim in an alabaster sea; there, climbing apes from the Ganges swing at the end of the nave of the Church of São Pedro. Ostriches from Brazil flap their wings around the Cross of Golgotha. Tears flow from coats of arms. Marble *mappae mundi*, astrolabes and set-squares appear alongside crucifixes, nautical axes, shields and ladders...[5]

When the monastery at Belém was restored after the Portuguese Civil War (1828–34), the architects and masons quite naturally interpreted the damaged parts of the building in light of what their own generation understood the ornament to represent: the maritime exploration and trade of the sixteenth century. In the late nineteenth century restoration, important parts of the building were removed that had been built (in the later sixteenth century) in a more classical, non-Manueline, style. All of the ornament that now seems to refer directly to maritime exploration, such as the ropes, ships, and astrolabes, is in the parts of the building restored in the nineteenth century.

Conversations with the Past

By the year 1600, publications and travel shaped a canon of architects worthy of study. Vasari's treatise was the first such listing of excellent artists and architects, but the emerging architectural treatises in the sixteenth and seventeenth centuries created a further group. For the English architect Inigo Jones (1573–1652), engaged in a self-directed programme of study of the best in European and classical architecture, Sebastiano Serlio, Philibert de l'Orme, Michelangelo, Jacopo Barozzi da Vignola, and Andrea Palladio could all be studied without leaving London. He owned books by, or about, all these architects, in addition to an extensive library of books on ancient culture. When he travelled to Italy in 1613–14, he studied the buildings of Palladio, travelling with Palladio's treatise in hand [**149**].[6] By the first decades of the seventeenth century, architects saw that in the previous century the experiments with ornament, and the development of building types, offered their generation a range of models which was as varied and rich as antiquity itself.

149

Andrea Palladio, Villa Capra, *I quattro libri dell'architettura*, Venice, 1570, with annotations by Inigo Jones

Jones read and annotated Palladio's treatise before he ever saw the buildings of Palladio in Italy. The book allowed Jones to study the plan and details of Palladio's architecture, and then to compare the printed image with the building itself. In his annotations, Jones made much of the discrepancy between Palladio's treatise and Italian building practice. For other architects and patrons who never travelled, architectural treatises allowed them to study ancient architecture and modern designs. A growing audience emerged in the sixteenth century, eager for each new book that appeared on ornament and the orders, antiquities, modern practice, and architectural culture.

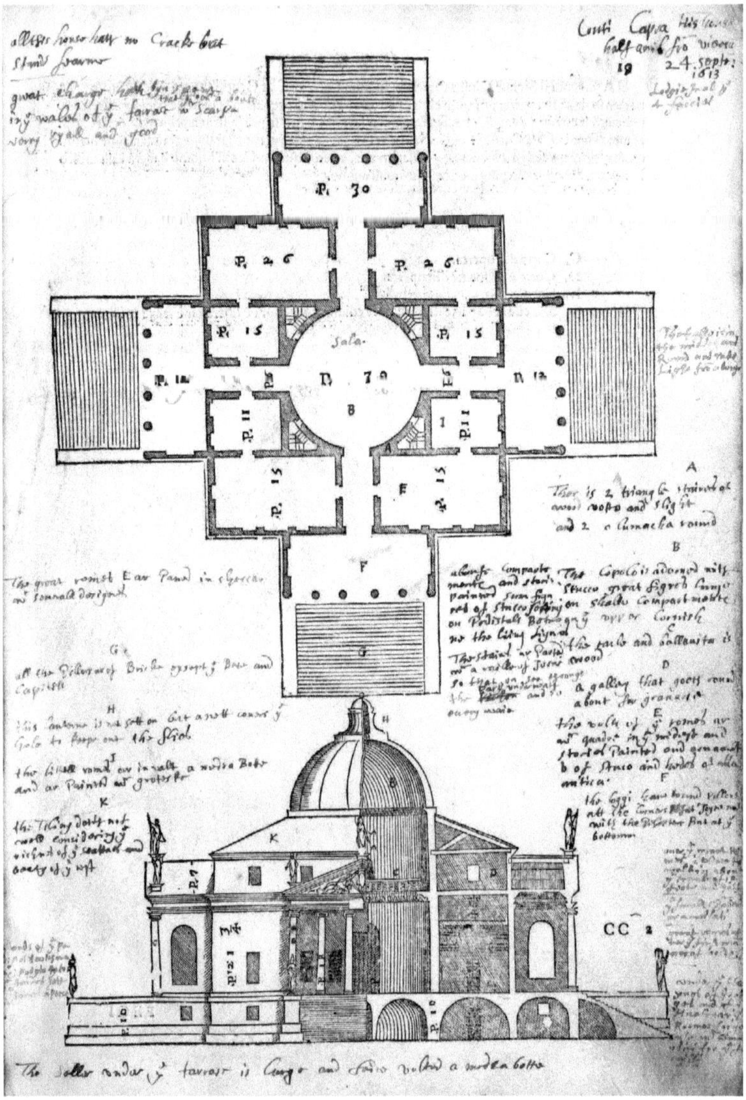

Training for architects had also evolved. Royal and private academies were founded that offered aspiring architects a formal counterpart to the apprenticeships available to craftsmen. Training might involve periods of study in Rome, deemed ever more important for intense study of antiquities as part of a classical training. François Blondel (1628–86) published the lectures he gave to the Académie Royale d'Architecture as *Cours d'architecture* (1675), making available his scientific explorations of the principles of architectural beauty.[7] Debates between architects such as that on best principles between Blondel and Claude Perrault could now be played out on a more public stage given the increased status and visibility of architects designing public commissions, and the easier access to print.

In the changing intellectual and scientific climate of the seventeenth century, the place of the allied disciplines also shifted in relation to architecture. New areas of investigation in statics, biology, civil engineering, and even astronomy all affected not only architectural theory but also its practice. Architecture had always, since the time of Vitruvius, been understood to draw on virtually every discipline. Yet those aspirations were never fulfilled in any tangible way. By the seventeenth century academies and royal societies brought together practitioners of various interests, and the similarities between disciplines offered rich areas for exchange. Christopher Wren, trained in mathematics and astronomy, brought that evidence-based approach to his work in architecture.

In the architecture and engineering projects of the seventeenth century, the scientific principles of Renaissance building encouraged construction on a larger scale, with ever more ambitious schemes projecting out into the surrounding landscape, a physical manifestation of the self-aggrandizing power of their patrons. The palace at Versailles, for example, transformed a small hunting lodge into a vast complex with the figure of the King at its conceptual centre. The most astounding development at Versailles, however, was the hydraulics systems created to fill the cisterns for the garden fountains. The Machine de Marly used fourteen paddlewheels to power 250 pumps to bring water from the Seine to the dry plains at Versailles by way of the Louveciennes Aqueduct [**150**].[8]

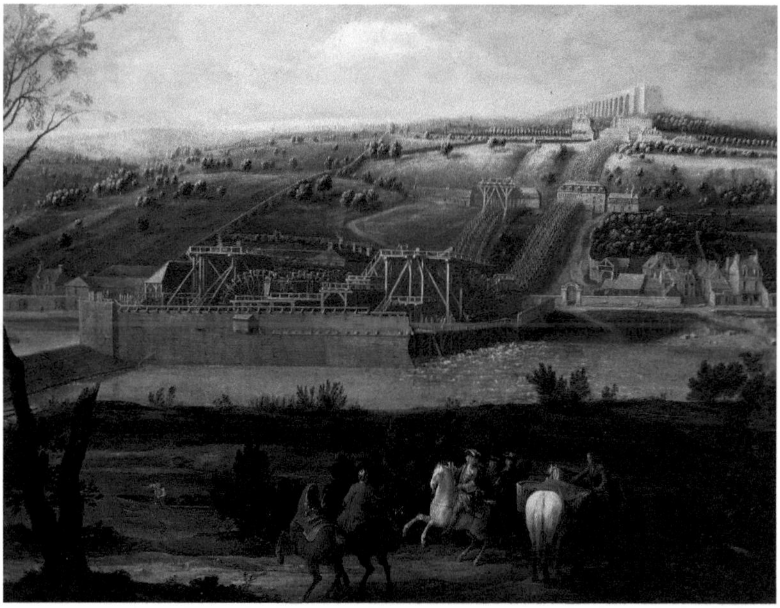

150

Machine de Marly, completed 1684, France

Only traces of this engineering marvel survive. The pumps, aqueducts, holding tanks, reservoirs, and pipes provided water for the fountains and gardens at Versailles.

Relevance to Contemporary Practice

The period I have covered in this book, the fifteenth and sixteenth centuries, is often referred to as part of the early modern period. That designation has the advantage of side-stepping some of the limitations in the term 'Renaissance': its implied exclusion of the merchant and labouring classes and concomitant focus on elite culture, its Eurocentrism, and its tendency to overlook factors such as the development of technology. The use of the term 'early modern' also suggests that the fifteenth to the eighteenth centuries can be seen as the precursor to modern culture. In the field of architecture and architectural history, this certainly has advantages. Alberti marks out, in his *De re aedificatoria*, a new attitude toward building as a process that begins first in the mind with the conceptualization of architecture, a psychological construction that includes both the practical aspects of planning but also the creation of the imaginary spaces of the psyche.

The work of the sixteenth-century architect Andrea Palladio has since the Renaissance received more attention than that of all other architects, on account of his seemingly rational and systematic development of architectural plans. If Palladio's architecture represented something essential for modern architects, then other fifteenth- and sixteenth-century architects were understood as more 'particular' and 'individual' talents. Before the Second World War, for example, the architecture of Giulio Romano (?1499–1546) in and around Mantua was largely ignored. His idiosyncratic use of ornament seemed an anomaly in a classical tradition that began with Brunelleschi. Yet buildings such as the Palazzo Te (from the mid-1520s) found new advocates in a climate that embraced a post-Freudian psychological interpretation of art and architecture.[9] Changing attitudes toward Renaissance architecture reveal as much about the changing interests of contemporary culture as they reveal about the buildings themselves.

Modern architects found in their studies of particular building types, such as the villa, models for the systematic invention of new rational architectural forms. Palladio's variations on a few limited plan types for domestic architecture served as one prototype for architects such as Le Corbusier in his design for a modern villa. In an essay on the relationship between the work of Andrea Palladio and the modern architect Le Corbusier, the critic Colin Rowe wrote this in 1947:

> As a constructor of architectural fugues, Palladio is the convinced classicist with a sixteenth century repertory of well-humanized forms; and he translates this received material with a passion and a high seriousness fitting to the continued validity that he finds it to possess. The reference to the Pantheon in the superimposed pediments of the Malcontenta, to the thermae in its

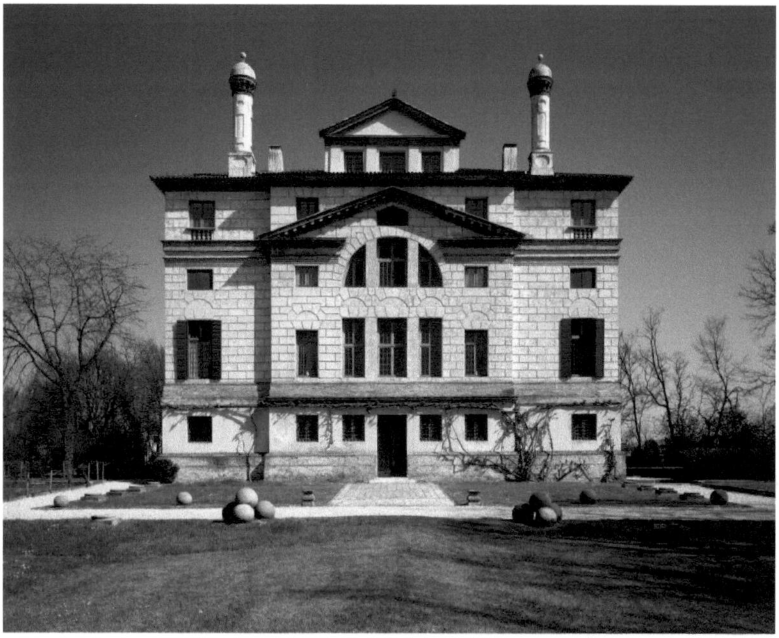

151

Andrea Palladio, Villa Foscari, begun *c.*1558, Malcontenta di Mira, Italy

Built for two brothers, Nicol' and Alvise Foscari, the Villa Malcontenta (as it is called) rises above the River Brenta on a tall podium, reminiscent of ancient temples. Unlike most of Palladio's other villas, this building has no agricultural connections: it is a regal retreat, easily accessible from Venice by boat. References to ancient architecture include the temple front on the main façade and the thermal (or half round) window on the back elevation. The memory of the front façade and Ionic porch is recalled in the pediment that embraces the thermal window and marks out the high entrance hall on the interior.

cruciform salon, the ambiguity, profound in both idea and form, in the equivocal conjunction of temple front and domestic block; these are charged with meaning, both for what they are and what they signify; and their impression is poignant. By such apparatus the ancient house is not recreated, but something far more significant is achieved: a creative nostalgia evokes a manifestation of mythical power in which the Roman and the ideal are equated.[10]

Rudolph Wittkower and Colin Rowe saw the value in Alberti and Palladio's architecture through the lens of current issues in twentieth-century architecture. In the simple geometries and formal rigour of Renaissance buildings they found the origins of modern architectural values [**151**]. For both, Renaissance design was not simply a process of stylistic recreation, or even a desire to make the past live again. In the references to antiquity and the rigour of formal planning, Rowe saw in Palladio a model, though an uneasy one, for the project of modernism. Embodied in Renaissance building was the poignancy of a past lost and only partially recovered, antiquity assimilated yet always incomplete. Whether or not we agree with Rowe's interpretation of Palladio's goals is beside the point. We cannot help but agree that Renaissance architecture is 'charged with meaning', while simultaneously knowing that that interpretation is always subject to change.

Notes

Chapter 1 Introduction

1. Giorgio Vasari, quoted on p. 214 in Erwin Panofsky, 'The First Page of Giorgio Vasari's "Libro": A Study on the Gothic Style in the Judgment of the Italian Renaissance', in his *Meaning in the Visual Arts* (London, 1970), 206–65.
2. See the recent collection Monique Chatenet et al., eds., *Le Gothique de la Renaissance* (Paris, 2011).

Chapter 2 The Voluptuous Pleasure of Building

1. Thomas Coryat, *Coryat's Crudities Hastily gobled up in five Moneths travells* (London, 1611; repr. Glasgow, 1905), 2.
2. Ibid. 306.
3. Ibid.
4. R. R. Bolgar, *The Classical Heritage and its Beneficiaries from the Carolingian Age to the End of the Renaissance* (New York, 1964), 317.
5. Deborah Howard, 'Attitudes to the Gothic in Renaissance Venice', in Monique Chatenet et al., eds., *Le Gothique de la Renaissance* (Paris, 2011), 103–20.
6. Richard Goy, *The House of Gold: Building a Palace in Medieval Venice* (Cambridge, 1992).
7. See the collection of essays in Lucy Gent, ed., *Albion's Classicism: The Visual Arts in Britain, 1550–1660* (New Haven, 1995).
8. See the collection of essays in Georgia Clarke and Paul Crossley, eds., *Architecture and Language: Constructing Identity in European Architecture, c.1000–c.1650* (Cambridge, 2000).
9. Nicola Camerlenghi, 'The *Longue Durée* and the Life of Buildings', in Robert Bork, William W. Clark, and Abby McGehee, eds., *New Approaches to Medieval Architecture* (Farnham, 2011), 11–20.
10. Cyriac of Ancona, *Itinerarium*, ed. L. Mehus (Florence, 1742), 54; cited in Peter Burke, *The Renaissance Sense of the Past* (London, 1969), 25.
11. *A direction for travailers. Taken out of Iustus Lipsius, and enlarged for the behoofe of the right honourable Lord, the Young Earle of Bedforde, being now ready to travell* (London, 1592), § $B4^r$–$B4^v$. See also the paraphrase of the above in Coryat, *Coryat's Crudities*, 9: 'Likewise the places wherein divers famous battels have beene fought, so much celebrated partly by the ancient Roman historiographers, and partly by other neotericke authors (many of which I exactly observed in my short voyage) when they are survayed by a curious traveller, doe seeme to present to the eyes of his mind a certaine Idea of the bloudy skirmishes themselves.'
12. James Ackerman, *Palladio* (New York, 1991), 177.
13. A. J. Toynbee, *A Study of History*, vol. ix (Oxford, 1954), 4; quoted in Jack Goody, *Renaissances: The One or the Many?* (Cambridge, 2010), 8.
14. Filarete, *Treatise on Architecture*, trans. John R. Spencer (New Haven, 1965), 15.
15. See Marcello Fantoni, George Gorse, and Malcolm Smuts, eds., *The Politics of Space: European Courts, ca.1500–1750* (Rome, 2009).
16. Francesco Colonna, *Hypnerotomachia Poliphili: The Strife of Love in a Dream*, trans. Joscelyn Godwin (New York, 1999), 59.
17. See the discussion of the yin and yang of Renaissance architecture in John Summerson, 'Antitheses of the Quattrocento', in *Heavenly Mansions and Other Essays* (London, 1949); and Christy Anderson, 'A Very Personal Renaissance', in Frank Salmon, ed., *Summerson and Hitchcock: Centenary Essays on Architectural Historiography* (New Haven, 2006), 69–84.

Chapter 3 The House of God

1. Leon Battista Alberti, *On the Art of Building in Ten Books*, trans. Joseph Rykwert, Neil Leach, and Robert Tavernor (Cambridge, Mass., 1997), Bk. VII, iii, p. 194.
2. Antonio di Tuccio Manetti, *The Life of Brunelleschi*, ed. H. Saalman, trans. C. Enggass (University Park, Pa., 1970), 106, quoted in Marvin Trachtenberg, 'On Brunelleschi's Old Sacristy as Model for Early Renaissance Church Architecture', in J. Guillaume, ed., *L'Église dans l'architecture de la Renaissance*, actes du colloque tenu à Tours, 28–31 May 1990 (Paris, 1995), 9.
3. See Giovanni Fanelli and Michele Fanelli, *Brunelleschi's Cupola: Past and Present of an Architectural Masterpiece* (Florence, 2004).
4. Paul Davies, 'The Madonna delle Carceri in Prato and Italian Renaissance Pilgrimage Architecture', *Architectural History* 36 (1993), 1–18.
5. Rudolf Wittkower, *Architectural Principles in the Age of Humanism* (New York, 1971), 21.
6.Joseph Leo Koerner, *The Reformation of the Image* (London, 2004), esp. 402–40.
7. Quoted ibid. 407.
8. Jacques Perret, *Des fortifications et artifices, architecture et perspective* (Paris, 1601) quoted in Per Gustaf Hamberg, *Temples for Protestants: Studies in the Architectural Milieu of the Early Reformed Church and of the Lutheran Church* (Gothenburg, 2002), 37.
9. Carol Herselle Krinsky, *Synagogues of Europe: Architecture, History, Meaning* (New York, 1985), 41.
10. Shalom Sabar, 'Jews and the Arts', in Paul F. Grendler, ed., *Encyclopedia of the Renaissance*, vol. iii (New York, 1999), 338–42.
11. See Krinsky, *Synagogues of Europe*, 200–5.
12. G. Isham, 'Sir Thomas Tresham and his Buildings', *Reports and Papers of the Northamptonshire Antiquarian Society* 65/2 (1966); J. A. Gotch, *A Complete Account, Illustrated by Measured Drawings of the Buildings Erected in Northamptonshire, by Sir Thomas Tresham, between the Years 1575 and 1605* (Northampton, 1883).
13. George Kubler, *Portuguese Plain Architecture: Between Spices and Diamonds, 1521–1706* (Middletown, Conn., 1978), 9.
14. Ruth Barnes, 'Relatives in Faith: Pilgrimage in Judaism, Islam and Christianity', in Ruth Barnes and Crispin Branfoot, eds., *Pilgrimage: The Sacred Journey* (Oxford, 2006), 12–41.
15. Ryan Gregg, 'The Sacro Monte of Varallo as a Physical Manifestation of the *Spiritual Exercises*', *Athanor* 22 (2004), 49–55.
16. Domenico Promis and Giuseppe Müller, *Lettere ed orazioni latine di Girolamo Morone* (Turin, 1863), 148–9, quoted in Alessandro Nova, ' "Popular" Art in Renaissance Italy: Early Response to the Holy Mountain at Varallo', in Claire Farago, ed., *Reframing the Renaissance: Visual Culture in Europe and Latin America 1450–1650* (New Haven, 1995), 112–26.
17. George Kubler, 'Sacred Mountains in Europe and America', in Timothy Verdon and John Henderson, eds., *Christianity and the Renaissance: Image and Religious Imagination in the Quatrrocento* (Syracuse, NY, 1990), 413–41.
18. Deborah Howard, 'Cultural Transfer between Venice and the Ottomans in the Fifteenth and Sixteenth Centuries', in Henry Roodenburg, ed., *Cultural Exchange in Early Modern Europe*, iv: *Forging European Identities, 1400–1700* (Cambridge, 2007), 138–77.
19. On Sinan, see Gülrü Necipoğlu, *The Age of Sinan: Architectural Culture in the Ottoman Empire* (Princeton, 2005), esp. 331–45.

Chapter 4 Theories and Practices: The Case of St Peter's, Rome

1. See Alina Payne, *The Architectural Treatise in the Italian Renaissance* (Cambridge, 2000).
2. Ingrid Rowland, 'The Fra Giocondo Vitruvius at 500 (1511–2011)', *Journal of the Society of Architectural Historians* 70 (2011), 285–9.
3. Ingrid D. Rowland, 'Vitruvius in Print and in Vernacular Translation: Fra Giocondo, Bramante, Raphael and Cesare Cesariano', in Vaughan Hart and Peter Hicks, eds., *Paper Palaces: The Rise of the Renaissance Architectural Treatise* (New Haven, 1998), 105–21.
4. Francesco Paolo Fiore, 'The *Trattati* on Architecture by Francesco di Giorgio', in Hart and Hicks, eds., *Paper Palaces*, 66–85.
5. Alexander Nagel and Christopher S. Wood, *Anachronic Renaissance* (New York, 2010), 51–70; and earlier, Richard Krautheimer, 'Introduction to an "Iconography of Medieval Architecture" ',

Journal of the Warburg and Courtauld Institutes 5 (1942), 1–33.
6. Catherine Wilkinson, 'Renaissance Treatises on Military Architecture and the Science of Mechanics', in J. Guillaume, ed., *Les Traités d'architecture de la Renaissance*, actes du colloque tenu à Tours, 1–11 July 1981 (Paris, 1988).
7. Olga Medvedkova, *Bibliothèques d'architecture* (Paris, 2009).
8. Howard Burns, 'Building and Construction in Palladio's Venice', in Jean Guillaume, ed., *Les Chantiers de la Renaissance*, actes des colloques tenu à Tours, 1983–4 (Paris, 1991), 191–226.
9. Anthony Blunt, *Philibert de l'Orme* (London 1959), 148; quoted in Henri Zerner, *Renaissance Art in France: The Invention of Classicism* (Paris, 2003), 402.
10. See Mark Girouard, *Elizabethan Architecture* (New Haven, 2009), 57–60.
11. Joseph Rykwert, 'On the Oral Transmission of Architectural Theory', in Guillaume, ed., *Les Traités d'architecture de la Renaissance*, 31–48.
12. Antonio Filarete, *Treatise on Architecture*, ed. J. R. Spencer (London, 1964), 198.
13. Pamela O. Long, *Openness, Secrecy, Authorship: Technical Arts and the Culture of Knowledge from Antiquity to the Renaissance* (Baltimore, 2001), 240–2.
14. Giacomo Grimaldi, *Descrizione della basilica antica di S. Pietro in Vaticano*, Codice Barberini Latino 2733 (Rome, 1972), quoted in Dale Kinney, 'Spolia', in William Tronzo, ed., *St. Peter's in the Vatican* (Cambridge, 2005), 35.
15. Frédérique Lemerle, *La Renaissance et les antiquités de la Gaule* (Turnhout, 2005), 51–81.
16. John Onians, *Bearers of Meaning: The Classical Orders in Antiquity, the Middle Ages and the Renaissance* (Princeton, 1990), 330.
17. See Georgia Clarke, 'Architecture, Languages and Style in Fifteenth-Century Italy', *Journal of the Warburg and Courtauld Institutes* 71 (2008), 169–89.
18. Sebastiano Serlio, *On Architecture*, vol. i: Books I–IV of 'Tutte l'opere d'architettura et prospetiva', in *Sebastiano Serlio on Architecture*, trans. Vaughan Hart and Peter Hicks, 2 vols. (New Haven, 1996), 254.
19. *Les Annotations de Guillaume Philandrier sur le De architectura de Vitruve, livres I à IV*, ed. Frédérique Lemerle (Paris, 2000).
20. Harry Francis Mallgrave, 'Dancing with Vitruvius: Corporeal Fantasies in Northern Classicism', in George Dodds and Robert Tavernor, eds., *Body and Building: Essays on the Changing Relation of Body and Architecture* (Cambridge, Mass., 2005), 126–37.
21. Paul Crossley, 'The Return to the Forest: Natural Architecture and the German Past in the Age of Dürer', in Thomas W. Gaehtgens, ed., *Künstlerischer Austausch: Artistic Exchange*, vol. ii (Berlin, 1993), 71–80. Also see Ethan Matt Kavaler, 'Nature and the Chapel Vaults at Ingolstadt: Structuralist and Other Perspectives', *Art Bulletin* 87 (June 2005), 230–48.
22. Letter dated January 1547. Michelangelo Buonarroti, *Letters of Michelangelo*, trans. E. H. Ramsden (Stanford, Calif., 1963), 69.
23. Leon Battista Alberti, *On the Art of Building in Ten Books*, trans. J. Rykwert, N. Leach, and R. Tavernor (Cambridge, Mass., 1988), Book II, 1, pp. 33–4.
24. Susan O. Thompson, 'Paper Manufacturing and Early Books', *Annals of the New York Academy of Sciences* 314 (1978), 167–74.
25. Richard Goldthwaite, *The Building of Renaissance Florence* (Baltimore, 1980), 370.
26. Howard Burns, 'Building against Time: Renaissance Strategies to Secure Large Churches against Changes to their Design', in Jean Guillaume, ed., *L'Église dans l'architecture de la Renaissance*, actes du colloque tenu à Tours, 28–31 May 1990 (Paris, 1995), 107–31.
27. Ann Huppert, 'Envisioning New St. Peter's: Perspectival Drawings and the Process of Design', *Journal of the Society of Architectural Historians* 68 (2009), 158–78.
28. Christof Thoenes, 'Renaissance St. Peter's', in William Tronzo, ed., *St. Peter's in the Vatican* (Cambridge, 2005), 85–6.
29. Christoph Luitpold Frommel, 'Il cantiere di S. Pietro prima di Michelangelo', in Guillaume, ed., *Les Chantiers de la renaissance*, 175–90.

Chapter 5 The Architecture of Ascendancy: Buildings and Power

1. Martin Warnke, *The Court Artist: On the Ancestry of the Modern Artist* (New York, 1993).
2. Marcello Fantoni, 'The City of the Prince: Space and Power', in Marcello Fantoni, George Gorse, and Malcolm Smuts, eds., *The Politics of Space: European Courts ca.1500–1750* (Rome, 2009), 39–57.

3. Fernando Marías, 'Gótico y neogótico en la Castilla del siglo XVI', in Monique Chatenet et al., eds., *Le Gothique de la Renaissance*, actes des quatrième Rencontres d'architecture européenne Paris, 12–16 June 2007 (Paris, 2011), 149–72.
4. Krista De Jonge, ' "Anticse Werken": Architecture in the Ancient Manner 1500–1530', in Krista De Jonge and Konrad Ottenheym, eds., *Unity and Discontinuity: Architectural Relationships between the Southern and Northern Low Countries (1530–1700)* (Turnhout, 2007), 31–2.
5. Dagmar Eichberger, 'A Noble Residence for a Female Regent: Margaret of Austria and the "Court of Savoy" in Mechelen', in Helen Hills, ed., *Architecture and the Politics of Gender in Early Modern Europe* (Aldershot, 2003), 29–33.
6. Ethan Matt Kavaler, 'Margaret of Austria, Ornament, and the Court Style of Brou', in Stephen J. Campbell, ed., *Artists at Court: Image-Making and Identity 1300–1550* (Boston, 2004), 124–37.
7. Malcolm Smuts and George Gorse, 'Introduction', to Fantoni, Gorse, and Smuts, eds., *The Politics of Space*, 19.
8. See George Kubler, 'A Sixteenth Century Meaning of the Escorial', *Diogenes* (1981), esp. 231–4.
9. Fray José de Sigüenza, *Historia de la Orden de San Jerónimo* (1605; 1905); new edn. of 3rd part, *Fundación del Monasterio de El Escorial* (Madrid, 1963).
10. Sigüenza, *Fundación del Monasterio de El Escorial*, 321, 322–3; quoted in Kubler, 'A Sixteenth Century Meaning', 245–6.
11. Alexander Nagel and Christopher S. Wood, *Anachronic Renaissance* (New York, 2010), 198–200.
12. Christopher S. Wood, *Forgery Replica Fiction: Temporalities of German Renaissance Art* (Chicago, 2008), 227–8.
13. Marian C. Donnelly, *Architecture in the Scandinavian Countries* (Cambridge, Mass., 1992), 98–100; Birger Mikkelsen, *Kronborg* (Helsinør, 1997).
14. Jiřina Hořejší, *The Vladislav Hall of the Prague Castle* (Prague, 1973).
15. Henry-Russell Hitchcock, *German Renaissance Architecture* (Princeton, 1981), 41, 43, 60–1.
16. Evelyn Welch, 'Between Italy and Moscow: Cultural Crossroads and the Culture of Exchange', in B. Roek and H. Roodenberg, eds., *Cultural Exchange in Early Modern Europe*, vol. iv (Cambridge, 2007), 59–99.
17. William Craft Brumfield, *A History of Russian Architecture* (Cambridge, 1993), esp. 92–101.
18. Joycelyne G. Russell, *The Field of Cloth of Gold: Men and Manners in 1520* (New York, 1969); Glenn Richardson, 'Entertainments for the French Ambassadors at the Court of Henry VIII', *Renaissance Studies* 9 (1995), 404–15.
19. Simon Thurley, 'The Palaces of Henry VIII', in Jean Guillaume, ed., *Architecture et vie sociale: l'organisation intérieure des grandes demeures à la fin du Moyen Âge et à la Renaissance*, actes du colloque tenu à Tours, 6–10 June 1988 (Paris, 1994), 97–106.
20. Egon Verheyen, 'Jacopo Strada's Mantuan Drawings of 1567–1568', *Art Bulletin* 49 (1967), 62–70.
21. Henry-Russell Hitchcock, *German Renaissance Architecture* (Princeton, 1981), 168.

Chapter 6 Corporate Identity

1. Philibert de l'Orme, *L'Architecture* (Paris, 1567), fos. 329^{v}–330; quoted in Henri Zerner, *Renaissance Art in France: The Invention of Classicism* (Paris, 2003), 417.
2. The psychological aspect of groups in the Renaissance is discussed in Hannah Chapelle Wojciehowski, *Group Identity in the Renaissance* (Cambridge, 2011).
3. See the collection of essays on corporate identity in the Renaissance: Richard C. Trexler, ed., *Persons in Groups: Social Behavior as Identity Formation in Medieval and Renaissance Europe* (Binghamton, NY, 1985).
4. Quoted in John A. A. Goodall, *God's House at Ewelme: Life, Devotion, and Architecture in a Fifteenth-Century Almshouse* (Aldershot, 2001), 1.
5. Ibid. 3.
6. Richard Mulcaster, *Positions* (London, 1581), 229. Quoted in Maurice Howard, *The Building of Elizabethan and Jacobean England* (New Haven, 2007), 87.
7. James S. Ackerman and Myra Nan Rosenfeld, 'Social Stratification in Renaissance Urban Planning', in Susan Zimmerman and Ronald F. E. Weissman, eds., *Urban Life in the Renaissance* (Newark, Del., 1989), 33.
8. John Newman, 'The Physical Setting', in James McConica, ed., *The History of the University of Oxford*, iii: *The Collegiate University* (Oxford, 1986), 607–44.
9. Stanley Gillam, *The Divinity School & Duke Humphrey's Library at Oxford* (Oxford, 1998), 29–39.

10. Eunice Howe, 'The Architecture of Institutionalism: Women's Spaces in Renaissance Hospitals', in Helen Hills, ed., *Architecture and the Politics of Gender in Early Modern Europe* (Aldershot, 2003), 63–82.
11. On Rolin as patron, see Marie-Thérèse Berthier and John-Thomas Sweeney, *Le Chancellor Rolin 1376–1462: ambition, pouvoir et fortune en Bourgogne* (Précy-sous-Tils, 1998), esp. 181–288.
12. Philip Gavitt, *Charity and Children in Renaissance Florence: The Ospedale degli Innocenti, 1410–1536* (Ann Arbor, 1990).
13. Maurice Howard. 'The Ideal House and Healthy Life: The Origins of Architectural Theory in England', in Jean Guillaume, ed., *Les Traités d'architecture de la Renaissance*, actes du colloque tenu à Tours, 1–11 July 1981 (Paris, 1988), 425–33.
14. Nicholas Terpstra, 'Confraternities', in Paul F. Grendler, ed., *Encyclopedia of the Renaissance*, vol. ii (New York, 1999), 65–72.
15. Francesco Sansovino, *Venetia, città nobilissima* (Venice, 1580), trans. and quoted in Richard Goy, *Venice: The City and its Architecture* (London, 1997), 214.
16. Deborah Howard, *The Architectural History of Venice* (New Haven, 2002), 141–3.
17. James Ackerman, *The Architecture of Michelangelo* (Chicago, 1986), 95–119.
18. David Hemsoll, 'The Laurentian Library and Michelangelo's Architectural Method', *Journal of the Warburg and Courtauld Institutes* 66 (2003), 29–62.
19. Deborah Howard, *Jacopo Sansovino: Architecture and Patronage in Renaissance Venice* (New Haven, 1987), 17–28.
20. Marilyn Dunn, 'Spaces Shaped for Spiritual Perfection: Convent Architecture and Nuns in Early Modern Rome', in Helen Hills, ed., *Architecture and the Politics of Gender in Early Modern Europe* (Aldershot, 2003), 151–76.
21. Quoted in Paulo Pereira, *Jerónimos Abbey of Santa Maria* (London, 2002), 16.
22. Maurice Howard, *The Building of Elizabethan and Jacobean England* (New Haven, 2007), 13–45.

Chapter 7 Shaping the Renaissance City

1. Nicola Coldstream, *Medieval Architecture* (Oxford, 2002), 126–7; Adrian Randolph, 'The Bastides of South-West France', *Art Bulletin* 76 (1995), 290–307.
2. David Friedman, *Florentine New Towns: Urban Design in the Late Middle Ages* (Cambridge, Mass., 1988).
3. Quoted in James D. Tracy, 'Introduction', in James D. Tracy (ed.), *City Walls: The Urban Enceinte in Global Perspective* (Cambridge, 2000), 1.
4. Simon Pepper and Walter Smith, 'City Gate', *Grove Art Online: Oxford Art Online*, 15 November 2010, <http://www.oxfordartonline.com.myaccess.library.utoronto.ca/subscriber/article/grove/art/T017889>.
5. Nicholas Adams, 'The Construction of Pienza (1459–1464) and the Consequences of *Renovatio*', in Susan Zimmerman and Ronald F. E. Weisman, eds., *Urban Life in the Renaissance* (Newark, Del., 1989), 50–79.
6. Helmut Puff, 'The City as Model: Three-Dimensional Representations of Urban Space in Early Modern Europe', in Arthur Groos, Hans-Jochen Schiewer, and Markus Stock (eds.), *Topographies of the Early Modern City* (Göttingen, 2008), 193–217.
7. Henri Zerner, *Renaissance Art in France* (Paris, 2003), 179–82.
8. Otto Lohr, s.v. 'Liber chronicarum', in *Gothic and Renaissance Art in Nuremberg 1300–1550*, exh. cat. (New York, 1986), 233–5.
9. Robert Bork, *Great Spires: Skyscrapers of the New Jerusalem* (Cologne, 2003), esp. 1–23.
10. Quoted in Douglas Biow, *The Culture of Cleanliness in Renaissance Italy* (Ithaca, NY, 2006), 83.
11. Francesco Guicciardini, 'Francesco Guicciardini's *Report from Spain*', trans. Sheila ffolliott, *Allegorica* 7 (1982), 68–9; quoted in Biow, *The Culture of Cleanliness*, 75.
12. Yvonne Elet, 'Seats of Power: The Outdoor Benches of Early Modern Florence', *JSAH* 61 (December 2002), 444–69.
13. Jean Favière, *L'Hôtel de Jacques Cœur à Bourges* (Paris, 1992).
14. See the excellent discussion in Susie Nash, *Northern Renaissance Art* (Oxford, 2008), 259–60.
15. Fabrizio Nevola, 'Home Shopping: Urbanism, Commerce, and Palace Design in Renaissance Italy', *JSAH* 70 (2011), 153–73.
16. Max Weber, *The City*, trans. Don Martindale and Gertrude Neuwirth (New York, 1958), 65, quoted in Christopher R. Friedrichs, *The Early Modern City 1450–1750* (London, 1995), 21.
17. Andrea Palladio, *I quattro libri dell'architettura* (Venice, 1570), II, 3.

18. Konrad Ottenheym, 'Meat Halls and Fish Markets in the Dutch Republic', in Konrad Ottenheym, Monique Chatenet, and Krista De Jonge, eds., *Public Buildings in Early Modern Europe* (Turnhout, 2010), 273–84.

19. Peter Stabel, 'Public or Private, Collective or Individual? The Spaces of Late Medieval Trade in the Low Countries', in Donatella Calabi, ed., *Il mercante patrizio: palazzi e botteghe nell'Europa del rinascimento* (Milan, 2008), 37–54.

20. Susan Mosher Stuard, *A State of Deference: Ragusa/Dubrovnik in the Medieval Centuries* (Philadelphia, 1992).

21. Nada Grujić, 'Dialogue Gothique–Renaissance dans l'architecture ragusaine des XVe et XVIe siècles', in Monique Chatenet et al., eds., *Le Gothique de la Renaissance*, actes des quatrièmes Rencontres d'architecture européenne Paris, 12–16 June 2007 (Paris, 2011), 124.

22. Timothy Clifford, 'Dubrovnik: Italian Art, *c.*1400–1800', in *Croatia: Aspects of Art, Architecture and Cultural Heritage* (London, 2009), 155.

23. Donatella Calabi and Derek Keene, 'Merchants' Lodgings and Cultural Exchange', in Donatella Calabi and Stephen Turk Christensen, *Cultural Exchange in Early Modern Europe*, ii: *Cities and Cultural Exchange in Europe, 1400–1700* (Cambridge, 2007), 315–48.

24. Benjamin C. I. Ravid, s.v. 'ghetto', in Paul F. Grendler, ed., *The Encyclopedia of the Renaissance* (New York, 1999), iii. 49.

25. Quoted in Richard Sennett, *Flesh and Stone: The Body and the City in Western Civilization* (New York, 1994), 233–4.

26. George L. Gorse, 'A Classical Stage for the Old Nobility: The Strada Nuova and Sixteenth-Century Genoa', *Art Bulletin* 79 (1997), 301–27.

27. Katherine W. Rinne, 'The Landscape of Laundry in Late Cinquecento Rome', *Studies in the Decorative Arts* 9 (2001–2), 34–60.

Chapter 8 Architecture in the Natural World

1. Agostino Gallo, *Le dieci giornate della vera agricoltura e piceri della villa*, Day VIII (Venice, 1566). Translated and quoted in James Ackerman, *The Villa: Form and Ideology of Country Houses* (Washington, DC, 1990), 129.

2. James Ackerman, 'The Villa as Paradigm', *Perspecta* 22 (1986), 11–31. Also see Amanda Lillie, 'The Humanist Villa Revisited', in Alison Brown, ed., *Language and Images of Renaissance Italy* (Oxford, 1995), 193–215.

3. Deborah Howard, 'Chasse, sports et plaisirs autour des châteaux d'Écosse', in Jean Guillaume, ed., *Architecture, jardin, paysage: l'environnement du château et de la ville aux XVe et XVIe siècles* (Paris, 1999), 295–305.

4. Alberti, 'Works of Individuals', V (17), p. 145. Quoted in Matthew Hardy, ' "Study the warm winds and the cold": Hippocrates and the Renaissance Villa', in Barbara Kenda, ed., *Aeolian Winds and the Spirit in Renaissance Architecture* (London, 2006), p. 65 n. 23.

5. Alvise Cornaro, *Discorsi della vita sobria* (Padua, 1558), trans. John Goadby Gregory as *The Art of Living Long* (Milwaukee, 1903). Quoted in Rebecca Williamson, 'The Breath of Cities', in Kenda, ed., *Aeolian Winds*, 156.

6. Quoted in Vaughan Hart and Peter Hicks, 'On Sebastiano Serlio: Decorum and the Art of Architectural Invention', in V. Hart and P. Hicks, eds., *Paper Palaces: The Rise of the Renaissance Architectural Treatise* (New Haven, 1998), 142.

7. Myra Nan Rosenfeld and James Ackerman, 'Social Stratification in Renaissance Urban Planning', in Susan Zimmerman and Ronald F. E. Weissman, eds., *Urban Life in the Renaissance* (Newark, Del., 1989), 21–49.

8. P. Bracciolini, *Lettere*, ed. H. Harth, vol. i (Florence, 1984), 109–10; quoted and trans. in Georgia Clarke, *Roman House–Renaissance Palaces: Inventing Antiquity in Fifteenth-Century Italy* (Cambridge, 2003), 136.

9. Pliny the Younger, *Epistles*, v.vi.45; quoted in Ackerman, *The Villa*, 13.

10. David R. Coffin, 'The Plans of the Villa Madama', *Art Bulletin* 49 (1967), 111–22.

11. Christy Anderson, *Inigo Jones and the Classical Tradition* (Cambridge, 2006).

12. Rudolf Wittkower, *Architectural Principles in the Age of Humanism* (1949; New York, 1971), 72.

13. Deborah Howard and Malcolm Longair, 'Harmonic Proportion and Palladio's Quattro libri', *JSAH* 41 (1982), 116–43. Also see Alina Payne, 'Rudolf Wittkower and Architectural Principles in the Age of Modernism', *JSAH* 53 (1994), 322–42.

14. See Deborah Howard, 'Reflections on Palladio's "soave armonía" ', in Maria

Beltramini and Caroline Elam, eds., *Some Degree of Happiness: studi di storia dell'architettura in onore di Howard Burns* (Pisa, 2010), 383–92 and Elwin C. Robison, 'Structural Implications in Palladio's Use of Harmonic Proportions', *Annali di architettura* 10–11 (1998–9), 175–82.
15. Quoted in James Ackerman, *Palladio* (London, 1966), 161.
16. See Maurice Howard, *The Building of Elizabethan and Jacobean England* (New Haven, 2007), 155–63 for a discussion of women as patrons in English building.
17. Matthew Johnson, *Behind the Castle Gate: From Medieval to Renaissance* (London, 2002), 75–8.
18. Alice T. Friedman, 'Architecture, Authority, and the Female Gaze: Planning and Representation in the Early Modern Country House', *Assemblage* 18 (1992), 41–61.
19. Rosalys Coope, 'The Gallery in England and its Relationship to the Principal Rooms (1520–1600)', in Jean Guillaume, ed., *Architecture et vie sociale: l'organisation intérieure des grandes demeures à la fin du Moyen Âge et à la Renaissance*, actes du colloque tenu à Tours, 6–10 June 1988 (Paris, 1994), 245–55.
20. See Pamela O. Long, 'Objects of Art/ Objects of Nature: Visual Representation and the Investigation of Nature', in Pamela H. Smith and Paula Findlen, eds., *Merchants & Marvels: Commerce, Science, and Art in Early Modern Europe* (New York, 2002), 63–82.
21. Henry Wotton, *The Elements of Architecture* (London, 1624), 3.
22. See Lyle Massey, ed., *The Treatise on Perspective*, Studies in the History of Art 59 (Washington, DC, 2003).
23. Claudia Lazzaro, 'The Sixteenth-Century Central Italian Villa and the Cultural Landscape', in Guillaume, ed., *Architecture, jardin, paysage*, 29–44.
24. Claudia Lazzaro, *The Italian Renaissance Garden* (New Haven, 1990), 177–84.

Chapter 9 Distant Shores

1. See Pamela H. Smith and Paula Findlen, eds., *Merchants & Marvels: Commerce, Science, and Art in Early Modern Europe* (New York, 2002).
2. See Katie Jakobiec, 'Merchant Builders and the Materials of Building: Polish Architecture *c.*1600' (Ph.D. dissertation, University of Toronto, 2012).
3. Alice Wilson Frothingham, *Tile Panels of Spain 1500–1650* (New York, 1969), 77–83.
4. Paulo Pereira, *Jerónimos Abbey of Santa Maria* (London, 2002), 45–53.
5. Edgar Quinet, *Mes vacances en Espagne* (Paris, 1954) quoted in Pereira, *Jerónimos Abbey*, 46.
6. Christy Anderson, *Inigo Jones and the Classical Tradition* (Cambridge, 2006).
7. Anthony Gerbino, *François Blondel: Architecture, Erudition, and the Scientific Revolution* (London, 2010).
8. On Marly and hydraulics see *Les Maîtres de l'eau d'Archimède à la machine de Marly* (Marly-le-Roi, 2006)
9. E. H. Gombrich, 'Zum Werke Giulio Romanos', *Jahrbuch des Kunsthistorischen Sammlungen in Wien* NS 8 (1934), 79–104; ibid. 9 (1935), 121–50.
10. Colin Rowe, 'The Mathematics of the Ideal Villa', in his *The Mathematics of the Ideal Villa and Other Essays* (Cambridge, Mass., 1982).

Timeline

Date	Political and religious	Culture and architecture
1350	*c.*1237–*c.*1450: Domination of the Golden Horde 1309–77: Papacy based at Avignon *c.*1322–1547: Grand Principality of Moscow (Muscovy) 1328–1589: Valois rule in France 1337: Hundred Years War between England and France begins 1348: Black Death 1369–1477: Duchy of Burgundy 1385: Portuguese victory over the Spanish at the Battle of Aljubarrota 1386–1572: Jagiellonian Dynasty, Kingdom of Poland and Grand Principality of Lithuania 1397–1523: Kalmar Union uniting kingdoms of Denmark, Norway, and Sweden 1390s: Manuel Chrysoloras (*c.*1353–1415) travels to Italy and teaches at the University of Florence	1334–60: Bell tower built for the Florence Cathedral 1338–90: Alhambra, Granada 1357: Merchant Adventurers Hall, York 1374–82: Loggia della Signoria, Florence 1379: New College founded 1386–8: Bodiam Castle
1400		1403: Lorenzo Ghiberti (*c.*1378–1455) wins a competition that secures a commission for the bronze doors of the Baptistery of San Giovanni, Florence 1404: Leonardo Bruni's *Laudatio Florentinae urbis* published 1405: Christine de Pisan (1365–*c.*1434) publishes *La Cité des dames* 1409: Groot Vleeshuis (Ghent)
1410	1416: Prince Henry 'the Navigator' (1394–1460), youngest son of João I of Portugal (reg. 1385–1433), establishes a naval base and a school of navigation at Sagres	1418: Beginning of rebuilding of San Lorenzo, Florence
1420	1420: Pope Martin V settles in Rome 1429: King Eric of Pomerania institutes Sound Dues for ships in the Øresund	1423: Gentile da Fabriano (*c.*1370–1427) paints his *Adoration of the Magi*

(*continued*)

Date	Political and religious	Culture and architecture
1430	1430: Capture, trial, and execution of Joan of Arc 1430: Philip the Good creates the Order of the Golden Fleece *c.*1430–*c.*1520: Influence of the Hanseatic League 1439: Union of Florence	1432: Jan van Eyck completes the Ghent Altarpiece 1436: Completion of dome for cathedral in Florence 1437: William and Alice de la Pole establish an almshouse in Ewelme
1440	1443: Alfonso V, King of Aragon and Sicily (reg. 1416–58), is named King of Naples 1444: Federigo da Montefeltro (1422–82) becomes Duke of Urbino 1444: Humphrey, Duke of Gloucester, donates books and money to Oxford 1447: Nicholas V (reg. 1447–55) elected pope	1440s: Nicholas V initiates restorations of Vatican Palace, St Peter's, and Senators' Palace in Rome 1440: Juan Guas arrives in Spain from Brittany 1443: Nicolas Rolin establishes the Hôtel-Dieu at Beaune 1444: Michelozzo begins Palazzo Medici, Florence 1445: Filarete creates bronze doors for old St Peter's Cathedral 1446: Rucellai Palace, Florence
1450	1449–1783: Khans of the Crimea (vassals of the Ottoman Empire, 1475–1783, annexation by Russia, 1783) 1453: Ottomans capture Constantinople 1453: The Hundred Years War ends. Calais is the only English possession on continental Europe 1455: The Wars of the Roses begin in England	1450s: Leon Battista Alberti (1404–72) writes *De re aedificatoria* 1451: Completion of house for Jacques Cœur (Bourges) 1452: Leonardo da Vinci born in Tuscany 1455: Johann Gutenberg prints the first of his bibles on his new printing press 1459: Pope Pius II (1458–64) visits his birthplace, Corsignano
1460	1462: Ivan III crowned in Moscow 1469: Isabella, Infanta of Castile and heir to the throne, and Ferdinand of Aragon are married at Valladolid (Spain)	1461–4: Filarete (*c.*1400–*c.*1465) writes his *Tratatto di architettura* 1462: Corsignano renamed Pienza 1464: Work begins on the Holstentor in Lübeck
1470	1474: Federico da Montefeltro given title of duke 1477: Mary of Burgundy's marriage to Holy Roman Emperor Maximilian I (reg. 1493–1519) and she becomes regent of the Low Countries (reg. 1477–82) 1478: The Pazzi Conspiracy, where members of the Pazzi family and Pope Sixtus IV devise a plot to oust the Medici from power in Florence 1479–1516: Kingdom of Castile and Aragon	1473: Work begins on the Sistine Chapel 1474: An earthquake destroys the Cathedral of the Dormition, Moscow 1475: Aristotele Fioravanti arrives in Moscow from Italy 1476: Construction begins at San Juan de los Reyes, Toledo (Spain)

1480	1482: Maximilian I of Hapsburg, Archduke of Austria and Holy Roman Emperor from 1493 until 1519, becomes ruler of the Low Countries 1483: Tomás de Torquemada (1420–98) is appointed to the post of inquisitor-general for Castile and Aragon 1483–91: Margaret of Austria serves briefly as Queen of France 1485: The Wars of the Roses end and the Tudor dynasty begins	1482: Leonardo da Vinci leaves Florence for Milan, entering the service of Ludovico Sforza 1482: Francesco di Giorgio (1439–1501/2) writes his architectural treatise 1483: Raphael born in Urbino 1483: Hugo van der Goes's Portinari Altarpiece is sent to the church of Sant'Egidio, choir of the hospital of Santa Maria Nuova, in Florence 1485–99: Giuliano da Sangallo appointed architect for the church of Santa Maria delle Carceri, Prato 1486: Matthäus Roriczer publishes his book on Gothic architecture
1490	1492: Granada falls to Ferdinand and Isabella; and Jews expelled from Spain 1494: Charles VIII of France (reg. 1483–98) invades Italy and seizes Naples 1494: Medici expelled from Florence 1494–1559: Hapsburg–Valois Wars 1495: Cardinal Francisco Jiménez de Cisneros (1436–1517) expels Muslims from Granada 1497–9: Vasco da Gama (*c.*1460–1524) travels to India	1492: Duke Ercole I begins construction in Ferrara 1493: *Liber chronicarum* published 1499: *Hypnerotomachia Poliphili* published in Venice 1499: Donato Bramante settles in Rome
1500	1503: Giuliano della Rovere is elected Pope Julius II (reg. 1503–13) 1504: Emperor Charles V (reg. 1519–56) accedes to Hapsburg throne 1506: Margaret of Austria moves her court to Mechelen 1508–16: War of the League of Cambrai	1500: Bramante arrives in Rome 1501: Michelangelo carves *David* 1501: Construction begins at the monastery at Belém 1502: Construction begins on Bramante's Tempietto at San Pietro in Montorio, Rome 1502: Vladislav Hall completed, Prague 1505: Work begins on the Cortile del Belvedere in the Vatican 1506: Foundation stone laid for new St Peter's, Rome 1508: Jan Gossart (*c.*1478–1536) visits Italy
1510	1510: Martin Luther visits Rome 1512: Medici return to power in Florence 1515: Francis I comes to power and rules until 1547 1516: Kingdom of Spain under Hapsburg rule 1516: Erasmus (*c.*1466–1536) publishes his edition of the New Testament in Greek and Latin	1511: Fra Giovanni Giocondo publishes new edition of Vitruvius 1512: Albrecht Dürer devises triumphal arch for Maximilian I 1514: Bramante dies 1514–15: Raphael writes to Pope Leo X about drawings and antiquities 1517: Jakob Fugger begins housing project in Augsburg

(*continued*)

Date	Political and religious	Culture and architecture
	1516: Venetian Senate requires Jews to live together in the *Ghetto Nuovo*	1519: Château Chambord begun 1519–34: Michelangelo designs the New Sacristry for San Lorenzo, Florence
1520	1520: Francis I and Henry VIII meet in France 1520–66: Reign of Süleyman 1527: Sack of Rome 1528: Francis I establishes Paris as principal residence 1528: Andrea Doria leads revolt against the French in Genoa	1523: Michelangelo begins the vestibule for the Laurentian Library 1527: Francis I (reg. 1515–47) undertakes the expansion of his hunting lodge at Fontainebleau 1529: Guillaume Budé (1467–1540) publishes his *Commentaries on Greek Language*
1530	1531: Stock exchange established in Antwerp 1536: John Calvin completes *The Institutes of the Christian Religion* 1536: Henry VIII begins the dissolution of the monasteries	1530s: Maarten van Heemskerck travels from the Low Countries to Italy 1531: Restoration of the aqueduct in Évora (Portugal) 1533: Protestant chapel built at Hartenfels Castle, Torgau 1539–46: Antonio da Sangallo designs new model for St Peter's, Rome
1540	*c.*1540: Ignatius of Loyola (1491–1556) and his followers found the Society of Jesus, or Jesuits 1545–63: Council of Trent 1549: King Henry II and Marie de' Medici arrive in Paris	1540: Metalsmith Benvenuto Cellini (1500–71) is invited to Paris by King Francis I 1541: Palladio makes his first trip to Rome 1549: Joachim du Bellay (1522–60) publishes his *Defense and Illustration of the French Language*
1550	1550: Duke Albrecht V moves his capital to Munich 1550s: John Calvin initiates religious reforms in France 1556: Charles V resigns the crown, divides the vast territorial holdings of the Hapsburgs between his brother Ferdinand, who succeeds him as emperor, and his son Philip, to whom he gives Naples and Milan (1554), the Netherlands (1555), and Sicily and Spain (1556) 1558: Elizabeth I crowned 1559: The Treaty of Cateau-Cambrésis, by which rule of Sicily and Milan is granted to Spain	1550–7: Construction of Süleymaniye in Istanbul by Sinan 1550–8: Strada Nuova, Genoa 1552: Work begins at Anet for Diane de Poitiers 1558: Alvise Cornaro, *Discorsi della vita sobria* 1559: Construction begins at El Escorial
1560	1560: John Calvin's *Institutes of the Christian Religion* published in Dutch	1560: Giorgio Vasari designs the Palazzo degli Uffizi

	1561: Philip II establishes Madrid as capital 1568–73: Marc'Antonio Barbaro serves as ambassador from Venice to the Ottoman court	1561: Philibert de l'Orme publishes his *Nouvelles Inventions pour bien bastir et à petits fraiz* 1563: The first art academy, the Accademia del Disegno, is founded in Florence 1563: John Shute publishes *The First and Chiefe Groundes of Architecture* (London) 1566: Villa Capra 1567: Juan de Herrera becomes architect at El Escorial 1569: Work begins on the Antiquarium in Munich
1570	1572: Catherine de' Medici (1519–89) orders the assassination of Huguenot leader Admiral Gaspard de Coligny in an attempt to maintain Catholic hegemony in France 1579: the northern provinces and some southern territories form the Union of Utrecht and declare independence from Spain in 1581	1570: Publication of Andrea Palladio's *I quattro libri dell' architettura* (Venice) 1572: Luís de Camões publishes *The Lusiad*
1580	1580: John White travels to North America 1588: Philip sends 130 ships to England in an attempt to overthrow Elizabeth's rule 1589: Anne of Denmark marries King James VI of Scotland at Kronborg Castle, Denmark	1580: Andrea Palladio dies 1580s: Michel de Montaigne (1533–92) publishes his three-volume *Essays*
1590	1598: Edict of Nantes grants Protestants freedom of worship under Henry IV (reg. 1589–1610) 1598: Philip II dies	1590: Fray José de Sigüenza publishes a history of El Escorial 1590–7: Hardwick Hall, England
1600	1609: Thomas Coryat leaves England for France	1611: English translation of Sebastiano Serlio's *L'architettura* 1613–14: Inigo Jones travels to France and Italy

Further Reading

From the nineteenth-century Germanic tradition, the history of Renaissance architecture has primarily been a history of Italian buildings and their architects. And still today, the majority of new scholarship is on central Italy. Therefore, the literature on those places and people is larger and growing. To understand the reasons behind this one must look both to the priority given to the history of classicism as well as the institutional structure of European and North American universities where this material is studied and taught. A good introduction to this topic is by Tod Marder in his article 'Renaissance and Baroque Architectural History in the United States', in E. B. MacDougall, ed., *The Architectural Historian in America*, National Gallery of Art, Studies in the History of Art 35 (Washington, DC, 1990), 161–74.

Two ongoing projects approach Renaissance architecture as a European phenomenon. Since 1983, André Chastel and Jean Guillaume began the publication of essays and monographic studies in the series *De architectura*, produced by Picard in Paris. More recently, Krista De Jonge and Piet Lombaerde have edited the series *Architectura moderna: Architectural Exchanges in Europe, 16th–17th Centuries*, published by Brepols in Turnhout (Belgium). These essays, and the conferences out of which they are gathered, have reshaped the study of Renaissance architecture and encouraged more studies with a broader geographical scope.

In addition to the book-length study, specialized articles are an important source for further information. The *Journal of the Society of Architectural Historians* (USA) publishes articles on all areas of architectural history, including the Renaissance, as does *Architectural History*, the journal of the Society of Architectural History of Great Britain.

The Centro Internazionale di Studi di Architettura di Andrea Palladio, based in Vicenza, Italy, the centre of Palladio's building activities, produces many exhibitions and books on Renaissance architecture, on Palladio as well as many other architects of the early modern period. They also publish *Annali di architettura*, a yearly journal on architecture in early modern Europe.

Grove Art Online, a comprehensive encyclopedia and available through Oxford Art Online, is an excellent starting point for further information on specific architects and buildings.

The list of titles below includes works primarily in English that I have found essential in writing this book, in addition to the references cited in the footnotes. Foreign-language books are included when there is nothing comparable and more recent in English, or it is too essential to ignore for its references, primary documents, or images.

History and Cultural Background

Aston, Margaret, ed., *The Panorama of the Renaissance* (New York, 1996). Excellent images, organized by topics.

Barkan, Leonard, *Unearthing the Past: Archaeology and Aesthetics in the Making of Renaissance Culture* (New Haven, 1999).

Brown, Alison, *The Renaissance* (London, 1999).

Burckhardt, Jacob, *The Civilization of the Renaissance in Italy* (New York, 1958).

Burke, Peter, *The European Renaissance: Centres and Peripheries* (Oxford, 1998).

—— *The Renaissance Sense of the Past* (London, 1969).

Chartier, Roger, ed., *A History of Private Life*, iii: *Passions of the Renaissance* (Cambridge, Mass., 1989).

Findlen, Paula, ed., *The Italian Renaissance* (Oxford, 2002).

Grendler, Paul F., ed., *Encyclopedia of the Renaissance*, 6 vols. (New York, 1999). An essential resource.
Hale, John, *The Civilization of Europe in the Renaissance* (London, 1993).
——*A Concise Encyclopedia of the Italian Renaissance* (New York, 1981).
Huizinga, Johan, *The Waning of the Middle Ages: A Study of the Forms of Life, Thought, and Art in France and the Netherlands in the Fourteenth and Fifteenth Centuries* (London, 1924).
Jardine, Lisa, *Worldly Goods: A New History of the Renaissance* (New York, 1996).
Lestringant, Frank, *Mapping the Renaissance World: The Geographical Imagination in the Age of Discovery* (Cambridge, 1994).
Muir, Edward, *Ritual in Early Modern Europe* (Cambridge, 1997).
Porter, Roy, and Teich, Mikuláš, eds., *The Renaissance in National Context* (Cambridge, 1992).
Richie, Robert, *Historical Atlas of the Renaissance* (New York, 2004).
Rublack, Ulrika, *Dressing Up: Cultural Identity in Renaissance Europe* (Oxford, 2011).
Ruggiero, Guido, ed., *A Companion to the Worlds of the Renaissance* (Malden, Mass., 2007).

Guidebooks

Drawing on the knowledge of conservators and curators who know the buildings from the ground up, guidebooks are invaluable resources to specific buildings and local traditions. Often only available on site or through the local historical commission, these books offer the most up-to-date information. For English architecture, for example, the books published by English Heritage and the National Trust of buildings under their care often include essays by leading scholars, excellent photographs, an inventory of objects, genealogies of the owners, excerpts from archival documents, and a bibliography. The following have been especially relevant for this book.

Favière, Jean, *L'Hôtel de Jacques Cœur à Bourges* (Paris, 1992).
Girouard, Mark, *Hardwick Hall* (London, 1989).
Mikkelsen, Birger, *Kronborg* (Helsingør, 1997).
Pedrosa Dos Santos Graça, Luís Maria, *Convento de Cristo* (Lisbon, 1994).
Pereira, Paulo, *Jerónimos Abbey of Santa Maria* (London, 2002).

Primary Texts

There is a list of treatises, their editions, and translations in Hanno-Walter Kruft, *A History of Architectural Theory from Vitruvius to the Present* (Princeton, 1994). A few are listed below.

Alberti, Leon Battista, *On the Art of Building in Ten Books*, trans. Joseph Rykwert, Neil Leach, and Robert Tavernor (Cambridge, Mass., 1988).
Colonna, Francesco, *Hypnerotomachia Poliphili: The Strife of Love in a Dream*, trans. Joscelyn Godwin (1499; London, 1999).
Dee, John, 'Mathematical Preface', in *Elements of Geometrie*, by Euclid and trans. Henry Billingsley (London, 1570).
Dürer, Albrecht, *The Writings of Albrecht Dürer*, trans. and ed. William Martin Conway (New York, 1958). Contains selections from Dürer's writings on proportion and fortifications.
Filarete, Antonio, *Treatise on Architecture*, ed. J. R. Spencer (London, 1964).
Palladio, Andrea, *The Four Books on Architecture*, trans. Robert Tavernor and Richard Schofield (1570; Cambridge, Mass., 1997).
Scamozzi, Vincenzo, *Vincenzo Scamozzi, Venetian Architect: The Idea of a Universal Architecture. Book III, Villas and Country Estates*, ed. K. Ottenheym, trans. P. B. Garvin, M. J. Obbink, and H. J. Scheepmaker (1615; Amsterdam, 2003).
——*Vincenzo Scamozzi, Venetian Architect: The Idea of a Universal Architecture. Book VI, The Architectural Orders and their Application*, ed K. Ottenheym, trans. Patti Garvin (1615; Amsterdam, 2008).
Serlio, Sebastiano, *Sebastiano Serlio on Architecture*, trans. Vaughan Hart and Peter Hicks, 2 vols. (New Haven, 1996–2001).
——*Serlio on Domestic Architecture*, ed. Myra Nan Rosenfeld (New York, 1978).
Shute, John, *The First and Chief Groundes of Architecture* (1563; London, 1972).
Vitruvius, *Ten Books on Architecture*, trans. Ingrid D. Rowland (New York, 1999).

General Renaissance Architectural Surveys

The following books include buildings from across Europe.

Beltramini, Guido, Burns, Howard, Forster, Kurt W., Oechslin, Werner, and Thoenes, Christof, eds., *Palladio and Northern*

Europe: Books, Travellers, Architects (Milan, 1999).
Benevolo, Leonardo, *The Architecture of the Renaissance*, trans. J. Landry, 2 vols. (Boulder, Colo., 1978).
Burckhardt, Jacob, *The Architecture of the Renaissance*, ed. P. Murray (London, 1985).
Busch, Harald, and Lohse, Bernd, eds., *Buildings of Europe: Renaissance Europe* (London, 1961).
Markschies, Alexander, *Icons of Renaissance Architecture* (Munich, 2003).
Millar, John Fitzhugh, *Classical Architecture in Renaissance Europe 1419–1585* (Williamsburg, Va., 1987). Book of drawings of buildings across Europe.
Murray, Peter, *Renaissance Architecture*, History of World Architecture (Milan, 1978).
Pauwels-Lemerle, Frédérique, and Pauwels-Lemerle, Yves, *L'Architecture à la Renaissance* (Paris, 1998). A broad survey, with up-to-date text and excellent photographs. Only available in French.
Swaan, Wim, *The Late Middle Ages: Art and Architecture from 1350 to the Advent of the Renaissance* (Ithaca, NY, 1977).
Tafuri, Manfredo, *L'architettura dell'umanesimo* (Bari, 1969). An important study, to date only available in Italian and French translations.
——*Interpreting the City, Princes, Cities, Architects*, trans. Daniel Sherer (New Haven, 2006).
Thomson, David, *Renaissance Architecture: Critics, Patrons, Luxury* (Manchester, 1993).

Britain

Anderson, Christy, 'Learning to Read Architecture in the English Renaissance', in Lucy Gent, ed., *Albion's Classicism: The Visual Arts in Britain, 1550–1660* (New Haven, 1995), 239–86.
Brunskill, R. W., *Brick Building in England* (London, 1990).
Clifton-Taylor, Alec, *The Pattern of English Building* (London, 1962).
Fawcett, Richard, *The Architectural History of Scotland: Scottish Architecture from the Accession of the Stewarts to the Reformation, 1371–1560* (Edinburgh, 1994).
Friedman, Alice T., 'Did England Have a Renaissance? Classical and Anticlassical Themes in Elizabethan Culture', in *Cultural Differentiation and Cultural Identity in the Visual Arts*, Studies in the History of Art 27 (Washington, DC, 1989).
Girouard, Mark, *Elizabethan Architecture: Its Rise and Fall, 1540–1640* (New Haven, 2009).
Howard, Maurice, *The Building of Elizabethan and Jacobean England* (New Haven, 2007).
Salzman, L. F., *Building in England down to 1540* (Oxford, 1967).
Summerson, John, *Architecture in Britain, 1530–1830* (New Haven, 1993).
Wells-Cole, Anthony, *Art and Decoration in Elizabethan and Jacobean England: The Influence of Continental Prints, 1558–1625* (New Haven, 1997).

Croatia

Croatia: Aspects of Art, Architecture and Cultural Heritage (London, 2009). Essays by Marcus Binney, Timothy Clifford, Donal Cooper, and David Ekserdijan discuss aspects of Renaissance architecture in Croatia.
Supičić, Ivan, ed., *Croatia in the Late Middle Ages and the Renaissance: A Cultural Survey* (London, 2008). An extensive survey of all aspects of Croatian culture in the Renaissance, with excellent photos and essays.

France

Blunt, Anthony, *Art and Architecture in France 1500–1700* (New Haven, 1993).
——*Philibert de l'Orme* (London, 1958).
Pauwels, Yves, 'The Rhetorical Model in the Formation of French Architectural Language in the Sixteenth-Century: The Triumphal Arch as Commonplace', in Georgia Clarke and Paul Crossley, eds., *Architecture and Language: Constructing Identity in European Architecture c.1000–c.1650* (Cambridge, 2000), 134–47.
Perouse de Montclos, Jean-Marie, *Histoire de l'architecture française: de la Renaissance à la Révolution* (Paris, 2006).
——*Philibert de l'Orme: architecte du roi, 1514–1570* (Paris, 2000).
Zerner, Henri, *Renaissance Art in France: The Invention of Classicism* (Paris, 2003).

Germany and Eastern Europe

Białostocki, Jan, *The Art of the Renaissance in Eastern Europe, Hungary, Bohemia, Poland* (Ithaca, NY, 1976).
Feuer-Tóth, Rózsa, *Renaissance Architecture in Hungary* (Budapest, 1977).
Fučiková, Eliška, et al., *Rudolf II and Prague: The Court and the City* (London, 1997).
Günther, Hubertus, *Deutsche Architekturtheorie zwischen Gotik und Renaissance* (Darmstadt, 1988).

Hitchcock, Henry-Russell, *German Renaissance Architecture* (Princeton, 1981).
Kaufmann, Thomas DaCosta, *Court, Cloister & City: The Art and Culture of Central Europe 1450–1800* (Chicago, 1995).
Knox, Brian, *The Architecture of Poland* (New York, 1981).
——*The Architecture of Prague and Bohemia* (London, 1962).
Matthew Corvinus, the King: Tradition and Renewal in the Hungarian Court 1458–1490, exh. cat. (Budapest, 2008).
Ullmann, Ernst, *Renaissance Deutsche Baukunst 1520–1620* (Leipzig, 1995).

Italy

The revised editions of Ludwig H. Heydenreich's *Architecture in Italy, 1400–1500* and Wolfgang Lotz's *Architecture in Italy, 1500–1600* contain up-to-date bibliographies by Paul Davies and Deborah Howard, respectively. Some of the most important books, including some that have appeared since, are included here.

Ackerman, James, 'The Planning of Renaissance Rome, 1450–1580', in P. A. Ramsey, ed., *Rome in the Renaissance: The City and the Myth* (Binghamton, NY, 1982), 3–18.
Burroughs, Charles, *From Signs to Design: Environmental Process and Reform in Early Renaissance Rome* (Cambridge, Mass., 1990).
Clarke, Georgia, 'Architecture, Languages and Style in Fifteenth-Century Italy', *Journal of the Warburg and Courtauld Institutes* 71 (2008), 169–89.
Concina, Ennio, *A History of Venetian Architecture*, trans. Judith Landry (New York, 1998).
Frommel, Christoph, *The Architecture of the Italian Renaissance*, trans. Peter Spring (London, 2007).
Gorse, George L., 'A Classical Stage for the Old Nobility: The Strada Nuova and Sixteenth-Century Genoa', *Art Bulletin* 79 (1997), 301–27.
Goy, Richard, *Venice: The City and its Architecture* (London, 1997).
Hersey, George L., *Alfonso II and the Artistic Renewal of Naples, 1485–1495* (New Haven, 1969).
Heydenreich, Ludwig H., *Architecture in Italy, 1400–1500*, introd. Paul Davies (New Haven, 1996).
Howard, Deborah, *The Architectural History of Venice* (New Haven, 2002).
Lieberman, Ralph, *Renaissance Architecture in Venice 1450–1540* (New York, 1982).
Lotz, Wolfgang, *Architecture in Italy, 1500–1600*, introd. Deborah Howard (New Haven, 1995).
——*Studies in Italian Renaissance Architecture* (Cambridge, Mass., 1977).
McAndrew, John, *Venetian Architecture of the Early Renaissance* (Cambridge, Mass., 1980).
McLean, Alick M., *Prato: Architecture, Piety, and Political Identity in a Tuscan City-State* (New Haven, 2008).
Magnuson, Torgil, *Studies in Roman Quattrocento Architecture* (Stockholm, 1958).
Millon, Henry A., and Lampugnani, Vittorio Magnano, *The Renaissance from Brunelleschi to Michelangelo: The Representation of Architecture* (London, 1994). An important catalogue with comprehensive essays and detailed catalogue entries.
Murray, Peter, *Architecture of the Italian Renaissance* (New York, 1963).
Nevola, Fabrizio, *Siena: Constructing the Renaissance City* (New Haven, 2007).
Partner, Peter, *Renaissance Rome 1500–1559: A Portrait of a Society* (Berkeley, 1979).
Rowe, Colin, and Satkowski, Leon, *Italian Architecture of the 16th Century* (New York, 2002).
Welch, Evelyn S., *Art and Authority in Renaissance Milan* (New Haven, 1995).
Westfall, C. W., *In this most perfect paradise: Alberti, Nicholas V and the Invention of Conscious Urban Planning in Rome, 1447–1455* (University Park, Pa., 1974).

On Individual Italian Architects

Alberti

Choay, Françoise, 'Alberti: The Invention of Monumentality and Memory', *Harvard Architecture Review* 4 (1984), 99–105.
Grafton, Anthony, *Leon Battista Alberti: Master Builder of the Italian Renaissance* (Cambridge, Mass., 2000).
Johnson, Eugene J., *S. Andrea in Mantua: The Building History* (University Park, Pa., 1975).
Tavernor, Robert, *On Alberti and the Art of Building* (New Haven, 1998).

Bramante

Bruschi, Arnaldo, *Bramante* (London, 1977).

Brunelleschi

Hyman, Isabelle, ed., *Brunelleschi in Perspective* (Englewood Cliffs, NJ, 1974).

Prager, Frank D., and Scaglia, Gustina, *Brunelleschi: Studies of his Technology and Inventions* (Cambridge, Mass., 1970).
Saalman, Howard, *Filippo Brunelleschi: The Buildings* (University Park, Pa., 1993).

Michelangelo

Ackerman, James S., *The Architecture of Michelangelo* (Chicago, 1986).
Elam, Caroline, ' "Tuscan dispositions": Michelangelo's Florentine Architectural Vocabulary and its Reception', *Renaissance Studies* 19 (2005), 46–82.

Palladio

More literature regularly appears on Palladio than any other architect. In 1980 Deborah Howard wrote a review, 'Four Centuries of Literature on Palladio' (*Journal of the Society of Architectural Historians* 39 (1980), 224–41), that remains an excellent starting point for any student of his architecture, writings, and reception. The Centro Internazionale di Studi di Architettura di Andrea Palladio in Vicenza (<www.cisapalladio.org>) publishes studies of Palladio and offers an excellent resource to his architecture on their website.

Ackerman, James S., *Palladio* (Harmondsworth, 1966).
Beltramini, Guido, and Burns, Howard, eds., *Palladio* (London, 2008).
Boucher, Bruce, *Andrea Palladio: The Architect in his Time* (New York, 1998).
Burns, Howard, with Lynda Fairbairn and Bruce Boucher, *Andrea Palladio 1508–1580: The Portico and the Farmyard*, exh. cat. (London, 1975).
Cooper, Tracy E., *Palladio's Venice* (New Haven, 2005).
Mitrović, Branko, *Learning from Palladio* (New York, 2004).
Travernor, Robert, *Palladio and Palladianism* (London, 1991).

Sansovino

Howard, Deborah, *Jacopo Sansovino: Architecture and Patronage in Renaissance Venice* (New Haven, 1975).
Tafuri, Manfredo, *Jacopo Sansovino e l'architettura del' 500 a Venezia* (Padua, 1969).

Low Countries

Belozerskaya, Marina, *Rethinking the Renaissance: Burgundian Arts across Europe* (Cambridge, 2012).
De Jonge, Krista, and Ottenheym, Konrad, eds., *Unity and Discontinuity: Architectural Relationships between the Southern and Northern Low Countries (1530–1700)* (Turnhout, 2007).
Hitchcock, Henry-Russell, *Netherlands Scrolled Gables of the Sixteenth and Early Seventeenth Centuries* (New York, 1978).
Kuyper, W., *The Triumphant Entry of Renaissance Architecture into the Netherlands*, 2 vols. (Leiden, 1994).

Ottoman Turkey

Blair, Sheila S., and Bloom, Jonathan M., *The Art and Architecture of Islam, 1250–1800* (New Haven, 1996).
Goodwin, Godfrey, *A History of Ottoman Architecture* (Baltimore, 1971).
Necipoğlu, Gülru, *The Age of Sinan: Architectural Culture in the Ottoman Empire* (Princeton, 2005).
——ed., *Sinan's Autobiographies: Five Sixteenth-Century Texts*, trans. Howard Crane and Esra Akin (Leiden, 2006).

Russia

Brumfield, William Craft, *A History of Russian Architecture* (Cambridge, 1993).
Voyce, Arthur, *The Moscow Kremlin: Its History, Architecture and Art Treasures* (Berkeley and Los Angeles, 1954).

Scandinavia and the Baltic

Christianson, John Robert, *On Tycho's Island: Tycho Brahe, Science, and Culture in the Sixteenth Century* (Cambridge, 2003).
——'Terrestrial and Celestial Spaces of the Danish Court, 1550–1650', in Marcello Fantoni, George Gorse, and Malcolm Smuts, eds., *The Politics of Space: European Courts ca.1500–1700* (Rome, 2009), 91–118.
Det Danske Selskab, *The History of Danish Architecture*, trans. Frederic R. Stevenson (Copenhagen, 1963).
Donnelly, Marian C., *Architecture in the Scandinavian Countries* (Cambridge, Mass., 1992).
Kavli, Guthorm, *Norwegian Architecture Past and Present* (Oslo, 1958).
Kirby, David, *Northern Europe in the Early Modern Period: The Baltic World 1492–1772* (London, 1990).
Kodres, Krista, Lindpere, Piret, and Näripea, Eva, eds., *The Problem of the Classical Ideal in the Art and Architecture of the Countries around the Baltic Sea.* Conference of the Estonian Academy of Arts, 9–10 November 2001 (2003).

Norberg-Schulz, Christian, *Nightlands, Nordic Building*, trans. Thomas McQuillan (Cambridge, Mass., 1996).
Paulsson, Thomas, *Scandinavian Architecture: Buildings and Society in Denmark, Finland, Norway and Sweden from the Iron Age until Today* (London, 1958).

Spain and Portugal

Bury, J. B., 'The Italian Contribution to Sixteenth-Century Portuguese Architecture, Military and Civil', in K. J. P. Lowe, ed., *Cultural Links between Portugal and Italy in the Renaissance* (Oxford, 2000), 77–107.
Kamen, Henry, *The Escorial: Art and Power in the Renaissance* (New Haven, 2010).
Kubler, George, *Portuguese Plain Architecture: Between Spices and Diamonds* (Middletown, Conn., 1972).
——and Soria, Martin, *Art and Architecture in Spain and Portugal and their American Dominions 1500–1800* (Harmondsworth, 1959).
Smith, R. C., *The Art of Portugal* (London, 1968).
Wilkinson-Zerner, Catherine, *Juan de Herrera, Architect to Philip II of Spain* (New Haven, 1993).

Chapter 2: The Voluptuous Pleasure of Building

Braudel, Fernand, *Out of Italy* (Paris, 1974).
Guillaume, Jean, ed., *L'Invention de la Renaissance: la réception des formes 'à l'antique' au début de la Renaissance*, actes du colloque tenu à Tours, 1–4 June (Paris, 2003).
Howard, Deborah, and Moretti, Laura, *Sound and Space in Renaissance Venice: Architecture, Music, Acoustics* (New Haven, 2009). Part of an emerging interest in architectural experience and the senses.
Kaufmann, Thomas DaCosta, *Toward a Geography of Art* (Chicago, 2004).
Panofsky, Erwin, *Renaissance and Renascences in Western Art* (New York, 1960).
Payne, Alina A., 'Rudolf Wittkower and Architectural Principles in the Age of Modernism', *Journal of the Society of Architectural Historians* 53 (1994), 322–42.
Pérez-Gómez, Alberto, *Built upon Love: Architectural Longing after Ethics and Aesthetics* (Cambridge, Mass., 2006).
Summerson, John, 'Antithesis of the Quattrocento', in his *Heavenly Mansions and Other Essays* (London, 1949), 29–50.
Tafuri, Manfredo, 'Discordant Harmony from Alberti to Zuccari', in Joseph Rykwert, ed., *Leonis Baptiste Alberti* (AD Profiles 21), *Architectural Design* 49 (London, 1986).
Wittkower, Rudolf, *Architectural Principles in the Age of Humanism* (New York, 1962).

Travel accounts of visitors in the early modern era offer first-hand descriptions of buildings.

Coryat, Thomas, *Coryat's crudities: hastily gobled up in five moneths travells in France, Savoy, Italy, Rhetia commonly called the Grisons country, Helvetia alias Switzerland, some parts of high Germany and the Netherlands* (1611; Glasgow, 1905).
Dallington, Robert, *The View of Fraunce, 1604* (London, 1936) and *A survey of the great Dukes state of Tuscany, in the yeare of our Lord 1596* (London, 1605).
Montaigne, Michel de, *Montaigne's Travel Journal*, trans. Donald M. Frame (San Francisco, 1983).

For more on travel, see:

Chaney, Edward, '*Quo vadis?* Travel as Education and the Impact of Italy in the Sixteenth Century', in *The Evolution of the Grand Tour: Anglo-Italian Cultural Relations since the Renaissance* (London, 1998), 58–101.
Kamps, Ivo, and Singh, Jyotsna G., eds., *Travel Knowledge: European 'Discoveries' in the Early Modern Period* (New York, 2001).

On medieval architecture and the continuity of the Gothic:

Chatenet, Monique, et al., eds., *Le Gothique de la Renaissance* (Paris, 2011). Offers essays on the continuity of Gothic architecture.
Coldstream, Nicola, *Medieval Architecture* (Oxford, 2002).
Kavaler, Ethan Matt, *Renaissance Gothic: Architecture and the Arts in Northern Europe, 1470–1540* (New Haven, 2012).

Two recent books explore the issue of time in Renaissance architecture and art:

Nagel, Alexander, and Wood, Christopher S., *Anachronic Renaissance* (New York, 2010).
Trachtenberg, Marvin, *Building-in-time: From Giotto to Alberti and Modern Oblivion* (New Haven, 2010).

Chapter 3: The House of God

Ackerman, James, 'The Gesù in the Light of Contemporary Church Design', in his *Distance Points: Essays in Theory and Renaissance Art and Architecture* (Cambridge, Mass., 1991), 417–51.
Alexander, John, *From Renaissance to Counter-Reformation: The Architectural*

Patronage of Carlo Borromeo during the Reign of Pius IV (Rome, 2007).
Bangs, Jeremy Dupertuis, *Church Art and Architecture in the Low Countries before 1566* (Kirksville, Mo., 1997).
Barrie, Thomas, *The Sacred In-Between: The Mediating Roles of Architecture* (London, 2010).
Buxton, David, *The Wooden Churches of Eastern Europe: An Introductory Survey* (Cambridge, 1981).
Chatenet, Monique, and Mignot, Claude, eds., *L'Architecture religieuse européenne au temps des Réformes: héritage de la Renaissance et nouvelles problématiques*, actes des deuxièmes Rencontres d'architecture européenne Château de Maisons-sur-Seine, 8–11 June 2005 (Paris, 2009).
Coster, Will, and Spicer, Andrew, eds., *Sacred Space in Early Modern Europe* (Cambridge, 2005).
Courtright, Nicola, *The Papacy and the Art of Reform in Sixteenth-Century Rome: Gregory XIII's Tower of the Winds in the Vatican* (New York, 2003).
Evans, Robin, 'Perturbed Circles', in his *The Projective Cast: Architecture and its Three Geometries* (Cambridge, Mass., 2000), 3–54.
Fanelli, Giovanni, and Fanelli, Michele, *Brunelleschi's Cupola: Past and Present of an Architectural Masterpiece* (Florence, 2004).
Frishman, Martin, and Khan, Hasan-Uddin, *The Mosque: History, Architectural Development & Regional Diversity* (London, 1994).
Gaimster, D., and Gilchrist, R., eds., *The Archaeology of Reformation 1480–1580* (Leeds, 2003).
Gorringe, T. J., *A Theology of the Built Environment: Justice, Empowerment, Redemption* (Cambridge, 2002). Although not directly on the Renaissance, an interesting approach to religious spaces.
Guillaume, Jean, ed., *L'Église dans l'architecture de la Renaissance*, actes du colloque tenu à Tours, 31 May 1990 (Paris, 1995).
Hamberg, Per Gustaf, *Temples for Protestants: Studies in the Architectural Milieu of the Early Reformed Church and of the Lutheran Church* (Gothenburg, 2002).
Jones, Barry, Sereni, Andrea, and Ricci, Massimo, 'Building Brunelleschi's Dome: A Practical Methodology Verified by Experiment', *Journal of the Society of Architectural Historians* 69 (2010), 39–61.
Kaplan, Benjamin J., 'Fictions of Privacy: House Chapels and the Spatial Accommodation of Religious Dissent in Early Modern Europe', *American Historical Review* 107 (2002), 1031–64.
Koerner, Joseph Leo, *The Reformation of the Image* (Chicago, 2004).
Krinsky, Carol Herselle, *Synagogues of Europe: Architecture, History, Meaning* (New York, 1985).
Meek, H. A., *The Synagogue* (London, 1995).
Nussbaum, Norbert, *German Gothic Church Architecture*, trans. Scott Kleager (New Haven, 2000).
Randall, Catherine, *Building Codes: The Aesthetics of Calvinism in Early Modern Europe* (Philadelphia, 1999).
S. Sinding-Larsen. 'Some Functional and Iconographical Aspects of the Centralized Church of the Italian Renaissance', *Acta ad arte et architecturam pertinentum (Norvegiae)* 2 (1965), 203–52.
Smith, E. Baldwin, *The Dome: A Study in the History of Ideas* (Princeton, 1971).
Spicer, Andrew, ed., *Lutheran Churches in Early Modern Europe* (Aldershot, 2012).
Yates, Nigel, *Liturgical Space: Christian Worship and Church Buildings in Western Europe 1500–2000* (Aldershot, 2008).
Wilson, Christopher, *The Gothic Cathedral: The Architecture of the Great Church 1130–1530* (London, 1992).

Chapter 4: Theories and Practices: The Case of St Peter's, Rome

On St Peter's:

Millon, Henry A., and Smyth, Craig Hugh, *Michelangelo Architect: The Façade of San Lorenzo and the Drum and Dome of St. Peter's*, exh. cat. (Milan, 1988).
Thoenes, Christof, 'St Peter: Erste Skizzen/St. Peter's: First Sketches', *Daidalos* 5 (1982), 81–98.
Tronzo, William, ed., *St. Peter's in the Vatican* (Cambridge, 2005).

On treatises, books and architectural writing:

Blunt, Anthony, *Artistic Theory in Italy 1450–1600* (London, 1940).
Carpo, Mario, *Architecture in the Age of Printing: Orality, Writing, Typography, and Printed Images in the History of Architectural Theory*, trans. Sarah Benson (Cambridge, Mass., 2001).
Corbett, Margery, 'The Architectural Title-Page: An Attempt to Trace its Development from its Humanist Origins up to the Sixteenth and Seventeenth

Centuries, the Heyday of the Complex Engraved Title-Page', *Motif* 12 (1964), 48–62.
Davies, Paul, and Hemsoll, David, 'Sanmicheli's Architecture and Literary Theory', in Georgia Clarke and Paul Crossley, eds., *Architecture and Language: Constructing Identity in European Architecture c.1000–c.1650* (Cambridge, 2000), 102–17.
Erickson, Roy, *The Building in the Text: Alberti to Shakespeare and Milton* (Pennsylvania, 2001).
Guillaume, Jean, ed., *Les Traités d'architecture de la Renaissance*, actes des colloques tenus à Tours, 1–11 July 1981 (Paris, 1988).
Hart, Vaughan, and Hicks, Peter, eds., *Paper Palaces: The Rise of the Renaissance Architectural Treatise* (New Haven, 1998). An essential collection of essays on all of the major treatises and authors of the Renaissance.
Jarzombek, Mark, *On Leon Baptista Alberti: His Literary and Aesthetic Theories* (Cambridge, Mass., 1989).
Kanerva, Liisa, *Between Science and Drawings Renaissance Architects on Vitruvius's Educational Ideas* (Helsinki, 2006).
Kruft, Hanno-Walter, *A History of Architectural Theory from Vitruvius to the Present* (Princeton, 1994).
Lombaerde, Piet, ed., *Hans Vredeman de Vries and the Artes Mechanicae Revisited* (Turnhout, 2005).
McPhee, Sarah, 'The Architect as Reader', *Journal of the Society of Architectural Historians* 58 (1999), 454–61.
Mallgrave, Harry Francis, Beasley, Gerald, Baines, Claire, and Raine, Henry, *The Mark J. Millard Architectural Collection*, iii: *Northern European Books, Sixteenth to Early Nineteenth Centuries* (Washington, DC, 1998).
Middleton, Robin, Beasley, Gerald, and Baines, Claire, *The Mark J. Millard Architectural Collection*, ii: *British Books, Seventeenth through Nineteenth Centuries* (Washington, DC, 1998).
Payne, Alina A., *The Architectural Treatise in the Italian Renaissance: Architectural Invention, Ornament, and Literary Culture* (Cambridge, 1999).
Pollak, Martha D., *The Mark J. Millard Architectural Collection*, iv: *Italian and Spanish Books, Fifteenth through Nineteenth Centuries* (Washington, DC, 2001).
——*Military Architecture, Cartography and the Representation of the Early Modern City: A Checklist of Treatises on Fortification in the Newberry Library* (Chicago, 1991).
Rykwert, Joseph, 'On the Oral Transmission of Architectural Theory', in Jean Guillaume, ed., *Les Traités d'architecture de la Renaissance*, actes du colloque tenu à Tours, 1–11 July 1981 (Paris, 1988), 31–48.
Saalman, Howard, 'Early Renaissance Architectural Theory and Practice in Antonio Filarete's *Trattato di Architettura*', *Art Bulletin* 41 (1959), 89–106.
Smith, Christine, *Architecture in the Culture of Early Humanism: Ethics, Aesthetics, and Eloquence 1400–1470* (Oxford, 1992).
Wiebenson, Dora, *Architectural Theory and Practice from Alberti to Ledoux* (Chicago, 1982).
——and Baines, Claire, *The Mark J. Millard Architectural Collection*, i: *French Books, Sixteenth to Early Nineteenth Centuries* (Washington, DC, 1993).

On architectural practice and the profession:

Ackerman, James, 'Architectural Practice in the Italian Renaissance', in his *Distance Points: Essays in Theory and Renaissance Art and Architecture* (Cambridge, Mass., 1991), 361–84.
Ettlinger, Leopold D., 'The Emergence of the Italian Architect during the Fifteenth Century', in Spiro Kostof, ed., *The Architect: Chapters in the History of the Profession* (New York, 1977), 96–123.
Goldthwaite, Richard, *The Building of Renaissance Florence: An Economic and Social History* (Baltimore, 1980).
Hollingsworth, Mary, 'The Architecture in Fifteenth-Century Florence', *Art History* 7 (1984), 385–410.
Kostof, Spiro, *The Architect: Chapters in the History of the Profession* (New York, 1977).
Nevola, Fabrizio, 'Lots of Napkins and a Few Surprises: Francesco di Giorgio Martini's House, Goods and Social Standing in Late-Fifteenth-Century Siena', *Annali di architettura* 18–19 (2006–7), 71–82.
Parsons, William Barclay, *Engineers and Engineering in the Renaissance* (New York, 1939).
Tussenbroek, Gabri van, *The Architectural Network of the Van Neurenberg Family in the Low Countries (1480–1640)* (Turnhout, 2006).
Wilkinson, Catherine, 'The New Professionalism in the Renaissance', in Spiro Kostof, ed., *The Architect: Chapters in the History of the Profession* (New York, 1977), 124–60.

Zervas, Diane F., 'Brunelleschi's Political Career', *Burlington Magazine* 121 (1979), 630–93.

On construction and the science of building:

Coldstream, Nicola, *Masons and Sculptors* (London, 1991).
Fitchen, John, *Building Construction before Mechanization* (Cambridge, Mass., 1986).
Gerbino, Anthony, and Johnston, Stephen, *Compass and Rule: Architecture as Mathematical Practice in Early Modern England, 1550–1750* (New Haven, 2009).
Guillaume, Jean, ed., *Les Chantiers de la Renaissance*, actes des colloques tenus à Tours, 1983–4 (Paris, 1991).
Mark, Robert, ed., *Architectural Technology up to the Scientific Revolution: The Art and Structure of Large-Scale Buildings* (Cambridge, Mass., 1993).
Opačić, Zoë, *Diamond Vaults: Innovation and Geometry in Medieval Architecture* (London, 2005).
Pagliara, Pier Nicola, and Piana, Mario, eds., *Palladio construttore: tecniche, materiali, cantieri*. XXXIX Corso sull'architettura palladiana, Vicenza, 8–10 September 1997. Essays collected in *Annali di architettura* 10–11 (1998–9), 231–334.
Robison, Elwin C., 'Structural Implications in Palladio's Use of Harmonic Proportions', *Annali di architettura* 10–11 (1998–9), 175–82.
Schlimme, Hermann, ed., *Practice and Science in Early Modern Italian Building: Towards an Epistemic History of Architecture* (Milan, 2006).

On drawing:

Ackerman, James, 'The Origins of Architectural Drawing in the Middle Ages and Renaissance', in his *Origins, Imitation, Conventions: Representation in the Visual Arts* (Cambridge, Mass., 2002), 27–66.
Bork, Robert, *The Geometry of Creation: Architectural Drawing and the Dynamics of Gothic Design* (Aldershot, 2011).
Brothers, Cammy, *Michelangelo, Drawing, and the Invention of Architecture* (New Haven, 2008).
Burns, Howard, 'The Lion's Claw: Palladio's Initial Sketches', *Daidalos* 5 (1982), 73–80.
Elam, Caroline, 'Drawings as Documents: The Problem of the San Lorenzo Façade', *Studies in the History of Art* 33 (1992), 98–114.
Lotz, Wolfgang, 'The Rendering of the Interior in Architectural Drawings of the Renaissance', in his *Studies in Italian Renaissance Architecture* (Cambridge, Mass., 1977), 1–65.
Scaglia, Gustina, 'Drawings of Roman Antiquities in the Metropolitan Museum of Art and in the Album Houfe, Ampthill', *Annali di architettura* 4–5 (1992–3), 9–21.

On the orders:

Benelli, Francesco, ' "Variò tanto della commune usanza degli altri": The Function of the Encased Column and what Michelangelo Made of it in the Palazzo dei Conservatori at the Campidoglio in Rome', *Annali di architettura* 21 (2009), 65–78.
Guillaume, Jean, ed., *L'Emploi des ordres dans l'architecture de la Renaissance*, actes des colloques tenus à Tours, 9–14 July 1986 (Paris, 1992).
Hersey, George L., *The Lost Meaning of Classical Architecture: Speculations on Ornament from Vitruvius to Venturi* (Cambridge, Mass., 1988).
Onians, John, *Bearers of Meaning: The Classical Orders in Antiquity, the Middle Ages, and the Renaissance* (Princeton, 1988).
Rowland, Ingrid D., 'Raphael, Angelo Colocci, and the Genesis of the Architectural Orders', *Art Bulletin* 76 (1994), 81–104.
Rykwert, Joseph, *The Dancing Column: On Order in Architecture* (Cambridge, Mass., 1996).
Summerson, John, *The Classical Language of Architecture* (Cambridge, Mass., 1963).
Tzonis, Alexander, and Lefaivre, Liane, *Classical Architecture: The Poetics of Order* (Cambridge, Mass., 1986).

On architecture and the body:

Dodds, George, and Tavernor, Robert, eds., *Body and Building: Essays on the Changing Relation of Body and Architecture* (Cambridge, Mass., 2005).
Hedrick, Donald Keith, 'The Ideology of Ornament: Alberti and the Erotics of Renaissance Urban Design', *Word & Image* 3 (1987), 111–37.
Hersey, George L. *Pythagorean Palaces: Magic and Architecture in the Italian Renaissance* (Ithaca, NY, 1976).
Lowic, L., 'The Meaning and Significance of the Human Analogy in Francesco di Giorgio's Trattato', *Journal of the Society of Architectural Historians* 42 (1983), 360–70.

On antiquity:

Aston, Margaret, 'English Ruins and English History: The Dissolution and the

Sense of the Past', *Journal of the Warburg and Courtauld Institutes* 36 (1973), 231–55.
Bolgar, R. R., *The Classical Heritage and its Beneficiaries from the Carolingian Age to the End of the Renaissance* (New York, 1964).
Bosman, Lex, *The Power of Tradition: Spolia in the Architecture of St. Peter's in the Vatican* (Hilversum, 2004).
Brilliant, Richard, and Kinney, Dale, eds., *Reuse Value: Spolia and Appropriation in Art and Architecture from Constantine to Sherrie Levine* (Aldershot, 2011).
Burns, Howard, 'Quattrocento Architecture and the Antique: Some Problems', in R. R. Bolgar, ed., *Classical Influences on European Culture A.D. 500–1500* (Cambridge, 1971), 269–87.
Curran, Brian, *The Egyptian Renaissance: The Afterlife of Ancient Egypt in Early Modern Italy* (Chicago, 2007).
Gombrich, E. H., 'The Style *all'antica*: Imitation and Assimilation', in his *Norm and Form: Studies in the Art of the Renaissance* 1 (London, 1985), 122–8.
Grafton, Anthony, Most, Glenn W., and Settis, Salvatore, eds., *The Classical Tradition* (Cambridge, Mass., 2010).
Howard, Deborah, 'Responses to Ancient Greek Architecture in Renaissance Venice', *Annali di architettura* 6 (1994), 23–38.
Jacks, Philip, *The Antiquarian and the Myth of Antiquity: The Origins of Rome in Renaissance Thought* (New York, 1993).
Karmon, David, 'Preserving Antiquity in a Protestant City: The Maison Carrèe in Sixteenth-Century Nîmes', in Virginia Chieffo Raguin, ed., *Art, Piety and Destruction in the Christian West, 1500–1700* (Farnham, 2010), 113–35.
—— *The Ruin of the Eternal City: Antiquity and Preservation in Renaissance Rome* (Oxford, 2011).
Lemerle, Frédérique, *La Renaissance et les antiquités de la Gaule: l'architecture gallo-romaine vue par les architectes, antiquaires et voyageurs des guerres d'Italie à la Fronde* (Turnhout, 2005).
McGowan, Margaret M., *The Vision of Rome in Late Renaissance France* (New Haven, 2000).
Weiss, Roberto, *The Renaissance Discovery of Classical Antiquity* (Oxford, 1988).
Wunder, Amanda, 'Classical, Christian, and Muslim Remains in the Construction of Imperial Seville (1520–1635)', *Journal of the History of Ideas* 64 (2003), 195–212.

Chapter 5: The Architecture of Ascendancy: Buildings and Power

Asch, Ronald G., and Birke, Adolf M., eds., *Princes, Patronage, and the Nobility: The Court at the Beginning of the Modern Age, c.1450–1650* (London, 1991).
Coffin, David R., *Pirro Ligorio: The Renaissance Artist, Architect, and Antiquarian* (University Park, Pa., 2004).
Cole, Alison, *Virtue and Magnificence: Art of the Italian Renaissance Courts* (New York, 1995).
Dickens, G., ed., *The Courts of Europe: Politics, Patronage and Royalty 1400–1800* (New York, 1977).
Fantoni, Marcello, Gorse, George, and Smuts, Malcolm, eds., *The Politics of Space: European Courts ca.1500–1700* (Rome, 2009).
Fraser Jenkins, D., 'Cosimo de' Medici's Patronage of Architecture and the Theory of Magnificence', *Journal of the Warburg and Courtauld Institutes* 33 (1970), 162–70.
Goldthwaite, Richard, *Wealth and the Demand for Art in Italy 1300–1600* (Baltimore, 1993).
Guillaume, Jean, ed., *Architecture et vie sociale: l'organisation intérieure des grandes demeures à la fin du Moyen Âge et à la Renaissance*, actes du colloque tenu à Tours, 6–10 June 1988 (Paris, 1994).
——ed., *Demeures d'éternité: églises et chapelles funéraires aux XVe et XVIe siècles*, actes du colloque tenu à Tours, 11–14 June 1996 (Paris, 2005).
Hollingsworth, Mary, *Patronage in Renaissance Italy: From 1400 to the Early Sixteenth Century* (London, 1994).
Holme, B. *Princely Feasts and Festivals: Five Centuries of Pageantry and Spectacle* (New York, 1988).
Strong, Roy, *Art and Power: Renaissance Festivals, 1450–1650* (Woodbridge, 1984).

On Urbino:

Heydenreich, L. H., 'Federico da Montefeltro as a Building Patron: Some Remarks on the Ducal Palace of Urbino', in *Studies in Renaissance and Baroque Art Presented to Anthony Blunt on his 60th Birthday* (London, 1967), 1–6.
Rotondi, P., *The Ducal Palace of Urbino* (London, 1969).
Westfall, C. W., 'Chivalric Declaration: The Palazzo Ducale in Urbino as a Political Statement', in H. A. Millon and L. Nochlin, eds., *Art and Architecture in the Service of Politics* (Cambridge, Mass., 1978), 20–45.

On the Hapsburg and Spanish patronage:

Brothers, Cammy, 'The Renaissance Reception of the Alhambra: The Letters of Andrea Navagero and the Palace of Charles V', *Muqarnas* 11 (1994), 79–102.
Eichberger, Dagmar, 'A Noble Residence for a Female Regent: Margaret of Austria and the "Court of Savoy" in Mechelen', in Helen Hills, ed., *Architecture and the Politics of Gender in Early Modern Europe* (Aldershot, 2003), 25–46.
Howard, Deborah, 'Bramante's Tempietto: Spanish Royal Patronage in Rome', *Apollo* 136 (1992), 211–17.
Kubler, George, *Building the Escorial* (Princeton, 1982).
——'A Sixteenth Century Meaning of the Escorial', *Diogenes* 29 (1981), 229–48.
Rosenthal, Earl, *The Palace of Charles V in Granada* (Princeton, 1985).
Wilkinson, Catherine, 'Juan de Herrera's Orders', in Jean Guillaume, ed., *L'Emploi des ordres dans l'architecture de la Renaissance* (Paris, 1992), 263–72.

On Pius II and Pienza:

Mack, Peter, *Pienza: The Creation of a Renaissance City* (Ithaca, NY, 1987).
Pieper, J. 'Architecture Grows out of Stone: Metaphors of Transformation in the Palace of Pius II in Pienza', *Daidalos* 31 (1989), 76–87.

On England:

Anglo, Sydney, *Spectacle, Pageantry and Early Tudor Policy* (Oxford, 1969).
Richardson, Glenn, 'Entertainments for the French Ambassadors at the Court of Henry VIII', *Renaissance Studies* 9 (1995), 404–15.
Russell, Joycelyne G., *The Field of Cloth of Gold: Men and Manners in 1520* (London, 1969).
Thurley, Simon, *The Royal Palaces of Tudor England: Architecture and Court Life, 1460–1547* (New Haven, 1993).

On Francis I:

Chatenet, Monique, *Chambord* (Paris, 2001).
Knecht, R. J., *Renaissance Warrior and Patron: The Reign of Francis I* (Cambridge, 1994).

Chapter 6: Corporate Identity

Kent, F. W., 'Individuals and Families as Patrons of Culture in Quattrocento Florence', in Alison Brown, ed., *Language and Images of Renaissance Italy* (Oxford, 1995), 171–92.
Martin, John Jeffries, *Myths of Renaissance Individualism* (Basingstoke, 2004).
Trexler, Richard C., ed., *Persons in Groups: Social Behavior as Identity Formation in Medieval and Renaissance Europe* (Binghamton, NY, 1985).
Wojciehowski, Hannah Chapelle, *Group Identity in the Renaissance* (Cambridge, 2011).

On schools and universities:

Gillam, Stanley, *The Divinity School and Duke Humphrey's Library at Oxford* (Oxford, 1988).
Grendler, Paul F., *Books and Schools in the Italian Renaissance* (Aldershot, 1995).
King, Margaret L., *Women of the Renaissance* (Chicago, 1991).
McConica, James, ed., *The History of the University of Oxford*, iii: *The Collegiate University* (Oxford, 1986).

On the Fuggers:

Häberlein, Mark, *The Fuggers of Augsburg: Pursuing Wealth and Honor in Renaissance Germany* (Charlottesville, Va., 2012).
Kluger, Martin, *The Wealthy Fuggers: Pomp and Power of the German Medici* (Augsburg, 2003).
Tietz-Strödel, Marion, *Die Fuggerei in Augsburg: Studien zur Entwicklung des sozialen Stiftungsbaus im 15. und 16. Jahrhundert* (Tübingen, 1982).

Hospitals and almshouses:

Gavitt, Philip, *Charity and Children in Renaissance Florence: The Ospedale degli Innocenti, 1410–1536* (Ann Arbor, 1990).
Godfrey, W. H., *The English Almshouse* (London, 1956).
Goodall, John A. A., *God's House at Ewelme: Life, Devotion, and Architecture in a Fifteenth-Century Almshouse* (Aldershot, 2001).
Henderson, John, *The Renaissance Hospital: Healing the Body and Healing the Soul* (New Haven, 2006).
Terpstra, Nicholas, *Abandoned Children of the Italian Renaissance: Orphan Care in Florence and Bologna* (Baltimore, 2005).
Thompson, John, and Goldin, Grace, *The Hospital: A Social and Architectural History* (New Haven, 1975).

Religious communities:

Dunn, Marilyn, 'Spaces Shaped for Spiritual Perfection: Convent Architecture and Nuns in Early Modern Rome', in Helen Hills, ed., *Architecture and the Politics of Gender in Early Modern Europe* (Aldershot, 2003), 151–76.

Lehfeldt, Elizabeth A., 'Spatial Discipline and its Limits: Nuns and the Built Environment in Early Modern Spain', in Helen Hills, ed., *Architecture and the Politics of Gender in Early Modern Europe* (Aldershot, 2003), 131–49.
Lowe, K J. P., *Nuns' Chronicles and Convent Culture in Renaissance and Counter-Reformation Italy* (Cambridge, 2003).
Roffey, Simon, *Chantry Chapels and Medieval Strategies for the Afterlife* (Stroud, 2008).
Strocchia, Sharon T., *Nuns and Nunneries in Renaissance Florence* (Baltimore, 2009).
Tafuri, Manfredo, 'The Scuole Grandi', in his *Venice and the Renaissance*, trans. Jessica Levine (Cambridge, Mass., 1995), 81–101.
Thomas, Anabel, *Art and Piety in the Female Religious Communities of Renaissance Italy: Iconography, Space, and the Religious Woman's Perspective* (Cambridge, 2003).
Wisch, Barbara, and Cole Ahl, Diane, eds., *Confraternities and the Visual Arts in Renaissance Italy: Ritual, Spectacle, Image* (Cambridge, 2000).

Chapter 7: Shaping the Renaissance City

Primary Texts

Alberti, Leon Battista, *Delineation of the City of Rome (Descriptio vrbis Romae)*, trans. Peter Hicks, ed. Mario Carpo and Francesco Furlan (Tempe, Ariz., 2007).
De Góis, Damião, *Lisbon in the Renaissance (Urbis Olisiponsis descriptio)*, trans. Jeffrey S. Ruth (1554; New York, 1996).
Palladio, Andrea, *Palladio's Rome*, trans. Vaughan Hart and Peter Hicks (New Haven, 2006).
Stow, John, *A Survey of London Written in the Year 1598* (1598; Dover, NH, 1994).

Secondary Texts

Ackerman, James S., and Rosenfeld, Myra Nan, 'Social Stratification in Renaissance Urban Planning', in Susan Zimmerman and Ronald F. E. Weissman, eds., *Urban Life in the Renaissance* (Newark, Del., 1989).
Adams, Nicholas, and Nussdorfer, Laurie, 'The Italian City, 1400–1600', in Henry Millon, ed., *The Renaissance from Brunelleschi to Michelangelo: The Representation of Architecture* (London, 1994).
Argan, Giulio C., *The Renaissance City*, trans. S. E. Bassnet (New York, 1970).
Benevolo, Leonardo, *The History of the City* (London, 1980).
Bork, Robert, *Great Spires: Sky Scrapers of the New Jerusalem* (Cologne, 2003).
Cowan, Alexander, *Urban Europe, 1500–1700* (London, 1998).
De Vylder, Jochen, 'The Grid and the Existing City: Or How New Civic Buildings and Interventions on Confiscated Grounds Transformed the Medieval City in Early Modern Times. A Focus on Antwerp (1531–84)', in Piet Lombaerde and Charles Van Den Heuvel, eds., *Early Modern Urbanism and the Grid: Town Planning in the Low Countries in International Context. Exchanges in Theory and Practice 1550–1800* (Turnhout, 2011), 77–93.
Elam, Caroline, 'Lorenzo the Magnificent and the Urban Development of Renaissance Florence', *Art History* 1 (1978), 43–66.
Friedman, David, *Florentine New Towns: Urban Design in the Late Middle Ages* (New York, 1988).
Friedrichs, Christopher R., *The Early Modern City 1450–1750* (London, 1995).
Gaunt, William, *Flemish Cities: Their History and Art* (New York, 1969).
Kubler, George, 'Open-Grid Town Plans in Europe and America', in Richard P. Schaedel, Jorge E. Hardoy, and Nora Scott Kinzer, eds., *Urbanization in the Americas from its Beginnings to the Present* (The Hague, 1978), 327–42.
McClung, William Alexander, *The Architecture of Paradise: Survivals of Eden and Jerusalem* (Berkeley, 1983).
Nijenhuis, Wim, 'Stevin's Grid City and the *Maurice Conspiracy*', in Piet Lombaerde and Charles Van Den Heuvel, eds., *Early Modern Urbanism and the Grid: Town Planning in the Low Countries in International Context. Exchanges in Theory and Practice 1550–1800* (Turnhout, 2011), 45–62.
La piazza del medioevo e rinascimento nell'Italia settentrionale. IX Seminario internazional di storia dell'architettura, Vicenza, 3–8 September 1990. Essays collected in *Annali di architettura* 4–5 (1992–3), 113–229.
Rosenberg, C. M., *The Este Monuments and Urban Development in Renaissance Ferrara* (Cambridge, 1997).
——'The Erculean Addition to Ferrara: Contemporary Reactions and Pragmatic Considerations', *The Early Renaissance, Acta* 5 (1978), 49–67.
Saalman, Howard, *The Transformation of Buildings and the City in the Renaissance* (Champlain, NY, 1996).
Sennett, Richard, *Flesh and Stone* (New York, 1994).

Thomson, David, *Renaissance Paris* (Berkeley, 1984).
Tittler, Robert, *Architecture and Power: The Town Hall and the English Urban Community, c.1500–1640* (Oxford, 1991).
Trachtenberg, Marvin, *Dominion of the Eye: Urbanism, Art, and Power in Early Modern Florence* (Cambridge, 1997).
Trio, Paul, and De Smet, Marjan, eds., *The Use and Abuse of Sacred Places in Late Medieval Towns* (Leuven, 2006).
Tuohy, T. J., *Herculean Ferrara, Ercole d'Este (1471–1505) and the Invention of a Ducal Capital* (Cambridge, 1995).

Infrastructure:

Rinne, Katherine W., 'Fluid Precision: Giacomo della Porta and the Acqua Vergine Fountains of Rome', in Jan Birksted, ed., *Landscapes of Memory and Experience* (London, 2000), 183–201.
—— *The Waters of Rome: Aqueducts, Fountains, and the Birth of the Baroque City* (New Haven, 2011).

Public space:

Ackerman, James S., 'Palladio, Michelangelo and *publica magnificentia*', *Annali di architettura* 22 (2010), 63–78.
Muir, Edward, and Weissman, Ronald F. E., 'Social and Symbolic Places in Renaissance Venice and Florence', in John A. Agnew and James S. Duncan, eds., *The Power of Place: Bringing Together Geographical and Sociological Imaginations* (Boston, 1989).
Ottenheym, Konrad, Chatenet, Monique, and De Jonge, Krista, eds., *Public Buildings in Early Modern Europe*, vol. ix of *Architectura moderna: Architectural Exchanges in Europe, 16th–17th Centuries* (Turnhout, 2010).
Rinne, Katherine W., 'The Landscape of Laundry in Late Cinquecento Rome', *Studies in the Decorative Arts* 9 (2001–2), 34–60.
Schofield, John, 'Social Perceptions of Space in Medieval and Tudor London Houses', in Martin Locock, ed., *Meaningful Architecture: Social Interpretations of Buildings* (Aldershot, 1994), 231–52.
——'Architecture and the Assertion of the Cult of Relics in Milan's Public Spaces', *Annali di architettura* 16 (2004), 79–120.
Symmes, Marilyn, ed., *Fountains Splash and Spectacle: Water and Design from the Renaissance to the Present* (New York, 1998).
Trachtenberg, Marvin, *Dominion of the Eye, Urbanism, Art and Power in Early Modern Florence* (Cambridge, 1997).

Fortifications:

De La Croix, Horst, *Military Considerations in City Planning* (New York, 1972).
Pepper, Simon, and Adams, Nicholas, *Firearms & Fortifications: Military Architecture and Siege Warfare in Sixteenth-Century Siena* (Chicago, 1986).
Pollak, Martha, *Cities at War in Early Modern Europe* (Cambridge, 2010).
Tracy, James D., ed., *City Walls: The Urban Enceinte in Global Perspective* (Cambridge, 2000). Includes essays by Simon Pepper, Martha Pollak, and Geoffrey Parker on siege warfare; George Milner on prehistoric North America and Richard Kagan on cities in colonial Spanish America; Michael Wolfe on walls during the French wars of religion.

Festivals and entries:

Arnade, Peter, *Realms of Ritual: Burgundian Ceremony and Civic Life in Late Medieval Ghent* (Ithaca, NY, 1996).
Bergeron, David M., *English Civic Pageantry, 1558–1642* (Columbia, SC, 1971).
Mitchell, B., *Italian Civic Pageantry in the High Renaissance: A Descriptive Bibliography of Triumphal Entries and Selected Other Festivals for State Occasions* (Florence, 1979).
Smuts, R. Malcolm, 'Public Ceremony and Royal Charisma: The English Royal Entry in London, 1485–1642', in A. L. Beier et al., eds., *The First Modern Society: Essays in Honour of Lawrence Stone* (Cambridge, 1989), 65–93.

Markets:

Calabi, Donatella, *The Market and the City: Square, Street and Architecture in Early Modern Europe* (Aldershot, 2004).
Postles, David, 'The Market Place as Space in Early Modern England', *Social History* 29 (2004), 41–58.
Welch, Evelyn, *Shopping in the Renaissance* (New Haven, 2005).

Houses and palaces:

Chastel, André, and Guillaume, Jean, eds., *La Maison de ville à la Renaissance: recherches sur l'habitat urbain en Europe aux XVe et XVI siècles*, actes du colloque tenu à Tours, 10–14 May 1977 (Paris, 1983).
Clarke, Georgia, 'History, Politics, and Art on Palace Façades in Early Sixteenth-Century Rome', in Maria Beltramini and Caroline Elam, eds., *Some Degree of Happiness: studi di storia dell'architettura in onore di Howard Burns* (Pisa, 2010), 233–58.

——*Roman House–Renaissance Palaces: Inventing Antiquity in Fifteenth-Century Italy* (Cambridge, 2003).
Cooper, Tracy E., 'Palladio and his Patrons: The Performance of Magnificenza', *Annali di architettura* 22 (2010), 89–100.
Goldthwaite, Richard, 'The Florentine Palace as Domestic Architecture', *American Historical Review* 77 (1972), 977–1012.
Goy, Richard J., *The House of Gold: Building a Palace in Medieval Venice* (Cambridge, 1992).
Kent, F. W., 'Palaces, Politics and Society', *I Tatti Studies* 2 (1987), 41–70.
Lindow, James R., *The Renaissance Palace in Florence: Magnificence and Splendour in Fifteenth-Century Italy* (Aldershot, 2007).
Schmitter, Monika, 'Falling through the Cracks: The Fate of Painted Palace Façades in Sixteenth-Century Italy', in Christy Anderson, ed., *The Built Surface*, i: *Architecture and the Pictorial Arts from Antiquity to the Enlightenment* (Aldershot, 2002), 130–61.

Chapter 8: Architecture in the Natural World

Ackerman, James S., 'The Belvedere as a Classical Villa', *Journal of the Warburg and Courtauld Institutes* 14 (1951), 70–91.
——'The Tuscan/Rustic Order: A Study in the Metaphorical Language of Architecture', in his *Distance Points: Essays in Theory and Renaissance Art and Architecture* (Cambridge, Mass., 1991), 495–545.
——*The Villa: Form and Ideology of Country Houses* (Princeton, 1990).
Bentman, Richard, and Muller, Michael, *The Villa as Hegemonic Architecture*, trans. Tim Spence and David Craven (Atlantic Highlands, NJ, 1992).
Chatenet, Monique, ed., *Maisons des champs dans l'Europe de la Renaissance*, actes des premières Rencontres d'architecture européenne, Château de Maisons, 10–13 June 2003 (Paris, 2006).
Coffin, David R., *The Villa in the Life of Renaissance Rome* (Princeton, 1979).
Cooper, Nicholas, *Houses of the Gentry 1480–1680* (New Haven, 1999).
Friedman, Alice, *House and Household in Elizabethan England: Wollaton House and the Willoughby Family* (Chicago, 1989).
Girouard, Mark, *Robert Smythson & the Elizabethan Country House* (New Haven, 1983).
Howard, Maurice, *The Early Tudor Country House: Architecture and Politics 1490–1550* (London, 1987).
——'The Ideal House and Healthy Life: The Origins of Architectural Theory in England', in Jean Guillaume, ed., *Les Traités d'architecture de la Renaissance*, actes du colloque tenu à Tours, 1–11 July 1981 (Paris, 1988), 426–33.
Johnson, Matthew, *Behind the Castle Gate: From Medieval to Renaissance* (New York, 2002).
——'Reconstructing Castles and Refashioning Identities in Renaissance England', in Sarah Tarlow and Susie West, eds., *The Familiar Past? Archaeologies of Later Historical Britain* (London, 1998), 69–86.
Lillie, Amanda, *Florentine Villas of the Fifteenth Century: An Architectural and Social History* (Cambridge, 2005).
Muraro, Michelangelo, *Venetian Villas* (New York, 1986).
Pounds, N. J. P., *The Medieval Castle in England and Wales: A Social and Political History* (Cambridge, 1990).
Rykwert, Joseph, *On Adam's House in Paradise: The Idea of the Primitive Hut in Architectural History* (Cambridge, Mass., 1981).
Shearman, John, 'A Functional Interpretation of Villa Madama', *Römisches Jahrbuch für Kunstgeschichte* 20 (1983), 313–27.
Thompson, M. W., *The Decline of the Castle* (Cambridge, 1987).
——*The Medieval Hall: The Basis of Secular Domestic Life, 600–1600 AD* (Aldershot, 1995).
Wheeler, D., et al., *The Châteaux of France* (London, 1979).

On gardens:

Adams, W. H., *The French Garden, 1500–1800* (New York, 1979).
Beneš, Mirka, and Lee, Michael G., eds., *Clio in the Italian Garden: Twenty-First-Century Studies in Historical Methods and Theoretical Perspectives* (Washington, DC, 2011).
——and Harris, D., eds., *Villas and Gardens in Early Modern Italy and France* (Cambridge, 2001).
Coffin, David R., ed., *The Italian Garden* (Washington, DC, 1972).
Comito, Terry, *The Idea of the Garden in the Renaissance* (New Brunswick, NJ, 1977).
Cosgrove, Denis, *The Palladian Landscape: Geographical Change and its Cultural Representation in Sixteenth-Century Italy* (Leicester, 1993).
Guillaume, Jean, ed., *Architecture, jardin, paysage: l'environnement du château et de la villa aux XVe et XVI siècles*, actes des colloques tenus à Tours, 1–4 June 1992 (Paris, 1999).

Hardy, Matthew, ' "Study the warm winds and the cold": Hippocrates and the Renaissance Villa', in Barbara Kenda, ed., *Aeolian Winds and the Spirit in Renaissance Architecture* (London, 2006), 48–69.
Henderson, Paula, *The Tudor House and Garden: Architecture and Landscape in the Sixteenth and Early Seventeenth Centuries* (New Haven, 2005).
Hunt, John Dixon, *Garden and Grove* (London, 1986).
Jellicoe, G., Jellicoe, S., Goode, P., and Lancaster, M., eds., *The Oxford Companion to Gardens* (Oxford, 1986).
Lazzaro, Claudia, *The Italian Renaissance Garden: From the Conventions of Planting, Design and Ornament to the Grand Gardens of Sixteenth-Century Central Italy* (New Haven, 1990).
Leslie, Michael, and Hunt, J. D., 'Garden and Architectural Dreamscapes in the *Hypnerotomachia Poliphili*', *Word & Image* 14 (June 1998).
Mosser, M., and Teyssot, G., eds., *The History of Garden Design: The Western Tradition from the Renaissance to the Present Day* (London, 1991).
Neil, Erik H., 'A Green City: Ideas, Conditions, and Practices of the Garden in Sixteenth Century Palermo', in A. Casamento and E. Guidoni, eds., *L'urbanistica del Cinquecento in Sicilia* (Rome, 1999), 227–35.
Nova, Alessandro, 'The Role of the Winds in Architectural Theory from Vitruvius to Scamozzi', in Barbara Kenda, ed., *Aeolian Winds and the Spirit in Renaissance Architecture* (London, 2006), 70–86.
Strong, Roy, *Renaissance Gardens in England* (London, 1994).

Chapter 9: Distant Shores

These books and articles offer a window onto global architecture in the fifteenth and sixteenth centuries.

Anderson, Christy, 'Without Art, Without Order: Ideas of Architecture in the New World', *Architecture and Ideas* 2 (2000), 58–73.
Dean, Carolyn, *A Culture of Stone: Inka Perspectives on Rock* (Chapel Hill, NC, 2010).
DeCorse, Christopher R., *An Archaeology of Elmina: Africans and Europeans on the Gold Coast, 1400–1900* (Washington, DC, 2001). A study of the castle at Elmina in Ghana, central in the Atlantic slave trade.
Fraser, Valerie, *The Architecture of Conquest: Building in the Viceroyalty of Peru, 1535–1635* (Cambridge, 1990).
Goody, Jack, *Renaissances: The One or the Many?* (Cambridge, 2010).
Howard, Deborah, *Venice & the East: The Impact of the Islamic World on Venetian Architecture 1100–1500* (New Haven, 2000).
McAndrew, John, *The Open-Air Churches of Sixteenth-Century Mexico* (Cambridge, Mass., 1965).
Muchembled, Robert, ed., *Cultural Exchange in Early Modern Europe*, 4 vols. (Cambridge, 2006–7).
Parker, Charles H., *Global Interactions in the Early Modern Age, 1400–1800* (Cambridge, Mass., 2010).
Pearson, Michael N., *Port Cities and Intruders: The Swahili Coast, India, and Portugal in the Early Modern Era* (Baltimore, 1998).
Russell-Wood, A. J. R., *The Portuguese Empire, 1414–1808: A World on the Move* (Baltimore, 1992).
Saunders, John J., ed., *The Muslim World on the Eve of Europe's Expansion* (Englewood Cliffs, NJ, 1996).
Sloan, Kim, *A New World: England's First View of America* (London, 2007).

Historians and critics of modern architecture have often looked back to Renaissance architecture for insights into the contemporary architectural condition.

Eisenman, Peter, *Eisenman Inside Out: Selected Writings, 1963–1988* (New Haven, 2004).
Hersey, George, and Freedman, Richard, *Possible Palladian Villas (Plus a Few Instructively Impossible Ones)* (Cambridge, Mass., 1992).
Hildner Jeffrey, 'Remembering the Mathematics of the Ideal Villa', *Journal of Architectural Education* 52 (1999), 143–62.
Rowe, Colin, *The Mathematics of the Ideal Villa and Other Essays* (Cambridge, Mass., 1982).
Sabatino, Michelangelo, *Pride in Modesty: Modernist Architecture and the Vernacular Tradition in Italy* (Toronto, 2010).
Tafuri, Manfredo, *Theories and History of Architecture*, trans. Giorgio Verrecchia (London, 1980).
Venturi, Robert, *Complexity and Contradiction in Architecture* (New York, 1966).

List of Illustrations

1. Michele Sanmicheli, Palazzo Grimani, commissioned 1556–7, completed 1575, Venice. © Palazzo Grimani a S. Luca, Venice/The Bridgeman Art Library.

2. Giovanni and Bartolomeo Bon, Ca d'Oro, 1420s, Venice. © Didier Descouens/ Wikimedia Commons.

3. Gatehouse, St Osyth Priory, late 15th century, Essex, England. © Edifice Photo Library/Philippa Lewis.

4. Azay-le-Rideau, 1518–28, near Tours, France. www.all-free-photos.com.

5. Francesco Colonna, *Hypnerotomachia Poliphili* (Venice, 1499). The Bodleian Library, University of Oxford (Douce C. subt. 174, sig. i 7).

6. Alfonso Domingues and Huguet, S. Maria da Vitória, 1388–1438, Batalha, Portugal. © Peter Zaharov/iStockphoto.

7. Huguet, Capella do Fundador, S. Maria da Vitória, 1402–38, Batalha, Portugal. © Jose Elias/Lusoimages - Landmarks/ Alamy.

8. Filippo Brunelleschi, Old Sacristy, 1419–28, San Lorenzo, Florence, Italy. © Scala, Florence.

9. Pantheon [Palladio, *I quattro libri dell'architettura*, Venice 1570; Bk. IV, p. 81]. Courtesy of the Library of Congress.

10. Brunelleschi, Santa Maria del Fiore, dome constructed 1420–36, Florence, Italy. © Vladimir Badaev/Shutterstock.com.

11. Giuliano da Sangallo, Sta Maria delle Carceri, 1485–99, Prato, Italy. © Scala, Florence.

12. Nicholas Gromann, Chapel, Schloss Hartenfels, 1543–4, Torgau, Germany. © Berthold Steinhilber/laif, Camera Press London.

13. Le Paradis, a Calvinist Temple, 1564. © The Art Archive/Alamy.

14. Old Synagogue, 16th century, Kazimierz [Krakow], Poland. © Robert Harding Picture Library Ltd/Alamy.

15. Donato Bramante, Tempietto, San Miniato al Monte, *c.*1505, Rome. © Angelo Hornak/Corbis.

16. Triangular Lodge, Rushton, 1595, Northamptonshire, England. © Powered by Light/Alan Spencer/Alamy.

17. João de Ruão, Fountain, Manga Cloister, *c.*1535, Santa Cruz Monastery, Coimbra, Portugal. © Massimiliano Pieraccini/Shutterstock.com.

18. Sacra Monte, Varallo, Italy. © MARKA/ Alamy.

19. Andrea Palladio, Il Redentore, begun 1576, Venice, Italy. © Adam Eastland Italy/ Alamy.

20. Plan, Andrea Palladio, Il Redentore, begun 1576, Venice, Italy. Courtesy of Scott Gilchrist/stock.archivision.com.

21. Interior, Andrea Palladio, Il Redentore, begun 1576, Venice Italy. © Pediconi/Scala, Florence.

22. Sinan, İsmihan-Sokollu mosque, 1571–2, Kadırgalimanı, Istanbul. © Salvator Barki/ Getty Images.

23. Sinan, Plan, İsmihan-Sokollu mosque, 1571–2, Kadırgalimanı, Istanbul. Reproduced with permission from *The Age of Sinan: Architectural Culture in the Ottoman Empire,* by Gülru Necipoglu (Reaktion Books, London, 2007), p. 334.

24. Sinan, View of the *qibla* wall, İsmihan-Sokollu mosque, 1571–2, Kadırgalimanı, Istanbul. © Leyla Ismet/ depositphotos.

25. St Peter's, Rome. © Scala, Florence.

26. Vitruvius, *De architectura*, Fra Giovanni Giocondo edition, published in Venice in 1511. By permission of the British Library (C.107.f.4. Bk X, 102r).

27. Cesare Cesariano, *Di Lucio Vitruvio Pollione de architectura*, Como, Italy, 1521. © Bibliotheque Nationale, Paris/Giraudon/ The Bridgeman Art Library.

28. Francesco di Giorgio, Face inscribed within entablature, *c.*1490. Beinecke Rare Book and Manuscript Library.

29. Raphael, Garden Loggia, Villa Madama, Rome. © The Author.

30. Attributed to a member of the Sangallo family, Pseudodipteral temple, *c.*1530–45, pen and dark brown ink. © 2012 The Metropolitan Museum of Art/Art Resource/ Scala, Florence.

31. Philibert de l'Orme, Allegory of the Good Architect, *Le Premier Tome de l'architecture*, Paris 1567. The Provost and Fellows of Worcester College, Oxford.

32. Étienne Dupérac, Twisted columns from St Peter's, drawing *c.*1575. © 2012 bpk, Berlin/Scala, Florence.

33. Amphitheatre, Nîmes, Jean Poldo d'Albenas, *Discours historial de l'antique et illustre cité de Nismes*, Lyons, 1560. By permission of the British Library (GRC 183.d.11., after f.120).

34. Henry Parke, *Student measuring the Temple of Castor and Pollux in Rome*, 1819. Courtesy of the Trustees of Sir John Soane's Museum, London/The Bridgeman Art Library.

35. Sebastiano Serlio, *Regole generali di architettura* (1537), Bk. IV, 127^{r}. © The Art Gallery Collection/Alamy.

36. Gate of Honour, Gonville and Caius College, Cambridge, England, completed 1575. © Anna Stowe Landscapes UK/ Alamy.

37. Erhard and Ulrich Heydenreich, Church of Our Lady, 1510–20, Ingolstadt. © Bildarchiv Monheim GmbH/Alamy.

38. Wendel Dietterlin, *Architectura*, Nuremberg, 1598. The Bodleian Library, University of Oxford H 3.3(1) Art., plate 29).

39. Basilica of Maxentius, Rome, in Bernardo Gamucci, *Le antichita della città di Roma*, Venice, 1569. The Bodleian Library, University of Oxford (8∞ G. 25 Art. Seld., p. 37).

40. Antonio da Sangallo and Antonio Labacco, wooden model for St Peter's, 1539–46. © St. Peter's, Vatican/The Bridgeman Art Library.

41. Bramante, Project for the centring of pier arches, St Peter's, *c.*1509. © 2012 Scala, Florence, courtesy of the Ministero Beni e Att. Culturali.

42. Maerten van Heemskerck, St Peter's exterior from the north, 1532/6. © 2012 bpk, Berlin/Scala, Florence.

43. Cristofo Foppa Caradosso, Foundation medal for St Peter's, 1505. © The Trustees Of The British Museum.

44. Michelangelo, Drawing of blocks for the San Lorenzo façade. © 2012 Scala, Florence.

45. Leonardo da Vinci, Embryo in the womb, 1510. The Royal Collection © 2011 Her Majesty Queen Elizabeth II/The Bridgeman Art Library.

46. Baldessare Peruzzi, Bird's-eye perspective view of project for St Peter's, *c.*1535. © Scala, Florence,courtesy of the Ministero Beni e Att. Culturali.

47. Michelangelo, Drawing for dome of St Peter's, probably 1546–7. © PBA, Lille, Dist. RMN-GP/Jacques Quecq d'Henripret.

48. Piero di Cosimo, Italian, 1461-1521, *The Building of a Palace*, *c.*1515–20. Oil on panel, 32 1/2 x 77 1/2 inches, SN22. Bequest of John Ringling, 1936, Collection of The John and Mable Ringling Museum of Art, the State Art Museum of Florida, Florida State University.

49. Juan Guas, Chapel, San Juan de los Reyes, 1477–1504, Toledo, Spain. © Bernard Gagnon/Wikimedia Commons.

50. Juan Guas, Upper cloister, San Juan de los Reyes, 1477–1504, Toledo, Spain. © Scala, Florence.

51. Anthonis Keldermans I, Palace for Margaret of Austria, begun 1506, Mechelen, northern Netherlands. © Victor Englebert/photographersdirect.com.

52. Lodewijk van Boghen, Jan van Roome, and Conrat Meyt, Tomb of Margaret of Savoy, 1516–30, Church of St Nicholas, Brou, France. © Henning Frhr. v. Vogelsang.

53. Juan Bautista de Toledo and Juan de Herrera, San Lorenzo el Real de Escorial, 1563–84, El Escorial, Spain. © DEA/W. Buss/Getty Images.

54. San Lorenzo el Real de Escorial, 1563–84, El Escorial, Spain. © Album/Oronoz/akg-images.

55. Pedro Machuca, Palace for Charles V, 1533–61, Granada, Spain. © Album/Miguel Raurich/akg-images.

56. Arch of Augustus, 27 BC, Rimini, Italy. © Scala, Florence.

57. Leon Battista Alberti, Church of San Francesco, enlarged 1450–6, Rimini, Italy. © Scala, Florence.

58. Albrecht Dürer, Triumphal Arch of Maximilian I, 1512–18. © Private collection/The Bridgeman Art Library.

59. Urbino, Italy. © Angelo Hornak/Alamy.

60. Luciano Laurana and Francesco di Giorgio Martini, Cortile d'Onore, 1467–72, Urbino. © The Art Archive/Alamy.

61. Staircase, Urbino. © Alinari/TopFoto.

62. Anthonis Obberghen, Kronborg Catle, 1574–85, Helsingør, Denmark. © Denis Caviglia/hemis.fr/Getty Images.

63. Riddersal, Kronborg, 1579, Helsingør, Denmark. © OJPHOTOS/Alamy.

64. Benedikt Ried, Vladislav Hall, finished 1502, Hradčany, Prague. © David Coleman/Alamy.

65. Benedikt Ried, Vladislav Hall, finished 1502, Hradčany, Prague. © Hervé Champollion/akg-images.

66. Aristotele Fioravanti da Bologna, Cathedral of the Dormition, Kremlin, *c.*1476, Moscow. © Daniel Kruczynski/Wikimedia Commons.

67. Chambord, France. © Bruno Morandi/Getty Images.

68. Roof pavilions, Chambord, France. © R. A. (Dick) White.

69. Double spiral staircase, Chambord, France. © Chad Bontrager/Shutterstock.com.

70. Tent design for the Field of the Cloth of Gold, June 1520. © The British Library Board (Cotton Ms. Augustus III. 18).

71. Jacopo Strada and Bernhard and Simon Zwitzel, Antiquarium, Residenz, begun 1569, Munich, Germany. © 50u15pec7a70r/Shutterstock.com.

72. Almshouse, 1437, Ewelme, England. © Paul Felix Photography/Alamy.

73. Chapel of St John, St Mary the Virgin, 1437, Ewelme, England. © Aidan McRae Thomson.

74. Old Hall, Berkhamsted School, begun *c.*1544, Hertfordshire, England. © Jbou.

75. Attr. Sebastian Loscher, Drawing for Fuggerkapelle (consecrated 1518), St Anna, Augsburg, 1509–10? Kunstsammlungen und Museen Augsburg.

76. Thomas Krebs, Fuggerei, 1517–23, Augsburg, Germany. © Adam Woolfitt/Corbis.

77. Kuiperspoort, Middelburg, Holland. © Peter Hoeks, www.hollandfoto.net, Amsterdam.

78. New College, 1379–86, Oxford, England, in David Loggan, *Oxonia illustrata* (1675). The Bodleian Library, University of Oxford (Vet. A3 b.22, New College).

79. William Orchard, Divinity School, begun 1420, continued 1480–3, Oxford, England. © Mark Wilson (@Sparks68).

80. Antón and Enrique Egas, Hospital Real, 1501–11, Santiago de Compostela, Spain. © Javier Larrea/Prisma.

81. Hôtel de Dieu, 1443–51, Beaune, France. © Peter Horree/Alamy.

82. Grande Salle de Pauvres, Hôtel de Dieu, 1443–51, Beaune, France. © Erich Lessing/akg-images.

83. Filippo Brunelleschi, Ospedale degli Innocenti, 1419–24, Florence, Italy. © 2006 Alinari/TopFoto.

84. Antonio di Pietro Averlino called Filarete, Ospedale Maggiore, 1456–65, Milan, Italy. After a redrawing from Filarete, Treatise on Architecture, *c.*1464. Copyright holder not traced.

85. Great Hall, Merchant Adventurers Hall, 1357–61, York, England. © 2005 Woodmansterne/TopFoto.

86. Pietro and Tullio Lombardo and Giovanni di Antonio Buora, Antonio Rizzo, and Mauro Codussi, Scuola di San Marco, 1489– , Venice, Italy. © age fotostock/SuperStock.

87. Michelozzo di Bartolomeo, Library, after 1438, Monastery of San Marco, Florence. © Erich Lessing/akg-images.

88. Michelangelo Buonarroti, Reading Room, Biblioteca Laurenziana, 1525, San Lorenzo, Florence. © 2006 Alinari/TopFoto.

89. Michelangelo Buonarroti, Entrance vestibule and stair, Laurentian Library, begun 1533–4, San Lorenzo, Florence, Italy. © Andrea Jemolo/Scala, Florence.

90. Section, Laurentian Library, San Lorenzo, Florence, Italy. The Bodleian Library, University of Oxford 941. 2 Ste (la. fol), Lorenzo Library).

91. Jacopo Sansovino, Library San Marco, begun 1537, Venice, Italy. Courtesy of Scott Gilchrist/stock.archivision.com.

92. Diogo Boitaca and João de Castilho, S. Maria de Belém, Jerónimos Abbey, 1501–22, Belém, Portugal. © Jose Elias/ Lusoimages - Landmarks/Alamy.

93. Diogo Boitaca and João de Castilho, Cloister, Jerónimos Abbey, 1501–22, Belém, Portugal. © Fotosearch/SuperStock.

94. Brunetto Latini, *Le Livre du trésor*, 1450–75. Bibliothèque de Genève (Ms. fr. 160, fol. 82).

95. John White, *Town of Pomeiooc*, 1585. © The Art Gallery Collection/Alamy.

96. Dubrovnik, Croatia. © age fotostock/ SuperStock.

97. Holstentor, 1464–78, Lübeck, Germany. © Shestakoff/Shutterstock.com.

98. Michele Sanmicheli, Porta Nuova, 1533, Verona, Italy. © Interfoto/Alamy.

99. Pienza, Italy. © 2006 Alinari/TopFoto.

100. Master of the St Lucy Legend, *Virgin of the Rose Garden*, 1475/80. © Detroit Institute of Arts, USA/Founders Society purchase, General Membership Fund/The Bridgeman Art Library.

101. Jakob Sandtner, Model of the city of Munich, 1570. © Brian J. McMorrow.

102. Cornelis Floris and Willem Paludanus, Town Hall, 1561–5, Antwerp. © Hemis/ Alamy.

103. Granaries, 15th–18th centuries, Grudziądz, Poland. © Patryk Kosmider/ Shutterstock.com.

104. Arch of the Saint-Denis Gate for the entry of Henry II and Catherine de' Medici into Paris: *C'est l'ordre qui a este tenu a la nouvelle et ioyeuse entrée, que . . . le roy treschrestien Henry deuxieme de ce nom, a faicte en sa bonne ville [et] cité de Paris* (Paris, 1549). By permission of the British Library (C.33.k.2; p. 7).

105. Jacques Androuet du Cerceau, *Fontaine des Innocents*, 1550–75. Bibliothèque nationale de France, Paris.

106. *Strasbourg* from Hartmann Schedel, *Liber chronicarum*, 1493. © ullsteinbild/ TopFoto.

107. Loggia della Signoria, 1376–81, Florence. © 2006 Alinari/TopFoto.

108. Michelozzo di Bartolomeo, Palazzo Medici, 1444, Florence. © Rogério Marques.

109. Courtyard, House of Jacques Cœur, 1443–51, Bourges, France. © Palais de Jacques-Coeur, Bourges, France/Giraudon/ The Bridgeman Art Library.

110. Plan, House of Jacques Cœur. Redrawn from Eugène Viollet-le-Duc, Dictionary of French Architecture from the 11th to 16th Century, 1856.

111. Donato Bramante, Palazzo Caprini, 1510, Rome. © RIBA Library Drawings & Archives Collections.

112. Sebastiano Serlio, City dwellings for artisans in the Italian and French manner. Courtesy of Avery Library, Columbia University, New York.

113. Latin School, 1610, Alfeld-an-der-Leine (Germany). © Werner Otto/Alamy.

114. Hendrick Martensz. Sorgh, *De Vismarkt*, *c.*1650. Collection Rijksmuseum, Amsterdam.

115. Groot Vleeshuis, 1409, Ghent. © Arterra Picture Library/Alamy.

116. Paskoje Miličević and Nikola and Josip Andrijić, Sponza Palace, 1516–21, Dubrovnik, Croatia. © Kris Ubach/Prisma.

117. Houses of foreign merchants, Bruges, from A. Sanderus, *Flandria illustrata*, 1641. © The British Library Board (177.h.10).

118. Zamosc, founded 1580, Poland. © David Sutherland/Corbis.

119. Plan, Ercole additions, Ferrara. Redrawn from Leonardo Benevolo, The History of the City, Rome: London: Scolar, 1980. © Leonardo Benevolo.

120. Corso Ercole I, 1492, Ferrara. © Gordon Sinclair/Alamy.

121. Biagio Rossetti, Palazzo Diamanti, begun 1493, Ferrara. © Scala, Florence.

122. Strada Nuova, 1550–8, Genoa. © 2006 Alinari/TopFoto.

123. Sebastiano Serlio, Tragic Stage Set, from his *De perspective: Il secondo libro di prospettiva*, Paris, 1545. © c./Shutterstock.com.

124. Domenico Fontana, Fontana dell'Acqua Felice, 1587, Rome. Marie-Lan Nguyen/ Wikimedia Commons/Public Domain.

125. Vitruvius, origins of building from Jean Martin, *Architecture, ou Art de bien bastir de Marc Vitruve Pollion Autheur* (Paris, 1547). Bibliothèque nationale de France, Paris.

126. Bodiam Castle, 1386–8, Sussex, England. © Marbo/Dreamstime.com.

127. Andrea Palladio, Villa Capra, begun 1565, Vicenza, Italy. © The Author.

128. Andrea Palladio, Villa Capra, begun 1565, Vicenza, Italy. © Jochen Jürgensen.

129. Sebastiano Serlio, Ancy-le-Franc, 1544–50, near Tonnerre, France. © A.J.Cassaigne/Photononstop.

130. Giuliano da Sangallo, Poggio a Caiano, begun 1485, near Prato, Italy. © Niccolò Rigacci/Wikimedia Commons.

131. Raphael, Antonio da Sangallo, Giulio Romano, and others, Villa Madama, from 1517, Rome. © The Author.

132. Villa Madama, plan. From *Raphael*, by Roger Jones and Nicholas Penny (1983). © 1983 Yale University Press.

133. Donato Bramante, Cortile del Belvedere, begun 1505, Vatican. © The Trustees of the British Museum.

134. Raphael, Antonio da Sangallo, Giulio Romano, and others, Garden Loggia, Villa Madama, from 1517, Rome. © Andrea Jemolo/akg-images.

135. Andrea Palladio, Villa Emo, begun 1559, Fanzolo di Vedelago, Italy. Fondazione Villa Emo Onlus.

136. View through loggia toward fields, Andrea Palladio, Villa Emo, begun 1559, Fanzolo di Vedelago, Italy. Fondazione Villa Emo Onlus.

137. Grotte des Jardins des Pins, 1541–3, Fontainebleau, France. © RMN-GP/ Gérard Blot.

138. Giulio Romano, Palazzo Te, from 1524, Mantua, Italy. © The Art Archive/Alamy.

139. Drawing by Jacques Androuet du Cerceau, Chateau of Anet, before 1576. © The Trustees of the British Museum.

140. Philibert de l'Orme, Gate, Chateau d'Anet, 1552, Eure-et-Loire, France. © Hervé Champollion/akg-images.

141. Robert Smythson, Hardwick Hall, 1590–7, Derbyshire, England. © Sue H. J. Hasker.

142. Plan, Hardwick Hall. From *The Country House in Perspective* by Gervase Jackson-Stops (Pavilion, 1990). Copyright holder not traced.

143. Long Gallery, Hardwick Hall, 1590–7, Derbyshire, England. © NTPL/Andreas von Einsiedel.

144. Niccolò Tribolo and Giorgio Vasari, Grotto of the Animals, Villa Medici, 1538, Castello, Italy. © Bildarchiv Monheim/ akg-images.

145. Francisco de Arruda, Tower, 1514–21, Belém, Portugal. © age fotostock/ SuperStock.

146. Casa de las Pilatos, rebuilt from 1509, Seville. © Alex Goethals.

147. Tiles from Casa de las Pilatos, Seville. © Manuel Cohen/The Art Archive.

148. Detail: Cloister, Jerónimos Monastery, Belém. © John Sie Yuen Lee.

149. Andrea Palladio, Villa Capra, *I quattro libri dell'architettura*, Venice, 1570, with annotations by Inigo Jones. The Provost and Fellows of Worcester College, Oxford.

150. Machine de Marly, completed 1684, France. © The Art Archive/Alamy.

151. Andrea Palladio, Villa Foscari, begun *c.*1558, Malcontenta di Mira, Italy. © Cameraphoto/akg-images.

The publisher apologizes for any errors or omissions in the above list. If contacted, they will be pleased to rectify these at the earliest opportunity.

Index

Note: References to illustrations and captions are in italics. There may also be textual references on the same page

Renaissance Architecture

Oxford History of Art

Christy Anderson is an architectural historian with a special interest in the buildings of Renaissance and Baroque Europe. The author of *Inigo Jones and the Classical Tradition* (2006), she has taught at Yale University, the Courtauld Institute, and MIT, and is currently an Associate Professor at the University of Toronto.

Oxford History of Art

Titles in the Oxford History of Art series are up-to-date, fully illustrated introductions to a wide variety of subjects written by leading experts in their field. They will appear regularly, building into an interlocking and comprehensive series. In the list below, published titles appear in bold.

WESTERN ART

Archaic and Classical Greek Art
Robin Osborne

Classical Art From Greece to Rome
Mary Beard & John Henderson

Imperial Rome and Christian Triumph
Jas Elsner

Early Medieval Art
Lawrence Nees

Medieval Art
Veronica Sekules

Art in Renaissance Italy
Evelyn Welch

Northern Renaissance Art
Susie Nash

Art in Europe 1700–1830
Matthew Craske

Modern Art 1851–1929
Richard Brettell

After Modern Art 1945–2000
David Hopkins

WESTERN ARCHITECTURE

Roman Architecture
Janet Delaine

Early Medieval Architecture
Roger Stalley

Medieval Architecture
Nicola Coldstream

Renaissance Architecture
Christy Anderson

Baroque and Rococo Architecture
Hilary Ballon

European Architecture 1750–1890
Barry Bergdoll

Modern Architecture
Alan Colquhoun

Contemporary Architecture
Anthony Vidler

Architecture in the United States
Dell Upton

WORLD ART

Aegean Art and Architecture
Donald Preziosi & Louise Hitchcock

Early Art and Architecture of Africa
Peter Garlake

African-American Art
Sharon F. Patton

Nineteenth-Century American Art
Barbara Groseclose

Twentieth-Century American Art
Erika Doss

Australian Art
Andrew Sayers

Byzantine Art
Robin Cormack

Art in China
Craig Clunas

East European Art
Jeremy Howard

Indian Art
Partha Mitter

Islamic Art
Irene Bierman

Japanese Art
Karen Brock

Native North American Art
Janet Berlo & Ruth Phillips

The Pacific Arts of Polynesia and Micronesia
Adrienne L. Kaeppler

WESTERN DESIGN

Twentieth-Century Design
Jonathan Woodham

Design in the USA
Jeffrey L.Meikle

Fashion
Christopher Breward

PHOTOGRAPHY

The Photograph
Graham Clarke

American Photography
Miles Orvell

WESTERN SCULPTURE

Sculpture 1900–1945
Penelope Curtis

Sculpture Since 1945
Andrew Causey

THEMES AND GENRES

Landscape and Western Art
Malcolm Andrews

Portraiture
Shearer West

Eroticism and Art
Alyce Mahon

Beauty and Art
Elizabeth Prettejohn

REFERENCE BOOKS

The Art of Art History: A Critical Anthology
Donald Preziosi (ed.)

Oxford History of Art

Renaissance Architecture

Christy Anderson

OXFORD
UNIVERSITY PRESS

OXFORD
UNIVERSITY PRESS

Great Clarendon Street, Oxford, OX2 6DP,
United Kingdom

Oxford University Press is a department of the University of Oxford.
It furthers the University's objective of excellence in research, scholarship,
and education by publishing worldwide. Oxford is a registered trade mark of
Oxford University Press in the UK and in certain other countries

First Edition published in 2013

British Library Cataloguing in Publication Data
Data available

ISBN 978–0–19–284227–5

Printed and bound by CPI Group (UK), Ltd, Croydon, CR0 4YY